Newsgirls

Gutsy Pioneers in Canada's Newsrooms

Donna Jean MacKinnon

Copyright © 2017 by Donna Jean MacKinnon. All rights reserved. No part of this book may be reproduced or transmitted in any form or by any means, electronic or mechanical, including photocopying, recording, or by an information storage and retrieval system—except by a reviewer who may quote brief passages in a review to be printed in a magazine, newspaper, or on the Web-without permission in writing from the publisher.

Photo Credits:
The Canadian Press
Marilyn Dunlop
Joan Hollobon
Kay Kritzwiser
Augusta Vineberg Solomon
PNG Library
Toronto Reference Library / Toronto Public Library
Torstar Syndication Services
Toronto Star Photograph Archive

Library and Archives Canada Cataloguing in Publication

MacKinnon, Donna Jean, author
Newsgirls: gutsy pioneers in Canada's newsrooms / Donna Jean MacKinnon.

Includes index.
Issued in print and electronic formats.
ISBN 978-1-988170-04-6 (softcover).--ISBN 978-1-988170-05-3 (PDF)

1. Women journalists--Canada--Biography. 2. Women in journalism--Canada--History--20th century. I. Title.

PN4912.M335 2017   070.4'30922   C2016-907840-X
                                           C2016-907841-8

Leaping Lion Books Publishing
4700 Keele Street Toronto, ON M3J 1P3
Leaping Lion Books is a department of York University that strives towards quality publication and the development of literary excellence.
www.yorku.ca/llbooks/

Printed and bound in Canada.

"In days of yore, print reporters would 'cut each other's throats' to be the first to have a story hit the street." – Dorothy Howarth

CONTENTS

Preface	7
Introduction	9
1 — Kay Kritzwiser	13
2 — Dorothy Howarth	27
3 — Olive Dickason	41
4 — June Callwood	51
5 — Simma Holt	69
Gallery	87
6 — Stasia Evasuk	91
7 — Angela Burke	103
8 — Marilyn Dunlop	121
9 — Joan Hollobon	135
10 — Augusta Vineberg	153
Endnotes	165
Index	171

PREFACE

Newsgirls tells the stories of ten 'pioneer' female reporters who brazened it out in Canadian newsrooms from the late 1920s into the 1960s and succeeded in a male milieu long before the word "feminism" was invented.

This book provides insight into a bygone era of Canadian press, along with cameos from the larger-than-life men who ran the Canadian newsrooms. The individual histories of these newsgirls, revealed through personal interviews, provide a window into the world of the working girl long before the Canadian *Charter of Rights* and equal opportunity existed.

By the mid-60s, a new breed of women flooded into the newsrooms where they encountered a modern working experience. Well before this movement took place, our youngest newsgirl, Dusty Vineberg, embarked on her career in 1956.

The idea for this book came about after a lengthy lunch held at the University Women's Club in Toronto. In 1995, Catherine Smyth, an alumna of the *Toronto Star*, had invited fashion reporter Stasia Evasuk, food writer, Mary McGrath, and myself to lunch. This is when Evasuk began to reminisce.

I was fascinated by the romance of the newspaper world she described, which was so different from the lean, mean newsrooms of my generation of reporters. During my tenure at the *Toronto Star* (1986-2009), newsroom cuts included sharing desks and computers and the elimination of taxi chits. Evasuk was treating us to a slice of social history and I realized that the women who started out as reporters several decades ago had unique stories to tell.

After dozens of conversations with newsroom veterans, there emerged an image of lady reporters, ghettoized in the women's department of all major Canadian newspapers. No matter—segregation be damned—these reporters enjoyed every minute of their careers; whether tripping around Europe on expense accounts, or honing a voice that would eventually shape the identity of the modern liberated woman.

A few of the reporters I approached, as they were writers themselves, intimated they would write their own books at some undefined time in the future. After getting over that hurdle, each newsgirl shared with me stories filled with candour and vigour.

Mind you, many cocktails were involved.

As I explained to fashion editor Olive Dickason, then seventy-five, and art critic, Kay Kritzwiser, then eighty-five, I would only be interviewing and telling the story of those still living. Thus the stories collected are from the horse's, or rather, the mare's mouth. Each interviewee was invited to talk about her background and how she became a "newshen." I encouraged each one of them to share any experiences (good and bad) that were milestones in her career. These biographical accounts are embroidered with comments from people who knew the reporter in her heyday. Some anecdotes are flattering; some are entertaining, while others are downright mean. Secondary sources, such as newsman and author, Pierre Berton, and *Toronto Star* reporter, Ben Rose (later editor of the *Jewish Daily News*) threw in their two-cents-worth. I also gathered a heap of juicy scuttlebutt.

In its final analysis, *Newsgirls* is an uplifting account of talented, working women, rather than a strident rant about oppressive male bosses. Nor is it an insider's potpourri. The stories, told by these reporters, are set within the historical and social framework of the working conditions in pre-feminism Canada and the major news events of the 20th century.

Since I started this project, many of the people I interviewed have died, including Stasia Evasuk, Olive Dickason and Kay Kritzwiser. A few of my newsgirls, like June Callwood and Simma Holt, were always in the public eye, but the rest of the ladies I came to know had rarely been asked about their lives as professional reporters. I can only add, I am chuffed that I persevered with this book. Without my diligence, these journalists would have expired—their experiences and contributions untold.

It is important to note that this book is limited to women working in the English-speaking press, as I believe the French-Canadian experience requires an entire book of its own.

INTRODUCTION

Once upon a time, there was a Lois Lane...

In times past, the female reporters in Canada's newsrooms would don a fancy hat and toddle out to report on a Trousseau Tea or a Hunt Club ball. At the *Toronto Star*, in the 1940s, spare hats and white gloves were kept in a filing cabinet in the Women's Department for fast forays into society en route to cover a late-breaking bulletin from the Opera Guild. But make no mistake, these women in their little hats were tough. Each one had a raw sense of humour, a penchant for cigarettes and a stomach for strong drink. The lady reporters who started out before World War II and into the early 1960s were gutsy in a world run by male editors who were condescending, hard-drinking and sexist, before the word was invented.

Tiny fashion reporter, Stasia Evasuk—nintey pounds soaking wet—had the *Toronto Telegram* and the *Toronto Star* competing for her services in the early '60s. Although she stayed with the *Star*, she spunkily told managing editor, Martin Goodman, "to stick it," when he offered her a five-dollar raise. "I told him, if the *Star* is that badly off you can keep it."

Catherine Smyth, a rookie reporter at the *Toronto Star*, will never forget the moment when city editor, Tommy Lytle, assigned her to cover the visit of a female Polish politician in the early '50s. "He described the Polish woman as a nickel-plated bitch," said Smyth, with a chuckle. She added that Lytle and his father, sports editor Andy Lytle, were rough-talking guys in brimmed hats who kept bottles in their desk drawers.

Arch-feminist and socialist, Michele Landsberg, started out at the *Globe and Mail* over fifty-years ago. She remembers the round table at the Lord Simcoe Hotel on King Street where "Globians" met after a hard day at the typewriter. There, legendary columnist Richard Needham—known for his sentimental epistles to feminine pulchritude—entertained the ladies. He bragged that when he travelled, all he took was a toothbrush. Author David Hayes, in his book, *Power and Influence* (1992), described Needham as a, "rumpled and pickled" man who wore thrift store clothes and, "drank gin daily."[1] Landsberg described Needham as lacking personal hygiene and a harasser of women. But as she said, this is the way it was. No one bothered about it.

Fast-forward forty-three years to November 1995, when Landsberg, with her grey locks and bifocals perched atop her nose, was an eminence grise. Not only was she a *Toronto Star* columnist, but she was also a keynote speaker at a "Women in the Media" conference in Toronto. She introduced her remarks with a snapshot of the days before the feminist movement. "In the 1950s, when I was a girl, we had bimbos, McCarthyism, lots of DDT but we didn't know the difference. We also wore wide cinch belts, crinolines and girdles even, so we didn't jiggle."

Newsgirls

To the superior guffaws of a liberated generation of journalists, she also explained that health class was based on a modest booklet called, "What Every Girl Should Know." "It outlined a girl's role in life. It instructed young women to be dainty and to change pads frequently so as not to be offensive. The '50s teen was cautioned that, 'virgins never wear tampons.' We were also advised to memorize football scores as this shows interest in your date."

Landsberg also pointed out that only three percent of Canada's women ever went to university, and those who did, did so by "sheer luck."

Print was *the* medium for news until the late '60s, so celebrities relied on reporters for publicity. As a result, many a Canadian gal, born on a pioneer farm or in a mining town, ended up rubbing shoulders with the likes of Aristotle Onassis and hobnobbing with royalty (hatted and gloved, of course).

Evasuk talks of lunching with Peggy Guggenheim, an American art collector and socialite, in her Venetian palazzo as if it were a common event for a miner's daughter from Cape Breton Island. *The Toronto Star* had sent Evasuk to cover a glamorous fundraiser organized to save the sinking buildings of Venice. Once there, she teamed up with jet-set photographer, Roloff Beny, and Guggenheim invited the both of them to dine with her. "We went to a writers' lunch hosted by Peggy. After lunch, everyone else went for a siesta and Peggy's son, Sinbad, and I went to a park and drank wine all afternoon," recalled Evasuk. That was only the beginning of Evasuk's 1968 fairy-tale Venetian assignment, which was forever etched into her storehouse of glittering memories.

Many of the careers documented in *Newsgirls* are classic Horatio Alger stories—in this case, poor *girl* makes good in the big city. The teenaged June Callwood arrived at the *Globe and Mail* in 1942, in a handmade, green-checkered suit; each stitch sewn with a needle and thread by Callwood herself. "We were poor and no, we didn't even have a treadle machine," said Callwood, who was a celebrated journalist for almost seventy years.

Eighteen-year-old Olive Dickason, later Professor Emeritus at the University of Alberta, came out of the Manitoba bush able to discuss Plato and the Battle of Thermopylae because an eccentric, Scottish remittance man arrived in the wilds with a classical library he shared with Dickason and her sister.

Before Dickason set out on the path to academe where she became Canada's foremost authority on North American Indigenous history, she spent twenty-one years as a reporter and editor. As *Globe and Mail's* women's editor, Dickason won the prestigious Elizabeth Arden award for fashion writing in 1956 and again, in 1958. In those years she wrote and produced fashion spreads on beachwear, mink (her favourite subject) and, "The Triumph of the Blouse."

In the 1950s, the agenda of women's editors, like Dickason and her counterpart Maureen Keller, at the *Toronto Star*, went more or less unnoticed because the ideas and the stories in the women's sections were not taken seriously by the overlords in Canada's newsrooms. Girl reporters were left alone in the women's pages to do "whatever women did", and to pursue stories of female interest that had nothing to do with the big, male world of hockey and national politics. Quietly, the women's pages in the dailies, became family sections and later, feminist thinkers such as Landsberg and Doris Anderson—the chair of the *Royal Commission on the Status of Women* and later editor of *Chatelaine* magazine—ended up using Canada's biggest newspapers as platforms for their ideas.

Thanks to these feminist writers and a new breed of female reporters, women's issues were noticed and Canadian society was forced to confront a lot of dirty national laundry.

Keller made a comment, that in 1960, she was still required to get permission to use the word "sex" in her section. Landsberg recalled that in 1962 at the *Globe,* she had to go to the wall to use the word "masturbation" in a story about an emotionally disturbed nine-year-old girl. In 1995, the *Star's* entertainment editor, Kathleen McKenna, was suspended for one week for allowing the word "fuck" to appear in a direct quote.

Although Keller had to fight to print the word "sex," there was plenty of it in the nation's newsrooms. Life being full of ironies and contradictions, several girl reporters of yesteryear, who ended up with the most spectacular careers, admit their public lives would not have happened without the help of a paternalistic man. But make no mistake, the help was only offered because these women were attractive.

Landsberg, for one, admits that she was indeed, "a sexy little number." "Quite frankly, if I hadn't been cute and pretty my career never would have happened," she said, then a middle-aged woman who had given a lot of thought to the topic of women and careers.

Although June Callwood would not admit that it was her long legs, stunning smile and starlet good looks that made all the reporters at the *Globe and Mail* help her through her first three years on the paper, others will vouch for this fact. Author and columnist Pierre Berton remembered Callwood as a "flibbertigibbet" in those early days. Callwood's "apprenticeship," as she called it, would not have happened if she had been pimply and plump. It is also unlikely that she would have married Trent Frayne, a handsome *Globe* reporter, who galloped on his white charger to tutor the new delectable cub reporter. In retrospect, if it hadn't been for Callwood's charms, Toronto's crusading St. June of Digger House (Yorkville hippies), Casey House (AIDS) and Nellie's hostel (for abused women), would not have existed.

Unlike the *Globe,* the *Star* managed to keep the temptresses out of the newsroom until the 1950s. Marjorie Earl, one of the *Star's* first "newshens," as they were often called in the past, used to reminisce about the 1940s when she and Alexandrine Gibb, the only other female newsie around at the time, were not allowed to sit in the city room with the men in case they "inhibited," "vamped" or "distracted" them. Earl enjoyed saying, "We were maintained in modest isolation at enormous cost and inconvenience. A special switchboard had to be set up connecting our telephones to the editorial room."

Ross Harkness wrote in his 1963 book, *J.E. Atkinson of the Star,* that Joseph Atkinson, the publisher of the *Toronto Star*, never thought much of girl reporters. However, he did marry Elmina Elliott, who wrote for the *Globe* under the nom de plume Madge Merton. Atkinson believed the only use for a woman on a newspaper was for such feminine jobs as writing social notes and describing weddings. Harkness said, "There was usually a sob-sister available for general assignments, but her desk was in the zenana of the social department, safe from the contaminating influence of male speech and manners. After his (Atkinson's) death, the number of women reporters was increased and they were given better assignments."[2]

In 1951, a scant three years after Atkinson died, the glamorous blonde, Angela Burke, became the first female reporter to sit in the *Toronto Star's* newsroom. But she was more than just a pretty face; Burke made news. In 1955, when she attended the first press conference ever held in the Kremlin, she was the first member of the Western press during the Cold War era to film the mysterious Soviet leaders.

In the copy she wired to the *Star*, Burke said, "No one stopped me from bringing my cameras into the room, which was remarkable. As [Nikolai] Bulganin began reading his statement, I decided to chance it, and with my 16 mm. movie camera, I began."

Star readers also followed the adventures of the perky Burke through the '50s as she covered the marriage of Prince Rainier to movie star Grace Kelly and partied with Frank Sinatra, Cary Grant and Sophia Loren.

In Canada's Centennial Year, 1967, W.K. Kesterton—a journalism professor at Carleton University—wrote a 300-page book titled, *A History of Journalism in Canada.* Exactly two female reporters were mentioned: *Regina's* Mrs. Kay Kritzwiser—her name spelled incorrectly—gets a total of six words, and Mrs. Simma Holt is mentioned in connection with the "editorial strength" of the *Vancouver Sun* during the 1950s.

Women may have received little respect from professors and the cowboys running the nation's newspapers, but by the time seventeen-year-old Kay Kritzwiser started out at the *Regina Leader-Post* in 1930, with a pay-rate of $40 a month, newsgirls were receiving decent pay for their work. It was never quite as much as the boys, but it was well within the national average. Statistics Canada reports that at that time, the average weekly wage for women was $12, (men $20). And in 1942, when Callwood went to the *Globe and Mail,* for $25 per week, the national average was $21 for women (men $35).

The gals enjoyed good wages and hard liquor in those pre-feminist days, but they also produced hard-hitting stories. Reporters like Burke and Dorothy Howarth filed international scoops. In 1959, Dorothy Howarth, on a hunch, rooted out the mysterious schoolgirl who was to be the bride of Crown Prince Akihito of Japan and revealed this secret to the world. Today, Michiko Shoda and Emperor Akihito are still going strong. Yes, in the past there were several Lois Lanes in Canada's newsrooms and today, building on their legacy, an army of smart women continue to deliver our daily news.

KAY KRITZWISER
Regina Leader-Post, 1931-1956. Globe and Mail, 1956-1980.

1910-2009

> "I was skinny and homely, but I had eyelashes and I batted them. I still do and I still get a response."

At eighty-eight, Kay Kritzwiser, retired *Globe and Mail* art critic, was still wearing the stiletto heels favoured by a generation of women that believed teetering on pumps made a girl look glamorous. "Curiosity is engraved across my chest," declared Kay with a fluttering of hands. As she explained why curiosity meant everything to her, she caressed flowers with long delicate fingers. This gesture, cultivated over decades, used to indicate one was *artistic*.

"Men," Kay went on, with a coquettish parting of scarlet lips, "Men were very much involved in my career and every good thing that happened to me. Dic Doyle and darling John Fraser. I met John when he came to the *Globe* as a winning little reporter. John is one of my treasures. He always called me Mrs. Super Kay. He had a puppy dog's tail that wagged. Everybody loved him."

The winning little John Fraser recently retired from his post as Master of Massey College at the University of Toronto.

Richard "Dic" Doyle, then Editor-in-Chief, picked up on Kay's self-image as a vamp when he met her, in the *Globe* newsroom, in the 1950s. In his book, *Hurly Burly: My Time at The Globe and Mail,* Doyle painted a picture of Kay as a femme fatale, much to her delight. "The lady knows how to bat an eyelash, swivel a hip, show off an ankle or arch an eyebrow. A rustle of silk announces her arrival, a breathless voice begins the interview, a laugh like Bacall's punctuates the questions. Tiny gasps greet the most mundane of responses to her guileless prodding into the dark recesses of the hapless fellow on the other side of her note pad. How gently she receives the confessions... And then she is gone. She swirls away, leaving a blur of her scarlet shawl; the fragile scent of Joy—or is it Chanel—to prolong the enchantment."[1] Whoa! Mr. Doyle.

Almost fifty years later, bright eyes glistening with the joy of dressing up, donning her best jewellery and dining out in a smart Toronto restaurant, Kay launched into her story.

"The way I started in newspapers, it just wouldn't happen today. I left high school in Grade 10 and took a six-month secretarial course at Scott College in Regina. My family didn't know. They thought I was at the Sacred Heart Convent School. I got zero on an algebra exam and decided the convent wasn't for me. I was a rebel."

The convent had worked for Kay's older sisters, who were born in Scotland. Her family roots, however, were in Ireland. Kay's father, Joseph Mullan, was born in Limavady, Ireland. He enlisted in the British army and spent eight years in Bombay where he served as an officer's orderly. After Mullan left the army, the colonel he had served hired him to work as a servant in his grand house in the English countryside. Mullan joined the below-stairs staff, and lived a life

Newsgirls

not unlike the servants and maids in the TV series, *Downton Abbey*. Kay's future mother, Lucy, was a cook in the officer's household, so it was inevitable the couple would meet. Joseph and Lucy married and moved to Dunoon, Scotland. After opening a butcher shop, they had four children. When the Mullans decided to move to Canada, Joseph went on ahead and found work at Armours, a meat packing plant, in Saskatoon. After the family reunited, Kathleen Mullan was born in Saskatoon in 1910. While Kathleen was still an infant, the Mullans moved to Regina.

"Obviously after that long separation, I was their love child. I never really had any connection to my older siblings who were born in Scotland. Besides, they all went to the convent school and I refused," said Kay, adding another daughter was born after her.

Kay's father had a magnificent tattoo of a skimpily clad Indian girl dancing a nautch on his forearm. "I used to be so embarrassed about it. When he was in his cups, he would flex his arm and the girl would dance. Her hips swayed," laughed Kay.

Because Mullan was a butcher, his six children never went hungry during the prairie droughts of the 1920s and The Great Depression in the 1930s.

> Nautch: a dance still performed today by girls, mainly in North India.

Novice Writer

The year was 1926 and, after learning to type and take shorthand, Kay worked at an insurance company, where she spent her noon hours writing letters to all the actresses in Hollywood. "I identified with Virginia Lee Corbin. She was a little blonde child. I had a doll with a mended china head I called Virginia. The doll became my alter-ego. This was pre-Shirley Temple," explained Kay.

At age fourteen, the romantic Kathleen Mullan had already started writing professionally for the *Regina-Leader Post*, under the byline "Betty Lou of the Lighthouse."

"I always used poetry. What the hell did I know about lighthouses living in Regina? Betty Lou of the Lighthouse, indeed," guffawed Kay, swirling the red wine in her glass. But Betty Lou's poetry and the lighthouse gig turned out to be her entree into the world of adult newspapers. Kay became editor of a children's weekly page, called *The Torchbearers' Club*, with its banner cry "Carry On! Carry On!" The imaginative teen also wrote fiction with titles such as *Lavender of the Lighthouse*, *The Taming of Betty Lou* and *O Hara San's First Christmas*, a story about a Japanese girl's first encounter with Christmas—a festival, the mature Kay laughingly admitted, was unknown to the Japanese in those days.

> Teenaged star of *Aladdin and the Wonderful Lamp* and *Sinner in Silk*. Corbin died in 1942 at thirty-one.

After Betty Lou and Lavender's lighthouse, Kay worked under Isabel Turnbull, Social Editor of the *Leader-Post* and editor of the *Torchbearer*. Shortly after Kay was hired by the newspaper, Turnbull married James Jeffrey Dingman. Once married and pregnant, Turnbull had to give up her job—according to the rules of the day—and Kay, at the untried age of seventeen, was catapulted into the editorship of the women's pages by A.M. Raymond, Managing Editor of the morning edition of the *Leader-Post*.

"My father and mother were delighted with my new job. I got $40 a month and, after room and board, my mother gave me back $15. A.M. Raymond gave me a chance to do everything. It was a great job. Later, I wrote three columns a week. I wasn't ahead of my time. At the *Post*, there was an awareness of women's capabilities and David B. Rogers, who was the big boss, was also supportive."

The *Leader-Post* sent Kay on her very first travel assignment. She travelled by train to the Banff Highland Games and, true to character, Kay had the correct costume made especially for the excursion—a Scottish tartan skirt and a black velvet jacket. "It was the first time ever I travelled myself. I had to ask my mother if I could go. I was so unsophisticated."

In 1933, Kay was a founding member of the Regina chapter of the *Canadian Women's Press Club* (CWPC). It grew out of a women's press club Kay and three other female reporters had formed in 1928. The next year, she attended the national meeting of the press club, in Edmonton, and was entertained in the home of Canada's great suffragette, Nellie McClung.

"I was thrilled. As a child, I had read her book *Sowing Seeds in Danny*.[2] She lived in a ranch-y type of house. Mrs. McClung was a lovely, warm person with grace and a sense of humour," Kay said, adding the CWPC played a big part in forming her working life.

> McClung's book made $25,000 (over $300,000 in today's money).

Kay Kritzwiser

In 1912 the first chapter of the CWPC was formed in Winnipeg, with Nellie McClung as president. When McClung moved to Edmonton, Alberta, in 1915, she was still involved with the press club and it was here she started lobbying Members of Parliament to have women appointed to the Senate. The British North American Act said only persons interpreted as "he" could be considered for federal government posts. By extension, women were "*shes*." By 1927 McClung had joined forces with four other women, known as the *Famous Five*, and they went to court to prove that women were *persons*—a bid the ladies lost. The Supreme Court deemed since women were *not* persons they could not sit in the Senate and it also decided they could not vote. This decision was overturned, on October 18, 1929, and set Canada on the road to universal suffrage.

Until the 1950s, great ladies visiting Regina were invited, by the CWPC, to take tea at the Hotel Saskatchewan. Kay remembers meeting the legendary Cora Hind, who, as agriculture reporter for the *Winnipeg Free Press,* earned a worldwide reputation for accurately predicting wheat crop yields. Hind always strode around in men's clothes and could out-tramp any hardened farmer in the prairie fields. "I found her a frightening woman. I met her in the hotel in the Spanish Tea Room. That's where I also met Eleanor Roosevelt in 1950. My most vivid memory is that Eleanor's hemline dragged beneath her fur coat," said Kay, ever sartorially correct.

And in fact, Kay wrote, for the *Leader-Post*, a long schmaltzy description of Mrs. Roosevelt, wife of former U.S. President Franklin Roosevelt, when Mrs. Roosevelt appeared in the Regina legislature chamber. The account is written in flowery Victorian prose, without one iota of news. At one point Kay alluded to Eleanor Roosevelt's "contributions to humanity," but didn't name them.

Eleanor Roosevelt once said: "I had a rose named after me and I was very flattered. But I was not pleased to read the description in the catalogue: no good in a bed, but fine up against a wall."

At the Regina chapter of the CWPC, Kay also met Kate Aitken, who was Queen of the Muffin Pans and the Canadian airwaves, from the 1930s to the 1960s. Aitken, born with a wooden spoon in her mouth, makes Martha Stewart look like a slacker. Aitken wrote fifty books about cooking, travel and etiquette, employed 12 secretaries and wrote weekly columns for the *Globe and Mail*, the *Toronto Telegram* and the *Montreal Standard*. She also convinced Mussolini to buy Canadian wheat, raised prize-winning white Wyandottes ran cooking schools in Montreal, the Canadian Maritimes and the Canadian National Exhibition. On top of all that during her long career, Aitken made more than 9,500 cross-Canada radio broadcasts including weekly ones from Regina.[3]

Kay also did a bi-weekly broadcast at CKCK, a radio station in Regina, in the '30s, under the pseudonym *Betty Beehive*. Two evenings a week, after supper, Kay would ride her "beautiful" CCM bicycle back to the *Leader-Post* building, the location of the radio station. Once behind the microphone, she would read her columns on the *Betty Beehive Show*, a women's program sponsored by the St. Lawrence Corn Starch Co. "Kate used to smoke behind a potted tree before going on stage at CKCK in Regina" said Kay, recalling the days when all radio broadcasts were live and liberated women smoked.

Kay was at the *Regina Leader-Post* the first time the CCF (Canadian Commonwealth Federation) ran candidates for federal office. "The *Leader-Post* was Liberal. They were all Liberals except me. D.B. Rogers, the managing editor, came out of his office and said could he put me down for the Liberals. It was the deep depression and the world was falling apart. I had voted CCF and was afraid I would be found out. But it was necessary. I felt about it as some people, today, might feel about the NDP. The CCF offered so much for a young person and I liked Tommy Douglas. He had panache."

In 1933, while still at the *Leader Post*, Kathleen Mullan married newspaperman Harold Kritzwiser who worked for the same paper. Apparently, all through Kay's girlhood, the Kritzwiser family lived around the corner from the Mullans and, because he was eight years Kay's senior, Harold had always regarded Kay as just another skinny neighbourhood kid. But that changed one day when he had a close look at the vivacious Kay and a romance began. Poetry had always been Kay's greatest pleasure and, at the drop of a hat, she would recite old favourites. One day

---

The province of Manitoba granted women the right to vote in 1916.

Wyandottes are an American breed of chicken developed in the 1870s and named for the indigenous Wyandot people of North America.

Tommy Douglas, founder of the CCF, was elected to the House of Commons for Regina in 1935. He later became Premier of Saskatchewan and is venerated in Canada as the Father of Medicare. In 1961, the CCF disbanded, regrouped and emerged as the National Democratic Party (NDP), which embraces a socialist agenda similar to the old CCF.

Kay and her "swain" were looking at a "beautiful scene of nature" and she was moved to recite a poem by Edna St. Vincent Millay. She claimed that is why Harold proposed to her. After the wedding, the couple moved to Windsor, Ontario, where Kay's only child, David, was born. Kay was widowed, in 1946, when Harold died of heart disease, leaving her with a six-year-old to raise. Kay always described her son as the "light of her life." David Kritzwiser, an advertising consultant, has lived most of his life in Vancouver.

After her husband died, Kay took David back to Regina. Rogers was still running the *Leader-Post* and he gave the grieving widow a job. "Mr. Rogers gave me many opportunities. He gave me royal tour coverage and instigated the opportunity to write an editorial page column. It was called KMK's column," said Kay, adding that Rogers and she never had "a bad word, quarrel or altercation."

In one column, written in 1948, Kay lamented the demolition of Regina's old isolation hospital. As she looked at the "sad-eyed hulk of the hospital with its innards gone," she recalled her stay there when she was a four-year-old, suffering from diphtheria. "The nurse had cleaned and cut my fingernails; I remembered that, because I didn't like the feel of newly-cut nails and kept my fingers folded into fists…And when I got home there were a lot of people looking at me. They were my father and sisters. But there were too many of them. There seemed to be two of each. There was a picture on the wall of two ladies in pink dresses. The diphtheria had left my eyes temporarily crossed."

In another KMK column, from the same period, Kay profiled Campbell Tinning, a young artist who had returned to the prairies after the flesh pots of Europe and Vancouver to try to capture the wheat lands on canvas. Kay wrote, "The other day, the young artist brought the first of his work back to Regina. There was the bird's eye view of the Lorlie countryside, painted as he perched on the roof of the grain elevator. He painted outside the town's general store and in front of the small white church and from the gate of an empty farmyard.

"He watched the [Indigenous people] come down from the reserve to meet the train and saw their citron shirts and cyclamen scarves. This prairie native finally captured the West in his work and managed to sell a picture of Lorlie station to a private collector."[4]

This portrait of an artist was a harbinger of a career opportunity that would come Kay's way in the near future.

Kay also wrote several columns, in the early 1950s, revolving around her young son David. Kay quaintly referred to herself as *we* throughout these pieces. In one, she described a Christmas Eve party: "We found ourselves assigned to the direction of Christmas carols and we were down on our knees to do this job properly, when the eight-year-old host discovered the soul of the conductor's shoe was fine for striking a match on." In another one, Kay talked about taking two wee boys to a carnival. She ends the column in the 18th century style of a genteel diarist: "Do not approach us from the rear, mute the voice. Deal gently with us. It isn't every day we have a hangover from an evening with the boys."

Kay covered a rodeo in Swift Current and treated *Leader-Post* readers with her usual flamboyant descriptions: "Feature attractions included Gibb Potter, who is a trick roper and three times Canadian trick champion. In his pearl-grey chaps, bright red boots and blue shirt, he spun a 50-foot lariat or whirled three at a time (one in his mouth), lassoed racing horses and gave an eye-filling show."

Although Kay was a young widow, she admitted everywhere she went she was fortunate and made no apology about using her feminine wiles to get ahead. "When the war was on and the men were away, that helped with my career. I was skinny and homely and had no bones, but I had eyelashes and I batted them. I still do and I still get response. Don't you, bat your eyelashes," Kay asked, as if eye-batting was a given for any woman worth her salt.

Thinking back on her rookie self, Kay also commented, "I never wore glasses until I married. Now I thought, I have my man, I can wear glasses." This, of course, brings to mind another lady, who was also a writer in the 1930s. Dorothy Parker, American author, wit and satirist, is famous for her assertion, "Men never make passes at girls who wear glasses."

In 1954, *Liberty Magazine* listed Kay as one of ten best-dressed women in Canada, along with Signy Eaton, wife of department store magnate John David Eaton. The *Liberty* spread featured a portrait of Kay, taken by peripatetic Canadian photographer Roloff Beny. Kay was snapped sitting in her humble living room, in Regina, sporting a big picture hat. "The very idea! There I am, the struggling widow from Regina, with a son to raise, next to the rich Signy Eaton. I'd been on a royal tour and *Liberty* saw me with several members of the *Canadian Women's Press Club*. I was well turned out. I wore gloves and hats; I always had good clothes because I was homely. It was my armour."

Kay was an ardent admirer of Diana Vreeland, the gawky, rake-like editor of *Vogue* magazine in the 1960s. Vreeland, despite her plain face, managed to be one of the most influential women of style in the post-war era. Kay did not deny that she fancied herself somewhat of a provincial Vreeland. She affected the same over-sized glasses, red nails and cigarettes. In 2012 a delightful documentary about Vreeland's life—*The Eye Has to Travel*—was launched at the Cannes Film Festival. Kay's frivolity in many ways emulated Vreeland, she of the entertaining throwaway line. Vreeland's stance is right up there with Kay's eye-batting comment. Who can deny the self-confidence and sophistication of a woman who said, "Unpolished shoes are the end of civilization," "I adore frivolity. I always have," "To be contented. That's for the cows," to quote a few of Vreeland's gems.

During her second stint at the *Regina Leader-Post* (1946-1956), Kay made Regina, then a small prairie town, sound like the hub of the civilized world—a whirl of famous personalities and cultural events. In the early '50s, she directed plays and acted "like crazy" at the Regina Capitol Theatre.

"We did *The Desert Song* and some plays I wrote. It was so fulfilling and wonderful. Shirley Douglas, the daughter of Tommy Douglas, was in one of my plays. It was a pantomime. She was the princess and I was the court jester," said Kay, digging out a picture of the players and pointing to Shirley.

Kay, the quintessential reporter, meticulously documented, not just her travels, but her whole life in dozens of notebooks and photo albums that cover every minute of her sixty-three-year-long career. As well as acting in plays, Kay performed in an amateur dance company with her friend Nancy Graham (Caldwell). Kay kept a plethora of theatre programs. All her life Kay cherished a 1936 playbill, from the Capitol Theatre, featuring the Grace Tinnings Dance Troupe. Along with *The Desert Song* program, from those early days, she had kept one from a 1956 production of *The Barretts of Wimpole Street* that she directed. Kay had always been a thespian and that's why it was easy for her to position herself as a *femme fatale*, a role she played until the end, with the aforementioned high heels, vivid lipstick, sultry voice and languid hand movements.

Kay also kept an original copy of *The Torchbearer*, the little paper that launched her career. In it, Kay had written a sanctimonious editorial about truth and falsehoods and signed her diatribe, "Your Editor." The copy is crammed with clichés that had Kay giggling, seventy years later. "Two wrongs don't make a right" and "honesty is the best policy," are written, as if she made up these platitudes herself.

"What a pompous young ass I was! I told you earlier and I've always said I was a seventeen-year-old rebel. But that doesn't sound like the way a rebel would write." More giggling!

In the early '50s, Kay fell in love again, this time with a Polish immigrant. But as luck would have it, in 1956, Richard Needham travelled across Canada trolling for fresh reporters for the *Globe and Mail*. He met Kay and later that year, Tommy Munns, managing editor of the *Globe,* wrote Kay a letter, asking her to join his staff in Toronto. This meant Kay would have to leave behind her prestigious column (KMK) and her lover.

"I took three weeks to answer because I was so involved with my Polish lover. I had to tell my darling George—who was a surveyor in Saskatchewan. He was lovely. But I knew I would have another dependent relationship in my life, so I decided to take the job offer from the *Globe*. I gave him up. I was so sorry about going to Toronto to start my new life," said Kay, with the air of a thwarted Juliette, "But I've had lots of lovers and lots of men in my life. I've always loved men, enjoyed them and been on their side."

Then, in her own defense, Kay added that everybody had lovers in those days, but she admitted for most of her adult life, she preferred homosexual male friends. "They are cultured

---

Eaton's was founded in Toronto in 1869 by Irish immigrant Timothy Eaton. The Eaton stores and its catalogue service, both Canadian institutions, went bankrupt and closed in 1999.

Capitol Theatre, Regina: Built in 1921; demolished in 1992.

In 1997, while Kay was tlaking about the *Desert Song*, Shirley Douglas was strutting her stuff on stage at Toronto's Royal Alexandra Theatre in the role of Amanda in *The Glass Menagerie*. Her real-life son, Keefer Sutherland, was playing Amanda's son, Tom.

and you don't have to kick them in the balls to get them out of your living room. I have to have men in my life. My sister's church ladies are charming. But..." Kay trailed off, waving around a linen napkin, at a dinner in her apartment.

Life at the Globe

After Kay was established in the *Globe* newsroom, feminist Michele Landsberg recalled, from her fledgling days as a *Globe and Mail* reporter, Needham—a man Kay counted as one of her beaux—as a "sexual harasser."

In an interview with me, in March 1995, Landsberg chatted about the Captain's Table at the Simcoe Hotel where *Globe* reporters and legendary columnist Richard Needham regularly hung out. Needham's musings appeared on the editorial page for about twenty years, ending in 1983. His columns were noteworthy for their flowery sentiments about female pulchritude and satirical comments about current affairs.

"He was a real sexual harasser and really creepy; he used to flatter women and was always holding court at the Simcoe Hotel. There was harassment at the *Globe*, but in those days, it was part of being a woman. There was an old guy in the foreign wire service; he had pornographic—actually erotic poetry. He tricked me into going into his territory a few times and he would leer, grab and sidle up. I learned to stay away from the foreign wire room," said Landsberg. "I wouldn't think of complaining. Harassment at the *Globe* was part of being a woman."

David Hayes in his 1992 book, *Power and Influence: The Globe and Mail and the News Revolution*, about the inner workings of the *Globe*, described Needham as "a cynical chain-smoking curmudgeon... who was rumpled and pickled on gin." Hayes also wrote by the time Needham's column was cut, in the 80s, "he was the *Globe*'s equivalent to a senile uncle to be ignored most of the time."[5] Chacun à son goût.

Even though Needham stayed in his marriage until his death in 1996, he was also the lover of *Globe* travel writer Beverly Gray, according to Kay. She first met him when she was hired as his secretary at the *Calgary Herald*. When Needham signed on with the *Globe and Mail*, Gray followed him to Toronto. Thanks to Needham's "connections" she became a well-published travel writer. In 1965, the *Globe* sent Gray and photographer Erik Christensen around the world. The trip involved nine countries. And giving Gray her due, she filed fifty stories.

Flash forward to 1996. Kay was still addicted to the charming 19th century prose style she used from her Regina days. In a bread-and-butter letter, dated July 29, she wrote (to me): "I can't believe that two Sabbaths have rushed by without a Thank You note to you for that exquisite Sunday evening. Fancy being invited to share such special delights—that beauteous salmon bedecked with lemon, the wicked dessert and the even wicked-er wine with such gallant guests, even better male cavaliers.

"How could I not have written my thanks? The only excuses from Kritzwiser stems from the sad interruption of the sad death of Needham—long-time cherished since 1956 when he was instrumental in beginning my long-time chapters with the *Globe and Mail*...You see how Kritzwiser was distracted from pen and paper."

Kay commented, although she was close to Needham, it never interfered with her relationship with Gray, who died a year after Needham. In Gray's obituary, in the *Globe*, Kay described their relationship as *simpatico*. "We shared an interest in literature and world affairs rather than in gossip and office politics."[6]

After the *Globe* recruited Kay, it was Dic Doyle who shortened her name from Kathleen to Kay and handed Kay her first big-city assignment. It was a wading pool opening and, later in December 1958, she had a front-page story about gift-buying for Christmas featuring an assortment of items ranging from TTC tokens for the needy to a $35,000 sable for sale at Creeds on Bloor St. But Kay was indignant. After all, she *had* gone from three weekly columns, in Regina, to the lowest junior assignments in the newsroom. However, things did pick up.

As an aside, when Michael Ignatieff, former leader of the Liberal Party of Canada, was 17 he landed a summer job at the *Globe and Mail*. In 2004 he wrote a column about his summer at the *Globe*: "Dic Doyle, the editor, was God almighty in that office when I turned up...

He pointed to a nasty-looking eight-inch nail sticking up on the rewrite desk and told me that was where bad copy went to die.

"By late August I was on the lobster shift (midnight to 8 a.m.) listening to the police radios in case another world war was declared, in which case I was to wake Dic Doyle out of bed. Nothing so exciting happened."[7]

Kay made her first major impact at the *Globe* when Doyle assigned her to write a project called "The Ones Who Never Grew Up," a series that examined society's failure to provide protection to the helpless. Kay's stories, written before the existence of Medicare and government welfare departments, were about neglected babies and children in Ontario. Kay's hard-hitting examination of social injustices elicited a huge response from *Globe* readers. According to Doyle, there was also response in the newsroom—surprise that such a weighty assignment was given to Kritzwiser "who wasn't known as a heavyweight," but rather as a reporter skilled in frothy subjects such as fashion, royal tours and exotic travels.

Kay's opening story was about a baby girl born into a wretched family, near Pembroke, in the Ottawa Valley. "When Shirley Ann Barnhardt died on January 27 in the seventh month of her life of malnutrition, dehydration and pneumonia, an icy wind blew in a broken window of the squalid cabin...A mummy child, puny and marked by sores, at the time of her death Shirley Ann was 6 lbs. 14 ounces...She died in a shirt and a ragged diaper."[8]

Hayes, in *Power and Influence,* observed: "Women were forced to fit one of two stereotypes: woman-page fare or the so-called sob sisters." A tradition carried on by Rosie DiManno, at the *Toronto Star*, and *National Post* columnist Christie Blatchford, when she was at the *Toronto Sun.* Hayes wrote that Kay belonged to a third category, "post-emancipation and pre-feminism," which meant she was competing with men "at half their salaries."[9]

According to Hayes, Kay was part of Doyle's "re-tooling" at the *Globe*, a restructuring that reflected concerns with urban social problems. Under this mandate in 1958, Kay had several bylines in the *Globe Magazine*, an insert in the regular newspaper. In one issue, Kay addresses the question: What's become of the Hungarians who arrived in Canada after the Soviet occupation that precipitated an uprising in Hungary in 1956. Kay's reportage starts: "On a warm mid-May morning last year, Zoltan Saary, a lean young Hungarian with glistening black hair, slumped like an old man in his chair in a classroom and shivered...an exam paper in basic English lay before him. He huddles over it as though the chill of October 23, 1956 blew across him."

Saary told newshen Kay that he received a letter that morning saying his father had been thrown into prison. Kay followed Saary's story and later reported his father had been released and the young immigrant was studying engineering at the University of Toronto. Saary was also adjusting to the lifestyle in Canada. "He has learned to eat celery and no longer regards carrots as filler for the barnyard silo. He is no longer puzzled by cornflakes."[10]

In February 1959, Kay wrote another human-interest story for the *Globe Magazine* that is legendary for its 600-word lead. The story, about Bertha "Mom" Whyte, a woman who sheltered unwanted children, starts, "The children call her Mom Whyte and they say it fast, the way the bird flutes it, all day long, 'Momwhyte, Momwhyte, Momwhyte.'"

Hayes commented: "What was striking was the way the opening ran nearly 600 words—the length of many hard-news reports in their entirety—before the reader even learned what the story was about."[11]

In 1963 Kay was still producing pieces for the *Globe Magazine* and it was Editor Colin McCullough who assigned Kay her famous Marshall McLuhan interview. The University of Toronto professor had just won a Governor General's Award for his book, *The Gutenberg Galaxy*, and was fast becoming a public figure. Kay's McLuhan profile was published, in the magazine, on January 4, 1964. Kay had chatted with McLuhan in his home and started her story, not with a statement about McLuhan's cutting-edge theories and pronouncements, but with a domestic observation. In her lead, Kay described visiting children swarming up a chair to touch a wooden mask, on a wall in the McLuhan living room. Kay, who had just visited Greece, drifted off into a riff about the mask. "It is a mask of Tiresias, a Theban of Greek legend who saw Athena bathing and was struck with blindness when she splashed water in his face...Athena was unable to restore his sight. Instead she gave him the power of soothsaying. She opened his ears so he could understand the language of the birds."

Admittedly, they were 21st century versions, producing prose spiced up with profanities and pornographic details in order to appear as hard-hitting as the newsroom boys.

After waxing poetic in her airy-fairy way, Kay re-focused on McLuhan and described him as casting "a shadow like a television tower on the University of Toronto."

Kay also wrote: "McLuhan's now global reputation as a communications authority credits him with the power to see as few do, to hear a new language and to walk confidently in the strange and frightening world of the electronic age...While McLuhan is the plaint core of a number of worlds, he finds the world he likes best is the narrow house on Toronto's Wells Hill Ave. with its tangle of bicycles on the front steps and the homey smell of baking pie coming from the kitchen." Kay continued on about McLuhan's six children and the healthy clatter and clutter they created in the house.

Hayes accused Kay of presenting McLuhan, the great communications' guru, in "a Norman Rockwell-like setting."

The Art Critic

As a reporter, Kay belonged to a simpler time, when everyone was nice—just like the people she grew up with in unpretentious Regina. Looking back through her interviews, Kay never criticized, rarely judged and there are no hard edges in her copy. Kay accepted everyone she interviewed, from Saary, to McLuhan, to Truman Capote, unconditionally, as they presented themselves to her. And later, when she became art critic for the *Globe*, Kay talked about each artist's view of his work, uncritically, and with an untrained eye. But nevertheless, it was as an art critic that Kay's career really took off, and she hung on to that prestigious beat from 1964 until her retirement, on her seventieth birthday, in 1980.

Pearl McCarthy, who had written the *Globe*'s art criticism for decades, died on a Thursday night and Kay was asked to provide a fill-in story for Saturday. She was assigned to interview artist Ken Danby best known, in future years, for *At the Crease*, a painting of a masked hockey goalie in full regalia. Danby was a mere twenty-four years of age and had just left his job as a graphic artist after winning the Jessie Dow Prize, a Montreal art award worth $250.

Danby was as green as Kay, when she went calling. The artist recalled that Kay mentioned her inexperience when she arrived at his Rosedale apartment in April, 1964. "But we got along fine and her enthusiasm and keen interest made me feel comfortable. Since that beginning, she established a strong reputation as a knowledgeable and fair arts critic-reviewer," he said, forty years later.

Kay, with her eye for domestic detail, started off her first art review with the carton of eggs that Danby kept in his refrigerator. She told readers: "On a normal day, Danby counts on using at least three egg yolks, which he mixes with the care of a cook with pure pigment and water."

Kay recalled that Danby had a furry creature of some kind. According to her interview, it was a black cat named Kimbo, the subject of the picture that netted Danby the Dow prize. Kay wrote: "Kimbo, an instinctive model, curls on an orange tablecloth and prompts some of Danby's current preoccupation with the school of magic realism." The next year Kay wrote a flattering review of Danby's first major exhibition, at the Columbus Centre, in Toronto. In the next two decades, Kay would review Danby's work many times as both their reputations grew.

Thirty-four years after Kay introduced Danby in print and miles of ink later, the *Globe and Mail* ran a coloured spread, by Val Ross, about Danby's comeback after thirteen years without a Canadian show. Ross was less flattering than Kay and somewhat baffled about the appeal of the artist's photo-like images. Under the head: "*They Like him, they really like him,*" (meaning the Philistines) Ross wrote, "Danby makes a carefully managed return with some all-too-familiar images. And his fans will no doubt be thrilled...Danby is a showman; in his first self-portrait in years, he has depicted himself in a Svengali-like pose, his left hand extended to the viewer as if attempting to conjure some magic." The entire review oozes contempt for what Ross called Danby's work as "cornily Canadian."[12]

Kay decided, after her toe-wetting Danby interview, that she liked the art beat and just managed to grab it out from under the nose of Elizabeth Kilbourn, wife of Toronto art and architecture historian William Kilbourn. "One day I saw Elizabeth sitting there outside the managing editor's office. She had come to apply for the art critic's job. I said to Dic Doyle, 'if this job is up for grabs, may I have it?'"

As it turned out, the job was Kay's for the asking and thirty years later, she admitted, she still felt bad about Kilbourn when she ran into her at luncheons, at the *Arts and Letters Club,* in Toronto.

Iris Nowell, author of several art books, bumped into Kay after she landed the art beat. Kay, confident she knew all about art, told Nowell, "I went to the library, over the weekend, and read everything about art. I start on Monday."[13]

And start she did. Doyle recalled a rocky transition from McCarthy to Kritzwiser. After McCarthy's death, a cabal of art advertisers and gallery owners indicated to the *Globe* they wanted Kilbourn to be the new critic as she had done some flattering freelance reviews. "After Kay got the job, the lobby group withdrew their art advertising from the *Globe* for several months," said Doyle. "But, in time, Kay managed to win the hearts of the art establishment with her enthusiastic reviews and the advertisers came back with more ads that ever."

Soon Kay was interviewing all the stars in the art firmament. In the summer of 1967, she interviewed Alexander Calder, the American sculptor commissioned to create a mobile for Expo 67 in Montreal. That year was also Canada's Centennial year and the country was choc-a-block with visiting celebrities.

Kay trailed after Henry Moore when he journeyed to Canada to dedicate *The Archer,* his controversial bronze sculpture erected in front of Toronto's brand new City Hall. She visited Bauhaus artist Josef Albers, in Connecticut, and he gave Kay a signed print, a memento that had a place of honor in her Davisville apartment. Kay also interviewed Sir Antony Blunt, art consultant to Queen Elizabeth II, who, in 1963, was exposed as a KGB operative, along with four other homosexual intellectuals from his Cambridge days.

Our peripatetic art reporter also wrote a profile of Alex Tilley, now "the Hat Man." Back in 1971, Tilley was billing himself as owner of *Fine Art Consultants of Canada Ltd.*, an enterprise that Kay described as a rolling rental gallery on wheels. In those days, Hippie Tilley framed pictures and sold art from the back of a van equipped with a skylight and carpeting.

In 1986, Tilley told *Toronto Star* reporter Ellen Bott, "I think that fabric made of natural fibres is a fad." Thus, Tilley's duds were made from endurable poly-cotton.

Doyle sent lucky Kay to the Venice Biennale in 1972. She said: "It was something to be sent by the *Globe*. Artist and sculptor Walter Redinger from London, Ontario, was representing Canada that year. The Canadian Pavilion was so unreal; It didn't look like a place you'd find art. The Pavilion was designed, in 1952, by a firm of Milan-based architects and looked like a public washroom made of particle board and rough barn board."

In Venice, Kay linked up with her old friend, photographer Roloff Beny, who took her to meet wealthy American art patroness, Peggy Guggenheim. Beny introduced Peggy to Kay on the banks of the canal. "She looked like a dowdy, frumpy little housewife. She was wearing ankle socks," commented Kay who was scandalized. Four years earlier, Beny had introduced the *Toronto Star's* fashion reporter, Stasia Evasuk, to Peggy when the pair went to Venice to cover a glittering benefit to raise money to save the city from sinking. Unlike Kay, Evasuk was smitten with Guggenheim's chic little black dresses.

Beny, a callow youth from the Canadian Prairies, had met Guggenheim, in his 20s, when he was a struggling artist in Rome. Eventually, he gave up painting and picked up a camera. Guggenheim introduced Beny around and his career as an acclaimed photographer was launched. His renowned portraits include Henry Moore, Vivien Leigh, Tennessee Williams and Federico Fellini.

Earlier, Kay had reviewed Beny's show *The Pleasures of Photography: The World of Roloff Beny,* mounted at the Art Gallery of Toronto, in June 1966. She wrote: "In this setting, the enlarged black and white stills from the artist-photographer's camera became a visit into a world of piercing beauty. Beny's camera becomes an extension of his inner world." She also described her dear friend Beny as having tidy good looks and a tidy way of wearing casual clothes. After Beny's death, in 1984, The Royal Ontario Museum, named its photography gallery for him. At that time Kay donated all of her signed Beny books and photographs to the museum's collection.

Losing to Kay didn't thwart Kilbourn; In 1978, she was the first woman in Canada to become an Anglican priest. In 1986 and 1993, she let her name stand in diocesan elections in hope of becoming the first female bishop. Kilbourn failed in both attempts.

Reputedly, the iconic Tilley hat is a knock-off of the ones worn in the '60s by Singapore mailmen.

On the same Venetian trip, Kay, ever a romantic, recalled chatting with sculptress Anne Mirvish, wife of millionaire Toronto merchant, Honest Ed Mirvish. "Anne and I sat on one of those little bridges and she told me the story of her life, in the semi-dark. It was a strange place with other people's voices in the background. So unreal and intimate. The time, the place, accentuated our intimacy. It was a brief encounter," said Kay, who remembered every word, as if it were yesterday.

In June 1975, Kay was photographed with Truman Capote in his room, at Sutton Place Hotel. "The first thing I asked him was how to pronounce his name. He took to me," Kay said, while rummaging around for her copy of Capote's book, *The Grass Harp* (made into a Hollywood movie in 1995), with a personal dedication on the flyleaf.

Kay seemed to take on almost all the artists she interviewed as friends, in the heady days of the '60s and '70s, when Toronto had a thriving art scene. In the many interviews, conducted in Kay's apartment, Kay spoke glibly about dozens of Canadian artists and dealers including Rita Letendre, Koso, Isabel McLaughlin, Dorothy Cameron, Gordon Rayner, Harold Town. "I have to accept that I did contribute something to their careers,"

But the best friends she made, in the local art scene, were the hip art dealer Jack Pollock, who introduced Anishinaabe artist Norval Morriseau to Toronto cognoscenti, and Pollock's lover Bernie Taylor. For years, Pollock, Taylor and Kay were a threesome. They wore a path between their adjacent apartment buildings on Davisville Ave. The trio often travelled to Britain and Europe together for holidays and to check out the art scene.

At the AGO's Cinema Ball in 1969, Kay and Taylor caused a sensation when they went costumed as "The End"—he in black tie and she in evening gown. A show-stopper photo, taken that night, shows the couple sporting life-like plastic bare bums, tied to their respective rumps. THE END is written on their ersatz bums.

Kay certainly gave Pollock his share of ink. In 1978, three years after Josef Albers died, Pollock and Kay travelled to Orange, Connecticut to visit Albers' widow, who was also an artist. The purpose of the visit was to secure a selection of Anni Albers' prints and pencil drawings to sell in Pollock's Toronto gallery. It seems the elderly Mrs. Albers was recovering from a fall. Kay wrote in the *Globe*: "It had been a long day for Anni Albers, lying there in her bedroom, so elegant in her blue robe, despite a mended hip and her left arm in a cast...She has brown eyes, young as a girl's, despite her seventy-nine years."

Kay told readers she and Pollock were looking at a portfolio of prints, fresh from the printer. "They had been completed by Mrs. Albers with loyalty to discipline and a fierce disregard of the pain of broken bones...She hasn't much patience for what passes as art in *New York Now*." Her creed: "'An artist has a duty to make order out of things. I believe in human order. Today's art seems to need so many words and the words are meaningless.'" Kay also informed the public that the Albers' collection hangs in the Pollock Gallery, at 122 Scollard St. until November 3.[14]

In a 1988 profile of Pollock for the *Toronto Star*, Bruce Blackadar described Pollock as a "junkie" hooked on cocaine. But the purpose of the piece was to praise Pollock's contribution to the Toronto art scene. In 1960, Pollock opened a gallery in Gerrard Village, Toronto's first edgy location featuring avant garde galleries and coffee houses patronized by beatniks. After Gerrard Village was knocked down by developers, Pollock re-opened a gallery on Dundas St. West and later "pioneered" the Mirvish Village, on Markham Street. Pollock's last gallery was the one, on Scollard, in Yorkville. That gallery closed and soon after Pollock had a breakdown and was hospitalized. He went to France to heal and to paint.[15]

After Pollock, a debauched and troubled personality, died of AIDS in 1992, Taylor moved to Calgary, but Kay and he remained close friends. In a telephone interview, Taylor recalled many devil-may-care good times with Kay. In Toronto, the jaunty friends haunted Antoine's, a by-gone restaurant, on Eglinton Ave. "We knew the owner and after the restaurant closed, we would turn up the music and dance. One time we were jitterbugging and I missed Kay. She ended up in hospital with two broken ribs."

On another occasion, while dancing around the pool at the elegant Cipriani Hotel in Venice, Kay caught her heel in her gown and most of the garment ended up on the tiles.

Taylor also described a trip to the south of France for Pollock's birthday. "Kay arranged only champagne and oranges for the party. She dramatically peeled one orange for Jack, but the rest of us had to peel our own." said Taylor, admitting part of Kay's charm was her eternal role as Drama Queen.

Taylor was well-connected with the Canadian art scene and, from this perspective, opined that Kay was a much-loved and well-respected critic. "She was an honest and upright critic. She never set out to really criticize any artist or to destroy anyone. She was supportive."

Toronto author Margaret McBurney knew Kay well. She commented: "Critique never. Kay was a cheerleader for all the nice young arty men in town. Even [artist] William Ronald, who was unpleasant but needed publicity, was nice to her. Her non-threatening demeanour and niceness resulted in dozens of gifts of art and jewellery."

Both Kay and McBurney were invited to join the snooty Arts and Letters Club, on Elm St. in Toronto, after it opened its doors to the fair sex in 1985. McBurney said, rather caustically: "I received a handsome pin from the Arts and Letters Club to commemorate *I* was the *first* woman accepted into this male milieu. But I didn't parade around, like Kay, and put a banner across my bosom. I was discreet."

One bleak January evening in 2001, I was at Kay's apartment having a supper of parsley ("It keeps me going," she said) and take-out barbecue chicken. Kay had dusted off her Waterford champagne saucers, for the wine, and set out lovely vintage linen napkins. "I love ironing them. My dear sister embroidered them for my hope chest, over sixty years ago. They are so organic. They respond. Linen is of the earth,"

Kay was always on the move, one trip after another, most of them financed by her employers. Over the years, she had complied a dozen scrapbooks of memorabilia devoted to lavish press junkets and luxurious freebies that would make a contemporary reporter's head spin. After the barbecued chicken, Kay hauled out all her travel diaries. She had a record of every trip she ever took, from her 1933 wedding trip to Quebec to a flight to Vancouver, in the 1990s, to spend Christmas with her sister. In between there's a record of some 125 journeys. In the early 1950s, Kay took a fabulous trip, on the *Empress of Lima*, to South America. Kay also had two major trips in 1958—one to Antigua, with a group of ten newspaper women, and the other to Switzerland, aboard Trans-Canada Airlines' inaugural flight to that country. There was also a jaunt to Hawaii, in 1961, and another to Ecuador.

"The *Globe* would send me anywhere I wanted to go. I could do anything I wanted to at the *Globe*," bragged Kay. "We had the world by the tail. It was simple. If the managing editor couldn't go, he'd send one of us. In 1963, that's how I got to go aboard the Canadian Pacific Airlines inaugural flight to Mexico and then on another one to Peru. That time I visited Machu Picchu, Cuzco and Lima. Between Royal Tours and inaugural flights, who could ask for anything more."

In 1970, the *Globe* sent Kay, who was never interested in wine (vodka, yes), to Beaujolais, for one whole week to a wine-tasting sponsored by the French Government. At the end of this sybaritic adventure, Kay and four other Canadian journalists were awarded a wine-tasting certificate and a sterling silver sommelier's cup. Both hung on Kay's kitchen wall for decades.

But it wasn't just ocean liner and airplane trips to exotic destinations. There were also endless theatre tickets, invitations to balls, openings and cocktail parties with the rich and famous. In 1970 Rothman's cigarettes sponsored an art show at the Shakespearean Festival, in Stratford, Ontario. The tobacco merchants sent a limousine to ferry Kay, from Toronto, to the festival. A telling photograph of her, in evening gown, stepping from the vehicle with the air of an empress, reveals how much Kay thrived on VIP treatment.

In his memoir, Doyle commented, back then *Globe* reporters thought nothing of accepting freebies. "Nowadays, a *Globe and Mail* staffer can't accept candy from a stranger without paying for it, but in our early days it would have been pretty dull without passes for theatres, trains, hotel functions, you name it. No favours were expected in return. None given. But we never accepted money."[16]

There were dozens of pictures of Kay with a roster of celebrities including Jazzman Oscar Peterson (c1961), Sculptor Henry Moore and Novelist Truman Capote. Looking at a

> That is, unless you're in the sports department of a newspaper. These reporters feed at champagne troughs and travel with expense accounts befitting a nineteenth-century maharajah.

photo of herself and millionaire art collector and dealer David Mirvish, taken in 1970 "when he had massive hair," Kay remarked about Mirvish: "He always had a wonderful sense of entrepreneurship. He was one of the first to appreciate Frank Stella. David must have a collection worth one million dollars."

In fact, David Mirvish has an art collection worth many millions. It was Mirvish who turned Markham Street into a Greenwich Village (NYC) style destination for aficionados of modern art. And while running his own gallery (1963-1975), Mirvish amassed a fine collection of American abstract paintings in the Color Field school. Today, he is still collecting and dealing in contemporary art.

In 1987 Mirvish took over the directorship of his father Edwin Mirvish's Toronto empire. This included Honest Ed's department store, the Royal Alexandra and Princess of Wales theatres. In 2000 Mirvish Jr. added condominium developer to his list of lucrative endeavours and, in 2012, entered into a partnership with uber-architect Frank Gehry. The partners are developing a stretch of King St. West, a project that includes a ninety-two-story condominium.

The fact that Kay's belief that a million dollars was a staggering sum of money is indication of her eternal naiveté and inability to grasp reality. She never rocked the boat. Almost never said a negative thing about any interviewee or boss. Rarely ever picked up a bill or paid her way. Never questioned the ethics of all the payola she garnered or who footed the bill for all the *free* luxuries that came her way. Life was a fantasy—a stage play like the ones she wrote in Regina—with herself cast as the glamorous soigné gal-about-town. Kay never learned to cook, but dined out on her stories. As mentioned, she lived, in her sunset years, on parsley along with tea and martinis. She always had vodka chilling and a fresh bouquet of the herb in the middle of her table and nibbled at it constantly.

Throughout her *Globe and Mail* days, Kay affected a cigarette holder and owned a stash of gold cigarette cases. "Every time I was asked to speak or make a presentation, they gave me a case as a thank you," she said. "I smoked DuMauriers and red-tipped Sobranies. I could blow beautiful smoke rings. It was so elegant," said Kay, making a big "O" with her mouth.

Kay, always in her own fantasies, meant elegant in the Hollywood sense. She was brought up in the era of black and white films when tough, but beautiful, career gals smoked cigarettes and threw back the odd whiskey. Also during her career, the newsroom culture dictated that you had to be able to drink and smoke with your colleagues way into the night. "I used to be a scotch drinker. Then I discovered 'wodka' and martinis. My smoking was principally decorative. Now I think of smoking as an invasion of privacy," admitted Kay.

Hayes confirmed, in *Power and Influence*, that Kay was often seen with a cigarette. He commented that she was "a social smoker and her prop was a Sweet Caporal (*sic*) that had a red filter tip that matched her lipstick."[17]

Old time newshens, like Kay, would never recognize or indeed enjoy the navel-gazing newsrooms of today, where repressed journalism-school-trained reporters live on mineral water and lettuce leaves. Hard drinking and smoking were as much part of the working press's image as the clickety-clack of the big black Underwood typewriters. Kay commented it was de rigueur to meet someone for a lunchtime interview and have a couple of martinis and many smokes.

Mad Men, the popular American TV series about *roués* in a Madison Avenue advertising agency launched in 2007, but set in the 1960s—Kay's heyday—has been instrumental in bringing back the classic vintage cocktails including the martini (Kay's favourite) and the Manhattan (Kay's second choice). Interestingly, the little black dress worn by Kay the Swinger is also fashionable again and these days, seen on the back of every chic female at every urban art gallery and cinema event.

Kay wasn't the only theatrical *Globe* staffer to live it up—sixties style. Editor-in-Chief Oakley Dalgleish and his gorgeous wife, Delsea, once a ballet dancer, dressed formally much like Nick and Nora Charles, Dashiell Hammet's sophisticated New Yorkers in *The Thin Man* mysteries. The Dalgleishs were dubbed Dal and Del: Once Dal and Del came up the freight elevator, into the *Globe* newsroom, for a nightcap and Doyle wrote in *Hurly-Burly*: "They were

---

October, 2013, David Mirvish announced the sale of Honest Ed's, Toronto's most beloved retail outlet opened by his father. From 1948, when the Bloor Street store opened, millions of immigrants, working poor and students left with bags crammed with bargains. The property was priced at $100 million.

dressed for the occasion and Del, in a clinging white gown that flared at the hem, got a round of whistles from the deskers at the (news) rim. She responded with a pirouette and a tiny bow." The flamboyant Mr. Dalgleish lunched every day at Winston's, a sophisticated Toronto bistro in the '60s and '70s, where Canada's richest and most influential men met. Habitually, their lunch meetings ended around 4 p.m. with Cognac and Montecristo cigars. Handily, Winston's was on Bay St. next door to the *Globe and Mail*.

"Dalgleish liked dogs, sleek cars, good scotch and ground lamb patties. Oscar Berceller (co-owner of Winston's) recognized the 'chief' with an entrée created in his honour. Steak Oakley, on Winston's menu for years, was served by white-gloved waiters."[18]

Tragically, Dalgleish died suddenly from a massive heart attack at age fifty-three.

The Freelancer

Kay kept one bulging scrapbook devoted to her retirement party and 70th birthday—surely one of the biggest galas thrown for a *Globe* employee, since reporters June Callwood and Trent Frayne held their wedding party, in the paper's cafeteria, in 1942. Kay's farewell fête was held at Toronto's Harbour Castle Hotel in 1980. Everyone was there and every man wore black tie. Dic Doyle, still managing editor, assigned Photographer Erik Christensen to follow Kay around for the evening. He captured Kay with a host of other well-known Toronto celebrities in by-gone years. John "Puppy Dog" Fraser, Jack Pollock, Richard Needham, Herb Whittaker, gossip Zena Cherry, Arnold Edinburgh, David Silcox. Everyone was smoking and photographed with a drink in hand. "The evening was so full of love," said Kay, years later, as she gazed at the pictures.

And indeed, such was the veneration of Kay's associates that they were able to entice seventy local artists to contribute a miniature work of art as her retirement gift. Kay had the pieces framed into two montages—"by the Tilley hat man before he got into hats." She later donated these works to the Robert McLaughlin Gallery in Oshawa where they still reside.

"I had them on my walls. I miss those pieces so much. But they are way out in Oshawa and I can't get there," Kay said, wistfully.

Coincidentally, one of the few negative comments, in print, written by Kay, was about the work of artist Isabel McLaughlin, who started painting in the 1930s. McLaughlin was a daughter of Colonel Sam McLaughlin, who formed General Motors of Canada from the old McLaughlin Carriage Co. In 1983, there was a retrospective of 40 years of Isabel's work, in Oshawa, at the Robert McLaughlin Gallery, named for Isabel's grandfather. Between describing the sketches and paintings with adjectives such as tantalizing, vigorous and daring, Kay commented: "Curators can seldom be persuaded that rough sketches are often tentative doodling...some of [McLaughlin's] wildflower sketches could have been left in the sketchbook." It is also worth noting this review was written as a freelance piece, three years after Kay retired.[19]

In retirement, Kay also produced travel and lifestyle pieces for the *Globe* and freelanced for *City and Country Home*, a glossy Maclean-Hunter publication that thrived in the '80s. A travel story in the *Globe*, about Hong Kong, started with one of Kay's trademark florid leads. "A Susie Wong at heart, I yearned to see the eight silvery Rolls Royces and there they were, lined up like self-assured gentry in front of the Peninsula Hotel...We have lunch. I resist the temptation to order a pink gin. I dare a martini after a long drought. By gad, it is a martini. I have chicken salad and French ice cream. I feel a traitor to the noon-day rice and Chinese beer I have acquired a taste for."[20]

Kay slowed down, a mite, after a dreadful accident which occurred Christmas 1983 when she took the bus to Bolton to spend the holidays with Nancy Caldwell, her girlfriend from the pre-war days in Regina. Nancy's husband, Spencer Caldwell, a founder of CTV, the first private Canadian television station, met Kay at the bus depot and on the way to the Caldwell farm a truck crashed into his vehicle, killing Caldwell and putting Kay in the hospital with head injuries. It took Kay months to recover, but it took Nancy longer. When Nancy finally came to terms with the tragic loss of her husband, she presented Kay with a

Luckenbooth pendant, a traditional Scottish love token, sold under the steeple of St. Giles Kirk in Edinburgh. These pendants feature a huge heart-shaped piece of amber, representing the heart of Mary, Queen of Scots. Spencer had given this token to his wife, and Nancy passed it on to Kay as a memento of her friendship with Spencer. Kay only wore it on state occasions like lunching (with me), at Grano, on Yonge St.

In 1992, Kay was awarded a Commemorative Medal for the 125th Anniversary of Canadian Confederation. The medal, presented by Prime Minister Brian Mulroney, was for "a significant contribution to Canada." By then Richard J. Doyle had left the *Globe* and had been appointed to the Canadian Senate, where he sat from 1985 to 1998. Doyle sent a letter to Kay, on Senate of Canada letterhead, congratulating her on the award. In it, he described Kay as "a demon reporter... who has ornamented journalism in Canada and furthered the cause of Canadian art. You are one of the few people these days who give the Irish a good name. Love, Dic."

Social Butterfly

Kay had another set-back on October 5, 1997. That evening, Kay and Nancy Caldwell toddled out to one of Kay's favourite neighbourhood haunts, the Barmalay, on Mt. Pleasant Rd. Kay loved this Russian restaurant because it offered both vodka and sentimental Russian music. As the old friends dined, a group of men celebrating the end of their baseball season arrived. One thing led to another and two "young men" asked Nancy and Kay, both aged 87, to dance.

"I was twirling around a bit and my rubber sole caught on the carpet and down I went. I guess I'm too old to jitter-bug...to hell with that. I'm not!" She later explained from her bed in St. Bernard's rehabilitation hospital. "You know, they took me to Mt. Sinai and I didn't even have a toothbrush. Thank goodness I had my lipstick, or I'd have killed myself."

Kay's local pub, the Barmaid's Arms on Yonge St., sent flowers, and the story spread to Ottawa, where her old boss, Senator Doyle, heard all about it. That Christmas, he sent Kay a card full of glee because one of the old guard could still *cut-the-mustard*. Well, almost.

By February 2000, Kay was back in fighting form and she had delightful photographs of herself, in a perky red tam, celebrating her 90th birthday. The shots were taken at both the Arts and Letters Club and the Art Gallery of Ontario.

In her mid-90s Kay moved to Briton House, a residence for seniors with small fridges for vodka chilling. Her room was outfitted with ugly IKEA furniture and walls full of the art given to her as gifts. Happily, it was located a few hundred yards from the Chicken Deli. Most evenings, Kay dressed, high heels and all and applied the red lipstick and made her way to the Deli. There she consumed a martini or two and a kindly waiter always helped her navigate her way home. Although this home was humble, there was no lack of richness and joy as Kay looked back on her life.

To the end, Kay's telephone never stopped ringing with friends calling to issue invitations for dinner and theatre. Kay remained in the loop and, with an astounding clarity of memory, would chat on about having tea with artist Louis de Niverville one Christmas, or about an upcoming date with her old beau Herb Whittaker, former *Globe* drama critic. Whittaker, born in 1910, the same year as Kay, died in 2006 thus predeceasing her by three years.

It would be remiss not to say something more about Kay's son. He rarely called her and he did not visit. By all reports, from people intimate with Kay, motherhood was another fantasy. She left the young boy alone while she pranced around town. He was left to his own devices and it is no wonder that once he started working in Vancouver, he stayed there. And when he married it was months before Kay found out.

At almost a century old, Kay read the *Globe* daily but was disgusted with its emphasis on people's marital problems and their whining or bragging about their privileged children on the back page of the *A* section. "It is my newspaper. I loved it. But now when I read it, I feel like throwing up. It doesn't deal with news in an objective way and has no stamp of originality. I have no feeling a personality is being delivered to my front door each day."

Hard words from a gentle soul.

Kathleen Mullan Kritzwiser died in Toronto, at Britain House, in 2009. She was ninety-nine.

DOROTHY HOWARTH
Regina Leader-Post, 1937. Toronto Telegram, 1943-1967.

1912-2009

"This is my advice to any girl who wants any: get married as soon as possible; to heck with the business life. I'm in newspaper work because I need money."

It was the Dirty Thirties when legendary news reporter, Dorothy Jean Howarth, at the untried age of eighteen, finished Normal School—teacher's college—in Moose Jaw, Saskatchewan. She found a teaching job in a rural community for the decent sum of $400 a year, but she never saw any of it. "The farmer took my board out of this and then he applied the rest against his taxes. It was all theory. There was no cash. No one was paid. I got promissory notes," said Dorothy who, at eighty-five, was still a strong, striding, strapping prairie girl, although transplanted to North Toronto. She added during a 1998 interview she never felt poor and couldn't understand "people on welfare squawking."

Dorothy was born in Weyburn, Saskatchewan, February 27, 1912. Her mother died soon after giving birth to a sister, Bertha, who was whisked away to Vancouver and adopted by an aunt. Dorothy's father, Thomas Howarth, re-married and Dorothy was brought up by a step-mother.

Her father ran a combination bowling alley, tobacco store, pool room and barber shop in Weyburn. In reality, it was the hamlet's (male) recreation centre, under the guise of a barbershop—until Howarth lost his livelihood in the Great Depression.

One of the few childhood memories Dorothy retained from her home town was canoeing with author W.O. Mitchell, who was also a Weyburnian. Mitchell became one of Canada's most celebrated authors and his novel *Who Has Seen the Wind* remains a Canadian classic.

In 1937, after eight years of teaching, Dorothy took a position in the advertising department of the *Regina Leader-Post*. She was assigned the humble job of measuring advertising linage for the paper. Luckily, the women's editor gave her a chance to do night assignments—concerts, meetings, and so on—giving Dorothy her first taste of seeing her words in print. Three years later, Dorothy moved as a reporter to the *Saskatchewan Farmer*, a supplement of the *Leader-Post*. There, she spent a few years answering letters in the women's section and handling the lovelorn column. Dorothy's next stop was the women's department at the *Saskatoon StarPhoenix*.

Dorothy Ventures East

Suddenly, Dorothy had an urge to go east. As soon as she managed to get together a grub stake of $400, Dorothy headed for Montreal. But, when she hit Toronto in 1943, she stopped and found work in a munitions' factory to keep body and soul together while trying her luck at landing a newspaper job. After she was turned down by the *Toronto Star*, the *Globe and Mail* and *Maclean's* magazine, Dorothy managed to find a position at the old *Evening Telegram* for $25 a week. Out of this, Dorothy paid $50 a month for room and board in a house on Laughton Blvd.

At the *Telegram*, Dorothy was placed in the women's department on a trial basis. She recalled that the ladies had their own office outside the newsroom, a safe distance from the boys who gathered the news.

"I wasn't crazy about the women's pages; it was all teas and bazaars, I didn't get as much money as the men, but I was living well enough on what I got. I paid for my board and only came home to sleep. I mostly worked and had no real life outside of the newspaper business. I wasn't a drinker, for one thing."

But Dorothy admitted she would mosey over to the Radio Artists Club on Bay St. now and then, where the newsboys in pork-pie hats hung out. "There was a bar and I sat along with the fellows–nothing romantic ever materialized; we just talked the same language. I would listen and learn. There was also a restaurant called Childs, on Bay St., where we gathered for black coffee after hours on a story."

Within months, Dorothy was in the newsroom as a general assignment (GA) reporter. Dorothy understood she never would have gotten out of the advertising department and into the newsroom if most of Canada's young men hadn't been off at war when she started out.

Dorothy landed the University of Toronto beat and that is where her newspaper career really began. Although she was the university reporter of a major newspaper, being a woman, Dorothy was not allowed into Hart House, a male bastion where dignitaries spoke and important debates were thrashed out. She endured the humiliation of begging for renditions of the speeches from privileged male reporters. No matter, in the next twenty years, Dorothy would deliver so many scoops that she was called "Front Page Dorothy," and nicknamed "The Sponge."

Dorothy started to tell her tales as she led me along North Toronto streets, towards a favourite restaurant on Bayview Ave. Still an Amazon—a bony, angular 5' 10"—it was hard to keep up. Dorothy assured me the place was only a few blocks away after I had been scampering beside her for fifteen minutes. Perhaps it's just as well our following interviews were conducted at her North Toronto home.

Dorothy recalled Editor Doug MacFarlane sending her to the University of Toronto to investigate rumours about the development of an atomic bomb in the summer of 1945. "The university science department explained that it was impossible. They said maybe in ten years. And that's the story I wrote. A few days later, August 6th, the A-Bomb was dropped on Hiroshima. MacFarlane was furious and said 'I should have dropped a bomb on you'. Then I went back to the scientist at the university and I told him I ought to drop a bomb on him," said Dorothy, as steamed as she ever got, commenting about one of the few stories she didn't snag for the front page.

Dorothy's stint on the university beat continued after the war, when the colleges were over-flowing with enlisted men returning from overseas. The return of thousands of battle survivors became a big social issue, both in the labour market and in education. Places had to be found for them, but they "had seen Hell" and returned home with a new perspective on authority and convention. These veterans were much older than the other students and many were small-town heroes with wives. They changed the face of the campus and caused much controversy; at one graduation ceremony, Dorothy lined up all the graduates and their babies—who took up the whole section in the front row—for a *Telegram* photographer.

"One controversy that I reported on involved the rule that men had to wear suit jackets and ties at Hart House. The boys, back from overseas, in their Eisenhower bomber jackets, objected, and the master [of Hart House] backed down. In the late forties, this was quite scandalous."

Hard News Beat

After moving from the university into news, Dorothy was a key player in one of the most sensational happenings of the 1950s: the saga of the infamous bank robbers, the Boyd Gang. Led by Edwin Alonzo Boyd, the gang's misadventures, prison escape and shooting of a policeman on College Street, kept Ontario readers on the edge of their seats through 1952.

"Sure, I worked on the Boyd Gang. Smirle Lawson, the coroner, asked me if I wanted to

---

In the dailies, the GA reporters are the news gatherers. This job is an apprenticeship in aggression and requiers running around all hours of the day and night and meeting a deadline at all costs. The GA reporter covers everything from infanticide to bake sales.

see the body of the dead policeman," said Dorothy, in a hard-boiled tone that provided a glimpse of the relentless newshen she once was.

After Sergeant Edmund Tong was shot, Dorothy and a *Telegram* photographer were right on the spot and followed the ambulance to the Toronto General Hospital, where Dorothy ran alongside the gurney right into emergency. "The shooting was in broad daylight; we knew right away this was a big story. Tong stopped two members of the Boyd Gang who had escaped from the Don Jail. They were in a stolen car and when Tong approached them, Steve Suchan panicked and shot him. Tong died in hospital several days later," explained Dorothy.

Swiftly, the *Telegram* reporters ensconced Evelyn Tong, the murdered officer's wife, in the royal suite at the King Edward Hotel. Dorothy befriended Ev Tong and filled the pages of the *Tely* with stories about how Mrs. Tong "bore the tragedy with the courage of her Highland Scot's nature." Dorothy also commented that "a policeman's wife has got to expect this."

But Dorothy wasn't the only newsgirl to befriend Ev Tong. Dorothy's colleague, Val Sears, reported that when he saw Mrs. Tong at the hospital visiting her dying husband, the distraught wife told Sears she wasn't lonely because she had a girlfriend with her. On inquiry, it turned out the "girlfriend" was none other than Dorothy's persistent rival Alexandrine Gibb of the *Toronto Star*. Meanwhile, the *Telegram* also got to Boyd's wife, Doreen Boyd, and stashed her and her three children in the King Edward Hotel before the *Star*'s Gibb grabbed her. Dorothy interviewed the woman several times, each time producing a sensational sob story about the bandit's wife left to bring up her little ones on her own.

Dorothy added what stuck with her, forty years later, was Mrs. Boyd telling her that robbing banks was okay because banks are insured.

Boyd was sentenced to eight life sentences, but was released on parole for good behavior in 1966. Suchan and Leonard Jackson, the shooters, were convicted of murder and given death sentences. "At the hanging of Suchan, I stood outside the Don Jail. It was the last hanging in Ontario," Dorothy said.

The Boyd story surfaced again in 1962 when the local newspapers were full of the hardships. Mrs.Tong suffered after the City of Toronto cut her widow's pension. This left her with an annual income of $3,230 to keep her son in school and to look after a chronically ill daughter. In November 1962, *Star* columnist Pierre Berton devoted a long column to the woes of the nice Mrs. Edmund Tong. He concluded: "Mrs. Tong deserves more than welfare. After all, her husband went to his death trying to protect his fellow citizens from armed thugs."[1]

Interestingly, the *Star* beat the *Telegram* to the punch on this follow up issue. Almost two months later, Dorothy was assigned to the pension story. She started with a strong emotional lead: "She gives without asking anything in return." Dorothy went on to tell about Mrs. Tong's volunteer work with epileptics and how she had never "asked the city for anything, not even ten years ago when her husband was shot down, at noon, by two dangerous and heavily armed bank bandits."[2]

Such is the power of the press that the widow's pension was restored.

The Boyd story certainly "had legs," as they say in Newspaper Land. Years later, in September 1996, *Toronto Star* reporter, Dale Brazao, was inspired to track down Edwin Boyd, who, after his release from prison in 1966, fell into obscurity. Brazao's sleuthing led him to a town in the Canadian West where Boyd, then eighty-two, lived with a second wife. He had a new name and did not want his neighbours to know about his past. Boyd told Brazao that, following his release, he learned to drive a bus and took a job ferrying disabled people around.[3]

Even Boyd realized how seriously the Toronto dailies lusted after sensational copy in the 1950s. He told Brazao that the exploits of the so-called Boyd Gang were really a creation of a circulation war between the *Daily Star* and the *Telegram*. "After a while, even I started to believe the things they were writing about me," Boyd said. "Half the time I didn't know what the hell I was doing."

By 1996, Doreen Boyd, who raised the two surviving Boyd children on her own after her husband went to prison, was living in a Toronto seniors' home. She told Brazao that she was still in love with Boyd.

After Dorothy read Brazao's cops-and-robbers story on the front page of the *Star*, she sent me a letter objecting to its excesses. Part of her critique included Brazao's use of the phrase

> Dorothy was not quite right. Suchan was hanged in Toronto's Don Jail in December 1952. Two more culprits were hanged in the jail in 1962. They were the last, although the death penalty was not removed from Canada's criminal code until July 14, 1976. In July 1976, Bill C-84 was read in the House of Commons and ultimately passes, abolishing the death penalty in Canada.

"wad of bills:" "I should think the haul would make a wad of only about $1,000—that's all the cash there was," wrote Dorothy. She also described Boyd as "a polite, well-spoken man, probably well-brought-up in England."

Later, in 1982, the CBC aired a TV documentary called *The Life and Times of Edwin Alonzo Boyd* and re-hashed the story all over again. But the Boyd saga wasn't over yet; in the summer of 2000, Brazao heard Boyd wasn't well and this time visited Boyd in his home, "Somewhere in B.C.," and found Boyd, then eighty-six, had become a Seventh-day Adventist. He described Boyd as "a man at peace with his God." Boyd died two years later.

Back in 1952, along with the Boyd scoop, Dorothy received first prize ($300) from the Toronto Firefighters' Association for her reportage in the *Telegram* about a fire at Lambert Lodge, an old folks' home on Christie St. "Miss Howarth talked to residents, giving readers a vivid word-picture of the elderly people watching their home burn."

Second prize ($200) went to a rookie reporter: "carrot-haired" Doug Creighton, 24. He wrote about a fire that resulted in the death of a young father and the "leap to safety of his wife and children." Readers were also told Creighton's prize money would help finance his honeymoon in June when he married Marilyn Chamberlain. This is the same Creighton that, in 1971, was a co-founder of the *Toronto Sun* along with Peter Worthington and Don Hunt.

In the mid-1940s, Dorothy joined the Toronto chapter of the *Canadian Women's Press Club*. The CWPC put out a monthly newsletter called the *By-Liner*. In the May, 1952 edition, Dorothy wrote a sour, rambling rant titled "*Small Town*" about the ugliness and stodginess of Toronto. It starts: "Toronto had the first [plumbed] bathtub in Canada 108 years ago. And it has been acting that way ever since."

"Governor John Simcoe Graves named the whole thing Muddy York and there's been no reason to change that name...Compared to the Festival of Britain, an exhibition of quality, the buildings at the Canadian National Exhibition (in Toronto) look like tired old outdated cardboard sets for a puppet show."

After many insults about how provincial, backward and pretentious Toronto is, Dorothy ends with a simile: "Toronto is like a well-worn wife. The façade once so beautiful (reference to fine historical buildings like Osgoode Hall) now has its ugly points...And though you may stray, caught by the loveliness and mystery of Rome, Paris and London, you will always come home to the staidness and order of Toronto."

This, from a woman brought up in the outback of pioneer Saskatchewan.

> Lambert Lodge was demolished in 1981 and all three *Sun* co-founders have since passed away.

Bell's Swim

Dorothy covered dozens of inspiring human-interest stories, as well as gripping tales of crime and death. The common denominator was the lengths the Toronto newspapers would go in the 1950s and early 1960s to scoop a story. Dorothy claimed she was always lucky, and that's why she ended up with one front-page story after another for the *Telegram*.

Dorothy scooped the *Toronto Daily Star* on Marilyn Bell's historical swim across Lake Ontario. This was one of the biggest Canadian stories of the 1950s and every old newsman from Pierre Berton to Jocko Thomas claimed they were principals in it. But it was Dorothy's audacity that got her the jump on her fellow newshounds on that one.

Marilyn Bell, Toronto's Sweetheart, was sixteen years old on September 8, 1954, when she set out to swim the forty miles from Youngstown, New York, to Toronto in an attempt to be the first person to conquer the icy, treacherous waters of Lake Ontario. The plan was for Marilyn to arrive, on the Ontario shore, near the annual Canadian National Exhibition. Bell was up against Florence Chadwick, a professional marathoner, who was the first person to ever swim the English Channel in both directions at one go. Chadwick was promised $10,000 when she crossed the finish line, but she became ill and was pulled out of the water before the Toronto shore came into view.

"The Marilyn Bell story was big. We called her the little girl with the big heart. She was a heroine. All Ontario school girls wrote away for an autographed photo of Marilyn. She was a sensation," said Dorothy.

Although the *Star* sponsored the teen's swim to the tune of thousands of dollars for boats and staff, plus prize money of $7,500, somehow Dorothy, a *Telegram* reporter and, thus by definition, arch-enemy of the *Star*, managed to get close enough to the swimmer to have her picture taken rubbing oil on Marilyn minutes before the girl slipped into the water at Youngstown. The picture, snapped by a *Telegram* photographer, ran on the front page. Even better, through deception and finding herself at the right place at the right time, Dorothy was able to beat the *Star*'s team of crack reporters with the news that Marilyn had completed her swim.

All through the swim, it had been a brutal struggle between the rival newspapers for every snippet of copy. During the crossing, the *Telegram*'s boat kept trying to intercept Marilyn's medical boat as well as the rowboat carrying her coach, Gus Ryder, and a bevy of *Star* reporters. Marilyn ended up near the Boulevard Club and so did her official yacht, the *Mona IV*, paid for by the *Star* and skippered by Dr. Bernard Willinsky, the official swim physician. The boat had kept pace with Marilyn as she battled her way across the lake. Dorothy followed Willinsky into the marine police station, near the club, and proceeded to listen to his minute-by-minute report of every inch of the twenty-one-hour swim.

"On shore, the *Star* went as far as hiring fifty-two Diamond taxis to jam the Harbour Police parking lot so we couldn't get in. Then, while I stood beside Willinsky as he told the fellow in charge everything Marilyn Bell said, the *Star* ambulance arrived for Marilyn. I climbed in, but the *Star*'s George Bryant recognized me and dragged me out. They claimed I was dressed as a V.O.N. (nurse). But I often wore a navy-blue suit, white blouse and a little pill box hat."

Dorothy explained that the big thing was the competition with the *Star*: "our editor, Doug MacFarlane, was a natural competitor. He said we had to get this story on the street before the *Star*. I had to find a phone and keep the line open to rewrite. The photographer and I would take turns guarding the phone booth. On every story, the first thing was to locate the phone and keep talking in order to keep the line open to the rewrite desk. A reporter would tie up the line as long as a story unfolded, filing copy to forward the story for each of the daily editions. Once the line was secured, the competition had to go further away from the scene to find its own telephone booth."

When MacFarlane realized Dorothy had the goods, he ordered her to write a first-person story that night. He also instructed his staff to feed every word, gesture and sound they heard to Dorothy for her first-person story. Meanwhile, the *Star* staff, thinking they had the story in the bag, figured they could wait until the next day for their exclusive interview. Dorothy cobbled together a first-person story from Marilyn Bell, while the exhausted swimmer slept at the Royal York Hotel–guarded by Bryant, who slept outside the door of her hotel room.

"I was busy, busy Dorothy while Marilyn slept. The *Telegram* sent someone up to Loretto Abbey, where Marilyn was a student, and asked the nuns to give us an essay with her signature," said Dorothy.

While the *Star* bided it's time, clever Dorothy pounded out a first-person account on her Underwood, using the details she had heard from Willinsky. Then the cagey *Telegram* deskers printed a copy of Marilyn's signature at the top of Dorothy's opus. Needless-to-say, when *Star* management saw Dorothy's nocturnal labours, they went bonkers.

"My story sold like hot cakes when the first edition hit the street. Yes, we would cut each other's throats on a story, but we were friends outside," Dorothy told me, with great satisfaction, decades later.

According to Ron Loman, a former RAF pilot who joined the *Toronto Star* as a reporter in 1946 and stayed for forty-four years, the *Star*'s first edition hit the street at 1 a.m. "The *Star* and *Telegram* trucks would race up Yonge St., starting at Front St. and throw bundles of papers to shops and newsboys as they went in an effort to be the first paper on the street with a breaking story. It was something to see."

Retired *Star* newsman Val Sears had a different version of the events of the Bell swim, as did every other vintage Toronto newshound. In his book "*Hello Sweetheart, Get Me Rewrite: The Last of the Great Newspaper Wars*," Sears wrote that MacFarlane told his troops: "Fight your way in if you have to. But get to [Marilyn] and get her into our ambulance. Dorothy Howarth, in her nurse's uniform, will be inside. We need words, any words that come from Marilyn, [coach] Ryder, her parents, anybody."[4]

MacFarlane also ordered *Telegram* reporters to get "every scrap of conversation, every message, every shout and every exchange between the *Star* guys." Sears went on to say that the *Tely* reporters and photographers commandeered a fleet of Yellow Cabs and ringed the life-saving station.

"I noticed three ambulances parked around the station. One was backed up right against the station door. That was ours. Howarth was crouched in the darkness …When the stretcher came on the slip, there was pandemonium. *Tely* men were everywhere. The stretcher went down and a reporter fell on top of Marilyn. Someone heaved him off; the stretcher handles were grabbed again and the *Tely* ambulance doors were invitingly open and Howarth, in her crisp uniform, beckoned the stretcher-bearers in."

Sears also reported that Alexandrine Gibb, the *Star*'s top sob sister, spotted Howarth and screamed, "Jesus Christ, don't put her there. That's Dorothy Howarth of the *Telegram*." Next, a *Star* man raced around the front of the *Tely* ambulance and, according to Sears, tore out the ignition wires. Sears concluded that when the *Star* squad finally succeeded in locking up Marilyn in a room in the Royal York, the *Tely* troops were done.

Sears also wrote in those days as-told-to stories were routine. "Dorothy's tale under the massive head MARILYN'S STORY- I FELT I WAS SWIMMING FOREVER, became a classic in the tight, little world of newspapering, not only because it was beautifully and quickly done, but because on top was a photocopy of Marilyn's signature." Sears added that the method of obtaining this scoop would "engage classes in journalism ethics for decades to come."

These Marilyn Bell tales were told, over and over again, by grizzled newsmen. On the 40th anniversary of the Bell swim, in September 1994, Pierre Berton and George Bryant reminisced with Peter Gzowski on CBC radio's *Morningside* about the swim. The glory days of the *Star* and the *Telegram* were guffawed over with lots of male bravado and much "those-were-the-days-eh-guys" comments as the trio re-hashed the swim. No one ever thought to call Dorothy about her version of the story, even though all the old guys mentioned her. As they boasted about the scallywags they were in those days, Dorothy was sitting at home, a few miles away from Gzowski's studio.

The 1950s was the decade of the Great Lake swims and one swimmer after another fascinated Ontario's newspaper-reading public. *Toronto Sun* columnist Peter Worthington—then a *Telegram* reporter—covered several swims. In a 1999 interview, he recalled one where he and Dorothy worked together. The *Tely* had brought a British swimmer, John Jeremy, to Toronto after Marilyn's swim. "After Jeremy's swim, the *Tely* had him stashed at the Waverly Hotel and Dorothy and I were up in the room with him. The *Star* had a reporter outside. Jeremy wanted Black Cat cigarettes and we sent a *Tely* photographer to get them. He came back, face streaming blood. He'd been beaten by Eddy, the *Star* reporter waiting outside. And then Jeremy refused the cigarettes because Mike had got the wrong brand." Worthington tells the story as means of emphasizing how serious the competition was to get the story first, and that meant before the *Star*.

Worthington also divulged that Jeremy had welts across his chest and the reporters suspected he had been towed across the Lake with piano wire, although it was never proven. The $5,000 purse—about a year's salary in the 1950s—was enough to inspire such torture.

Worthington confessed, after Dorothy's stellar coup with the Bell story, that sticking *authentic* signatures on top of a scoop became stock-in-trade for him.

For years, as contemporary visitors stepped off the elevator at the *Toronto Star*'s editorial offices on the 5th floor, at One Yonge St., the first thing they saw is a framed page of the Marilyn Bell story—reportage that the *Star* still considers one of its greatest moments even though the paper was scooped by the competition. The *Star* also had its version of the capture of the Boyd Gang framed beside the Bell story.

In 2017, it is hard to imagine a pre-television world where every citizen hung on the printed word. The medium was the newspaper and reporters would go to any length, as Dorothy has pointed out, to get a story and to have it in readers' hands first. In Dorothy's day, competition between Toronto's two big dailies was driven by the *Star*'s publisher H.C.H. Hindmarsh and at the *Telegram* by Managing Editor Doug MacFarlane and owner John Bassett.[5] Bunking down with victims, buying them liquor, exploiting their tragedies—anything was fair game to get that scoop. Ethics never entered the equation.

In 1955, Bell became the youngest person to swim the English Channel and a year later she swam the Strait of Juan de Fuca, British Columbia. Dorothy covered both events. She commented, in her crusty way: "I went across Juan de Fuca and the English Channel, with Marilyn, in a row boat. That was okay, but vacation cruises make me sick."

Perhaps this is because, until recently, reporting was never considered a profession like medicine, teaching or law, and a tertiary education was not a prerequisite for a job on a newspaper. What counted was a flare for snooping and colourful writing—a bill filled by a ragtag troop of scribblers who had, for the most part, survived the Great Depression and two World Wars. "We always laughed if someone called himself a journalist. We were reporters," stated Dorothy, proudly.

Charles Templeton, a managing editor at the *Toronto Star* in the early '60s, was a witness to newsroom shenanigans throughout this period. He commented in his 1982 memoir:

"Despite its excesses, the *Star* had many notable achievements in legitimate journalism. Its reporters were dispatched around the world. In pursuit of a breaking human-interest story, the *Star*'s efforts were sometimes awesome: it sent *teams* of reporters and photographers. It once hired an entire railroad train—to transport staffers to the site of a story and to keep its rivals out of the area. Reporters for the *Star* and the *Telegram* (whose standards were not much higher) sometimes kidnapped newsworthy persons, wining and dining them in locked hotel rooms to keep them from talking to the opposition. Gangs of 'kidnappers' sped across Toronto corralling Irish Sweepstakes winners and witnesses to bizarre murders. Hindmarsh formed a famed Flying Squad, complete with staff cars and a portable wire-photo unit. It was on call twenty-four hours a day, seven days a week, ready to go anywhere in pursuit of a story. The Flying Squad cars, jammed with reporters and photographers, would descend on a scene and drop off men at likely points to ferret out information and round up every available picture before the opposition arrived."

Ben Rose, later editor of the *Jewish Daily News*, was a *Toronto Star* reporter in the 1940s and 1950s. In those years, he often met Dorothy on assignment and remembered her as a great reporter. "Dorothy and I covered lectures at the Royal Canadian Institute together. But, as a *Star* reporter, I was always conscious, she was with the *Telegram*. And for any big story, I had to get there first."

Rose also confirmed that, in order to get a scoop, it was routine to lock key people up so the *Telegram* couldn't get at them. During the war, the *Star* sent Rose to Montreal to interview Canadian heroes returning from the European front. "We cloistered them in hotel rooms and we let them drink all the booze they wanted. The idea was to keep them away from the *Telegram* reporters," Rose said. "Another time, near the end of the war, reporters were sent, by train, to Halifax to interview Toronto sailors who arrived home off the warship *HMCS Haida*. They were heroes of a recent battle. We got them up to a hotel room and ordered booze. The party got out of hand and turned into a real brawl. One guy in the navy seriously tried to drown another fellow by holding his head in the toilet bowl. Finally, the military police came and broke it all up."

The upshot: the *Star* quietly picked up the bill. No questions asked.

On the subject of ethics, Sears had an anecdote about Dorothy, whom he described as a marvelous writer with "an interesting line in scruples." He remembered an occasion when Dorothy berated him for practically blackmailing a grieving mother into giving him a picture of her dead daughter. "Then, a few days later, while we were combing through the rubble of a fire, Dorothy came upon a bundle of love letters from the victim to her soldier husband. 'Listen to this,' she said, wonderful, sexy stuff, and began to read me the details. I was horrified. 'Dorothy, you can't use that. It's private, intimate correspondence,' I said. 'Like hell I can't,' said Dorothy and stuffed the bundle into her purse."[6]

Our Gal Travels

Although Dorothy did her fair share of local stories, the *Telegram* also gave her national and international assignments. In 1949, she travelled to Newfoundland to cover the British colony's entry into the Dominion of Canada—and guess what? Dorothy just happened to be on the Newfie Bullet and just happened to sit next to Joseph Smallwood, who was about to become Newfoundland's first premier. Naturally, Dorothy got an exclusive interview with him. "After we got off the train, I walked down the hill with him, to his little red frame house just below the Hotel Newfoundland. You just walked in. No one locked doors."

The Newfoundland railway operated for a little over a century and received its gently mocking term "The Newfie Bullet" after World War II.

Newsgirls

In a long profile printed in the *Telegram*, on April 1, 1949, Dorothy sketched Smallwood as a man of great bravado. He bragged to Dorothy that he could call 100,000 Newfoundlanders by name.

Dorothy said of her Newfoundland assignment that she lacked experience and that trip to Newfoundland was her first time in a foreign country. "The *Tely* took a chance on me. I was working against Bee (Beland) Honderich of the *Star*, but I beat out Bee. I liked him though and at one point we ended up in a hotel room talking together. Bee, Smallwood and I."

Dorothy also recalled, after the Newfoundland House of Assembly passed its Independence Bill from Great Britain, thus endorsing the colony's decision to become a province in the Commonwealth of Canada, there were black flags and arm bands worn all over St. John's by those against union with Canada. One citizen of St. John's told her: "We hate Canada and Canadians. You just come in here with your baby bonus and take us over and you'll name us a premier and a cabinet that are leopards that can change their spots."

Anyway, vitriol or not, Dorothy was determined to be the first reporter to file a story about the historic moment when the bill passed. "I stationed myself outside the assembly and had a taxi waiting. The minute the bill passed, I raced to the Marconi Tower on Telegraph Hill to cable my story."

Once Dorothy had filed all the breaking political stories, ushering in Canada's tenth province, she was allowed to pursue her real interest: the people in Newfoundland's outports. Dorothy ploughed through the spring ice on a mail boat to several outports and isolated fishing villages. "I was very curious about people and stayed with a family on St. Brennan's Island—an outport. I discovered it was like being in another country with another language like Gaelic in The Hebrides. In the outports people were so remote, they weren't the least bit concerned about independence and anyway, they couldn't vote on the issue because there were no ballots delivered to them."

Dorothy filed a series of stories, studded with vintage Newfoundland speech and delicious local colour, somewhat matched by E. Annie Proulx's 1993 best seller, *The Shipping News*. However, there is a big difference: Proulx's book is fiction and Dorothy's exuberant stories fact. A story datelined Glovertown starts: "The two masts of a fishing schooner rise above the ice. Beneath these masts, master builder Edgar Paul explained, 'I builds my ships like a woman knits. I knows how it should look and that's the way I builds it.'"

At Glovertown, Dorothy also talked with Hubert House, a woodworker, who showed her a piece of "shooky" lumber and explains that it is cracked because the wind shook the pine tree too much.

At Happy Adventure, a village in Newfoundland, Dorothy trailed after a Viennese doctor, Josephine Maiwald, a refugee from the Hitler War, who surfaced in Newfoundland. Dorothy reported that Dr. Maiwald, a roly-poly woman, charged $2 for a routine visit and $30 for a confinement. "Sometimes, when the way up to the house is steep, a man will get behind the fat little doctor and another in front to pull her up the path. On another occasion, two men harnessed themselves to a sleigh to pull the doctor to a remote house to see a sick woman."

The *Tely* also received files from Eastport, where the intrepid Dorothy followed Joseph Squires, a veteran sealer. Her story starts: "Cut roughly in the rock, along the shore of Eastport, is *1848 John Squires*. 'Me father cut that there when he came up the point with his fishing schooner from Salvage,' said Joseph Squires."

Squires told Dorothy that the young harp seals, at two to six weeks old, are easy to kill with a tap on the side of the head. He added, "Out there on the ice now they're borning. You'd think you were in a maternity ward, the squealing and groaning that goes on."

Dorothy talked to the hamlet's taxi service, Walter Squires. "He buys groceries, watches babies and transports half-quintals (112 pounds) of salt cod in his station wagon over the twenty-mile trail to Glovertown." Dorothy also wrote that the night before she met Walter, he had two passengers—one a corpse. The cabbie tells the big city reporter from foreign Canada in his droll way that "he bounced him some too, but I don't think he felt it."

The headline on another Newfoundland story, filed on April 4, 1949—the island's first day as a Canadian province—screamed: "They Dare Death for $100 a Week." What follows is

Dorothy's first-hand account of sealers arriving in St. John's Harbour with their harvest. A twenty-year-old sealer, pleased with the $350 he made on the perilous hunt on the ice floes, guided Dorothy around the deck of his boat. "Clarence moved over the pelt-packed deck with a rolling walk. The fat-backed skins moved under his rubber boots like jelly. He picked out a fine one and held it up with his hands stuck through the two holes near its head. 'You take a bedlamer like this.' He drew a sharp, short-bladed knife from the belt. 'Slit it down the stomach like this, and peel the pelt away like this. See, easy as peeling a banana.' He threw the reeking hide back on the pile."

Award-winning journalism? You bet. Dorothy's copy would stand up to today's standards anywhere in Canada. And, indeed, Dorothy won the first ever *National Newspaper Award* for her series on Newfoundland. Dorothy attributed the high quality of her prose and the wealth of detail to her own excitement and interest. "I was young and it was my first big trip. Everything interested me," she said. In 1949 she was also presented with the *Canadian Women's Press Club* award for her in-depth reportage of a knitting mills strike in Paris, Ontario.

On Friday, June 24, 1949, on page 3, the *Telegram* printed two photos of Dorothy and a feature crowing about her newspaper awards. "Newfoundland Series Hailed Nation's Finest" reads the headline. Oddly, in an interview for the in-house story, Dorothy beckons back to her days at the *Saskatchewan Farmer* when she answered letters to the lovelorn. She told the *Telegram* reporter that she could have had a husband any time. "There were hundreds of them for the taking," she said, adding that she was willing to hand out some current advice.

"This is my advice to any girl who wants any: get married as soon as possible; to heck with the business life. I'm in newspaper work because I need money," said Dorothy on the very day of the announcement of the award for her gutsy, insightful Newfoundland stories. The next day, when Dorothy flew to Vancouver to accept her award from the CWPC, she had another mission: to see a sister she never knew. After Dorothy's mother died in 1913, her newborn sister was sent to British Columbia and disappeared out of Dorothy's life. Dorothy was to see her sister, Mrs. William Murdoch, for the first time. Dorothy said, in print, that she wouldn't have much time in Vancouver "but I'm going to see my sister Betty (Bertha) or bust."

For the record, the *Telegram* published a photograph of Dorothy in the velvet evening gown that she wore to the National Newspaper Awards (NNA) ceremony on the women's page right above what she detested most—social notices. Under Dorothy's portrait, the personal notes gathered by the unnamed lady reporters in the women's department informed readers that Miss Heather Perry was among the passengers sailing from New York on the *Queen Mary*. The notes also provide a list of out-of-town guests at the Raper-Collins wedding, the guest list at Bangor Lodge, Lake Muskoka, and the news that the Harold Smiths were at home in celebration of their silver wedding anniversary.

In *Hello Sweetheart*, Sears described Dorothy, in her news-gathering days, as a "slim, elegant reporter with a puckish sense of humour." Dorothy snorted at being called elegant.

"We wore suits and hats. And as long as I had a decent suit, I didn't care what I wore," Then, thinking back, she said that she had two tailored suits, one pale blue and one dark red. They were made from wool woven on a handloom in a Quebec village. She also had a dark green suit with a matching top coat made by Hardy Amies, dressmaker to the Queen—a far cry from the skinny pants and black one-size-too-small tops favoured by today's crop of female reporters. Dorothy also remembered an evening dress she wore to a party in Karachi given by the Prime Minister of Pakistan for the Canadian Minister without Portfolio, J.M. MacDonnell. The minister was on a goodwill tour and reporters were invited to fill the empty seats on his government aircraft. This plum assignment took Dorothy around the world in twenty-six days, a fact trumpeted in a banner on the top of the front page of the *Toronto Telegram* on September 10, 1957.

When Dorothy embarked on her sensational trip, *Around the World in 80 Days*, starring David Niven, was playing in movie houses in Toronto and the paper took advantage of this to promote Dorothy's trip. Under the banner, a creative copy editor wrote: "Being an account of an aerial voyage taken by Miss Dorothy Howarth from Toronto to Toronto by way of Asia, Africa and Europe and other foreign places in an intended time of twenty-six days—considerably less time taken by the late celebrated Mr. Phileas Fogg. She tells of her adventures with thoroughness and great humour, beginning in this journal today."

> A bedlamer is a harp seal who is fourteen months of age and has reached beyond the young "beater" stage, but is not yet mature.

Newsgirls

The Karachi party for the Canadians was held in the palace grounds beside an outdoor swimming pool. There was a long table of buffet goodies served by a troop of male servants in dazzling white uniforms and turbans. Dorothy, ever the reporter, noted for *Telegram* readers outside the palace there "were bits of tin, canvas and other materials propped against the stone walls to make shelter for the poor starving families who were born, lived and died, curled under these shelters."

The gown that saw Karachi had a pale blue jersey bodice with a high neck and sleeves below the elbows. The skirt was made of several layers of different shades of blue tulle. "When I was dancing with our host, the Pakistani prime minister, he complimented me on my dress. Thinking about it later, I realized he was probably complimenting me on my cover-up. It was a Muslim country and, appropriately, only my head and feet weren't covered." Dorothy said.

Dorothy continued with the Canadian entourage to Malaya, until then a British Colony. MacDonnell's goodwill ambassadors, including Dorothy, attended a *very British* reception at the posh Penang Cricket Club. "The British Empire was breaking up and for the first time they started to put up the Malaysian flag. There was no cheering. A local dignitary next to me said, 'I'm British. My flag is the Union Jack' and he went inside to take tea."

> According to the Malaya Independence Act 1957, the British settlements of Penang and Singapore became independent sovereign countries within the British Commonwealth on August 31, 1957. Final Independence for all British Malaya was not achieved until August 31st, 1963.

Dorothy had one poignant assignment after another that took her, bodily and emotionally, to places beyond the dreams of most pre-feminism women. Imagine this twenty-six-day trip on an expense account at a time when air travel, for pleasure, was a luxury only the wealthiest could indulge in. Dorothy commented that the *Telegram* paid for everything without query. "I wasn't luxury oriented. But Doug MacFarlane said that he wanted his reporters to go first class and stay in the best hotels. There was no discrimination. I was treated same as every man on staff," she said, adding that it never crossed her mind that a woman couldn't do the stories men were doing. As one no-nonsense editor put it: "I don't care, if it's a man or woman behind the typewriter. It all goes out in the same truck."

Dorothy could get it into the truck in spades. She said when MacFarlane wanted her attention, he would yell from the city desk, "Howarth come-eeeree."

In a 1993 *Toronto Sun* column, Worthington praised the atmosphere of equal opportunity at the *Telegram* and reminisced about some of the best reporters he has known during his forty or so years in journalism and identified them as women: "In the old *Telegram*, women were not regarded as second-class in the newsroom. *Tely* publisher John Bassett, in negotiations with the union in the days when women were paid less than men, insisted women be paid the same. He felt if women did the same work as men, they should get the same salary. End of discussion.

"In the *Tely* newsroom, from the 1950s on, women were the equal of men, or better. In 1949, Dorothy Howarth became the first woman to win a National Newspaper Award—the year they were inaugurated. Arguably the worst speller in journalism, Dorothy went everywhere and took a back seat to no one."

> Phyllis Griffith (1905-1978), was a champion varsity basketball player during her student days in the 1920s. In 1927, she was hired by the *Telegram* and became the first woman in Canada to write a sports' column. She was a member of the *Canadian News Hall of Fame*.

Worthington also described Dorothy and Phyl Griffith, another *Telegram* female newshound, as awesome and dogged. "But they were not garbage mouths. They didn't want to compete with the men. They could mix with the guys and still be a lady,"[7] he wrote.

Sears wrote, (in *Hello Sweetheart*) in a similar vein, a revealing tongue-in-cheek passage: "The *Tely* and *Star* women were wily, proto-feminists who could steal a picture, vamp a cop, slug a rival or stitch a wound, entirely unaware that they were exploited and that the militant sisterhood (1960s feminism) was on the way to their rescue."[8]

> In 2011, Val Sears launched a newspaper in Ontario called the *Almonte Millstone*.

During her career, Dorothy also covered royal tours and, unlike *Globe and Mail* reporter Kay Kritzwiser who thrived on the gloves and pearls scene, Dorothy hated it. "They were all boring. The Queen came out and waved. And then I'd have to file reaction from the crowd and describe what she wore. It was women's page stuff," said Dorothy, with disdain. "We were crowded on the press car and the train stopped at every whistle stop and the Queen got out and shook hands with the mayor. It was awful."

There was little chance to get near the royal personage, but Dorothy managed to meet the Queen four or five times and Prince Phillip in casual moments. "There would be about forty of us on the royal train. We each had our own berth. The prince came to the press car to joke. But we had to promise what he said was off the record. He was a nice fellow. We got along."

Dorothy added; in those days, protecting celebrities and the movers and shakers was as much a policy of newspapers as was the protection of readers from words like sex and abortion.

"We never used underwear in print and no one undressed in our world. Also, in the press gallery, we all knew about all sorts of liaisons. We all knew what was going on between MPs and various ladies. And then there was Toronto Mayor Allan Lamport, who would go down with us to a favourite bootlegger after the pubs closed—a detail that never made the papers in, teetotaling *Toronto the Good*. We tacitly agreed that we wouldn't do these stories," Dorothy said.

> Lamport was instrumental in the construction of the Toronto subway system and Pearson International Airport.

During her years at the *Telegram*, although she met endless celebrities, Dorothy always maintained a sangfroid attitude about it all. And in a classic low-key, pioneer Canadian way, she insisted she was never impressed with exotic sights and the exalted people she met. "If I met Jesus Christ, I would regard him as just another person."

A good example of this attitude occurred in 1959 when the *Telegram* sent Dorothy to Japan. At that time for most Canadians, Japan was a mysterious remote island on a school map. Dorothy's job was to cover the wedding of Emperor Hirohito's son, Crown Prince Akihito, to Michiko Shoda, a commoner he met on a tennis court. Reporters were not allowed inside the palace grounds or anywhere near the royals. "But I found out that the bride had gone to a Catholic college. So, acting on a hunch, I went there. And sure enough, she was at the convent and I got an exclusive interview with her. She asked me to pray for her, as she was a commoner and would need help as an empress," recalled Dorothy.

The lovers married in April, 1959, and Emperor Akihito, now eighty-three, and Empress Consort Michiko, eighty-two, are still going strong. Through April and May of 2015, they attended ceremonies commemorating the 70th anniversary of the end of World War II.

Throughout the 1950s, Dorothy was the *Telegram*'s top feature person, according to Peter Worthington. He should know; Worthington and Dorothy went on several strenuous assignments together, including the mining disaster in Springhill, Nova Scotia, in 1958. On October 23, a coal mine exploded trapping 174 miners. Some seventy were killed and 100 others were saved, including twelve who were dug out after a week underground and another five were saved after nine days of entombment. Worthington was the junior member of the *Tely* team at the scene. One of his vivid memories was of the last man rescued from the mine, whose greatest worry was the fact that he lost his pants while surfacing.

In 1999, Worthington recalled the Springhill drama, over coffee, in the *Toronto Sun* cafeteria: "There was Phyl Griffith, Bert Petlock, Dorothy and I. We were standing around waiting with the wives. We were told to do a diary for the guys who were trapped. We were at it all night and had to have it done by 6 a.m. for the morning edition. The three were arguing about what happened and I was typing, on a manual portable. Dorothy and Phyl were in tears with frustration and exhaustion."

Worthington added that none of the team wanted to do the diary bit ordered by the editor because they were all ashamed of the idea because of its exploitation of the trapped men. When the diary format was finished, the reporters discussed having by-lines taken off their stories. Then, after the first edition, Doug MacFarlane called and said it was the greatest thing he ever saw. Once the accolades came in, Dorothy changed her tune about having her by-line on the piece. "We were all mortified when the diary of these trapped guys was submitted for a newspaper award," admitted Worthington.

Interestingly, in the past, the *Toronto Star* and the *Telegram* had as many as six editions daily. In a case like the Springhill disaster, the initial story would hit Toronto's streets as early as 1 a.m. After that, updates would be phoned in or wired from far-off places to the newsroom, where different copy editors on the re-write desk would cobble these snippets into the original story. Worthington and Dorothy were always on a news beat. They felt the only paper worth filing a decent story for was the morning edition. "After that, we filed running copy all day for the other editions and, by evening, it was a jumble," said Dorothy.

Then suddenly in late 1958, feeling stale, Dorothy went to the *Vancouver Sun*—a move she preferred to dismiss and not talk about. She admitted she didn't know what happened, but the move did not work out. She felt it was her own fault because she didn't "take to Vancouver and [she] didn't try." There Dorothy worked with *Sun* reporter Simma Holt who, like Dorothy, was one of an elite group of female newsgirls. Dorothy described Holt as a gutsy go-getter. "She wouldn't wait for assignments. She would go out and find stories and get on the front-page. I didn't get one front page out there," Dorothy said.

Dorothy wouldn't elaborate on her Vancouver experience, but there is a backstory to her move to Vancouver. In the 1950s, Dorothy's father was living with her in a duplex at Spadina and Bloor. He was sick with cancer, so Dorothy took him to Vancouver to see his daughter, Bertha. The *Vancouver Sun* offered Dorothy a job and eventually Dorothy decided to give it a try. "They didn't take things seriously there and it was a time of grief for me," was all Dorothy would say. One assumes her father had died.

Dorothy was considered a "big shot" from The East, and the *Sun* staffers resented her. The editors gave Dorothy a tough time and didn't assign her worthwhile stories, according to Holt, who eventually became a Liberal cabinet minister in Pierre Trudeau's government.

Dorothy lasted just over a year in Vancouver and, after the *Sun* fiasco, she returned to the *Telegram* where Publisher John Bassett had assured her there would always be a position for her. At Dorothy's going-away get-together, Bassett had said: "While I wish you every happiness and success in the world...if your situation in Vancouver should change, I do hope at some time it will be possible for you to come back to us."

Worthington recalled that the *Telegram* newsies collected money and bought Dorothy a Group of Seven painting as a bon voyage present. "Then she was back and quite shameless about keeping the painting. I said to her, for a painting, I'd quit too and come back," laughed Worthington.

Also at Dorothy's farewell party, she was presented with a mock front-page prepared by the newsroom wits. The headline on the page reads: DOT DASHES WEST: EAST HUNG OVER. Beside the headline, appears the trademark *Telegram* info—*The Pink Tely*, five big stars and the word *night* indicting this was the fifth edition of the day.

Under the date, it says: *Late Bulletin...Hurricane Howarth Terrorizes W. Coast* and from there the story proceeds like a legitimate weather report and hurricane warning, featuring Dorothy as the storm hitting British Columbia. A half-page photo of Dorothy shows her dressed in a hat and white gloves with a duffle bag and, over one shoulder, a huge purse. She's in a half squat picking up a suitcase and the double entendre caption screams, *She's Loaded!*

Forty years later, Dorothy explained as she showed off the Lawren Harris on her living room wall that she went to the Haines gallery on Bloor St. to pick out the picture. It cost $250. She later had it appraised and was offered $50,000 for it. At that point, Dorothy had arranged for the painting to go to the Art Gallery of Ontario when she died.

After Dorothy returned to the *Telegram*, she kept a low profile. "I wasn't as lively. Besides, it was the '60s and there was a whole new crop of bright young women in the newsroom."

Dorothy claimed she didn't travel much after she scampered back to the familiarity of the *Telegram*; nevertheless, she did travel enough to garner more front page stories. Besides the Japanese emperor's wedding, the ever-diligent Dorothy landed yet another scoop when she visited Poland. For some reason, in 1961, the *Canadian Press* was running around trying to find the whereabouts of Fred Rose, a Communist spy whose story caused a sensation in 1946, when he was arrested by the RCMP. Polish-born Rose (Rosenberg) was a Communist member of the House of Commons at the time.

His tribulations started when Igor Gouzenko, a cipher clerk in the Soviet Embassy in Ottawa, was recalled to the USSR. Instead Gouzenko defected to the west with documents indicating there was a Soviet spy ring in Canada and Rose was the ring leader. As a result, Rose spent six years in prison and was stripped of his Canadian citizenship. When he was released in 1956, he defected and went back to Poland. "Everyone was trying to find Rose. So I figured I'd better try to find him too. I just looked him up in the Warsaw phone book and found him. He wanted to hear about Toronto. He wouldn't tell anything about his activities—or couldn't because of fear. That interview was a front page story," said Dorothy, matter-of-factly, adding that when she got back to Toronto, everyone was in awe that she had run Rose to ground.

Beside the large, frivolous photo of Dorothy and the sillycopy about her, there are a few genuine stories of the day. Under one headline, "Parents Rejected Blood," the report is about a fourteen-year-old boy who died because the parents, Jehovah Witnesses, "turned a deaf ear to pleas of doctors to allow a life-saving blood transfusion."

Dorothy also flew to Berlin when it was still divided into four sectors: "I wrote stories about commie youth and work camps in the Russian zone and sent them back to the *Telegram*. Jim Nichols of the *Star* was also there and wrote about how scary it was, trying to get to the Russian sector. But I just got on the train with workers who commuted between zones and crossed to the Russian side. It never occurred to me to be afraid, even though a soldier asked me on the train if I had permission to go. I said sure. I shot holes in Jim's stories about what a dangerous assignment it was and he was quite annoyed," said Dorothy, with a bit of a swagger. "I'd walk up to the armed guards on the Brandenburg Bridge and talk to them. One gave me the red star insignia off his uniform. I still have it."

Dorothy had many incredible assignments during her time as a newsgirl. They had her interviewing Dr. Martin Luther King during the American civil rights uprisings. The *Telegram* even sent Dorothy to cover one of the most iconic events of the 1960s—President John Kennedy's funeral in 1963.

Toronto Telegram reporter Peter Worthington, along with Dorothy Howarth and Ken MacTaggart were sent to Dallas within a day of the assassination of President John F. Kennedy on November 22, 1963. The *Toronto Star* sent Rae Corelli. The *Telegram* reporters staked out various sites as the police hunted for the assassin, Lee Harvey Oswald. By a fluke, Worthington ended up witnessing police shooting Oswald. While this was going on, Corelli was asleep in his Texas hotel room. *Star* staffers saw Worthington in the TV newsreels from Dallas and "wondered where their guy was." They phoned Corelli's hotel and woke him up. Corelli had missed the story.[9]

"As punishment the *Star* suspended Corelli without pay for a couple of weeks," according to Worthington.

Matrimony

In 1966, at age fifty-four, Dorothy's life changed. She married Dr. Harold Richardson, sixteen years after she advised young women, in print, to grab a husband and forget the business world. Dorothy had been introduced to Richardson, chief medical officer at Women's College Hospital, by her pal Helen Allen, who was a *Telegram* staffer for forty-two years. The next year, Dorothy, now Mrs. Harold Richardson, left journalism forever and devoted herself to her husband until his death in 1995. And by all accounts, she spent her married years savouring the family life she missed as a young woman.

After her years of *snooping* and *scooping*, Dorothy did not continue writing once she exited the newsroom as many other newsgirls did. She proudly declared, "I was a serious news reporter, not a creative writer."

Besides, Dorothy felt her descriptive, slow-moving writing style had gone out of fashion, according to Marilyn Dunlop, who had arrived at the *Telegram* in 1949 as a cub reporter. Dorothy took Marilyn under her wing and the pair became life-long friends.

In 2001 hard-nosed Dorothy was inducted into the *Canadian News Hall of Fame,* where she joined the likes of her old editor, Doug MacFarlane, and fellow reporters Pierre Berton, Phyllis Griffith, Simma Holt and Peter Worthington.

As a widow, Dorothy kept herself busy with art classes, visiting Richardson relatives and lunching once a week with a clutch of girls, which included retired *Toronto Star* reporter, Marilyn Dunlop, and a friend from Dorothy's Saskatchewan school days—long ago in the 1920s. Dorothy died in Pickering, Ontario, July 14, 2009.

OLIVE DICKASON

Regina Leader-Post, 1941-1946. Winnipeg Free Press, 1946-1947.
Montreal Gazette, 1950-1955. Globe and Mail, 1955-1967.

1920-2011

"I always say it's better to be born lucky than with brains."

3

Despite earning her crust at four prominent Canadian newspapers, Olive Dickason had few fond memories of her first career. Post-journalism, she became Dr. Olive Dickason, a venerated Canadian scholar who gleaned accolade after accolade for her ground-breaking work about the Indigenous peoples of the New World.

Only a half-page of Olive's twenty-eight-page *curriculum vitae* mentioned her journalistic career even though she won six awards for her fashion spreads while Women's Editor at Toronto's *Globe and Mail* from 1956 to 1967. The glamorous world of fashion and collection launches in New York, Montreal and Paris left her unmoved. Olive was always thinking about her girls and what she could get for them. "There I was drinking, champagne in New York. But, at home, there was no bread and butter,"

Olive explained in an interview in 1997 that her husband, Tony Dickason, was a charming peripatetic newspaperman who left her with life-long debt. After the marriage disintegrated, she became a single parent—an uncommon situation in the 1950s. Her career as a reporter and editor was simply a means to an end. It enabled her to support her family. The one thing Olive remembered most clearly about those years was the lonely struggle to bring up her three daughters.

Olive came to the academic life late. It was a dream she only allowed herself to pursue after her children were born. Olive is most proud of being the first person in Canada to get a PhD in "Indian people" and rising to the rank of Professor Emeritus at the University of Alberta. But it was a long journey to Academia.

She was born Olive Patricia Williamson in Winnipeg in 1920. Her father, an Englishman from Manchester, was an exporter-importer for the Bank of Montreal. Her mother, Phoebe Philomene Cote, was Métis, but was "in denial about her Indian connection." When Phoebe Cote was young, there was a disrespectable expression—*a bit of the tar brush*—to describe people with mixed blood. As a result, Olive's mother, a school teacher, gladly left behind her native Métis heritage and the subject was never mentioned. It was a great social breakthrough for Phoebe to marry a gentleman from England.

As daughters of a professional couple, Olive and her sister, Alice, went to a private Catholic school in Winnipeg. But things changed when Frank Williamson was caught in the Great Depression. The stock market crashed in 1929 and his banking career with it. Williamson tried his luck at a florist shop. When it went broke, he moved his family to a mining property on Lake Wanipigow, north of Winnipeg. There he became involved with the San Antonio gold mines and went broke all over again. Olive was thirteen years old.

"My mother had been a teacher in south Saskatchewan. So, in the bush she knew how to survive. My father couldn't even shoot a deer," said Olive.

As a result, Olive and Alice learned the fine points of hunting and fishing from their mother. Olive commented that living in the bush also taught her that survival depended on assessing a situation before taking action.

She described their home in northern Manitoba as the most depressed place in the world. Luckily, the impoverished Williamson children were saved from eternal ignorance by a Scottish remittance man who came up the river one day and settled.

"Bob Hamilton was appalled by our lack of education. You know how the Scots are about learning. He had a very fine library sent over from Scotland and gave us the run of it. He also subscribed to the *London Observer* and the *London Times*. Hamilton was unstinting with his time and discussed Plato, Aristotle and Marx with us. It opened a whole world there in the bush," said Olive, adding in those days, a remittance man in a canoe was just as likely to have a copy of *Virgil* in his pocket as a length of string.

The scholarly gentleman, who arrived so serendipitously, was the first of Olive's two *fairy godfathers*. Ultimately, Hamilton drowned in a boating accident, but not before he had gone through his wonderful classical library with Olive.

Olive managed to complete Grade 10 by correspondence, but could not continue her schooling because there was a $60 charge for Grade 11—an impossible sum during the Depression years in Manitoba. At eighteen, Olive heard on the family's battery-run radio about the Munich crisis of 1938—one of the events leading to World War II—and figured something big was going to happen. "I thought I'd better get down the river, get into the action and save the world. So I went down to Winnipeg by boat," She had only the clothes on her back and no money, but she did come out of the bush with a passion for books and an ability to discuss Greek history, thanks to the eccentric Hamilton.

Survival

In Winnipeg, Olive hired out as a maid in order to buy books and clothes—in that order. But she left this post after her employer refused to advance her salary for books. "She said 'I'll give you money to buy clothes, but not books.' Times were very tough. I had second-hand clothes and we never ironed in the bush. I admit I looked like an unmade bed," said Olive wistfully.

In desperation, Olive joined a crew of four girls who were driven to rural areas where they flogged magazines, house-to-house. Their territory took in southern Manitoba and Saskatchewan. "It was deep Depression—sheer hell. In Saskatchewan, the average drop of farm income was 75 percent. We saw economic devastation. Kids without shoes. Not a speck of paint to be had anywhere. It was so depressing."

In her travels, the young Olive heard tales of a renegade priest known as "Père." Father Athol Murray, a scion of a wealthy Toronto family, provided education for impoverished boys in Wilcox, in the boondocks of Saskatchewan. Olive made her way to Murray and "blew him out of his chair" with her knowledge of classical philosophy. "Père wasn't interested in girls, but he was floored I could discuss Aristotle with him. I had no small talk and I was a social disaster, but I was intelligent," said Olive.

Murray decided that a few girls in class would make the boys behave better and so he took Olive into his make-shift school located on the Sioux Line, sixty miles south of Regina. At nineteen, Olive was thrown in with much younger children. She started Grade 11 in March and by June she had mastered that curriculum, along with the literature part of Grade 12. Immediately, Olive started studying for a bachelor's degree, mentored by Murray, who had named his frontier school Notre Dame College. Later, Murray had arranged an affiliation with the University of Ottawa. In 1943, Olive graduated with a B.A. in French and philosophy. "Murray, quite simply, gave me my life," said Olive of her second *fairy godfather*.

Olive was often a guest on CBC Radio's *Morningside,* where she never failed to mention *Père* to Peter Gzowski, the host from 1982-1997. In the fullness of times she and Gzowski would

After her death, Dickason's Libary went to the Athol Murry College of Notre Dame in Wilcox, Saskatchewan.

be memorialized at Trent University, in Peterborough, Ontario. At Trent, Aboriginal studies are held in the *First Peoples House of Learning* where students enjoy the *Olive Dickason Reading Room*. In 2003, Trent opened a new building and named it *Peter Gzowski College*.

A Paying Job

Olive always knew she would be a writer and, while studying for her degree, she freelanced for the *Regina Leader-Post*. In 1941, she wrote a piece defending the wolves' place in nature, long before Canadian author Farley Mowat became an advocate for wolves after observing the declining wolf population in the Arctic. Many years later, after Olive came to terms with her Métis heritage, she wondered if there was something in her DNA that made her relate to the wolf, a powerful figure in Amerindian myths that appears, like a deus ex machina, to aid people in desperate situations.

Once she had a shiny new B.A. in hand, Olive decided to head for "Lotus Land," as every Canadian east of British Columbia used to call Vancouver. "To get to Vancouver was the great goal for plains' dwellers. But the *Leader-Post* said they needed me. In those days, the jobs looked for you. You didn't look for the job. So I never did get to Vancouver," said Olive, echoing an experience common to the many women who broke into newspaper work during the Second World War. With most of the men enlisted in the armed forces, women were given unheard of opportunities. With the labour shortage, even girls were welcome employees.

Olive earned about $50 a month, the first real money she ever had. She paid $7.50 weekly for room and board and spent a nickel every day for coffee and toast. One of her first purchases was a pair of shoes. "I paid $5 for them. And you can bet they weren't sensible shoes. I was dying to get into high heels," she recalled, with a laugh.

At the *Leader-Post*, Olive was a general assignment (GA) reporter interviewing important people who came to town. The end of the war was etched in Olive's memory. She was sent out to cover reaction in Regina. "It was wild. Everybody was celebrating and shaking hands. People were leaning out of streetcars and at one point I was lifted up—kidnapped and taken away on a streetcar."

Olive proudly pointed out that she was *on the rim*—the command central of any newsroom—rather than in the women's department. "I had a wonderful time. I worked seven days a week, all day. I was in the center of the action and I loved it."

In Regina, Olive met some of her Métis relatives for the first time. This gave her an inkling about her mother's roots, but Olive was too busy getting on with life to ruminate about this connection. Also, at the *Leader-Post*, Olive's career-path crossed with that of the future *Globe and Mail* art critic, Kay Kritzwiser. During the war, Kritzwiser was busily writing a column on the *Post*'s editorial page. Kritzwiser commented in 1996: "Olive was a half-breed, you know. But we didn't say anything."

Everybody was aware of Olive's heritage by looking at her, but she was oblivious. However, Olive did remember as a child in Winnipeg, she was teased once. "When I was seven years old, I was taunted about being an Indian in the schoolyard by a boy. And he beat me up properly."

Kritzwiser added that Tony Dickason proposed to Olive in the Kritzwiser's living room. Kritzwiser reminded Olive about this fact at a lunch when the pair met in Toronto for the first time in decades. Olive admitted she had erased this occasion from her mind.

Shortly after the young couple's engagement, Tony Dickason took a job at the *Winnipeg Tribune*. Olive followed him to Winnipeg where they married in 1946. For a year, she worked as a reporter at the *Winnipeg Free Press*.

Then Olive's husband decided to move again and, with one child, they relocated to Montreal where Tony took a public relations' job at CIL, a paint company. During the three years the family lived in Montreal, Olive freelanced, mainly for industrial magazines. In the meantime, her second daughter was born. Then, in 1950, there was a brief move to Vancouver where Olive had another child. Then disaster struck. Tony abandoned her after a hectic marriage that lasted four years. "I had triplets the hard way. And I was still nursing a baby when the marriage broke up. The girls never saw their father again."

Olive took the children back to Montreal where she landed a job with the *Montreal Gazette*. During this period of her life, circumstances were so desperate, resulting in the Children's Aid placing the girls in a foster home—a trauma Olive never got over. "It was a very different period. It was a struggle to keep them together. I never let them be separated and I never accepted welfare. I simply didn't have enough money to go around. They were out in the country and I was a visiting parent. The eldest was twelve before I got them back," said Olive, who could hardly talk about the pain of those years, some forty-five years later.

After signing on at the *Gazette* in 1950 as a GA reporter, Olive also worked in a bookstore to make ends meet. She explained how there was no sympathy for single mothers and certainly no daycare, an issue Olive would later address in the pages of the *Globe and Mail*.

The only colleague Olive recalled from her *Gazette* days was the City Editor, Al Russia, from Stornoway, Scotland, whom she never saw sober.

Fashion Reporter

Personal struggle or not, luck was with Olive professionally. When the *Gazette*'s women's editor quit, Olive took over her job. "Simple as that. No striving to rise in the hierarchy; but, you have to remember, moving from the rim to the women's department was a downhill slide for me. But I realized that I'd have access to clothing factories as a perk. With three girls to clothe who would soon be teenagers, I took it," said Olive, who chortled at the irony of the *unmade bed* suddenly becoming women's editor and, by extension, fashion reporter travelling to the world's smartest fashion meccas.

When Olive signed up at the *Gazette*, she was paid $55 a week—an excellent salary, not just for a woman, but for anyone. Statistics Canada reported in 1953 that the income for a family of four was $50 a week. "If my salary was astronomical for a woman, bills were worse in 1950. I didn't have a towel, spoon or dish. But suddenly, with the fashion job, I had access to the clothing factories and wholesalers. That was equal to a boost in salary right there," she said, tartly, when confronted with the reality she had landed a decently paid job.

As fashion reporter, Olive often went to New York and, because of her fashion beat, she frequented the Stork Club, Park Plaza Hotel and the Pierre—all dazzling names associated with luxury and high living. Olive was unimpressed with the flesh pots of New York and the chic parties surrounding the fashion launches. She only ever thought about her girls in the foster home. She admitted it was a very unhappy, unsatisfactory time in her life, although her job would have been regarded by any other working girl as a dream come true.

"It may have been a dream job, but to me it was fluff. I didn't like it. People made a great deal over something that isn't very important." Olive added that she always looked okay, but she had no recollection of what she wore to those grand salons

While at the *Gazette*, Olive was driven by a desire to own a house so she and her children could live together. After much research into real estate, she targeted Toronto as the right place to settle her family. Olive saw Montreal as a city of apartments. "I knew Toronto had a better house market. It has always been a city of independent house dwellers." So, armed with this conviction, when the *Globe and Mail* advertised for a women's editor in 1955, Olive applied for the job and was hired.

Margaret Cragg, who interviewed Olive for the job, felt sorry enough for this single mother and her plight that she actually lent Olive the money for a down payment on a $19,500 house on Briar Hill Ave., where one of Olive's daughters still lives.

"After I came to Toronto, it was no more foster homes for my girls," declared Olive, adding, "although she realized her objective of owning a house, she was still upset that her children had to be *latchkey kids*."

Once at the *Globe*, Olive was careful to keep the fashion reporter's job for herself so that her source of free and discounted clothes wouldn't dry up. She was proud to say, looking back, that her girls were the best dressed kids at school. In those days, members of the fifth estate had no qualms about taking graft. Free trips, cases of booze at Christmas, tables at the best restaurants in town and complimentary theatre tickets were expected by the print media and considered part of the game.

As a fashion reporter, Olive wrote yards of copy about blouses, suits, hats and particularly fur—a must-have in the fashionable woman's wardrobe in the days before the environment was an issue. In the spring of 1956, Olive reported from the Château Frontenac in Quebec City, where the Fur Trade Association of Canada was holding its annual preview, that "slim lines were the rule. Coats, when full, were flat at the front and back with fullness worked in the sides. Whether in exotic ocelot or sheared black mouton, styling was done to please the eye rather than to startle." In June, 1957, Olive told *Globe* readers that little furs know no season; they are as fashionable at the racetrack as the opera and the Royal Winter Fair."

A small item about Princess Margaret appeared on the same page as Olive's fur reportage: "Princess Margaret is wearing a new hair style which British newspapers have dubbed the Malenkov curl. The curl was introduced last month when chubby ex-Premier Georgi Malenkov, Soviet power stations minister, came to London as head of a Russian delegation. A photograph of him, on arrival at the airport, with a windswept lock falling over one eye, gave London hairdressers the idea. It caught on and soon became a must for Britain's smartest debutantes…Last night Princess Margaret attended a ball at a West End Hotel. Nestling coyly over her forehead was a Malenkov curl."

All of Olive's fashion spreads, throughout the 1950s, feature models with hats, most often from milliner *Irene of Montreal*, who was the toast of Canadian fashion. She was known as much for the design of her smart little hats as for her chic kill-to-get-an-invitation parties. Dusty Vineberg, who was a reporter at the *Montreal Star* during Irene Burstyn's reign as Queen of Canada's Milliners, described Irene's shop on Sherbrook St. as the toniest address in Montreal. Irene made hats for the likes of Olive Diefenbaker, wife of Prime Minster John Diefenbaker, and for Maryon Pearson, wife of Prime Minister Lester Pearson. In press photos of Olive from this period, she too is wearing a smart little hat.

In one fashion editorial, dated October 4, 1958, Olive took a stab at analyzing the importance of fashion (meaning clothes from Paris) without insulting the provinciality of her readers. She started out benignly enough with the assertion that it is impossible to overestimate the psychological need of women to be in fashion. "Just as it's important for a woman to feel individuality in fashion, it's important that her city or country be up to the minute." Olive then plunged on with a pithy quote from a pompous Brit, who said, "A woman who is not in fashion is either too stupid to understand it or has thrown in the sponge. To be in fashion is to be at home in the world, or rather to be at home in one's epoch."

From there Olive opined that "haute couture is, after all, an expensive business, and no woman is going to pay $200 for an afternoon dress unless it expresses something she wants." From there the hapless reporter, who didn't really give two hoots about fashion, built up a case for Canadian—read Montreal—haute couture as representing Canada's growing self-confidence. Olive finally concluded: "Not that fashion is a national affair…in our Western World it belongs to all nations, each adding its own touch to the trends from Paris."

Also in 1958, in the Christmas issue of the *Globe Magazine*, beside a page advertising crinolines made of tiers of net and nylon, Olive wrote a feature on bejewelled shoes. It started: "The gaiety of the festive season is more likely this year to go to the fashionable woman's feet rather than her head." Then, trying to add a bit of educational information to her fluffy copy, Olive looked to the ancients. "Jewelled shoes have not always been the prerogative of women. Indeed, Heliogabalus, one of the more decadent Roman emperors, felt so deeply on the subject, he forbade them to women but bejewelled his own feet to the last point of space."

In the same edition of the *Globe Magazine*, Honest Ed's—a zany department store—was advertising boxes of chocolates for 73 cents and 8mm Kodachrome movie film for $1.99, and Schick was offering gift-boxed razors for $1.

In 1961, Toronto was King Tut mad and everything Egyptian was in. Everyone lined up outside the Royal Ontario Museum to gawk in wonder at the boy pharaoh Tutankhamun's gold funeral mask. Within months, Olive created a fashion spread for the *Globe Magazine* with the headline "*Wigs Come Back as a Top Fashion*" printed beside a picture of an Egyptian lady from the fourteenth century B.C. wearing a long wig. In her opening paragraph, Olive wrote, rather archly: "There have been times in the affairs of women—and of men—when coiffeurs have called for more expense and attention than clothes. There was such a period in ancient Egypt and another in ancient Rome. Coiffeurs changed from generation to generation, but dress styles remained fairly constant. Coins minted at the height of Roman power can be dated by the style of the emperor's hair."

In pre-electronic days, readers actually waded through all this kind of verbosity to get to the meat of a story. In Olive's wig opus, *Globe* subscribers needed to know what the latest in wig wear was in Toronto fashion circles and where to buy them. Yes indeed, in the '60s every gal with any style whatsoever had at least two wigs in her wardrobe. They were *de rigueur* when dressed for cocktails and dinner.

To the end, Olive felt a measure of contempt for her career in fashion. "I didn't adapt well, but I got nice fancy clothes and mastered the jargon." In fact, Olive mastered the subject well enough to win several awards. In 1956 and 1958, she received the top Elizabeth Arden Awards for fashion reporting, In the '60s, she won two Judy Awards for fashion writing and two *MacLarens*, technical awards for typography and page layouts.

"The reason I succeeded was because I didn't buy into fashion. I was objective. I never got involved in the behind-the-scenes manipulations of the fashion world," admitted Olive, who also kept her head down and never allowed herself to run afoul of *Globe* management.

Olive was also women's editor in the mid '60s when the ladies stuffed their *chapeaux* back into their hat boxes forever. Feminism, offering a brand new concept of a woman's place in society, bloomed and Olive tried to reflect the issues of this cataclysmic movement in the women's pages of the *Globe*. Her agenda was to cover the entire social scene. She assigned stories about concentration camp survivors, Aboriginal concerns and daycare issues. "That was something I sure knew something about," commented Olive, caustically.

Two reporters in Olive's department are worthy of mention. Michele Landsberg was hired by the *Globe* in 1962. In future years at the *Toronto Star*, Landsberg would morph into a committed feminist and one of the strongest public voices for the rights of women and underprivileged persons. Landsberg confessed, in a 1995 interview, she never had a career plan, but it was just "blind luck" that she ended up at the *Globe*. It also helped that she was the "cutest thing in shoe leather."

"We weren't brought up to have career plans. My parents didn't want me to go to university; they wanted me to do the traditional thing—marry and children. The domesticity credo was so dominant, but I was happy to do writing once I realized you get paid for it."

Like all cub reporters, Landsberg was dispatched across the city to cover assorted daily happenings like dull school board meetings and knocking on doors for photos of deceased accident victims. A more benign assignment that stuck in Michele's mind was coverage of the Canadian National Exhibition. "I went to the press building and got a press badge. I felt so special with my press badge. I remember feeling so lucky to have such a fun job. I got a front page by-line with a silly story about a cat show," Landsberg said.

She continued: "It never crossed my mind to ask for more challenging work. Then a features series came up about the working conditions of nurses because there was a movement afoot to unionize nurses. I discovered that registered nurses were paid less than the janitors in the hospitals. In those days, the paper really gave you tons of space and time to research full-page features. My articles helped change things and that, I discovered, was the exciting part of being a journalist."

By then, Landsberg was out of GA and in the women's section where she found her boss, Olive, to be warm and helpful. "I remember how Olive Dickason supported me in all issues. She was encouraging and always gave me time—up to three weeks to research something. I was so fortunate. She had a lovely tactful way to get you to change something," recalled Landsberg.[1]

Another highlight of Landsberg's neophyte stints at the *Globe* was a series of stories about emotionally disturbed children assigned, by Olive, in 1965. "People thought they were the same as retarded children and they were in institutions and tied to their beds. Lots were in correctional institutions and reform schools. I remember a nine-year-old girl, a chronic masturbator, who was in reform school. I was so heart-broken hearing about her. Masturbate! The *Globe* wouldn't let

---

On the cover of the Saturday *Globe* magazine containing the wig piece, there's a photograph of James Hoffa, the tough-guy boss of the American Teamsters' Union. After a questionable career, in 1957, Hoffa was last seen in the parking lot of a Detroit restaurant. He vanished without a clue. Ultimately Hoffa was presumed murdered and, in 1982, declared legally dead. To this day his fate is a mystery.

me use the word," shrieked Landsberg, thirty years later. "There was a big fuss in the women's section."

Landsberg also told me she "got bored doing the same things over and over at the *Globe*. "I used my first pregnancy as an excuse to quit. My husband Stephen (Lewis) was in politics and we were very involved. Now I would cling to my job. At the *Globe*, I was making more than Stephen. He was making $6,000 as a politician and I was making $9,000," recalled Michele.

Kay Rex, later at *Canadian Press* and a big wheel in the *Canadian Women's Press Club,* was also a reporter and copy editor in Olive's department. In 1995, after leaving the *Globe*, Rex published a history of CWPC. By then Olive was Dr. Dickason, Professor Emeritus, University of Alberta. A mellowed Olive contributed a promotional blurb, printed on the back cover of Rex's book: "Kay Rex's reminiscences of the CWPC and of the public spirited women who made it possible bring into clear focus the key role of women journalists in our society today."[2]

During her tenure as editor, Olive had to take stories from freelancers in order to fill the women's pages. Olive remembered freelancer Barbara Frum's efforts rather sourly. "Her copy was the worst I ever saw. She couldn't spell, for one thing, but maybe writing wasn't her medium." Bad writer; no matter. Frum, who had a blunt interviewing style, went on to become the television and radio personality most revered by CBC management. A year after Frum's death from cancer in 1992, the CBC opened its new Toronto broadcasting centre and named the atrium for her.

Toronto author, Iris Nowell, the author of several books about Canadian art and artists, remembered Olive as being short on charm. The first story Nowell ever sold was to the Women's Section of the *Globe*. It was a piece about the girls behind the scenes at Woodbine Race Track who worked as *hot walkers*. "Years later, I met Olive at a book launch, at the press club, and reminded her about that assignment and told her, she scared me shitless. Olive said *good* and that was the end of the conversation," recalled Nowell.[3]

In another interview in 2002, Olive admitted in retrospect her job was great. "But it was a means to an end. I was a closet intellectual. As women's editor of the *Globe and Mail*, I was in a squirrel cage going around and around. It was endless Independent Order of the Daughters of the Empire (IODE) and Junior League meetings. Also, I realized I wasn't getting anywhere in the newspaper business and for a long time there was, in the back of my mind, the notion I would do something else when I had my three kids launched. Mother beat into me the value of education and that stayed with me my whole life. She had come from a pioneer family and risen to become a teacher and that influence was still there," said Olive, summing up her twenty-six years in journalism—a term that did not exist in her early days.

In the fullness of time, Olive did leave her comfortable pew at the *Globe*. At forty-seven, she bought her freedom by cashing in her pension, which netted her $4,000. She promptly paid off debts and, for the first time since her collapsed marriage, she was financially clear. Olive said *ta-ta* to her grown up daughters and enrolled in several history courses at her old alma mater, the University of Ottawa. "People at the *Globe and Mail* thought I was mad, but I was always drawn to history. As they say, 'Journalism is the first draft of history'."

After leaving the *Globe* and Toronto behind, Olive secured a prestigious public relations job at the *National Gallery of Canada* that kept her in a pay cheque while she studied. Once again, her phenomenally good luck kicked in and the job turned out to be Olive's *Road to Damascus*. By chance, the *Museum of Man* was undergoing a renovation and the art gallery was forced to house some of the museum's artifacts. Among them were some early "Indian" pieces. This was a turning point in Olive's life: "The pieces spoke to me. I felt like I knew all about them. I guess it's what they refer to as racial memory,"

From that point on, Olive knew what she was going to do. She buried herself in libraries researching Native American history for her courses at the University of Ottawa. In 1972, her thesis, *French Indians at Louisbourg: A Study in Imperial Race Relations,* earned her an M.A. Olive had found her métier and continued her studies in Ottawa. In 1977, at the age of fifty-seven, Olive became the first scholar in Canada to earn a PhD in Aboriginal history. Her doctoral work, *The Myth of the Savage,* was published in book form in 1984.[4]

Meanwhile, Olive was lecturing at the University of Alberta and, by 1985, had tenure. Finally, she was where she wanted to be—at the pinnacle of her profession. But a mere ten years into her brilliant academic career, Olive turned sixty-five and was faced with mandatory retirement.

Olive Williamson Dickason hadn't worked like a galley slave all those years to be put out to pasture only months after reaching the top pay scale in Academia. Olive maintained that her biological age had no relevance to her professional age of ten. She decided to fight mandatory retirement as a human rights issue. Unfortunately, after seven years of legal jousting, the Supreme Court of Canada ruled against her and Olive was forced to retire.

The battle was lost, but not the war. Olive managed to remain in the field, producing groundbreaking work on the Aboriginal of the New World. In fact, the year of her legal defeat, Olive published *Canada's First Nations*, a tome that is now a university textbook.[5] Her output of six major books and dozens of academic articles, reviews, countless lectures and honours-galore established Olive as Canada's foremost expert on First Nations and Métis history. In 1992, she was honoured by the University of Alberta and given the rank of a Professor Emeritus in Canadian History. Also in recognition of her work, in 1996, the nation awarded Olive the *Order of Canada*.

After leaving Alberta, Olive was an adjunct professor at the University of Ottawa. Until her death in 2011, she worked on a series of tomes for Oxford Press about the first contacts between the North American Native (and other Aboriginal peoples) and Europeans and the resulting relationships.

Throughout the 1990s, as a respected academic, Olive contributed freelance pieces, mainly book reviews, to the *Globe and Mail*. One of the reviews was about *Stolen from Our Embrace*,[6] one of the first books about the Canadian Government's policy of abducting First Nations children and placing them into residential schools. This book and Olive's review addressed Aboriginal issues that are still hot topics in the media today.

She wrote: "'Killing the Indian in the child' resulted in adults disconnected from their communities...It became increasingly clear removing aboriginal children from their faltering families to non-aboriginal homes was not solving the problem. Children in foster care could be even more subject to abuse...And in turn become 'walking time bombs' who in turn abused their own children in a cycle passed from generation to generation."

Olive also wrote: "While there has been some encouraging progress, the healing of the damaged aboriginal societies (soaring suicide rates, broken homes, sexual abuse, alcoholism) has just begun," thanks to a 1996 report of the Royal Commission on Aboriginal Peoples. Olive supported the opinion voiced in the book that a healing process involves accepting responsibility and not blaming governments and others for abuses. "I abuse because I was abused" is no longer an acceptable excuse."

In her review, Olive did fault the authors of the book for idealizing the aboriginal traditional past as a Golden Age in Pre-Confederation times.

Olive concluded: "The authors' study of Canada's failed Amerindian social policy is generally well presented. As they demonstrate, the goal of social justice is easier to proclaim than to achieve in practice."[7]

Revered Elder

In March, 1997, Dr. Olive Dickason was Guest of Honour at a Drum Dance at the University of Toronto. She was presented with an eagle feather, much to her delight. Earlier in the year, on national television, she had received an *Aboriginal Life Achievement Award* from the Canadian Native Arts Foundation. Olive Dickason, the reporter and fashion editor, was long gone. In her place stood a woman who had reinvented herself as a Native role model and a *Grand Old Woman of Letters*. Professor Dickason had become a noted champion of Canada's Indigenous and an expert on New World history.

One May morning a year later, Olive was a guest at a Champlain Society Symposium at Victoria College in Toronto. She was clearly a favourite. After the reading of several earnest academic papers about *Aboriginal and Non-Aboriginal Histories: Parallel Paths and Convergences*, at the end of the afternoon, Olive rose to wrap up the theses presented throughout the day. This she did extemporaneously and with great wit. Olive had no notes and uttered no stodgy academic bromides. She took a middle ground, as becomes a wise elder, and mediated between political correctness and those presenting the tired Indian persecution message. Olive had no whinny axe to grind about the post-Columbus history of the Americas and adhered to no party line. Like a grey-haired Solomon she asked society members: What is history?

"You can throw a definitive history out of the window. It will always be rewritten. History is about identity and identity is grounded in the past, but differences in techniques—in how you record the past—produces a different history."

Olive sparkled as she continued and actually laughed as she became more excited about her subject. The audience was listening to an extrovert with an open, original mind. Taking the position history is in the *ear* of the beholder, Olive explained: "The word in an oral society has a different connotation. It is the person speaking. It is immediate instead of a second-hand presence. Rituals and story-telling—the interaction between teller and listener—is a form of history of that society."

Olive hit her stride with gusto and concluded: "There's a whole new field—totems and the marks of Aboriginal Canadians. What does this all mean? Our recorded history goes back much further than we think."

Everybody sat enthralled by this woman who had made her mark and who thrilled to the intellectual exercise of searching out and conjuring with old forgotten records and existences. After Olive sat down, everyone rushed forward to get her ear. Olive was elated, a new woman, who bore no resemblance to the disgruntled and resentful reporter she once was. Not at all, the worried woman columnist June Callwood observed, in the *Globe and Mail* newsroom, as "kind of a severe woman—remote, not one of the warm cozy ones."

Callwood also described Olive as having a reputation when she was in the *Globe* newsroom as "a whiner, a sad-sack and woe-is-me type."

In 2003, *Villagers Media Productions* produced a one-hour documentary, *Olive Dickason's First Nations*, "a profile of Canada's greatest Aboriginal historian." The film was to be launched at a splashy party. When Olive was asked in an interview for a *Toronto Star* profile what was she, a former fashion editor, intending to wear to a party where she would be the honoured guest. What else, but a chic little black dress. In fact, it was the same dress Olive had on when she received the Order of Canada.

The First Nations' project, shown on Vision TV, blossomed into a thirteen-part series based on Olive's book. She appeared as narrator and, after seeing herself on television, Olive, master of the wry and dry remark, commented "I realize I'm not God's gift to television."

Despite her dozens of awards, international travel as a celebrity scholar, honorary degrees and on-going accolades from Indian communities, Olive could hardly believe her good fortune and often commented mantra-style, she was born under a lucky star. "Imagine starting out in the bush, going to university in a backwater and becoming a fashion editor. When I was in the bush, I would have thought that all this is like going to the moon. Impossible. But I always say, it's better to be born lucky than with brains," remarked Olive, with a twinkle, as she contemplated the fortuitous opportunities her lucky star beamed her way—starting with Bob Hamilton and Athol Murray.

Looking back, Olive agreed sometimes the journey to fulfillment is a long rocky road—even with the help of Lady Luck. Nevertheless, like Tennyson's aging *Ulysses*, Olive "drank life to the lees" and "followed knowledge like a sinking star."

Olive Dickason died, in Ottawa, March 12, 2011, leaving behind a legacy that gives Canada's Native people a documented identity.

AFTERWORD

The drum beat goes on. In 2009, historian David McNab, a professor at York University, updated Olive's monumental tome, *Canada's First Nations: A History of Founding Peoples From Earliest Times*.[8] He attended a convention in Victoria, that June, where Olive's work was front and centre.

McNab, a colleague and dear friend of Olive, described her as an amazing woman. McNab believes the obstacles that Olive faced in her life were character-building and her Métis blood helped her overcome hardship and press on to her latter-day status. "She had a typical Aboriginal view of the world and a holistic sense that is pronounced in Aboriginal people. There was an internal Olive and an external Olive that was practical and faced reality. She also had the Indian seventh sense which is humour. It is the trickster-self that is non-judgmental and gently teases."

JUNE CALLWOOD
Bantford Expositor, 1942. Globe and Mail, 1942-1944.
Freelancer, 1946-2000s.

1924-2007

"I am subsidized by a forty-year marriage, which is a little like being a millionaire socialist."

"I hated the women's press club. There was not a woman there who could write. I guess there were a few. But the rest were silly," said June Callwood, a seventy-three-year-old woman who definitely had not lost her edge. It was 1997 and we were sitting in the chintz-covered lounge in Casey House Hospice, an AIDS facility Callwood had helped build as a monument to her deceased son Casey Frayne.

"My husband belonged to a real press club made up of professional writers and I could see how different it was. Anyway, I was so much younger than the other women and I didn't drink."

This ire, from one of Canada's most revered journalists and philanthropists goes back to the 1950s when June wrote a piece for *Maclean's* magazine about teenager Marilyn Bell, the first person to swim Lake Ontario. June submitted the article to a *Canadian Women's Press Club* (CWPC) awards' competition.

"I won second prize and they gave first to a woman, in the prairies, who wrote about her disabled child. That showed how silly they were. It was the best thing I ever wrote. I was as mad as anything. I thought they were unprofessional and then I was mad at myself for being mad at them," continued June, as New Age music drifted into the room.

June was in her late twenties when the CWPC failed to recognize her as first-prize talent. Some forty years later, June maintained that her favourite piece was still the Marilyn Bell story. "Sometimes a piece, you do it right. It just works out."

June forgot it was *Toronto Telegram* reporter Dorothy Howarth who, through cunning and tenacity, scooped everyone on that story. Howarth filed within hours of the bedraggled Marilyn Bell hitting the Toronto shore on September 8, 1954. June's re-telling of the Bell swim for *Maclean's* magazine was published in November well after the fact.

June did admit that during the swim she was in a privileged position—in a boat two miles out, with no less a personage than Allan Lamport, Mayor of Toronto, unlike *Toronto Star* reporter George Bryant and a host of others who actually spent twenty-one hours on the water in swaying boats beside the young swimming sensation. June described Bell as a great kid and commented it was the triumph of the girl's feat that inspired her to write her best-ever article.

June's Marilyn Bell story, with an introduction by populist writer Pierre Berton, can still be found in a 1950s anthology published by *Maclean's*. June bragged that she worked over night and interviewed Bell two days later. Meanwhile Howarth of the *Telegram* had crouched, clandestinely, in an ambulance waiting to pounce as the half-dead swimmer was fished out of the rollicking Toronto surf and taken to hospital for a routine check over.

"I was a hard worker—always a hard worker. No one worked harder than me and people used to say that," said June, her gorgeous slim legs crossed. She was wearing an elegant taupe suit. In the Casey House lounge, minions were attempting to move a big blue sofa as June bellowed at them: "Not there. Not there," creating mass confusion. Her shrieks added an interesting contrapuntal effect to the piped in New Age music.

The Journey Begins

June Rose Callwood was born into poverty in Chatham, Ontario, on June 2, 1924. Because of her ne'er-do-well father, Harold "Bing" Callwood, the family was peripatetic. One of the many ventures he failed at was re-tinning tops of milk cans. June's mother, Gladys Lavoie, was the daughter of a Metis bootlegger. By the time June was fifteen, she, her sister and mother had lived in Belle River, a Francophone community near Windsor, and from there moved to Kitchener and Regina before ending up in Brantford where June attended high school and wrote for the school newspaper. Hurt, because her mother accused her of being a financial drain, June quit her schooling and fortunately the principal found it in his heart to forge her graduation diploma.[1]

June was a voracious reader and, between ten and twelve years of age, she claimed she read the whole Kitchener library. June checked out books alphabetically and, because she was a speed reader, she could polish off five books a day.

"There was no money at home for clothes or anything like that. But I won a literary prize in high school, named for a young man who was killed in World War I. It was given by Judge Sweet, his father. The judge said 'let me know if you ever need any help.'"

June left home at the tail-end of the Great Depression and the beginning of the Second World War. She went to see Sweet, who was part owner of the *Brantford Expositor,* and he sent June to see W.B. Preston, the editor.

"He gave me a job. They were desperate as young men were still going off to war. Isobel Plant was there and she had worked out well, so they hired me at $7.50, for a six-day week," said June.

June took up her new position at the *Expositor* on a cold February morning in 1941. Thus was launched one of the longest careers in Canadian journalism. June recalled, along with Plant, who kept a prim hat in her drawer, there was another woman on the *Expositor*–Ethel Raymond, a traditional newspaper woman. "She was needy but well-born. Ethel did the society stuff and wore white gloves while she typed."

"I started at 7:30 a.m. reading galleys and proof reading. I would cover something and then wait until 9 p.m., then go to the post office to collect the farm news and write it up. Preston assigned me to a bomber base where they trained pilots. It took me a while to realize most of them later died," said June. "In between, while waiting for assignments, I taught myself to type by typing poetry. I also did some photography and learned to develop the film. It was a terrific experience. I was thrilled and delighted."

Out of her $7.50 salary, June paid her mother $3 weekly for board and she saved up for fabric to make clothes. "We were poor. I made my own clothes. I even made my own bathing suit. I made a green and white check suit with pleated skirt and jacket. It didn't look good. We didn't have a sewing machine, so I had made it all *by hand.* I remember buying a pair of shoes that cost $11. I paid for them on time. I used to walk down the street and think: there is $5.50 on one foot and $5.50 on the other. I also saved to buy stockings with seams."

In late summer 1942, June received a phone call from the *Toronto Star* with a job offer of $25 a week. June turned up at the *Star* on Bay St. in her precious eleven-dollar shoes.

"I wore my new high heels. My feet were quadruple A. The shoes were cheap and didn't fit properly, so my feet slid around. I arrived at the *Star* with bloody feet and my toes wrapped in cotton batten. At the *Star,* they had seen by-lines. Then when I arrived, they were shocked to see how young I was. Jim Kingsbury, the managing editor, said I was far too young to be a reporter and made me a secretary and then fired me two weeks later," recalled June.

But there's a bit more to this story. The *Star* assigned June to the rotogravure department, where her job was to answer mail and write cut lines for photographs. One day, June replied to a letter from a soldier stationed in Camp Borden. He pointed out a mistake under a picture of a tank. Spunky June wrote back saying she was amazed to discover sergeants could read. The *Star* was not amused; June was fired.

The only female reporter at the *Star*, that June could recall, was Marjorie Earl who covered crime and was also involved with forming a serious union for newspaper personnel. Being fired by the *Star* did not discourage June. "Anyway, I didn't know how to be a good secretary, so I went to the *Toronto Telegram* and they offered me a secretary's job as well. I knew I couldn't do it, so I filled out all the papers to enlist in the air force. I always wanted to fly and thought that I could learn. But they told me it was impossible and I withdrew my application."

> In 1948, there was an initiative at the *Toronto Star* to form a local of the *American Newspaper Guild*. Earl was a member of the negotiating committee for the newly formed Local 87. Her comrades-in-solidarity include Ben Rose, Beland Honderich, Dennis Braithwaite and Borden Spears. This union morphed into the Southern Ontario Newspaper Guild (SONG). Presently, SONG limps on at the *Star*.

Cub Reporter

Young and naïve, but persistent, June took herself to the *Globe and Mail*. "It was the only newspaper left. I sat in Bob Farquharson's office, the managing editor, and he said you look like someone who needs a job. He gave me a three-day assignment at the Ontario Medical Association convention at the Royal York Hotel. "I didn't know how to cover anything like that. Don Carlson (*Toronto Star*) wrote my three pieces. It was a piece of generosity. He allowed himself to be scooped by the *Globe*. That was September, 1942," said June matter-of-factly.

At the *Globe* in 1942, June's starting salary at age eighteen was $25 weekly or about $1,300 annually. More recently, across Canada, fulltime journalists earn $45,000 to $65,000.[2] June shared a two-bedroom apartment and the $50-a-month rent with three other girls including her best friend Marian Jackson (nick-named *Stoney* as in Stonewall Jackson). Jackson led a troubled life and died prematurely in her late 40s, a loss June still mourned decades later.

June was the only female in the *Globe* newsroom and among the first to jump to the aid of this lovely ingénue were Frank Tumpane, Bruce West and Ken MacTaggart. "They all helped me—I couldn't write leads, they would come over and talk me through. I couldn't figure out how to do this. The men were enormously kind. Every man in the paper wrote my leads for me. Then suddenly, I started to be not bad as a reporter. I gradually learned my business. It took about three years. I had a paid apprenticeship, I was a long-time learning. I got competent. I got a lot of good breaks. I was never resented by men."

Richard J. Doyle (1923-2003), in *Hurly-Burly: A Time at the Globe*, confirmed June's confusion when starting out. She told him in 1990, "I couldn't write. I'd just sit there and I couldn't get started...Frank Tumpane would tell me what to do, or maybe write a lead for me. People (men) were great."[3]

From the 1940s into the 1960s, Tumpane, a renowned newspaperman and CBC broadcaster, once told Robert Fulford, currently a *National Post* Columnist: "I could never work for a woman." And in 1967 at the height of the feminism battle for equality in the work place, Tumpane said: "Equality? Great—um, I think it is."

No wonder the men were falling all over themselves. Looking at vintage photographs of the delectable young June, one sees a knock-out with shiny hair, fresh young face and long slim legs. She was a June Allyson look-alike and although June Callwood denied it, it's hard to believe every man in the newsroom would be panting at the desk of a plain pimply teenager if she wasn't.

When June arrived at the *Globe*, there were a handful of women on the paper, but not in the newsroom where the tough hard-drinking guys reported the daily news. Until the late 1950s, the girls were separated from the boys. People writing arts, social and domestic science columns were delegated to different sections of a building. For June to be in the newsroom and a general assignment (GA) reporter in the 1940s was indeed something to crow about.

"In news, we were in a separate department. I rather enjoyed the snobbishness of not being in the women's department. I felt they did the soft stuff, not important work like writing the news."

June made friends with two of the pariah females at the *Globe*—fashion writer Lillian Foster, who was "fat, ugly and dressed like an un-made bed," and art reviewer Pearl McCarthy. She also befriended Alexandrine Gibb (1891-1958), a Boadicean tough news and sports reporter from the *Toronto Star*.

Newsgirls

These newsgirls supported each other, and June and *Gibby* often collaborated on stories. "We wore suits. Male-looking suits and as a matter of pride we didn't wear hats like the other pre-war female reporters in the women's department," June said.

This attitude about soft news persisted in Canadian newsrooms into the 21st Century. Everything, from lifestyle to entertainment to family issues, was considered *fluff*. And even worse, a lot of it was purveyed by self-indulgent *feminists*—a bad word in testosterone-run newsrooms. At the *Toronto Star*, the area designated for soft news was known as the *Pansy Patch*. As several Pansy Patchers used to ask, who's to say that a fifty-inch story about Down's syndrome is less important than an eight-inch story about a drunk who drops a lighted cigarette on his bed and burns to death?

> In defense of this attitude, there is a difference. Breaking news is the mark of a newshound on-the-run while the information-gathering for medical stories is leisurely. Hard news is gathered on the street and filed within hours of breaking. That is what separates the pansies from the hardcore reporters in the world of dead tree media.

As a GA reporter, June covered a wide spectrum of local news—everything from theatre to court hearings. The *Globe* editors were alarmed by her youth and her supposed fragility, so they often gave June easy stories to cover such as Empire Club speeches and happenings at the Board of Education. During June's apprenticeship, come Sunday, every shop and business in Toronto was tightly bolted. Pretty well, the only public buildings open were police stations, hospitals and churches. Sometimes on Sunday mornings, June was dispatched to various Protestant churches to cover sermons. "I was a Catholic at the time, and listened to one sermon where the Baptist minister asked the congregation to pray for the soul of someone dating a Catholic."

June also covered the troop trains pulling into Union Station with scores of wounded men from the battlefields of Europe. "The stories were up-beat; not well-written. They came back—arms and legs amputated and blind. It was considered bad form to dramatize. I remember Stalag 17. Germans captured about fifty escapees and shot them. I had to interview the widow of one of these men for the *bulldog* edition. It was very embarrassing to interview her."

The *Globe's bulldog* was really a morning paper, but a reporter's deadline was at 8 p.m., so the *bulldog* was ready to hit the street at 10 p.m., even though it had the next day's date on it. The idea was to out-scoop the *Telegram* and the *Star*. In those days, the rivalry was so fierce to get *the* story first that often scruples did not come into play. *Globe* management figured, even if the news in the bulldog wasn't accurate, when reporters gathered more facts, they could fix up the stories for the actual morning edition that came out after the bulldog was delivered. Meanwhile, *Globe* management would be chuffed by another one-up on their archrivals.

Through the war years, June found herself always writing about "tears of joy" and "welcomed" Red Cross packages. "It was all designed to be morale-building. It was a festive time. Decorated men, air force aces and movie stars came through Toronto to help raise money for Victory Bonds. Remember, those were the bleak days of the war and we escaped to movies like *Show Boat* and *Oklahoma* and radio comedies like *Our Miss Brooks*, *Amos and Andy* and the *George Burns and Gracie Allen Show*."

> Una Merkle was one of the many perky, pretty blondes MGM featured in escapist romances through the Depression and war years. Merkle appeared in *42nd Street* with Ginger Rogers in 1933, and later in *Destry Rides Again* where her role involved a catfight with Marlene Dietrich (Frenchie) over a husband. During the war, Merkle also toured with Gary Cooper and a stage company that later went overseas to entertain the troops.

June described Victory Bond assignments as thrilling. She met several movie stars and vividly recalled interviewing Charles Boyer and Tyrone Power, one-on-one, when they appeared at Massey Hall to encourage the crowds to buy government war bonds.

June also filled in for drama and movie critic Roland Young and, one evening, the *Globe* sent her to the Royal Alexandra Theatre to review a play. And like every small-town girl before her, June was smitten with the spectacle. "My family was very poor. I was deprived and had never seen a play. It was my first stage play and starred Una Merkle from Hollywood. Of course, I wrote it was wonderful because I had nothing to compare it to. I learned everything on the job."

June also recalled the second production she was told to review. It was a play starring Glenda Farrell. The delight June experienced from seeing these first live performances was etched in her mind for the rest of her life.

Another first for June, as a cub reporter, was witnessing the machinations of the Ontario court system.

> Glenda Ferrell was seen on the Silver Screen through the 1920s and 1930s. During the war, she went on the stage and toured different war zones. In 1933, she won an Emmy for Best Supporting Actress for her work on the *Ben Casey* TV series.

"I spent months in courts. There was a pressroom in Old City Hall—a great hangout. I was very proud that I was the only *Lady of the Press* in City Hall. The aldermen would come in and schmooze with the press. I really enjoyed it."

June never forgot one trial that would become a seminal experience in her later development as a social activist. It involved a woman who was arrested and accused of trying to give herself an abortion with Lysol. The pregnant woman hemorrhaged and was taken to hospital. Ultimately, she was sent to prison because abortions were against the law. June was horrified that this woman, a mother of four or five children, was imprisoned. This dose of reality opened June's eyes to the abortion issue, a subject verboten back then. But June admits it would be a long time into the future before women's issues, such as pro-choice, began to concern her.

On another occasion, June's job was to cover a series of sixteen trials involving heroin trafficking. It was a spectacular case that after a long investigation by the RCMP resulted in a roundup of a large gang of hoodlums. As their key witness in all these trials, the police used a seventeen-year-old girl (a prostitute), who was also an addict.

"I was the only other girl in the courtroom, so during the recess she went into the hall and I talked to her. She told me RCMP officers were supplying her with heroin. June, glibly, wrote this detail into her *Globe* story and the *Globe* printed it. We thought it was okay. Imagine doing that today," June said.

But it was *not* okay. It seems the judge read June's reportage and the next day threw out all the cases after declaring the witness unreliable. The police were furious. June learned it had taken months for them to gather the evidence and she wrecked it for them. As a novice reporter, it never occurred to June there would be "ramifications." Worse yet, the world-weary veterans manning the news desk who were responsible for editing what went into the paper, were either asleep at the switch or appeared not to be any savvier than their greenhorn, teenaged reporter.

But no matter how June messed up under the *Globe*'s banner, she admitted her cute little misdemeanors were always overlooked. "The *Globe* was very much a warm family during the 1940s. I was trusted. People always liked me and the paper would send me to do difficult interviews. I was scared, lonely, out-of-my depth, but the quirky people there were supportive. There was a lot of humour then and a lot of heavy drinking. But I was treated so kindly," said June. "There was a family feeling at the *Globe*. We were very, very close. Everyone helped. Men helped me. It was very much a family."

From those early years, author Pierre Berton described June as a "flibbertigibbet." As time went by, June earned Berton's respect and, in the 1960s, they became chums and colleagues.

Ben Rose, a *Toronto Star* reporter, had a different take on June from the get-go. "She used to wear little wee ankle socks. She was just a kid. But I was amazed at how good she was. She was so young and she asked surprising questions and got good stories." Of course, Rose was unaware of what went on behind the scenes at the *Globe*, where June's apparent competence was due to a lot of help from her friends.

When asked about June, Dorothy Howarth, known as "The Sponge" at the *Toronto Telegram* for her ability to scoop every hardboiled newsman, commented, "June used to ask the stupidest questions. But she was beautiful. More beautiful than a movie star."

The best coinage a girl could have in pre-feminist days was beauty. It trumped money. After all, a stunner could marry into dough. June's pulchritude did not go unnoticed by the *Globe*'s wealthy publisher, George McCullagh, a handsome roué who chased June around the newsroom while she was still a cub reporter.

June said: "He collected virgins and I was one at the time. Sexual advances. I thought it was part of working. You just made the decision to sleep with him or not. I was flattered but I didn't want to go to bed with him. I had started dating and was in a serious relationship. I heard later McCullagh wanted to fire me; but the M.E., Bob Farquharson, supported me. It sounds trite, but everyone wanted to protect me."

In fact, pretty June told city editor Dic Doyle, "He (McCullagh) chased me. He exuded sex. The switchboard operator was a friend of mine. She'd tip me off. 'The publisher is looking for you.' And I would go hide in the washroom."[4]

McCullagh hated the *Toronto Star* and bought the *Telegram* in order to go one-on-one with the *Star*. He told the world: "I'm going to knock that pedagogic shitrag right off its pedestal," according to David Hayes in his book, *Power and Influence*. Hayes also observed when it came to employees, McCullagh was paternalistic and "remarkably benevolent about retaining rascals and drunks. As a result, the *Globe*, at night, had a reputation for being a boozy shop."[6]

From the mouth of famous Canadian writer Pierre Berton. This word was used before "airhead" came into fashion.

The philanderer, McCullagh, started his newspaper career in the 1920s as a financial reporter. He had the wit to invest in gold. By age thirty, he was a millionaire and in 1936 bought two Toronto papers—*The Globe*, a conservative paper, and *The Mail and the Empire*, with Liberal leanings. McCullagh merged these journals and they became, and still are, the *Globe and Mail*—or as Torontonians used to say, the *Mope and Wail*. In 1948, a decade after this merger, McCullagh bought the *Toronto Telegram*, headquartered in a chunky brick edifice that earned it the moniker, *The Old Lady of Melinda Street*.[5]

At one point, McCullagh purchased several cottages on Lake Erie as an employee vacation camp. Catherine Smyth, a neophyte reporter, recalled seeing June at this camp wearing a silk scarf, Grace Kelly-style. "June looked like she arrived from Hollywood. She was gorgeous, so the other women went into their cabins to put on scarves, like hers, and of course they looked frumpy, like Russian peasants in babushkas," Smyth said.

It is interesting that another future feminist and social activist, Michele Landsberg, told a similar story about her initiation into the *Globe and Mail* newsroom in the early 1960s. She told me in 1995, "Yes, I was pretty and sexy. I never would have been a journalist if I hadn't been. There's no question, men helped me out," she said adding, "June Callwood was beautiful. She also benefited from having men take her under their wing. I know June sometimes denied it later on. Horse patooties! Beauty was hers and my first affirmative action and then we proved our worth."

Meanwhile, over at the *Toronto Star* in the early 1950s, Publisher H.C. Hindmarsh noticed a girl reporter, who was "overweight but highly productive." Hindmarsh said to city editor Borden Spears: "That girl is too fat. Fire her." Done. She was toast.[7]

In 1952, McCullagh's political machinations and tom-catting came to an unexpected end when he was found floating in the artificial lake at his Thornhill estate. He had committed suicide.[8]

Telegram cub reporter Marilyn Dunlop, who later became a foreign correspondent at the *Toronto Star*, saw June at McCullagh's funeral. "She was so beautiful in a big black hat. She looked as if she had just stepped out of *Vogue*."

It seems it wasn't only June's dynamite looks that attracted the cowboys in the *Globe* newsroom. Part of her allure was the fact that like every other worker during the war, she had a ration card for alcoholic libations. Because June was a teetotaler, the boys, including sports' reporter Trent "Bill" Frayne, took her along to the tavern so they could soak up her booze rations.

Love and Marriage

Frayne was also one of the smitten *Globe* men. He had galloped up on a white charger to tutor the alluring new cub when she first appeared in the newsroom. Eventually, Frayne made his move and scooped up June and married her in June, 1944. Later, June would admit she had seen Frayne's by-line and photograph in the *Globe* and she had set her cap for him from the start.

"We had a *Globe and Mail* marriage. At our wedding party at the *Globe*, the whole floor was decorated and everyone at the paper came. Bob Farquharson gave me away because my father was overseas. I kept my single name because the *Globe* fired married people. People thought I was an early feminist. But I was the opposite; not an early feminist at all. It took me a long time understanding feminine barriers, because I was always seen as a reporter just like any other," said June without guile.

Dic Doyle described the wedding fiesta in *Hurly-Burly*: "For the happily-ever-after party, there were crepe-paper streamers, balloons and real flowers; six strong men were recruited to haul up a piano in the freight elevator for the singing and dancing. Just about everybody was there."[9]

In those days, all reporters expected to get presents. It was a bonanza at Christmas with lots of fortified beverages. "We expected to have our vacations paid for. No one thought anything of it," said June, implying her honeymoon trip was courtesy of their connections to the *Globe*.

June and Frayne honeymooned at Niagara Falls—then billed as the *Honeymoon Capital of the World*. The couple had their photo taken as they gazed out over the falls. June, age nineteen, wears a full skirt tightly cinched at the waist, and Bill wears the baggy pants and rolled up shirt sleeves favoured by matinee idols like Clark Gable. Three months later, June was pregnant. The policy then was to fire pregnant women. June was kept on the payroll because the war was still raging and they needed female help. By winter of 1945, she was gone to have her first baby.

"By then my salary was up to $35 or $45. My husband's was always $5 to $10 more, although sometimes we covered the same beat. That was my last salaried job. I did go back and freelance for the *Globe*. Since then, I've never had a story that didn't sell or I didn't have a market for."

Post-War Years

After the *Hitler War* ended in 1945, June returned to the *Globe* and was assigned on a freelance basis to write up fashion for the women's pages. When first interviewed, June claimed she remembered nothing about the fashion beat except fashion shows at the T. Eaton Co. and the Robert Simpson Co., rival department stores that faced each other on Queen Street. But with a bit of prodding, suddenly the memories poured out.

"Post-war, there was a tremendous interest in women's clothes because, during the war, there weren't any. It was an extravaganza of extra fabrics. Eaton's and Simpson's did two solid weeks of fashion shows, in the spring and in the fall, and because they paid for the back-page ads, we gave them plenty of coverage. It was very glamorous. I'd write, for example, that the theme is pink. At that time, there were also the first new appliances—like electric toasters."

Ruth Hammond, Women's Editor at the *Toronto Star*, confirmed during those years that Eaton's and Simpson's had an exclusive. The other major fashion retailers in Toronto—the Henry Morgan Co., Creeds, and Holt-Renfrew—could not be mentioned. Hammond recalled in a 1998 interview that she was often confronted with Harry Creed who asked why his fashions were never featured.

"Eaton's advertised on the back page of the *Star's* front section and Simpson's the back of Sports. If we gave one four columns and two pictures in a fashion story, the other had to have the same coverage. One word more or less and there was hell to pay." Hammond added her reporters could not mention any Canadian designers because *Star* management deemed that *too commercial*. However, her roster of newshens routinely wrote about Chanel, Givenchy, Balenciaga and St. Laurent—especially when Eaton's and Simpson's were stocking their frocks.

Although publisher Harry Hindmarsh always denied there was any connection between editorial and advertising and was highly insulted by the mere suggestion, the exclusivity of Eaton's and Simpson's was law at the *Toronto Daily Star*.

Ben Rose (1922-2008) confirmed the *Star*'s policy regarding Eaton's and Simpson's. Once, City Editor Tommy Lytle sent him out to write a story about an expansion at Eaton's. "Tommy said to me, 'I only want to hear those high notes,' meaning that he only wanted a favourable story," recalled Rose, later a staffer at the *Canadian Jewish News*.

As June indicated, during World War II there wasn't extra cloth available for frivolities like full skirts. Fabric was reserved for factories making uniforms, bandages and assorted supplies for the Allied warriors. After the war, in reaction to this deprivation, designers created dresses with yards of material in the skirts and jackets and with wavy peplums and exaggerated shoulders. These extravaganzas were matched with over-sized picture hats. This trend, propelled by Christian Dior in Paris, lasted until the end of the 1950s. Dior's shirtwaist dress, with circle skirt and smartly belted waist, is still a classic.

June also covered a municipal parade in 1948 in honour of Olympian Barbara Ann Scott, the first Canadian to win a gold medal for skating. That year, the Winter Games were held in St. Moritz, Switzerland, and twenty-year-old Scott skated her way into Canada's soul on mushy ice.

"Parades always went up Bay St. to City Hall. Barbara Ann had a hat everyone copied. It was white and had a small rolled brim, trimmed with red on the crown, and a daisy that stuck straight up. It was very cute," said June.

In 1955, Scott was inducted into Canada's Sports Hall of Fame. She died in 2012 at eighty-four years of age.

After the war, June would realize her dream of earning a pilot's license. Her flying lessons came about when she was at home with her baby, Jill. June's instructor was Violet Milstead (1919-2014), a woman who had signed on with the Air Transport Auxiliary, a World War II civilian outfit that flew planes to England. Milstead was one of a handful of lady pilots flying Spitfires overseas to support the Allied forces. Under the tutelage of Milstead, June earned her pilot's license in a single engine Aeronica Superchief. In 1946, the enterprising June parlayed her relationship with Milstead into a freelance piece about Milstead's *derring-do* during the war. This story was so well received in *Liberty* magazine that it kick-started June's life-long career as a freelancer. June recalled earning $50 for the Milstead profile—a huge sum at a time when

---

The T. Eaton Company was founded in 1869 by Timothy Eaton. In 1900, he made a deal with Joseph Atkinson (1865-1948), *Star* publisher and major stockholder, to position Eaton's daily advertisements on the back page of the paper. Except for a brief squabble in the 1920s, this policy continued until the bankruptcy of Eaton's department stores in 1999.[10]

In the dreary post-war years, Ottawa-born Scott was Canada's sweetheart. Girls sighed over Barbara Ann and Eaton's sold Barbra Ann Scott dolls, complete with little blue, silver or red skating costumes, trimmed with white fur—now worth at least $500 each. Barbara Ann Scott figure skates were on every Ontario girl's Christmas wish list and every one of them cut out magazine and newspaper pictures of Barbara Ann and pasted them into scrap books. Some six photos of Marilyn Bell, the teenaged swimmer.

the average household income in Canada was under $3,000 annually. The following year, June wrote a story about The Leslie Bell Singers, a women's choir. This piece, published in *Maclean's* magazine, led to a decades' long relationship with *Maclean's*.

In 1952, *Maclean's* assigned June to interview and write a profile of author Robertson Davies (1913-1995), who had just published *Tempest Tost*, the first book in his *Salterton Trilogy*. June found him haughty and hostile. But being June, she stood up to him and the interview was published. She figured Davies may have been "defensive" about her poking around in his life.[11]

In her profile in *Maclean's* magazine, June wrote: "Mrs. Davies is horrified when admirers suggest she must be a great help to her husband. But she does permit him to work uninterrupted evening after evening. "Permit!" snorts Davies. "I'll have you know that I am master in this house and it is run to suit me."

Callwood later commented: "When he said 'I am master of the house,' you have to remember it was the 1950s. This was the normal male prerogative...When he said it, I was offended. I was probably delighted that he was in character. The more he dug himself in, the better for my piece."

What June did *not* know at the time was Davies was a dyed-in-the wool misogynist and anti-feminist. This came clear some twenty years later when *Montreal Star* reporter, Dusty Vineberg, was also assigned to interview the *Great Man of Letters*, who by then was Master of Massey College at the University of Toronto.

Davies explained to Vineberg in February 1973, "that the basic element in male nature is *Logos*, or law and reason, while in women it is *Eros*, or feeling." This great intellectual also suggested girls should study things they are good at, like psychology, so they do not have to compete with men.[12]

One can only imagine Davies' arrogance and attitude when confronted by an unschooled woman, such as June, daring to interview him a decade prior to the Feminist Movement.

Meanwhile, June's own marriage was diametrically opposed to what went on in the Davies' household. The Frayne marriage was not just an at-home marriage. Husband and wife worked together on TV and in print. When the couple freelanced for *Maclean's*, they were deeply in love and June felt they were the luckiest people in the world. "We had young children and not much money. We always took two typewriters on vacation." Pierre Berton, also a *Maclean's* contributor, reckoned the Fraynes produced more pieces for *Maclean's* than anybody else.[13]

Throughout the 1950s and 1960s, both were consistently given space in *Maclean's* by Ralph Allen to jabber about whatever they fancied. In those days, *Maclean's* was published biweekly. In March 1959, June wrote a facile piece about a family holiday weekend in Ottawa and, in March 1963, June pontificated about emotions and her pal Pierre Berton penned a silly article, *Confessions of a Hotel Fancier*. By then, both contributors belonged to a small circle of celebrity reporters and writers with public profiles and big egos. June negotiated a deal with editor Ralph Allen for her emotions series. She was paid $1,000 per article at a time when *Maclean's* usually paid $500-$600.[14]

Later, June's series about emotions was cobbled into a book called, *Love, Hate, Fear, Anger and Other Lively Emotions* published by Doubleday, 1964.

June also wrote several well-researched articles on scientific subjects. In 1958, June contributed a piece to *Maclean's* about the plight of the Avro Arrow factory in Malton, Ontario. That year the proto-type of the Arrow, an innovative jet designed by the A.V. Roe Company, was launched. On February 20, 1959, a new Conservative government in Ottawa, led by Prime Minister John Diefenbaker, cancelled the Arrow project. More than 40,000 people lost their jobs and this aircraft, regarded as a thing of beauty, was greatly mourned by the industry and June.

By the mid-1950s, the charming Fraynes were also media personalities. They hosted an early talk show on CBC Television called *The Fraynes,* where June and Trent babbled about the joys of family and benign social problems. This cozy kitchen sink vanity fest took place after the Saturday night hockey games. It lasted one year (1954-1955).

June loved Royal Tours and, in the 1950s and 1960s, she managed to get herself assigned to five of them. Is this the same Miss Callwood who, in the 1940s, looked down her nose at the newshens in the women's department who specialized in these assignments? June claimed the tours were the hardest work of all because you have to "gather stuff and file it daily." One wonders what June thought run-of-the-mill GA reporters did every day. "We didn't have clothes. We were rough and ready, but you had to have one good outfit for your turn to attend a reception or go on the *Britannia*."

June recalled a tour in 1959 that centered on the opening of the St. Lawrence Seaway. The Seaway, a joint venture between Canada and the United States, connected a series of canals and locks from the Atlantic Ocean to Canada's Great Lakes. Queen Elizabeth II and Prince Philip travelled to Canada for this monumental occasion. They arrived in Newfoundland on June 18 and from there travelled to New York state, then on to Washington where the Queen was hosting a dinner at the Canadian Embassy in honour of U.S. President, Dwight Eisenhower. All this before the Seaway was formally opened on June 26, 1959, at St. Lambert, Quebec.

This meant that June's plum assignment as a freelancer for the *Toronto Star* included a trip to New York and Washington before the ribbon-cutting in Quebec.

"'I started in Newfoundland and a highlight was when I went on the *Britannia* in Quebec City. I was given the assignment because I was a pet of Ralph Allen (former *Maclean's* editor), who was then managing editor at the *Star*. But it was uncomfortable because Jeanine Locke counted on the Royal Tours and was mad at me for taking her wonderful assignment. Anyway, at Thunder Bay, I was so tired and sick that I quit and she got to take over," said June.

Never mind the bad feelings about pulling the *Star* assignment out from under Locke's feet, June remembers the press followers of the Royal Tours as "a camaraderie—a big press gang." There was a hierarchy of radio and pork-pie hatted newshounds from all over the world that sorted itself out into an elite clique. June found herself at the top of the pecking order because she was with a prestigious big-city Canadian newspaper. She was given a red badge which meant she was treated differently by the Mounties than the lowly reporters who belonged to the press rabble.

"We were on the trains and buses together. And for press conferences, we would pick different people from a pool to represent us. This person was responsible, on his honour, to tell all that happened and hold nothing back."

The same year as this tour, Angela Burke, a former *Toronto Star* reporter and *Newsgirl*, had written a piece for *Maclean's* in the May 1959 issue that slammed the monarchy and questioned its place in Canadian society. Burke's story spawned a rash of reporters flogging the same horse, including June who wrote an anti-monarchy article that was accepted by *Look* magazine, an American publication. June's diatribe had the head: "*Canada Indifferent to the Queen.*" The very day her *Look* story hit the newsstands, June was invited aboard the *Britannia*.

"I heard the Queen's staff bought fifty copies. This reception was unusual in that we were told the Queen would mingle. The press was all there and we hung back and the Queen waited for something to happen. She didn't know how to approach us any more than we knew how to approach her. Then one of her people singled me out and walked me across the deck to meet her. We had been in an open-pit mine that day where there was iron dust everywhere. We discussed trying to get the iron dust out of our hair and clothes. The Queen and I both talked about washing our hair and the water turning red from the particles. The Queen was far too classy to raise the issue of the *Look* story. I think she just wanted to look the upstart over.

"Anyway, the British gutter press had a field day with the encounter. They said things like I had a cigarette in my mouth while I talked to the Queen. The truth is I always used a white pen and would wave it about as I talked," said June.

June, pithily, dismissed Prince Philip as "a prick" and claimed she always avoided him. This opinion was seconded by Burke, who described the prince in her *Maclean's* rant as "inaccessible and antagonistic," while being wined and dined out of the Canadian public purse. (The *Toronto Star* assigned me to follow Prince Philip around the horse pavilion at Toronto's Royal Winter Fair in 1996. At the time, the Royal Consort seemed somewhat vacuous, but pleasant in a Monty Python, *Upper Class Twit of the Year,* manner.)

In 1960, Locke went to London, England, as the *Toronto Star's* bureau chief. In 1969, she was hired by the CBC where she was a writer and producer. Locke stayed with the broadcaster until she retired. She died in March, 2013, at eighty-seven years of age.

Meanwhile, Joyce Davidson, hostess of CBC's *Tabloid*, also weighed in with iconoclastic comments about the British royals on the *Today Show* in New York no less. Davidson confessed she was indifferent to the Queen and felt so were most Canadians. These turned out to be firing words and she was duly dispatched thanks to a witch hunt led by Toronto's mayor, Nathan Phillips. Davidson's career was ruined.

The Activist

The House of Windsor, homeless grubby teens, and everything else in between—is grist for the mill of any GA reporter or freelancer to this day. June garnered more press than even she could hope for due to her involvement in Digger House, a hostel for indigent hippies. It was located on Spadina Ave. in a fourteen-room house slated for demolition to make way for the never-built Spadina Road Extension. Supposedly, the extension would shoot Torontonians from downtown all the way up north to Lawrence Ave. Digger House had opened in February, 1967, and June herself raised $600 for the first month's rent. On top of that, another $600 was needed for a security bond. A clutch of Diggers collected $250—mostly in one-dollar bills and change—to help pay the bond. Later, June "kicked in $350 to help start Digger House and scraped her purse for $4 to buy a permit for its operation."[15]

There is a backstory here. June's sixteen-year-old son, Brant "Barney" Frayne, ran away from his comfortable home in Etobicoke, a middle-class establishment enclave, to hippydom in Toronto's Yorkville. Mother June followed him and found her son bunking in an accommodation she described as a pig sty. This reality was a catalyst for the Digger House project and June's interest in the hippy movement.

It turned out Brant Frayne was a budding film maker and eventually produced a documentary about a twenty-four-year-old drug addict charged with trafficking heroin. The defense lawyer, Clayton Ruby, a pal of June's, screened the documentary about this felon's unfortunate life in the courtroom as a defense ploy. June, a witness, insisted the druggie was not to be blamed for his crime. The judge gave the defendant twelve months in jail.[16]

June also read a series in the *Toronto Star* by Glen Allen about kids on the street, hungry and homeless. And she felt she could help.

"At first Digger House got a lot of attention. In 1966, when the Hippie Movement began, I was on the board of the Mental Health Association, so I had learned a lot about social agencies from this experience."

June added her involvement in Digger house was propelled by her own childhood experience. "I came from a shabby background of deprivation and I believed that these kids should at least have reasonable shelter and food. I thought it a simple matter at first and then realized they needed counseling as well. We got a federal grant for three years. It ended in 1971, and in 1972, we staggered along, but then had to close Digger House."

In Toronto, Digger House was part of the emerging hippy scene centered around Yorkville. While Spadina was not quite Yorkville, it was close enough—a ten-minute walk. Funding came initially through the *Company of Young Canadians*, a federal government agency set up in 1966 by Prime Minster Lester Pearson (he of the United Nations *Declaration of Human Rights*, 1948). The CYC paid hippy organizer David DePoe to manage the hostel. This initiative was also supported by two Toronto churches and two synagogues, including Holy Blossom temple whose Rabbi, Gunther Plaut, stood firmly in the forefront with June. This connection resulted in B'nai Brith giving June its *Woman of the Year* award in 1969.

The 1960s were a vibrant time in downtown Toronto. The neglected Victorian houses around Yorkville Ave. were turned into psychedelic night clubs and coffee houses, reminiscent of the Beat Generation with the likes of Jack Kerouac. It was also the era of public hootenannies, crammed with Flower Children in granny glasses, bell bottom trousers and flowered shirts. Males with long unkempt hair, on face and head, lugging guitars, were evident twenty-four hours a day. On one Yorkville corner, troubadour Gordon Lightfoot strummed his guitar in a fringed jacket while, a few feet away, hip chicks in wispy Indian cotton skirts sold their tie-dyed T-shirts and handmade jewellery with turquoise all the way from Afghanistan. Poets reading their odes to peace also *made the scene* on the streets of *Toronto the Good*.

Those who were *with it* went to Yorkville venues to listen to a roster of young entertainers forging their careers. At the Riverboat, they heard Joni Mitchell, Neil Young, Phil Ochs and Ian and Sylvia. At the Penny Farthing, there was Jose Felicano and, at the Purple Onion, Carley Simon and Buffy Sainte-Marie. Everyone stopped at the Mynah Bird, at 114 Yorkville, to gawk at the *Go Go Girls* in their white go-go boots, doing their energetic gyrations in a cage in the window.

Digger House was named for a group of people in 19th Century England who lived a simple life off the land and with minimal possessions. The Digger Movement, a naïve philosophy of life, popped up in the 1960s in San Francisco's Haight-Ashbury under the auspices of a contingent of Peaceniks and Flower Children. Like man! Brown rice. Free love and peace.

Plaut's is a whole other story of liberalism and social activism—from Nazi Germany to U.S. army Chaplain, reformist, scholar and free thinker. Plaut died in 2012 at age ninety-nine. Plaut wrote frequently for the Globe. *He was very much involved as an observer of crime, immigration and politics as well as the human spirit. When Doyle was M.E. at the* Globe, *he consulted Plaut for advice about how to handle "touchy social issues."[17]*

It was oh so risqué and, yes, empowering for a generation mostly born during World War II and who were just getting used to that new word "feminism."

Over the Victoria Day weekend, May 22, 1967, there was a major *Love-In* at Queen's Park. Hippies, peaceniks and flower children squatted on the lawns of the Legislature, participating in ad hoc hootenannies, until poet Leonard Cohen mounted a platform and spoke-sang *Suzanne* and Buffy Sainte-Marie sang *Universal Soldier.*

Then came July 10, 1968, where June earned her credentials as the friend of the hippy and homeless run-away. There was a sit-in on Yorkville Ave. in support of Dr. Benjamin Spock, the first celebrity pediatrician. He had been sentenced to two years for aiding and abetting young men evading the American draft. The Vietnam War was still raging and downtown Toronto was alive with American draft dodgers. (No! No! We won't go!) Several protesters sat on the road and police arrived to move them. June was there and described what happened. "I was trying to protect a kid the police were trying to take down an alley to beat up. They did this routinely. He was in the peace demonstration."

Apparently, June followed a policeman and the teen down the alley and when she did not "mind her own business," as ordered by the officer, she was arrested and charged with disturbing the peace.

Doyle of the *Globe and Mail* had a slightly different version of the night's events. "Police took a long-haired youth down a lane to a waiting cruiser... Miss Callwood joined a mob which surged behind the police, repeatedly asking why the youth was being arrested. 'Why don't you arrest me, too?' she asked. An officer said he might.

"'Oh, goody. This will be my first bust.' She followed police up and down the sidewalk, repeatedly asking to be arrested."[18]

June continued to harangue officers of the law. Eventually she got her wish and was put into a white patrol van along with another woman and a man. June was released by early morning.

Authoritative insiders and news photographers there that night confirm that June begged the police to arrest her because they figured she wanted her picture on the front pages. But that could be sour grapes. However, one *Toronto Star* archival photo does show a policeman holding June back from the police van.

Photographs of June were plastered all over the Toronto newspapers. There she is, our heroine, in a paddy wagon, dressed like Jackie Kennedy. After a night in the slammer, she appeared in court accompanied by Rabbi Plaut, political journalist Dalton Camp, her lawyer and her husband. Of course, June was granted bail and a trial set for three months hence. At her trial, no less a personage than reporter, author, TV personality and long-time buddy, Pierre Berton, testified on June's behalf.

A night or two after the arrest, comedian Frank Shuster hosted a party at his home. *Star* photographer Boris Spremo took photographs of the event and there is June holding court in a long green sleek gown (she said it was green), upswept hair and big bangle earrings. June is describing the sad lot of the young people at Digger House and explaining what a necessary haven it is for them.

In the photo, society artist Harold Town lurks behind June, and looking at her, enraptured, is a host of other congregants that included the usual high-profile suspects who surrounded June. The illustrious guests, movers and shakers, in Toronto at the time, wrote cheques for Digger House.

According to June, some important people didn't come to Shuster's soiree because they were so shocked. "They thought it was scandalous. I did too," said June, wryly.

In a CBC interview, two decades after her Yorkville protest, June talked about her arrest and stated she was held overnight in a cell where someone "had a bowel movement" and "smeared shit all over the walls and ceiling."[19]

"I was humiliated and felt disgraced. I was a middle-class woman in my forties. If they (the police) did this to me, what would they do to others?" In photographs taken in the morning at her court appearance, June is clad in a stylish coat and dress ensemble that makes her look like she just arrived from a high-society afternoon tea.

By the mid-1970s, Yorkville had deteriorated from beatniks to deadbeats and a hang-out for druggies and riff-raff. There was also a hepatitis scare or 'hip'-atitis alert, as

Newsgirls

By the 1980's, Yorkville was pretty much gentrified and today it is a bourgeois bastion of expensive bistros, designer duds and deluxe condominia.

some people referred to it, and the glory days were over. The Riverboat lasted until 1978 and then the lights went out.

In another CBC radio interview in the late 1970s, June described her Digger House involvement as a "watershed" experience. "I was entranced with what I saw in Yorkville. It's what I wanted when I was growing up." In this interview, June also said that by the 1970s, the Flower Children were safely gone and replaced by kids from Sudbury and Newfoundland with teeth rotted out of their heads. She was appalled by their condition, and told the interviewer she felt *despair* for the thousands of teenagers who never had a chance. She also claimed they were "so hated, they couldn't get treatment in (Toronto) hospitals."

June admitted it took decades for her to comprehend feminism, social needs and injustice. But 1975 found June freelancing for the *Globe and Mail*, writing a column about homelessness and a litany of social issues. That gig lasted until 1978 when Roy Megarry was appointed publisher and C.E.O.; Megarry looked around the newsroom and decided there were too many *lefties* for his liking. He described June as a "bleeding heart" and axed her column.[20]

June was shocked by the transition from the cozy family atmosphere in the newsroom of her innocent youth to the animosity thirty years later when Megarry waged an open campaign to dump her. She later claimed: "He wanted me fired; but I quit because they dropped my husband."

Linda McQuaig did not fit into Megarry's vision of the Globe either. She was writing offensive lefty stuff about lenient corporate taxation practices and she left the Globe for freelance work and the CBC. In the Toronto by-election in November 2013, McQuaig ran for the National Democratic Party (NDP) in Toronto Centre. She lost.

During Megarry's tenure, lasting until 1992, he also targeted Stevie Cameron, the *Globe and Mail's* national reporter and political columnist, who purveyed all the political scuttlebutt worth knowing. Her descriptions of the excessive lifestyle of Prime Minister Brian Mulroney and his unconscionable wife, Mila, were an affront to staunch Conservatives like Megarry and *Globe* owner Ken Thomson. Cameron told *Globe* readers about the over-the-top expenditure of taxpayers' money—Mrs. Mulroney's redecorating of 24 Sussex Dr. After that, Cameron's days were numbered and she was out the door. Cameron's celebrated book, *Corruption and Greed in the Mulroney Years,* appeared in 1984. In December, 2013, Cameron received an *Order of Canada,* "For demonstrating excellence for exceptional service in ways that bring special credit to the country."

Interestingly, when I interviewed June at Casey House in 1997, she bristled at the suggestion of lean, mean, discriminatory newsrooms and refused to discuss the subject, never mind her termination by Megarry.

"I'm still part of the *Globe* gang. I feel good at the *Globe*. People tell me how hard things are today, but I never experienced anything negative."

In 1977, at age fifty-three, June was host of another CBC television series called *In Touch*, which June described as a show about empathy. June was interviewed by Barbara McLeod in a promotion piece for *In Touch*. McLeod asked June about eschewing TV makeup and being up-front about her age. No matter, June looks fabulous in an online CBC clip. High cheekbones, tanned complexion, dark eyes and wavy hair. She could pass for thirty-eight. "It is to do with my philosophy about being truthful...Not artificial. Why am I pasting on these eye lashes, as I used to do...gradually I stopped using them...I thought 'Bill doesn't wear makeup so why am I doing this'."

June also claimed she had taken off her brassiere, previously, and never put it back on. And it sure looks like it in photographs taken in the 1960s. In one *In Touch* episode, June interviewed teenaged mothers clad in a frumpy cardigan and *sans* makeup.

Early in her career June dressed in chic clothes. At one point, she looked like a cross between Grace Kelly and Jackie Kennedy. "I was very interested in clothes and learned to appreciate good style and design as a result of being so deprived in my childhood. I had second-hand clothes, so I was always self-conscious about this and the reaction to my own appearance." But there was a period, in the 1970s, after June discovered feminism when she lapsed into shapeless long garb and plain tops, in the tradition of the Birkenstoked *Earth Mothers* who spear-headed affirmative action and organizations such as the National Action Committee and Organized Working Women. During this period, June also gave up the aforementioned makeup and bra. She later returned to a more stylish wardrobe, never mind the vanity skirts worn to display her legs.

After being turfed from the *Globe*, June continued to freelance for magazines and found other work as a ghost writer. She also became more deeply involved in community work. June's Digger House experience had catapulted her into social activism and she found that experience useful for Nellie's, her next cause célèbre. She stated: "I'd learned about how to do it from Digger house."

Nellie's, a hostel for battered women, opened in 1974. This sanctuary was named after suffragette Nellie McClung, who, in the 1920s, challenged the federal government on the *non-status* of women. At the time, women could not vote because they were not "persons" according to the Canadian constitution. McClung and four other militant Albertan ladies took their cause to court and won. Canadian women were declared persons and could thereafter vote.

Also, in the late 1970s, after the launch of Nellie's, June chaired a Task Force with a mandate to look into facilities for pregnant girls. The outcome was the opening of Jessie's Centre for pregnant teenagers in 1982. This hostel, now called the June Callwood Centre for Young Women, is currently on Parliament St., Toronto. It helps some two hundred girls annually.

Troubles

At Nellie's, June was one of a committee of women comprised mainly of active feminists and unionists who planned and fundraised for the cause. The women sprang into action after discovering there were only forty beds in the City of Toronto for homeless women, while there were 400 for men. Once Nellie's was established, June was on the Board of Directors until 1992, when she resigned after a scandal. It seems that at a board meeting in December 1991, Joan Johnson, a staff member, complained that women of colour, like herself, felt they weren't treated as well as the white women. June pointed out to Johnson, that she, herself, had been a recipient of help from Nellie's. Apparently, Johnson responded, "Do I have to be grateful the rest of my life?" For what it's worth, in "a tirade," June responded with, "Put aside your fucking differences...I don't want to hear that crap."[21]

There was a general hue and cry and June was accused of being a racist. It all came to a head six months later and June resigned from Nellie's board. Dear friends circled the wagons to defend June. "If Callwood is a racist, then we all are," wrote Berton, in his *Toronto Star* column, and CBC broadcaster Peter Gzowski made a similar statement.

Meanwhile, Michele Landsberg, the strident feminist columnist for the *Toronto Star*, did *not* rush solely to June's defense, but attempted to spread the blame around by shaking a finger at all Caucasians. Landsberg wrote: "By the year 2001, nearly half the population (in Toronto) will be visible minorities. Every one of us, and every one of our institutions will have to face the fact, the old unwritten assumptions of our white-dominant culture will no longer be acceptable—or workable."[22]

Finally, in July 1992, the *Star* published June's defense. The paper allowed her a thousand-word column for her magna apologia. June told her side of the story. She wrote she was "startled" that the women of colour not only demanded she resign from Nellie's board, but added requirements forbidding her to be on any Nellie's committees and barring her from the hostel premises.

"I have to keep reminding myself that this draconian measure was the result of two incidents—neither of which seems to me to merit reprisal of such magnitude...I disputed a black woman's shocking accusations against the white staff and I failed to apologize to her adequately." June goes on to list many of her good works and worthy supporters and ends her piece with the bromide: "A society in which everyone has an equal opportunity to flourish can only come about through collaborative effort...This period of destruction must cease. It's time to heal and build."[23]

June was *Toronto Life's* cover girl for the March 1993 issue. Inside was an article about June, written by Elaine Dewar. It featured terms such as "The Mother Theresa of Ontario." *Saturday Night* magazine also run a sympathetic story by Adele Freedman, who described June as *battered*.

Throughout the 1980s, both June and Frayne were back at the *Globe and Mail*, simultaneously, writing columns for the paper and *Maclean's* magazine. At the *Globe*, Frayne was writing for the sports section while June was producing a column called *This City*. Here, as a columnist, she hit her stride as a social advocate. June tapped out several hundred *Globe and Mail* columns in which she constantly beat her social-justice drum. One of the more memorable columns was her manifesto *The Country of the Poor*. Here, on November 21, 1987, June lists fifteen points regarding the sufferings of Canada's underclass. The list includes: "Most poor women have been beaten up by men on whom they depend... Everywhere, the poor live one day at a time with a fixed goal: to find at least one meal... Housing is seen everywhere as the key issue in the *nation of the poor*. However, no city in Canada yet has a sufficient supply of affordable permanent housing. There is therefore no hope for the homeless this winter or for those who occupy vile rooming houses and hotels. Some will die. The sick will get sicker; the well will become ill." In the 21st Century, these issues are still discussed in the media. Plus ça change, plus c'est la même chose.

In 1989, June was involved in yet another fiasco. It occurred at Roy Thomson Hall in Toronto, where PEN International was holding its annual congress. June, the incoming president of PEN Canada and the organizing committee had made sure the meeting was inclusive. Meanwhile, outside of the Roy Thomson Hall, two women handed out literature complaining about PEN's lack of a racial component. One of the pamphleteers was black writer Marlene (Nourbese) Philip. June told her to "fuck off."

Immediately, someone called the *Globe* to report June's verbal gut reaction. The paper put it on the front page, even though June was one of its popular columnists. The upshot: June's relationship with the newspaper, where she had learned her craft, ended once and for all.

June, a founding member of the *Writers' Union of Canada*, was involved in a third controversy in 1994. This one ended with her resignation from the Union. June had delivered the annual *Margaret Laurence Memorial Lecture*. Two writers complained about the content. One even compared June to Ezra Pound, who was known as a poet with fascist leanings. Again, June was accused of racism.

June told *Toronto Star* reporter, Nancy J. White, in a 1995 profile with the big splashy head, *Portrait of 'Saint June'*, that she loved to hug the babies at Jessie's. Although, she more or less stayed clear of Jessie's after the dust-up at Nellie's. In the same interview, June also shared with White, because of her reputation as a racist, she was suffering from loss of income due to lack of speaking engagements. However, on the same page as this *Star* story, happened to be an advertisement for a talk at Roy Thomson Hall, in the *Unique Lives* series: *June Callwood Fights back, Monday, Feb. 27th. Don't Miss Out. Call for Tickets.*

White also quoted June as saying about the Nellie's, PEN and Writer's Union debacles, "I wanted to be dead. I wasn't suicidal, but I wanted the pain to end."

During this period, June, who still had her pilot's license, learned to fly gliders. Looking back over her besmirching and disappointments, she explained "I turned to it as a metaphor, to get up above the shit; up, up, up."[24]

Tragedy

Sadly, June not only experienced professional and public pain, but she endured more than her share of family heartache. Her eldest daughter, Jill Frayne, was struck on her bicycle by a cement mixer and almost "cut in half." She did survive and is a family therapist and a writer. In 2002, Jill published an autobiography called *Starting Out in the Afternoon*. It documents Frayne's mid-life crisis, and a Cross-Canada camping trip ending in the Yukon. The author was endeavouring to find herself by communing with nature. June's other daughter, Jesse Frayne, is married and the mother of four children. In 2001, she authored a cookbook and in 2005 a novel, *Just Keep Breathing*. June's sons did not fare so well. Brant, nick-named Barney, has been disabled since he was diagnosed with MS in his forties and suffered a stroke when a brain operation went wrong. Today, Brant Frayne is a writer and an editor. June's youngest child, Casey, was killed by a drunk driver in April 1982 while riding his motorcycle to Queen's University in Kingston. He was only twenty-one. The woman who drove the car was charged with dangerous and impaired driving, paid a $500 fine and had her license suspended for three months. June

---

Philip is still active; her letter to the editor at Now *Magazine was published July 14, 2016. It talks about a black woman's protest staged at 2016 Toronto Pride Parade criticizing conservative author Michael Coren's attendance at the parade.*

had Casey's ashes buried under an apple tree in her backyard. "April is crappy. I hate April. I always thought nothing like that would happen to me." When asked why in a CBC interview, she answered, "I always thought nothing would happen to people I love."[25]

In the 1996 interview at Casey House, June also declared the best column she ever wrote was written in the fall of 1983 during her later tenure as a *Globe* columnist. "It was my second tour at the *Globe*," she said. "The column was about young men and motorcycles." This was obviously about the loss of her son, Casey.

In October 1983, June's wistful, breezy thoughts about motorcyclists were published in the *Globe*. Not once did she mention Casey's name. This piece must have broken—again—the hearts of the Frayne family and all those near to June and Casey.

"In a few weeks, the young men will be restoring their motorcycles for the winter. It had been a long lovely summer, riding free on the highways in the open air, unencumbered by the confinement of an automobile, alone under the sky, masters of their fate.

"The young men are full of nostalgic regret as they wax the machines one last time. The men are filthy, their hands black, but the motorcycles are spotless. The young men have always loved wheels...

"The motorcycle horrifies parents who can't understand it and won't ride it... They (young men) buy leather because if something goes wrong and they hit the pavement, they don't want to be flayed. The truth is if something does go wrong, the leather is irrelevant. On impact, if the motorcyclist hits the pavement, he slams down with the force... of being dropped from a building... Dying is what happens to someone else. Young men have believed this since human history began."[26]

During the seventy years the Fraynes were married, June emphasized more than once her career and simultaneously raising four children would have been impossible without the unfailing support of her husband. Although at one time a heavy drinker, Frayne managed to bring home the bacon. In October 1964, after an evening of excessive imbibing at Mohawk racetrack, Frayne crossed the median on Highway 401 while driving home and was found going the wrong way. He narrowly missed hitting a police car, but he did rear-end another vehicle. Frayne was arrested, fined $500 and his license suspended for two years. After this humiliating misdemeanor, Frayne gave up the demon drink forever, but not before this story reached legendary status among veteran sports' hacks who told and re-told it at the Press Club bar. There are several accounts of this peccadillo in print.[27][28]

But the supportive husband's career did not always benefit from the high-profile wife. In 1959, Frayne went to work at the *Toronto Star* as a features and sports writer. In the 1960s, he picked up an extra gig, producing publicity for the *Ontario Jockey Club* (1962-1968). After "righteous" Conn Smyth, Director of the Jockey Club, saw the newspapers with the photos of June being hauled away by police in the Yorkville incident, he fired Frayne.

Both the drunk-driving story and the Jockey Club firing were confirmed, in conversation with Frank Orr, revered *Toronto Star* hockey reporter and master of the spontaneous pun and quip. He once told me, "Yes. Frayne had the Jockey Club job, even though the only stud he knew was the one on his shirt front."

Off-the-cuff comments like this were typical of by-gone sports' scribblers, fueled by a cornucopia of grub and gallons of grog supplied to the working press by club owners during games in assorted cities. Days on the road together gave these reporters lots of time in a male milieu to chew the fat and exchange and embroider their tales for the reading public. In 1990, Frayne published a memoir of his fifty years in the "toy department" with the witty title, *The Tales of an Athletic Supporter*, and written with a broad Damon Runyon-esque flavour.[29]

In contrast, June's copy is over-earnest and humourless—no wit, double entendre, snappy puns or clever turn of phrase. That was Frayne's department.

June once told the *Toronto Star*, "My husband loves me. That makes me impregnable." Really! Mother of four children!

Through all of life's trials and tribulations, June often confided to anyone who would listen, she was comforted and succored by her life-long love affair with Frayne who she called "Bill" and referred to as "Dreamy" and "my guy."

June told author Susan Crean in 1985 that she was one of the highest paid freelance writers around because she had a husband. "Had I been alone, I wouldn't have been able to hold out for higher fees which I do every time, pushing up the price... I am subsidized by a 40-year marriage, which is a little like being a millionaire socialist."[30]

Survivor

In later years, June liked nothing better than giving interviews and chattering about her romance with *Dreamy*. Anthony Jenkins interviewed June in 1998 for *The Globe and Mail*'s Q & A feature, *Person, Place, Thing*, about Queen Elizabeth's 50th wedding anniversary. Question: "Philip is the Queen's consort. Is playing second banana to a spouse a fitting role for any man or woman. Answer: It depends whether the man's balls are nailed on or not. If they are going to fall off at the slightest hint that he's not running the show, you've got an immature man who's going to be a problem for anybody to be married to... If you think of marriage in terms of who is top banana, you are not talking marriage." June was also asked how her husband would react to being called her "consort." June smugly answered, she had a spouse who had been called Mr. Callwood and he thought it was funny. June had nothing positive to say about Prince Philip and QEII as a couple, and opined their children were "raised in a dysfunctional family." This echoes June's 1959 *Maclean's* article disparaging the British monarchy.

Casey House was June's last hurrah on the service front. From the get-go, she donated a percentage of proceeds from book sales, and also her time and influence to get the hostel rolling. In 1988, June was busy spear-heading the establishment of this respite for men dying from AIDS, and in 1994, she was designated honorary Director of the Casey House Foundation. As long as her health allowed, June continued to fundraise and participate in activities including gala cabarets. By all accounts, she was greatly loved by the Casey House administrators and patients. In 1988, June's book *Jim: A life with AIDS* appeared (Lester & Orpen Dennys, 1988.) This was ground-breaking in that AIDS was greatly feared at that time.

It would be wrong not to riff on June's legendary legs and her duds. Everyone who ever met June or wrote about her mentioned her physical appearance with admiration. June, a dedicated sun worshipper, was always tanned and, even in cold weather, she strode around the city wearing high heels and with her bare tanned legs showing under a short skirt. This conjures a remark by American wit Dorothy Parker: "If you wear a short enough skirt, the party will come to you."

The last time I ran into June, it was a chilly autumn evening outside of 21 Dale, a Rosedale condominium. We both had casseroles in hand. It turned out we were going to different pot luck suppers. I was bundled up—wool socks and boots—and there was June, almost eighty years old, with naked legs and spike heels.

When CBC radio commentator Michael Enright first laid eyes on June in the 1960s, he described her "as beautiful as blazes." Renowned gardener and writer Marjorie Harris likened the young Fraynes to a pair of movie stars. They were "jaw-dropping gorgeous." Both quotes are from *It's All About Kindness: Remembering June Callwood*, a book compiled by Margaret McBurney and published in 2012, five years after June's death. In this elegiac volume 58, people wrote about their joy in knowing June.[31]

June's other vanities also deserve a mention: her nifty little Miata sports cars and giving gifts of French champagne. Devon Stutt, a computer specialist who assisted June with her computer woes, was "rewarded" with bottles of champagne. Knowing June did not lock her doors, he would sometimes go into her house and June would come home to find Stutt seated at her computer. "After a big hug, she would go off to the cellar for another bottle of champagne. When she told me she was a Lay Bencher for the Law Society of Upper Canada and was helping select champagne for their cellar, I almost fell over. Would there be no end to champagne? By this time, I was in a small one-bedroom flat and the hall and closets were full of champagne." Apparently, Stutt solved the problem by finding June another techie who accepted dollars.[32]

If one may indulge in a bit of social psychology, June was the product of the Great Depression and World War II when Hollywood movie stars like Betty Grable were all the rage. Grable was the pin-up favourite of the American army and every post had a picture of her in a bathing suit and her long bare legs, made even sexier thanks to her high-heeled shoes. Dancers like Ann Miller (*Easter Parade, Kiss Me Kate*) and the Busby Berkeley chorus gals flitted across the silver screen—all legs and high heels. It appears June never got over the images of the dazzling movies and the glamour girls she first saw in the 1940s.

There is another aspect to June's personality that comes through. Poor or privileged, a female who has been told she is beautiful from her formative years usually learns how to parlay this admiration into unshakeable self-confidence. These women understand beauty is power. One wonders what made a school principal issue a fraudulent graduation certificate for June. Could it be because she was perky, clever and lovely to look at? In past centuries, these beauties would have been courtesans. Their characteristics include an enchanting smile and a controlled soft, alluring voice. When they speak to an individual, such women stare into the eyes and with glued attention make that human feel exceptional.

Interestingly, Jim Bratton, Executive Director of Casey House, shrewdly observed this quality, and wrote in his tribute to June: "Hi sweetie," she chirped as she struggled to my office. How are you doing? How are your kids? How's Casey House?"

"I felt special. I watched her in conversation with others: totally focused, gently caressing a hand, smiling, nodding her head. She had the knack... No matter what your station in life, when June Callwood was talking with you, she made you feel you were the most important person in her life; and at that moment, you were."[33]

June once explained to the *Toronto Star* that she did not have power. "I have influence which is different. I can phone a lot of people and get my call taken, but after that I had better have the goods."[34]

Sadly, in 2003 June was diagnosed with cancer. Towards the end, in 2007, Toronto writer John Lownsbrough asked to meet June for lunch. She explained she had a "leaky leg;" a wound that wouldn't heal and a nurse came in regularly to change its bandage.[35]

While June was living with cancer, Toronto Mayor David Miller decreed a laneway near Nellie's be named *June Callwood Way*. Located near Queen St. East and Broadview, people living in the lane had a Saulter Street address. Elizabeth Trout, a thirty-year resident in a converted factory in this laneway, was given a new address; *One* June Callwood Way. At the dubbing ceremony, Trout approached June and said she was now *Number One*. "You have to be very good to be number one," was June's curt reply, as she turned on her high heel.

In 2005, the University of Toronto inaugurated the June Callwood Professorship in Social Justice at Victoria College and June gave the first lecture. She said: "I'm missing a formal religion, but I am not without a theology, and my theology is that kindness is a divinity in motion." Currently, Toronto author Dr. Camilla Gibb is serving a three-year term in the Callwood professorship. She began her tenure in January 1, 2015.

June told George Stroumboulopoulos in a CBC TV interview, three weeks before she died, she had no regrets and she still had her pilot's license—certainly a highlight of her life. June was also asked about her 1969 Yorkville episode and commented, "if you have been arrested, as in Belle River, you are a bad person. I thought I was finished writing, but won the B'nai Brith award that year."[36]

By the time June died in April 2007, she had eighty-two very good years under her belt. June's *curriculum vitae* credits her with thirty books, belonging to sixteen professional organizations, ninety-nine miscellaneous organizations, twenty times acting as a judge for awards, delivering dozens of important lectures, receiving forty prestigious awards and twenty honorary degrees. Quite impressive for a high school drop-out. And that's not the half of it. June also ghost-wrote a plethora of volumes including the Barbara Walters's autobiography, *How to Talk to Practically Anybody About Practically Anything*, published in 1970.[37]

Quickly, post-mortem honours began to stack up. In 2008, Ontario Premier Dalton McGuinty declared June's birthday, June 2, *June Callwood Day*. A plot of land bordered by Fort York and owned by the City of Toronto was named *June Callwood Park*. The Garden Club

Trent Gardiner Frayne outlived June by five years. He died in 2012. Frayne was ninety-three years old.

of Toronto took on the project of planting eighty-nine crabapple trees and several flower beds on the site. At the park launch, in May 2012, a roster of some twenty local writers, activists and politicians praised June's many accomplishments at what can only be described as a *Love In*. But the final words go to June. "I like everything I ever did. I worked in a dime store on Saturdays, and I liked that too."

SIMMA HOLT

Winnipeg Free Press, 1941. Vancouver Sun, 1944-1974.
Member of Parliament, 1974-1979.

1922-2015

> "To me, in this age of conformity and political correctness, being something of a loose cannon is a term of respect."

5

"I'm furious with you. Putting my name on a list with all those spoiled PR types in Toronto. Toronto reporters who never did anything," veteran reporter Simma Holt screamed over the phone from 2,000 miles away in Vancouver. It was early 1995 and I was conducting the first of several interviews with Simma for *Newsgirls*. It was obvious she did not like the company she was to keep. "You can't put my name with the likes of Stasia Evasuk. It's here in the West where we did things. We were reporters. Pioneers. Do you know Lily Laverock, Kay Alsop, Murphy etcetera? They did it, not spoiled Toronto types. You don't know anything in the East. I'm insulted."

Simma, who adored every day of her life in the world of newspapers, wanted the world to know she was never one of the girls—always one of the boys. As far as she was concerned, the only female reporters worth a pencil were the old guard in the West. Simma viewed herself and her West Coast sisters as unique and she made it clear nobody east of the Rockies is worth a damn. Warming to her subject, Simma said she didn't know if she wants to be part of such weak company. "Write me and I'll think about it," she yelled.

I begged her to talk to me, to set the record straight about who's who in journalism. Simma tore on like a desert twister about attending a Canadian Women Journalists Conference in Vancouver where June Callwood was a keynote speaker.

"The women sat cross-legged on the floor. It was disgusting. Have you ever seen professional men do that? And they all shared rooms to save their employers money. Have you ever heard of men doing that?"

After hitting a crescendo, Simma stopped for a breath and I assured her she had a point. "At my age, I say what I want and if people don't like it, screw 'em." Before banging down the receiver, Simma continued: "It was hell for 30 years at the *Sun*. And now I'm telling all. Naming names!"

Getting on with naming names, Simma mentioned a list of personalities from yesteryear and various scandals. But she saved a sour grapes harangue about Toronto celebrity journalist June Callwood getting the Order of Canada, and by implication, Simma herself order-less, or as it's known in some circles - the *Odour* of Canada. "I say screw it. If June Callwood got it, it is worth nothing to me."

In 1996, shortly after this lusty outburst, Simma was informed she was to be received into the Order of Canada. It seems she was able to hold her nose long enough to collect her very own *Odour* pin and to crow about it with pride. Simma received this award from the Governor General for her "commitment to assisting those suffering from injustice, persecution and poverty."

At the time of the telephone eruption, Simma was in a bad mood, frustrated because she could not master the computer and get on with her latest book. Finally, she agreed to be an interviewee and was much calmer at the Vancouver Lawn Tennis Club, a prestigious Establishment stronghold. In fact, during that interview in October 1995, Simma was jolly, full of vim and talked non-stop. She appeared decades younger than her 73 years.

Even though Simma was the recipient of prestigious writing awards, a former Member of Parliament, worked for President George H. W. Bush's administration and authored five books, it wasn't enough. Neither was the slew of public honours that came her way including *Woman of the Year* from the Arts and Letters Club in 1964, and two Memorial Awards in 1958 and 1962 for hard news reporting from the *Canadian Women's Press Club.*

Simma's 30 years at the *Vancouver Sun* were her glory years and everything else paled. She was also irate and angry because she couldn't get a publisher for the book she wrote about U.S. President George H. W. Bush's backroom shenanigans. Simma lamented the fact she hadn't been able to land a proper job since her political career ended in 1978. She felt forgotten. Yesterday's woman! While other pensioners are relieved to leave their working lives behind, not our gal Simma, who at one time was known in Vancouver as the "Fastest Lip in the West."

Formative Years

But that was all in her future. Simma Milner was born in Vegreville, Alberta, on March 27, 1922. She was the sixth of eight children in the only Jewish family in town. Her father, Louis Simon Milner, an Ukrainian immigrant, settled in Alberta in 1909. He started his Canadian life peddling vegetables to the Cree. By the time the family moved to Vegreville, renowned today for having the world's largest Ukrainian Easter egg, Milner Trading Company was a thriving business and Louis was affluent enough to purchase the National Hotel, one of the two hostelries in town. By then a patriotic colonial Canadian, Milner changed the name to the Prince Edward Hotel for King Edward VII who reigned from 1901 to 1910 after the death of his mother, Queen Victoria. The hotel on the main drag was a multi-purpose centre with a beer parlour, general store and cafe. In those days, beverage rooms had separate entrances for men and women. God forbid they drink together. In her autobiography, *Memoirs of a Loose Cannon*, Simma told a story about her sister Hannah's husband, an American, being deported back to the States because he served liquor to a "half-breed" at the Prince Edward bar.[1]

Simma described her mother, Nassa Rachel Greenberg, as the first liberated woman she ever knew. "She was a typical prairie woman. They were liberated because the men needed them to survive. I had a very liberal upbringing. My parents believed that you had to serve the community you were born into. There was no anti-Semitism. In fact, when the town's people went after the Jehovah Witnesses, my father stood up for them and argued for their right to their religion.

"My parents let us go into churches. I was in the international choir and sang Christmas carols. I celebrated Christmas. We had shortbread with neighbours and we invited them in for Jewish specialties. It was a nice town. But because I always thought I had fat legs and was ugly, I missed a lot of joy," said Simma, looking at photos of her young self.

Murder came early into Simma's life. When she was four, her grandfather was shot and robbed by two teenagers in his general store in Edmonton. The haul was barely ten dollars. Her older sister Hannah was at the trial and she heard a woman say, "Why all the fuss? He's only a Jew."[2]

In the mid-1930s, Simma had her first whiff of printer's ink at the *Vegreville Observer*, when she became involved in the reportage of Vegreville's first murder. After school, it was Simma's habit to hang around the Observer office and watch the elderly man who was owner, reporter and publisher of the newspaper set type by hand. Conveniently, the newspaper was opposite the courthouse, so Simma had a front row view of the to-ing and fro-ing of a farmer and son accused of shooting their neighbour. Simma, then 11 or so, actually witnessed the accused being escorted in and out of the courthouse. Simma always considered this thrilling experience a formative event in her life.[3]

The family was affluent enough in 1939 at the end of the Great Depression to arrange to send Simma to Barnard College in New York. Unfortunately, World War II broke out and her U.S. visa never came through. Instead, Simma went to Winnipeg to attend the University of Manitoba. She graduated in 1944 with a Bachelor of Arts degree. "I was terrified when I first went into the stacks in the library and saw all the books. I just broke down because I couldn't believe there was so much to learn," Simma said.

During her freshman year, Simma heard John Dafoe, the university's chancellor, speak. He had been editor of the *Winnipeg Free Press*. His speech emboldened Simma and the next day she went to the *Free Press* to ask for a job. Right off the bat, the editor told her he couldn't stand university students. Nevertheless, he hired Simma as a part-time stringer. "The only reason I got hired and into journalism was the men were at war, so I wasn't taking a man's job," declared Simma. "I was already as cheeky as hell then, but today I would have told Coo to piss up a rope."

The editor in question was Abby Coo and Simma wasn't the only audacious university gal who asked Coo for a job. In 1941, Elizabeth (Beth) Paterson approached him at the *Winnipeg Free Press* and Coo said she had two strikes against her. "One, I don't like women for reporter jobs. Two, I can't stand university graduates. They know too much and I have to undo all they know. One more strike and you're out." But because of the shortage of men, even the crustiest misogynist editor had to take girls into his newsroom, so Miss Paterson was hired as a full-time reporter. At the *Free Press*, Paterson worked the 4 p.m. to midnight shift. She remembered Coo as a "fat man who constantly took his false teeth out and put then put them back in again."

As a rookie, Paterson's job was to hang around the local hotels and the train stations in order to discover if anyone important was arriving in Winnipeg. "I loved the job. It was something to see the steam engines huffing into the cold station with the hoar frost around them like a magical mist," she told me in a 1997 interview.

While Simma studied and worked at the *Free Press*, she boarded with Dr. Jack Lander and his wife. She paid the couple $25 a month for room and board, which left her $25 spending money.

As well as a stringer for the *Free Press*, during her student years Simma wrote for *The Manitoban*, the university's newspaper. Simma's first assignment for *The Manitoban* was to interview American singer Marian Anderson and violinist Isaac Stern at the City Hall Theatre. Simma shared this assignment with fellow student Enid Nemy. The pair of neophytes had one nickel and cannily managed to get around to both interviews on that sum. They also interviewed Sigmund Romberg (1887-1951), the composer of the great American operetta, *The Student Prince*. After graduation both girls landed jobs at *Canadian Press* (CP) located in Calgary.

"At university, Enid and I were good friends and when we were rookies at CP, I remember we both wobbled around in high heels that sunk into the asphalt in the summer. We thought we were so sophisticated and elegant," said Simma.

The girls also posed for a photograph with cigars hanging out of their mouths. It can be argued, as time proved, Simma came as close to a cigar-chomping newshound as a woman could. Nemy went to Ontario and after a stint at CBC TV, in 1963 she found a job at the *New York Times*. The clever Enid Nemy started out as a reporter but worked her way into a lifestyle columnist. Nemy officially retired in 2003, but still scribbles the odd column for the *Times*.

One of Simma's best tales harkens back to her fledgling days at CP where she had to cope with the wire service.

"I was a junior reporter. I had learned the ticker tape so they sent me on the train to Calgary. As luck would have it, I arrived on D-Day," recalled Simma with a shudder.[4]

The D-Day allied invasion landed on the Beaches of Normandy, France on June 6, 1944. There were over 1000 Canadian casualities. In those days, news was transmitted across the country by means of punched tape telegraphed, in sequence, from one bureau to another. On June 6, 1944, Simma was alone in the CP bureau. She was told to keep the lines clear. Simma couldn't operate their teletype system properly and panicked. "I heard on the wire, 'Hustle your bustle Calgary' and 'There's a woman in Calgary on the machine.' I've never been so scared in my life. You see it was D-Day. All D-Day news stopped while I tried to figure out why the teletype machine wouldn't work and the news was 20 minutes late going further west."

All through her life, Simma took great delight in saying that she tied up the war on D-Day for 20 minutes. After Simma's D-Day disaster in Calgary, she admitted she was scared that Ralph

Daley, the boss at CP, would come and hit her. After the D-Day incident, not only did Simma live in fear of Daley, but she received a wire from Gillis Purcell, a legendary boss at CP, saying she would be working nights starting Monday. "I said I'd no longer be working. He said, go home and they would help me. They gave me a week's pay–$22.50."

Vancouver – Here She Comes!

Simma had her eye on a job at the *Vancouver Sun*. She described her efforts to get into the *Sun* as a tough fight. She heard the usual line about having a baby. "Then when I finally got the job, the men said things like, 'We'll fix you up with a big black stud.' And they had a pool on who would get me into bed first," Simma said.

Simma also heard the old clichés—women are too emotional. Their place is in the bed and the kitchen and the best line—females rush to the washroom to cry when things don't go their way. Sexism aside, in November 1944, Simma received a telegram from Hal Straight, the managing editor at the *Vancouver Sun*, "Come immediately as assistant to the editor."

In her excitement Simma read the invitation as *Assistant City Editor*. She arrived at the *Sun* on the foggiest November day ever recorded in Vancouver's history. It was so dense, she couldn't see the sidewalks or buildings, but luckily she made her way to the *Sun* building on Granville St. Simma didn't realize there were mountains around the city and that it was situated by the sea until several days later. "Imagine in that fog, I went to the paper wearing a big brown picture hat. I thought you had to dress up. I wore a suit, pumps and that hat with my fat face. Yes, we did dress up. I had only one pair of shoes and would trudge through Chinatown's back alleys in my smart little pumps. But I wouldn't wear a sweater, I was too shy," said Simma. "I was paid $22 a week. After room and board, it took me six months to save the money to buy a radio."

Simma admitted she was always lucky and, during her apprenticeship at the *Sun*, three old-time newsmen took her under their wings. In time, they whipped her reporting into shape and they shaped her career. They were managing city editor Hal Straight, his assistant Himie Koshevoy—a squat man with a gnome-like face, according to Simma—and provincial editor Bill Short, a man who went on drinking jags and would disappear for days.

"Bill was always given a second chance," said Simma. "He eventually became a founder of Alcoholics Anonymous in Canada." In Tom Ardies' essay, published in *Canadian Newspapers: The Inside Story*, Ardies described Simma's mentors, Straight and Koshevoy, as interchangeable in the managing editor's post. He adds, Straight ran the *Sun* like his own empire and was a "devotee of plain language." This meant that Straight demanded short leads from his reporters. Accordingly, reporter Arnie Myers responded with a story that began, simply, "Dead." Second paragraph: "That's what the man found in the lane was." Straight loved it, according to Ardies. Ardies described Koshevoy as an "ugly little bugger." "Five foot nothing and all nose. Himie was once asked how much he would charge to haunt a house. Himie thought for a moment. 'How many rooms?'"[5]

Despite her mentors, the young Simma's career at the *Sun* didn't quite start out as she envisioned it. "I was the stooge on the city desk. I listened to the police radio—a great experience. I also took dictation from reporters in the field and looked through the war casualty list for local stories. But I did have the wit to eavesdrop on how Bill Short and Koshevoy asked questions."

According to Simma, after checking the national defence's casualty list and deciding on a local story, a reporter was assigned to obtain a photograph of the deceased – by hook or by crook. To this day, the City Desk insisting that a reporter hound relatives for a photograph of a murderer or slain relative is the bane of a GA reporter's existence.

The conversation goes like this: *This is the Toronto Star calling. I understand your teen-aged daughter was gunned down in a parking lot today. May we have a photo of her?* If there *isn't* a cheery "yes" to this request, the next step is pounding on the bereaved parents' door and demanding one.

If a City Editor demands a comment from the Prime Minister, the GA reporter is the one who has to get it. The M.O.: Call the switchboard operators who at major newspapers seem to have the phone number of every important human in the world. In times past, a canny *Toronto Star* operator could put you through to the PM's residence and manage contact even if he were in the bathtub. The reporter snaps, "the *Star* needs a statement." Mission Accomplished. This was true until the Stephen Harper regime set up camp in Ottawa with a sign saying: No reporters admitted.

Seeing that Canada was still at war in 1944, there were shortages and rationing of food and liquor. Citizens were issued ration books and Simma, at twenty-two, was old enough to obtain a government ration book for booze. What an opportunity for the newsroom boys! Weekly, she was deployed to pick up her liquor ration and deliver it to the City Desk. According to Simma, this was the only time she was noticed. Other than that, there were no adventurous forays into the city and certainly no sleuthing for Simma. She spent her neophyte years desk-ridden and taking dictation from the beat reporters who phoned in stories.

Historically, the desker rested the phone receiver on one shoulder and held it in place with the chin so their hands were free to type the spoken word from a GA reporter somewhere in a phone booth. Years of this usually results in neck pain and bad posture.

Finally, in 1945, the war was over and when the men were demobbed, girl reporters, like Simma, were expected to get back in the kitchen and rattle them pots and pans so the boys could slide into their jobs. As a result, in the post-war years, most newsrooms were peppered with roués who had been lucky enough to survive the bloody battlefields of Europe. Luckily, Simma was able to keep her job because at the time, Myers, the newsroom wit, was one of Simma's idols and also her champion. He protected Simma and she also had the support of her caregivers Koshevoy and Straight.

When Simma joined the *Sun*, there were another two rookies on-staff named Pierre Berton (1920-2004), and Allan Fotheringham. Both Fotheringham and Berton, a city editor at 21, were Simma's contemporaries. In those days, the *Sun* published seven editions daily, six days per week. Decades later, in 2000, Fotheringham wrote a nostalgic piece in *Maclean's* magazine about the early days at the *Sun*. He observed that after Berton and Hal Straight put out the morning edition, they habitually went to Stanley Park where they "finished off a 26-ouncer out of the neck of a bottle, then they would return and put out the afternoon edition. That was just the day. Then there were the night editions to get out."[6]

Berton, in his 1987 autobiography *Starting Out: 1920-1947*, wrote about his early years at the *Vancouver Sun*. He viewed himself as "Scoop Berton, a hard-drinking, hard-driving reporter with a hat on the back of his head."[7] It seems he did live up to his self-image.

With great disdain, Simma dismissed Berton and Fotheringham, who later ended up in the East with the same contempt she had for the lady reporters in Toronto. "There were more men like them, writing about drunks and other crap rather than anything worthwhile. Berton's wife, Janet, took all his calls. The phone was on her side of the bed and she covered for him no matter what he was up to," Simma said.

In future years, Berton urged Simma to write her autobiography and threw her a bone of praise. He said: "The foreword would read something like this; 'She never did the job the way a reporter should. She got too involved...but scooped us all.'"[8]

Crime and Mayhem

Once released from the desk from the get-go, Simma prowled around Vancouver in search of stories. On her own time, she followed any lead that came her way. "One day I got a tip on a story and wrote it. After Himie and Hal read it, Hal said, 'This is the greatest story. Now get the hell out of here and get the other side.' When I found the other side, my big story evaporated. It was the best lesson I ever had. I owe whatever success I've had to Himie. He was the wisest and most patient teacher I could ever have hoped for," confessed Simma.

Lop-sided story aside, in one week as a cub reporter, Simma claimed that she had five banner headlines resulting from tips heard on the police and ambulance radios. Simma bagged her first big scoop when she was twenty-two-years-old. There was a fire in Chinatown late one night, after deadline, and Simma was alone in the newsroom. The eager young reporter decided to go out to investigate even though "in those days when a Chinaman died, it was *just* a Chinaman." When she arrived, all the big guns were there including her fellow reporter from the *Sun*, Jack Webster.

"The press decided there was nothing here. But I decided to hang around a little longer even though my one pair of shoes were so wet, water was squishing through my toes. I followed some cats. They led me to the story of the elderly Chinese man who died. It turned out he had 58 cats and was burned trying to rescue them," recalled Simma.

Sidebar 1: During a recent visit to the *Toronto Star* newsroom, despite cell phones, tiny hand-held devices and computers, I spotted two reporters, necks cricked to hold old-fangled reciver as they keyboarded. The upshot, most newspapers now offer RSI physiotherapy to help heal wounded reporters with GA neck.

Sidebar 2: In *Starting Out*, Berton explained he had a casual romance with the easy going and tolerant Janet Walker. Eventually, he married her when he realized he need "an anchor, a helpmate, somebody sensible enough to curb my natural tendencey to waywardness." Berton's own words more or less confirming Simma's evaluation of the marital situation.

Newsgirls

It seems the man believed that his kindness to the felines would ensure a place for both the cats and him in heaven. The next day the *Sun*'s headline read: "Burnt Chinaman Rescues Cats so They Could Go To Heaven."

"Jack Webster got such hell for missing it," snorted Simma over a glass of wine at the tennis club. She added with bravado, "Jack Webster is still riding on his name."

Simma and Webster became friends and allies in their indignant fights against what they perceived as injustices. After Webster had left print and took up radio as his cudgel, Simma was often heard on his show on CKNW. Both of them were rabble rousers and when Simma was a guest, Webster would warn listeners by announcing: "Here comes terror in the name of Simma." This was the inspiration for the title of Simma's book about British Columbia's Doukhobor sect, *Terror in the Name of God*, published in 1964 by McClelland & Stewart

During the 1990s, Webster was a panelist on CBC TV's "Front Page Challenge," along with his old *Sun* cronies, Pierre Berton and Allan Fotheringham. Webster died in 1999.

In 1948 on a *Sun* assignment, Simma spent New Year's Day lurking on the shore of the Pacific Ocean with the Polar Bear Club, a group of masochists who specialized in plunging into the frigid water every New Year's Day. Simma plotted with a *Sun* photographer to fake a swim. As it turned out, a horde of people turned up to watch and Simma had to go into the 58°F water. She survived to see her picture on page one of the *Sun* and to write a story with the charming headline, "I Swam with The Polar Brrrs." Interestingly, the big news that day concerned Sir Winston Churchill who was ailing in Morocco. The *Sun* editors relegated Churchill to a bottom corner of the front page to make way for "Super Swimmer" Simma.

Later the same year, what started out to be yet another amusing caper like the Polar Bear swim, ended rather badly for Simma. It all began with the discovery of a new diet pill. Simma always felt she was fat, even though photos of her as a young woman show a curvaceous figure à la Marilyn Monroe. Through the 1940s and 1950s, this was the most desirable female body. Simma's diet and record of this experience was intended as another entertaining story for *Sun* readers. During her Battle of the Bulge, headlines included "Science Joins Fight Against Fat For Simma Holt" and "Pills Prescribed For Avoirdupois." The diet series started with a picture of Simma being weighed by a nurse in a spanking white uniform who also administered the first pill. Simma had to take these tiny miracle workers three times a day.

She confessed to a case of the "mind is willing, but the flesh is weak." She wrote: "I've gone on diets before. But each time my will took a beating and I succumbed to my passion for food...Now I have found a doctor who has the newest thing in diets—three little pills." Within days, Simma was recognized everywhere in Vancouver. She reported strangers would walk over to her in restaurants and gaze at her plate and make comments loud enough for her to hear. "Simma will never get slimma on that" and "That is a pretty heavy calorie count for Slimmin' Simma."

Simma began to lose weight, but after a few days she experienced fierce headaches, insomnia, fatigue and tension. "I knew I was losing self-control and feared I would blow up in public." It turned out this seductive diet pill was a dangerous methamphetamine. Simma went cold turkey, and, in time, did get back to her usual perky, pugnacious ways.[10]

At one point in 1949, Simma was offered a job by the *Toronto Star*. The *Star* was looking for a newshen who could compete with the *Toronto Telegram*'s Dorothy Howarth, an aggressive uber-reporter who constantly grabbed the biggest scoops in the city.

"You couldn't beat Dorothy Howarth at the *Telegram*. The *Toronto Star* asked me to come there to beat this woman. The petty little bastards in the West said I could never stand up against her," recalled Simma.

With thoughts of big money, the Big City and story opportunities dancing in her head, Simma, 27 and single, felt she had the "world on a plate" and went East for an interview. "But just as I was leaving I heard, but of course, you can't work out of the newsroom. Your desk will be in the women's department. I used the most colourful language I could muster and walked out. That was a turning point in my life," she said.

Ironically, 10 years later in 1958, Howarth left the *Telegram* and took a reporting job at the *Vancouver Sun*. Simma recalled Howarth arriving at the *Sun*. Her reputation, as one of the toughest reporters in the East preceded her. However, she did not last and, head bent low, went back to Toronto. "Dorothy was salty. But I saw her when she was abused in our business. They (men) always found ways to deliberately batter your copy. Women would go to the bathroom to

---

Sidebar:

Well, he should have been. Webster was a big shot in British Columbia and, eventually, across Canada. Webster, a Scot, emigrated to Canada after serving in the Middle East during World War II. He surfaced at the *Sun* in 1953 and later took over the labour beat. That ended when he had a set-to with editor Hal Straight.

According to Webster's autobiography, one day in foul mood, he walked into Straight's office and bellowed: "The day you die of overweight, I'll be one of the 10,000 people who will dance on your coffin. Straight promptly told Webster he was fired and Webster, natually replied with a snappy, "I quit."[9]

No matter, Webster went on to become a pioneer in broadcasting. He invented the radio talk show format. Such was his fame by 1963 that rioting prisoners in the British Columbia Penitentiary requested that Webster mediate for them. He did and the inmates released their hostages unharmed.

cry. But the meaner they got, the stronger I got," swaggered Simma. "The whining women, today, have really no idea what it was like."

Howarth admits her Vancouver venture was a dismal failure. She did not "take to Vancouver" and "didn't try." Looking back, Howarth compared herself to Simma Holt. "She would go out and find stories and get them on the front page. I didn't get front page there," said Howarth, who slunk back to the familiar turf at the *Telegram* and stayed there until she retired in 1966. Obviously, both Simma and Howarth felt like fish out of water when they found themselves in an unfamiliar newsroom in a foreign city.

Simma always claimed the male editors at the *Sun* never assigned her anything. "I found all my stories. Then I could always scoop reporters like Webster and I could still do it today. They were reactors, not researchers," said Simma, with chin jutting out. Others along with Howarth appear to agree this was no idle boast on Simma's part. Tom Ardies, in his essay about the *Vancouver Sun*, wrote "no one ever accused Simma Holt of being able to write. But, oh God, what a digger. She should have been a cop and once did apply for Police Chief."[11]

Chinatown, politics, crime—Simma had a nose for news no matter what the subject, but she loved best fires and firemen. Early in her career, Simma wondered at her peril how a fire truck reached people in dense Vancouver fogs. She actually phoned the fire chief and asked him. The next thing Simma knew she was in a fire hall and someone handed her a flashlight. Her job was to run ahead of the fire truck and shine it on the edge of the road. A few nights of this and Simma had more than her answer. In the name of research, she also carried water at a lumber mill fire. "I rode with the fire department to see what it was like. I'd stay overnight in Number 2 Fire Hall and pull on my overalls and go down the pole with the rest of them. Besides running in front of the trucks and carrying water, I also did first aid. I attended nintey-six calls with the rescue squad. I liked heroes and firemen were heroes," Simma wrote in her 2008 autobiography.[12]

In Canadian newsrooms, chasing fire trucks and ambulances is considered the most junior and déclassé job that every cub reporter has to go through as a rite of passage. Later these rookies look back on this experience with loathing or humour, depending on disposition. It's the Boot Camp in Newspaper Land, but not for Simma, who loved the shiny red fire trucks. She became a fixture at Vancouver fires and kept filing stories about the work of the firemen. At the time of Simma's reportage and participation, the thought of a female *fireperson* wasn't even a glimmer in any mayor's eye.

Simma was like a mascot and in 1953 she was named an Honorary Fire Chief of the Vancouver Fire Department's Rescue and Safety Squad. The department gave her an authentic fireman's hat and she wore it as often as she could. Simma took her position very seriously and this experience added fuel to her thirty-year-year romance with the fire department.

Also, during the 1950s, Simma recalled a Christmas party when Straight gave a speech about how impressed he was with the three lady reporters at the *Sun* and, consequently, he planned to hire more. Two of the newshens were presented with sewing boxes. Simma suspects because she was younger, she received a portable typewriter.

Simma remembered with admiration Mae Garnett, one of the recipients of a sewing box. Garnett was on the courthouse beat for thirty years and, reputedly, only had a grade eight education. Judges and leading lawyers would consult with her on precedent. The other newshen was Doris Milligan, an experienced City Hall reporter. She befriended the young Simma and her no-nonsense professionalism provided Simma with a role model for her entire career. It's interesting to note these *ladies of the press* stayed out of the newsroom—one holed up in the courthouse and the other in a City Hall niche. Both women phoned in their copy to the City Desk.

A little rain must fall into any life and in Simma's case it was Earl T. Smith. Simma described Smith, a desker and copy editor at the *Sun*, as "the biggest chauvinist pig" who ever worked in a newsroom. "He would put his own slug on my stories. I questioned him about this and he'd say 'you're fired.' After scenes like this, I used to go the women's washroom and cry. But Himie always said, 'okay you're not fired.' It was lucky that Himie and Hal Straight really liked my work. Smith also showed pictures of naked women and would ask, 'How do you like those lungs?'"

In the early 1950s, Smith's constant refrain, if only you could write, and the fact he never recognized her talent for bringing in a story, wounded Simma. She admitted this left a big scar and doubts about her writing abilities. Smith resented girls in the newsroom and Simma, as the only girl, was the target.

Ardies stated in his *Vancouver Sun* essay that all the reporters lived in mortal terror of Smith or ETS as he was known in the newsroom. "All those stories about tough city editors... eating cub reporters for breakfast, etc....He didn't just chew your ass off. He chewed all the way around it. It fell out by itself...He could destroy you with a word. A gesture."[13]

Years later, after she was well established, Simma liked to tell people she never allowed the men she worked with and interviewed to see her as a sexual being. Her male colleagues called her "the sexless wonder of Canadian journalism" and she liked it that way. Myers was an antidote to Smith's nastiness. He championed the young Simma and offered advice for dealing with abuse: "When it starts, tell them where to go and walk across to the Lotus Gardens lounge and get drunk." The Gardens, a Chinese-owned establishment opposite the *Sun* building, was long the watering hole of choice for parched *Vancouver Sun* scribblers. Myers remained a life-long friend and supporter and encouraged Simma to write her memoirs after she retired.

"At times I wanted to punch *them* out and not just deliver idle throw-away lines. I had so much anger. But I didn't want to give journalism up because I loved it," Simma said, adding she was lucky her husband supported her emotionally.[14]

Marriage?

Husband? Man? The nemesis and enemy of the talented Newsgirl! Well, it turned out Simma Milner married Leon Holt, a high school mathematics teacher, in 1949, five years after joining the *Sun*. But Simma loved to tell a pre-Leon story. Apparently, her mother was always trying to get Simma to take to the Jewish boys in Vancouver. "Finally, I would serve bacon and the boy would go home and tell his mother and that was the end of that," she guffawed. As amusing as the bacon ruse was, on the other side of the ledger, before her marriage, Simma suffered a trauma.

One evening, she took an after-dark walk with a friend along the sea shore at Point Grey. They were speculating about their futures, as young people do, unaware of rising water. Suddenly, her friend disappeared. The young man could not swim and panicked. Simma tried her best to save him. The next day searchers found his body in three feet of water. Serendipitously, within weeks of this terrible accident, Simma met Holt. He invited her to join a group aboard his sailboat. After many day trips to Bowen Island, they began dating and the rest is history. Simma became a married woman much to her mother's relief.

Because Simma "loved journalism so much," the couple agreed not to have children. The Holts were as close as only a childless couple can be and, for their entire marriage, they lived happily in the same apartment in Coquitlam. Simma became even more devoted to her husband after he suffered a heart attack in 1975. Leon, with all Simma's TLC, survived another decade and ultimately died in 1985 while playing doubles with three doctors at the Vancouver Lawn Tennis Club.

In 1959, still at the *Sun*, Simma took on the waterfront beat. Covering marine news and the business of an important seaport was traditionally a male domain. Only one other female reporter before her had ever worked the waterfront. A gal in Hawaii, according to Simma. This assignment caused resentment amongst the boys in the newsroom. Apparently, a few had their caps set for this challenging beat. Simma further stirred the pot by asking for a perk. She demanded a wardrobe for the chilly and hazardous working days at the harbour. In the end, the *Sun* paid for a cozy lined parka and warm slip-proof boots. Once dressed to satisfaction, Simma was ready to confront and consort with the stevedores, freighter crews, shipping executives, pilots and custom house staffs who would become grist for the Holt mill.

Simma vividly recalled the time she was assigned to cover a meeting of influential shipping executives in the board room of the ritzy Terminal City Club. It seems this establishment did not allow unescorted women into the club. After much carrying-on, Simma was taken to the kitchen where there was a door into the meeting room. The door turned out to be a divided Dutch door and the top half was locked, so Simma had to duck down to get under. Reporter Holt ended up crawling on her belly into the meeting, much to the amusement of the assembled male executives. Simma, predictably, was outraged and insulted and complained to the assigning editor. No sympathy. She was told if she ever entered a room that way again, she would be fired.

One of the more astonishing waterfront stories was Simma's reportage about her Christmas voyage on the *Northern Princess*, a small freighter. Annually the ship, laden with gifts and supplies, made a run to a few bleak coastal villages. Before returning to Vancouver Harbour, the crew of the *Northern Princess* had a tradition of lashing a Christmas tree to the top of the mast. That December, the Pacific was wild and a storm carried the small vessel miles out to sea, according to Simma. Although they got back to calmer waters, the ship continued to reel and heel so none of the men wanted to deal with the Christmas tree. Enter the intrepid Simma who volunteered to be hoisted to the top of the mast to secure the tree, despite the wild sea below. "It made good art and copy, and fear never inhibited me from going after a story," declared Simma.[15]

Death Row

During Simma's thirty years at the *Sun*, there were certainly a lot of stunts, but she also became involved in several sensational crime stories. As a result of her dogged digging and advocacy, three men were saved from the gallows. One of them, James "Jimmy" Carey, became a cause célèbre for Simma. Carey and his pal, Joe Gordon, killed a policeman during a drug war in Vancouver. Carey was sentenced to death by "Hanging Judge," Alec Manson. According to Simma, Carey was used by police and it was Gordon who actually shot the policeman. At the eleventh hour, thanks to Simma's articles in the *Sun*, Carey did not hang, but was re-sentenced to life in prison. Simma would visit Carey and Gordon in prison and give them chocolate bars. This attention won their trust and this is how she managed to get the true story, thus saving Carey's life.

Simma also delved into the case of Joey McKenna, who was given a death sentence for murdering an ambulance driver in a night club after the victim allegedly insulted McKenna's girlfriend. Due to Simma's bull-dog tenacity as a reporter, McKenna's sentence, like Carey's, was converted to life in prison. Ultimately, with the support of Simma and Leon Holt, McKenna was granted parole.

Simma became a familiar figure on Death Row, also befriending Charles Heathman, who was accused of killing a 10-year-old newspaper carrier, whose body was found in the Okanagan Valley in 1960. Heathman, a former army cook, confessed his crime to Simma during an interview. "I killed him all right," Heathman told Simma. "I just got the urge to kill somebody —anybody—and that kid just happened to be the first one who spoke to me."

In another interview, Heathman told Simma he enjoyed killing the boy and "prolonged it as long as he could." Heathman, who described himself as a psychopathic killer, himself after being released from a psychiatric hospital in 1991.[16]

In a *Toronto Star* article, columnist Joey Slinger pointed out that Simma Holt held the r the person who had witnessed the most executions in Canada. Oddly, although she was a pin-up girl for saving prisoners on Death Row, Simma championed capital punishment and voted as a Member of Parliament in the House of Commons to keep the death penalty.

While at the *Sun*, Simma also crusaded for rights for female prisoners and wrote a series of stories about incarcerated women under the headline "House of Horrors." Simma visited prisons in the U.S and Israel, as well as facilities in Canada, to research these articles. "Some of my best friends are killers," confessed Simma. "I made good friends. I always went back to people I interviewed. I wasn't a primadonna. I'm a citizen first. Thieves were all my friends. After I wrote the series about women in prisons, Penny MacNeil (an inmate) and I stayed friends. There is gold in every soul."

Peter Worthington commented, in a *Toronto Sun* column in 1993, that Simma was "perhaps the greatest woman reporter of her time." Worthington also gave Simma another plug in the same column. "She was *Canada's Woman of the Year* in the 1960s and wrote a column in the *Sun* and today is as feisty as ever...She left male counterparts at the gate. Simma's persistence saved three men from the gallows. She unearthed evidence of their innocence. Simma also wrote the definitive book on the Doukhobors."

And indeed she did. In 1957, Simma went to South America and interviewed Stefan Sorokin, the head of the Sons of Freedom, a sequestered Doukhobor sect. Every night, she shipped her copy to the *Sun* by airplane. Simma also covered the Doukhobors living in the

Kootenays in British Columbia. This sect was noted for demonstrating in the nude and refusing to send their children to school. By the 1960s, these people, originally from Russia, were involved in land disputes. This and other anti-social activities resulted in bombings and arson. The Doukhobor terrorists' trials of 1960-1962 in Vancouver ended with 120 of the terrorists serving time in the Mountain Prison, a provincial penitentiary at Agassiz.

In 1962, Simma received a newspaper award from the *Canadian Women's Press Club* for her Doukhobor stories in the *Sun*. It was one of five CWPC awards Simma garnered between 1955 and 1962. Simma served as president of the CWPC chapter in Vancouver in 1953. Out of Simma's Doukhobor *Sun* series came *Terror in the Name of God*, published in 1964 by McClelland & Stewart. It was later printed in the United States by Crown Publishers Ltd. Some 60 years later, Simma's book is still considered an important authority about the Doukhobors in Canada and the New World.

On a more frivolous note, Simma managed to grab a new angle on a royal visit – an assignment always given to a girl reporter because all there was to report were the white-glove teas, black-tie receptions and the royal hand wave. This particular time, Queen Elizabeth II and Prince Philip were visiting Vancouver. Simma's only job was to follow the Royals to the Shaughnessy Military Hospital. The padre happened to tell Simma there was an old man in the hospital and all this patient desired was to see the Queen before he died. "I watched the public bullshit. Then I asked to be taken to the old man's room. Reverend Turpin was inside. The Queen looked into this room and passed on, and then the old fellow died. You were called a sob sister if you wrote a human story like that," said Simma. She reckoned that time, she out sob-sistered everyone with her story about the old man dying in peace after seeing his Monarch. With a chuckle and a spark of wit, Simma described this episode as the "Ultimate *Deadliner*."

During her decades at the *Sun*, Simma also produced a heap of freelance pieces. She vividly recalled one assignment because it didn't quite work out. The story, destined for *Cosmopolitan* magazine, was suggested by the editor Helen Gurley Brown. It was supposed to be about men who fake orgasms with their wives after fooling around with other women. Simma did her due diligence and filed a story, ripe with nitty-gritty sexual details. It was a bit too risqué and detailed and so Brown rejected it.[17]

A similar thing happened after Doris Anderson, editor of *Chatelaine* magazine, called Simma and asked her to write a story about Margaret Sinclair Trudeau, the flighty young wife of Prime Minister Pierre Trudeau. The couple had married in a secret ceremony in March 1971, when Margaret was 22 and the groom 50. Margaret was the daughter of James Sinclair from West Vancouver. He had been a Liberal cabinet minister in the government of Prime Minister Louis St Laurent (1948-1957). When Simma was covering the waterfront, she had met Sinclair because he was Fisheries Minister at that time. Unfortunately, there was no help from this connection. Meanwhile Kay Alsop, a veteran *Sun* reporter, had been granted the only interview given by the Sinclairs after their daughter's marriage. Simma recruited Alsop to help her with the *Chatelaine* assignment. The result was a tell-all story about the prime minister's hippy-dippy bride and her lovely face graced the magazine cover.

According to Simma, Anderson would not publish the true account of Margaret's shenanigans as a student, as written by Alsop and herself. Apparently, Canadian readers were not ready for shocking descriptions of Margaret's get-together with Fidel Castro, her involvement in the drug scene in Cuba, nor her outré adventures in the Soviet Union, France and Morocco, for starters. So, *Chatelaine* published a cleaned-up version of the story. Later Simma was asked to write a piece for a South African publication, *Fairlady*, where she and Alsop pulled out all the stops and filed all the juicy details censored by *Chatelaine*. This foreign magazine, still in business, gleefully published the indiscreet antics of the Canadian prime minister's Flower Child wife.

During her three decades at the *Sun*, Simma figured she had written over 10,000 stories— pretty much all local content. Interestingly, she never took on any overseas or glamorous foreign assignments. This is unusual for a high-profile gutsy newsie, who in her later years could demand anything she wanted at the *Sun* and get it. The dream, for most girl reporters of Simma's generation such as newsgirls Marilyn Dunlop (*Toronto Star*), Dorothy Howarth, (*Toronto Telegram*) and Joan Hollobon (*Globe and Mail*), was to travel abroad. The ultimate assignment was a posting as a foreign correspondent in some far-off country. One can only assume Simma could not bear to disrupt her life with her beloved Leon.

The Candidate

In 1974, Simma left the *Sun* to venture into politics. But before she left, she started a campaign in the paper to have police women put on a street beat—not just employed as escorts or kept on desk duty. It all started out as a slam against the police chief for under-using well-trained police personnel. This initiative turned into an equal-rights-for-women battle. Simma took her crusade to City Hall and appeared before Vancouver City Council. The upshot was the resignation of the Police Chief. At one police station, the officers put up a sign that said: *Simma Holt for Chief*. Already a Fire Chief, the incorrigible Simma applied for the job. She filled out all applications along with a roster of male candidates. There was no response from the mayor, so Simma considered running for mayor with the slogan "*Vancouver needs a jolt from Holt.*" Ultimately this morphed into "*Why not a jolt from Holt?*" In Ottawa, when Simma's friend Marc Lalonde, a Liberal MP and confidante of Pierre Trudeau, posed the question, the Liberal answer was "*Ottawa needs a jolt from Holt.*" What began as a joke ended as a reality.[18]

Simma recalled when she was asked to run for the Liberals in the Vancouver-Kingsway riding, she was reluctant because she didn't like Liberal Leader Pierre Elliot Trudeau's public image. Simma's negative opinion of Trudeau started with an assignment for Webster's radio slot on CKNW. She agreed to cover a Trudeau press event at the Hotel Vancouver. "I held a strong dislike for the man. It was the first days of Pierre and the rose buds—that ever-present red rose bud in his lapel and the drink Perrier in his hand." Simma also said her resentment was heightened by the fact he was surrounded by a bevy of pretty young girls terraced, at different levels, on the steps up to the stage and arranged around him like a Hollywood production. "They were smiling, gushing and hugging him…These young women, apparently pubescent girls, were being used to promote a phony image of Canada's new sex god, aged 48." Simma likened Trudeaumania to the bobby sox hysteria aroused by the young Frank Sinatra in the 1940s.

To say the least, this Busby Berkeley-style girlie show and all the teenaged Trudeauboppers did not wash with Simma the feminist. After this scenario, she told CKNW listeners she did not approve of Trudeaumania and did not understand why women of all ages were "so turned on by this short wiry man with a bumpy face."[19]

A while later, Simma was persuaded to stand for Liberal candidacy after a friend dragged her to a publicity event Trudeau was holding in Vancouver. The 1974 election was in the offing and this time Simma met Trudeau *vis-a-vis*. It seems he had been briefed by Lalonde about Simma's potential as a candidate. Simma confessed after meeting with Trudeau and informing him she "might not toe the party line at all times and that her constituents would always come before the party or leader,"[20] she was impressed enough with Trudeau's liberality to run for office.

Simma also ventured to ask Trudeau if he had seen the *Chatelaine* article about Margaret. Being Simma she accused Trudeau, to his face, of "pulling a velvet curtain" when it came to information about Margaret. According to Simma, he blamed Margaret for the shut down and laughed. Apparently, this won Simma's heart and the campaign was on. Simma does not recall whether she asked Trudeau if he had seen the *Fairlady* piece. Regardless, Trudeau and Simma became good friends and she suspected he got a vicarious thrill out of Margaret's rebellious and non-conformist antics.[21]

Simma and Mrs. Trudeau paired up for campaigning and door-knocking. Simma described Margaret as a kind and caring woman. Together, they spied a woman looking out of the window of a retirement home and the duo went in and visited every resident. According to Simma, Margaret held everyone's hand, thus leaving behind her an atmosphere of "much happiness." At a party at Harrington Lake, Trudeau once commented to Simma that he could not understand why the media were so cruel to Margaret when she was such a "good person."[22]

By the time she ran for Parliament, Simma was well-connected in Vancouver's Chinese community and friendly with the owner of the Lotus Lounge and Hotel, the home away from home for parched *Sun* reporters. The owner was active in helping new arrivals settle in Canada and Simma took an interest in this process. Over the years, Simma also helped out the Chinese Benevolent Association and the Chinatown Merchants' Association. These involvements linked Simma to many prominent Chinese leaders. During her election campaign, her Chinese friendships held Simma in good stead. She was invited to every Chinese social function, weddings, the works – and introduced as *The Candidate* at every event.

Simma was fifty-two when she was elected and headed to Ottawa to take her place in the Liberal caucus in the House of Commons. She was the first Jewish woman in Canada to become a Member of Parliament.

Simma tells a story that reveals a prejudice or two of her own. Once in Ottawa, she had to hire an executive secretary. The second applicant she interviewed was a beautifully turned-out "gorgeous Hollywood-style blonde" who looked like Angie Dickinson. This vision had 11 years' experience with two other MPs and knew The Hill. "But I was uneasy. She was so attractive," said Simma admitting she would feel *safer* with a plain woman. In the end, Simma did hire this woman after learning she was a divorced single mother of a teenaged daughter and the clincher– Jewish. Shirley Strean was an excellent secretary and became a loyal friend.[23]

Canadian taxpayers certainly got their money's worth out of Simma. In Ottawa, she served under finance minister John Turner on six committees including Finance, Trade and Commerce, Justice and Legal Affairs and Regulations and Statutory Instruments. Peter Worthington, ever a Holt supporter, wrote in one of his *Toronto Sun* columns, "If Parliament were filled with Simma Holts it wouldn't much matter what party formed the government, one could be sure of getting straightforward, honest representation." Simma also travelled on the taxpayer's dime to Washington, European NATO bases, the European Union headquarters in Brussels and as part of the Canadian delegation to Golda Meir's funeral in Israel in 1974.

In her memoir, Simma described the House of Commons as a "silly place" where members, mostly lawyers, yakked on-and-on just to get their names in Hansard in order to make their constituents think they were doing something worthwhile.

Her fellow politicos may have been silly, but this could well be a case of the pot calling the kettle black. On *The Hill*, Simma continued her rabble-rousing ways and provided a plethora of hilarious copy for the scribes in the Canadian Press Gallery. One of the best moments in the House of Commons was the time Simma went on record insisting she was *not a lady*. In repartee in the House between Simma and Sean O'Sullivan, a Conservative MP from Hamilton, he offered an apology for interrupting a conversation between Mrs. Holt and Trudeau. O'Sullivan made the mistake of referring to Simma as "the honourable lady."

The reportage published by both *Canadian Press* and the *Toronto Star* on November 8, 1975 provides a chuckle or two. "Mrs. Holt, a former newspaper reporter, rose on a question of privilege. 'I hardly expected to be in this House and see the young gentleman– the handsome man in the grey suit...join the ranks of the front row of Neanderthals,' she began, as a dig at the men in the Conservative front ranks." The reporter ends with Simma's final statement: "I am here, gentlemen, as a Member of Parliament and NOT as a LADY of any description."[24]

Always a headline grabber. On another occasion, CP reported: "MP Simma Holt wants to fine members of the Commons $109.11 for every minute they waste the time of the House in "dilatory motions which they know to be unlikely to carry."

Previously, Simma had calculated the annual cost of running the House was $57,347,185.00 or $109.11 a minute. But fellow MP Jack Marshall rose and accused Simma of wasting $218.22. "I timed her," said Marshall to laughter from the Conservative benches, "and she wasted two minutes."[25]

The Faibish affair was much juicier. A headline in the *Toronto Star* on November 1, 1978, screamed "CRTC's FAIBISH 'ABUSES' MP." Underneath there's a head shot of MP Holt and one word "Horrified." It seems on this day of horror, Simma was at a meeting of the Canadian Radio-Television and Telecommunications Commission and a "vigorous conversation" occurred between Roy Faibish and Simma. It all had to do with the CRTC's bid to delete American television stations from cable services in British Columbia, an initiative that Simma`s constituents opposed. Simma was distributing buttons saying, *CRTC stay out of B.C.* A scene right out of "Monty Python's Flying Circus" ensued when Simma approached Faibish, who was a commissioner on the board of the CRTC. She attempted to pin a button on Faibish's lapel. Faibish grabbed Mrs. Holt`s hand, flung the button across the room and yelled at her in hysterical anger. Faibish also told Mrs. Holt several times to "shove the buttons up your ---." "I was horrified. I think we should all be concerned that a bureaucrat would treat a member like that," Simma reportedly said.

James Jerome, the House of Commons Speaker, agreed with Simma and threatened to charge Faibish with contempt of Parliament after Faibish admitted he did, indeed, throw one of Simma's buttons across the room. During the Commons discussion on this important national matter, several MPs came to Simma's defence, including the member from Cape Breton-The Sydneys who said "he was fed up with some of the actions of the flunkies, lackies and pseudo-intellectuals (like Faibish) who are appointed to boards like the CRTC."[26]

One or two days later the *Toronto Star*'s Ottawa correspondent, George Bain, wrote in his weekly column, *View from the Hill*, that Faibish later insisted he didn't say anything about Simma or make any anatomical reference at all. "He says what he said was that 'this is not a circus' and 'take that button away from here or I'll stick it down your . . .'" From here, the button incident progressed from "Monty Python" to "The Goon Show."

Bain, having a heck of a good time wrote: "It is important here to distinguish between . . . and - - -. In newspaper practice, a . . . denotes either the speaker's words were bitten off, unfinished, or an incomplete quotation. On the other hand, - - - means letters expunged out of delicacy." Bain rattles on to examine the rest of the unfinished quotations, by analysing the nuances of *shove* and *stick* and lots more silliness in the same vein. For sure, there was never a dull moment on Parliament Hill when Simma was in her prime.[27]

In the end, Jerome ruled Faibish could not be held in contempt of Parliament because MPs have special privileges. But he did agree Faibish's treatment of MP Holt was "shocking" and "very grave."[28]

> Bain should talk about silliness. He joined the *Star* in 1973, but started his career at the *Globe and Mail*. In the late 1940s, he drank an entire bottle of beer while standing on his head when he was at the summer camp the *Globe* had bought at Port Dover for its employees.[29]

In 1976, when Bill C-84 came before the House of Commons, Simma took an independent stance that revealed the girl with the jutting chin was still alive and kicking. Bill C-84 promoted abolishing the death penalty in Canada. The day before the final reading of the bill in the House, July 14, 1976, Simma proclaimed to the Ottawa press corps that during the 1950s and 1960s, when murder was punishable by hanging, a killer contract in Vancouver ranged between $2,000 and $2,500. "But a killer will now do the job for between $50 and $500. They feel freer to kill because they would not face the death penalty."[30]

Backing up a bit, in the *Sunday Sun*, June 27, 1976, Simma wrote a 1,200-word article stating her case against the Canadian judicial system for doing away with the practice of hanging murderers. Wearing her Cassandra hat, she screamed from the ramparts a warning to all Canadian citizens. The headline above her rant was "Execution will take place of hanging." In a nutshell, Simma's thesis goes like this: If there's no death penalty, the number of murders and street executions will increase exponentially in Canada.[31]

> The day of the vote—contrary to instructions to the Liberal caucus to vote for abolition—Simma, proud to be a maverick, voted nay. Interestingly, the bill just scraped through—130 MPs for and 124 against.

However, that's not the way it turned out. According to government statistics in 1975, homicides in Canada peaked. There were three killings per 100,000 population. By 2014, this had decreased to approximately 1.45 per 100,000 population. In 2014, StatsCan reported 516 homicides in the entire country, the lowest ever. So there went Simma's hysterical prediction along with the legitimization of her pride in being a renegade and who often voted against caucus.

Thirty years after she defied Prime Minister Trudeau and the Liberal caucus, Simma wrote in her memoirs that Trudeau, "a man amongst men and politicians," had told her that "he liked people who swim against the stream." And so she did in the case of Bill C-84. When considering Simma's reputation as a saviour of men on death row, her vote to hang onto hanging as punishment was seen, by some commentators, as a bizarre decision.

Parliament dissolved in 1978. In Simma's bid for re-election and thus keep her Commons' seat, she threw her full support behind Trudeau even though he was unpopular in Western Canada because of his new National Energy Program. Perversely, Simma had her photo taken with him everywhere in Vancouver during this campaign. In the end, she lost to NDP candidate Ian Waddell, but remained a loyal friend to Pierre Trudeau until his death.

In a 1992 interview, Simma told *Vancouver Sun* reporter Kayce White she always adored Pierre Trudeau. "But his Achilles heel was wanting a place in history. The worst thing he did was bring Canada's Constitution home without settling Quebec's role in it...Trudeau and Lester Pearson are to blame for the divisive concept of bilingualism and biculturalism in Canada." Fifteen years earlier, when it was announced that Margaret and Pierre Trudeau's marriage had crumbled, Simma told the National Council of Jewish Women in Toronto that Prime Minister Trudeau was broken-hearted. According to the reportage in the *Toronto Star* in May 1977, Simma Holt MP Vancouver-Kingsway also said "the break-up was the kind of problem many Canadian families face. The Prime Minister is not the arrogant man you may think he is. He's strong, direct and honest."

The *Star* report continued: "Meanwhile in Ottawa, Trudeau breezed through a business-as-usual day—kissing tourists and entertaining foreign visitors."[32]

After her political career, Simma maintained ties with Trudeau through her mother, Nassa Milner. Trudeau took a liking to Mrs. Milner, who died in 1986, and sent her several letters that Simma treasured all her days. One was a thank you note dated November 19, 1975: "Margaret and I were both very touched to receive the certificate that tells us 18 trees are growing in Israel as a tribute to our three young sons. What a thoughtful gesture for you to make...I have told Simma she must bring you to see me again when you come back to Ottawa. She is a fine girl (Simma was 53) and we value her highly, as you know."[33]

In 1979, Simma, the square peg in a round hole, hit the news again. She sued her old employer the *Vancouver Sun* for libel. In an editorial, a *Sun* reporter alleged that Simma conducted personal research for a book she was writing while she was in California as part of a parliamentary committee touring U.S. prisons. The editorial reported Simma interviewed Lynette "Squeaky" Fromme, a member of the Charles Manson Family cult, who was serving a life sentence for trying to assassinate former U.S. President Gerald Ford in September 1975. The problem was Simma, as an MP on a government-financed trip, had no authority to conduct personal business courtesy of the taxpayer and the insinuation was she would use this interview for a book she was writing.

Simma won the suit and the British Columbia Provincial Court awarded her $2,000. The Sun appealed and the court threw out the newspaper's lawyers, and upped Simma's award to $5,000 and a big fat apology from the Sun.[34]

Simma Moves On

Four years after her failed re-election bid, at age fifty-seven, Simma bitterly claimed she was all wiped out. Self-pity aside, somehow Simma mustered the strength to come back—like the proverbial bad penny—and serve on the National Parole Board from 1981-1985. This reminded Simma of a favourite story from this phase of her life. One Vancouver morning she was snowed in, "And there was Johnny, my bald-headed safe-cracker and robber, shovelling away. He said, 'you tell the Parole Board and I'll tell your mother I found pork and beans in your cupboard.'"

In the 1980s, Simma's sister Hannah Smith, a graphologist, also landed a job with the National Parole Board in British Columbia. Smith analysed prisoners' handwriting as a help to determine who was fit for parole. Perhaps, a little bit of nepotism here.[35] After the parole gig, Simma turned her wits to hosting radio and TV shows, and to writing political commentary, including a column for the *Ottawa Sun* that appeared until 1991. This re-incarnation, as an authoritative talking head, included a stint as a political advisor, researcher and writer for George Bush's presidential campaign in the 1980s.

Before Leon's death in November 1985, Simma had been introduced to Bill Wead, an American writer and political insider, who visited Vancouver with thoughts of starting a publishing company in British Columbia. This was an auspicious introduction and the Holts and Wead became friends. After Leon died, feeling bereft and alone in the world, Simma received a call that would put her on the fast track again. In September 1987, Wead contacted Simma to say his brother Jim had died (one of three Wead brothers) in North Dakota and would ask Simma to drive him to the Seattle airport. Wead and his other brother, Doug, a motivational speaker for Amway, amongst other things, were movers and shakers in Washington. They were busy working on the campaign for Vice President George H. W. Bush in the hope he would succeed Ronald Reagan as president. After the airport drive, Bill Wead kept in touch with Simma from Washington and provided her with insider information and gossip that he knew would never be printed in the U.S. because the American press was controlled by the White House. Bill collected these "truths" and floated a Byzantine plan that required Simma to write "these leaks" in Canadian publications so they could later be picked up by American reporters via Canadian agencies.

Simma became so involved with the Weads she moved to Arlington, Virginia to help Doug Wead with a book he was writing about the Bush family. The book called *George Bush: Man of Integrity* was to be released just as Bush Sr. announced he would run for President in the 1988 election.

During her Washington sojourn in 1987, Simma was invited to a top-drawer charity dinner and ball where Nancy Reagan was to be the honoree. Simma observed that most of the

Bush family were scattered throughout the crowd but Mrs. Reagan never turned up. Apparently, her mother had died and Reagan herself was ill. However, the cunning Simma managed to have her photo taken with Bill Wead, Laura Bush and George W. Bush (*Dubya*) who is seen with his arm around her back. Simma owned a copy of this picture autographed by *Dubya*.

When Wead's book was finished, Simma returned to Vancouver. A few months later, he called to say they needed a writer who understood Canadian and American politics and the relationship between the two countries. Once again, Simma, the gal from little Vegreville, packed for Washington and more insider power mongering.

Simma was there as a researcher for Bill Wead and produced massive reports on American political issues and responded to queries about Bush's position on abortion and prayer in schools. During this gig, Simma witnessed all manner of intrigue and endless backroom manoeuvres and manipulations involving George Bush Sr. and his son, George W. She observed, for example, a surprising number of liaisons with powerful Evangelicals—extreme Christian contingents—involving prayer and laying on of hands.

Simma believed the moguls in the Republic National Committee, the White House and the campaign headquarters, all shared information and all talked openly when she was around because she was a "fixture" at the campaign HQ and in the Weads' aura. "I was a Canadian, an old lady (then 65), overweight...They saw me as little more than a piece of furniture in the Wead household."[36]

Then came the parting of the ways when, in the name of Family Values, Bill Wead recruited Phyllis Schlafly as a Bush reporter. Apparently, he felt she would draw extra support from the "new right." Schlafly, as an author, national broadcaster and a constitutional lawyer, had credentials. She was also a Roman Catholic, a mother of six and a woman who had anti-feminist views and did not approve of homosexuals. Simma flipped. "That bitch...She hates everything I have fought for all my life...equality for women. I did not stop in my fury, and knew I was in serious conflict...I was torn between my beliefs and desire to help my friends (the Weads)," Simma later wrote in her autobiography.[37]

After Simma laid her feminist cards on the table, Bill and Doug Wead stopped speaking to her. Once it was obvious she had fallen out of favour, Simma said, "I was treated like a copy girl by snob journalists." In September 1988, Simma left the Sodom and Gomorrah that was Washington and never went back. Simma commented: "With the benefit of hindsight, I would realize the election victory of the first George Bush, in November 1989, was as contrived and manipulated by backroom power brokers as was the victory of George Bush the Second against Al Gore in November 2000." Simma concluded through various machinations, the elections of both George Bush (First) and George Dubya were—her word—"fraudulent".

Back in Canada, Simma wrote a column for the *Ottawa Sun* from 1988 to 1995. A year after this regular spout-off ended in May 1996, Simma was inducted into the *Canadian News Hall of Fame* along with TV anchor Knowlton Nash, and Peter Worthington, co-founder of the *Toronto Sun*. Worthington, who believed his old friend Simma could do no wrong, always indulged her and often allowed her a full page in the *Toronto Sun*.

So, in May 1996, Simma treated *Saturday Sun* readers to a vitriolic rant, headlined: "The Ugly Truth About Chrétien." Simma dredged up her impressions of Liberal Jean Chrétien (Prime Minister, 1993-2003) from the 1970s when she was part of the Liberal caucus. She accused him of being self-serving, a do-nothing prime minister and a man suffering from "blind ambition."

In this diatribe, Simma once again positioned herself as a Cassandra, this time warning Canadians about the scallywag we had for a Prime Minister. "As an MP, in the Trudeau government, I knew Chrétien could never be a Trudeau, but like Jean Marchand (Quebec MP, 1995-1976), he was part of the Little Boys' Club. And when he could not accept the will of the majority, in the election of John Turner as Liberal leader (Prime Minister, for four months, in 1984), it was apparent Chrétien cared for nothing or no one—only his own ego and ambition... Starting with blind ambition for his own personal agenda of fame, power and history...Chrétien proved he had little else. He could not even keep a promise to rid the nation of Brian Mulroney's cruel legacy, the GST." Simma also painted Chrétien as a cad and bounder within the Liberal ranks who "had no loyalty to the leader."[38] In her memoir, Simma took another whack at Chrétien. She described him as "a little man who nurtured pandering opportunists."

In the 1992 interview, with *Sun* reporter Kayce White, Simma said she had learned first-hand about power and politics. "I know what goes on in Ottawa and Washington and when I read a story I know what's behind it...I've fought for women's rights and I've learned that powerful women behave badly toward other women...I could have had the world on a platter, had I compromised with the power brokers and backroom boys. But I refuse to give up my integrity." Simma summed up her take on politics with an *outré* comment. "I still think politician is a dirty word, even after I was elected. Parliament is irrelevant. No matter what you do, the unelected, behind the scenes, run the country," declared Simma, the cynic.

Condo Woes

In her personal life, Simma was ready to move on. In 1999, Simma left her Coquitlam apartment, full of the happy memories she shared with Leon for thirty-six years, and moved to a condominium in Port Moody. She felt all was well there and was looking forward to this new phase of her life. But her sense of comfort was not to last. Simma described the condo purchase as the worst mistake of her life. The building suffered from leaky condo syndrome. The real estate agent lied, according to Simma, who was never allowed to see the garage where water damage was evident. The builders left buyers low and wet instead of high and dry and registered under a new name. Simma received a bill for $40,864 to pay for her share of the fix-up involving mould removal and several other repairs.[39]

She couldn't sleep or work on the premises due to on-going dampness, dust and mold, as well as constant racket from hordes of workmen who came and went. For the first time in her life, Simma developed a host of health problems including a terrible eye infection that morphed into low grade lymphoma. Also, the extra condo bills and lawyers' fees caused her life's savings to dwindle. All this ate away at Simma's quality of life and resulted in a state of depression. This led to enduring a series of medical treatments and visits to a psychiatrist.

Simma reported she had paid $110,000 for her condo. Seven years later, the assessed value was $50,000. There was also a compounded tax bill because she didn't pay annually while waiting to have the building fixed. For the first time in her life, at almost eighty, Simma was in debt. On top of all these woes her lawyer, a long-time friend, let her down.

The situation became extremely complicated and Simma took her problem to the powers-that-be in Ottawa. She had the nerve, after the evisceration in the *Sun*, to try to contact no less a personage than former Prime Minister Jean Chrétien, her old crony in the Liberal Party. No wonder he did not answer any of her calls and deftly side-stepped B.C.'s leaky condo issue by deeming it a provincial and not a federal matter. In the end, the condo crisis boiled down to a lack of a strict building code in British Columbia and the soggy Pacific coast climate; God's fault.

Simma felt "whipped." Then in August 2001, a victim no more, the gladiator in Simma bubbled to the surface and she decided to go to battle against the injustice done not only to her but to thousands of other British Columbians who bought faulty towers. She had heard there were 2,000 unliveable units and maybe 100,000 victims. Simma mobilized and joined the *Coalition of Leaky Condo Owners* (COLCO). Simma knew the ropes in Ottawa and, again, she and a delegation headed to the capital where they were recognized in the House of Commons and met with the Alliance party leader, Stockwell Day, and his sympathetic caucus. But nothing much was gained by this and in the final analysis Simma blamed Chrétien for the rotting condos in British Columbia. Apparently, during his watch as Minister of National Energy, Chrétien shepherded a national code that applied to every province in Canada. Simma could not forgive Chrétien for this because, as she pointed out, the bone-dry prairies and the central provinces do not have the same heavy rains as coastal B.C.[40]

Leaving the hopeless condo battle behind, Simma moved to a seniors' residence on Taylor Way in West Vancouver in 2012. She described herself as the resident celebrity. "They point me out on the elevator to their guests." Long pause: "I had a lot of practice being young—none being old."

In 2008, before her move to the seniors' facility, at the launch of her last book *Memoir of a Loose Cannon*, Simma told everyone present she liked being a loose cannon. "To me, in this age of conformity and political correctness, being something of a loose cannon is a term of respect," she said.

Peter Worthington, Simma's cheerleader for over fifty years, suggested the title. At the Ottawa launch, he described Simma as arrogant and the only octogenarian teenager he'd ever met. "Not a yes person, she never hesitated to criticize her own party or the prime minister when necessary, and Mr. Trudeau always recognized he would get the truth from Simma."[41] At the book fête, Simma got all het up about her current cause célèbre, the Falun Gong, a fringe sect enduring persecution by the Chinese government. She gave a short speech championing the rights of this group to practice their religion as they saw fit and not to have their organs harvested. Talk about channeling her father, Louis Milner! And shades of the old days at the *Vancouver Sun* and the Lotus Gardens where she first became aware of Vancouver's Chinese population.

Simma was also peeved that CBC's French language network had shown a TV documentary alleging the Falun Gong was a subversive force in Montreal's Chinatown. And there she is—the *Old War Horse*—in August 2012, microphone in hand at a Falun Gong rally in Vancouver, demanding that Canadian Prime Minister Stephen Harper take action to stop the persecution in China. Harper was in attendance and that wily opportunist, Simma Holt, managed to have her photo snapped with Mr. and Mrs. Harper. The picture was plastered all over the internet.[42] For the record, the last photos of Simma, at nintey-two, are not much different than those of the pretty young woman with sparkly eyes and a joyful expression, who sixty years before wore a Fire Chief's hat at a jaunty angle.

Loose cannon for sure, with lots of balls—fired.

AFTERWORD

Sadly, the endearing firebrand Simma Holt died January 23, 2015, two months short of her 93rd birthday, and one month after I last chatted with her. In a prior telephone conversation in November 2013, Simma had said after she finished her autobiography she gave a batch of her files and memorabilia from her career to the University of Manitoba. She indicated she had received a $75,000 tax credit for this archival material. Simma, the author, also left behind a legacy of illuminating books on Canadian subjects including *Sex and the Teen-Age Revolution*, (1971), *The Devil's Butler* (1971), *The Other Mrs. Diefenbaker* (1981).

After Simma's death, her nephew Nathan Smith, a B.C. Supreme Court Justice, told the *Vancouver Sun* that she had left strict orders to him and others that it was *never* to be said that she died "peacefully." Smith replied "Don't worry, you've never done anything peacefully in your life."[43] Well said, Mr. Smith.

Angela Burke flying with Bob Cummings, 1957. Photograph by Howard Anderson. Reprinted by permission of Special Collections and Archives, Toronto Public Library.

Women's Editor Olive Dickason with Elizabeth Arden Award for her "unique contribution to the promotion of Canadian fashion." January 8, 1959. Photo by Erik Schack. The Globe and Mail.

Angela Burke, with papoose, on assignment in Red Lake, Manitoba, July, 1952. Photo by Hal Barkley. Reprinted with permission of Special Collections and Archives, Toronto Public Library.

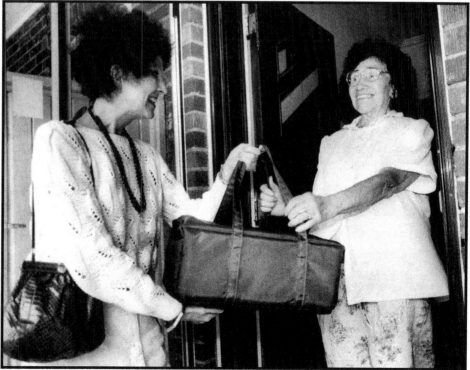
Stasia Evasuk delivering Meals on Wheels, *September 7, 1986. Photograph by Bernie Weil. Reprinted with permission of Torstar Syndication Services.*

June Callwood at Digger house, July 12, 1968. Photograph by F. Lennon. Reprinted with permission of Torstar Syndication Services.

Vancouver M.P. Simma Holt (1974-1979) chatting with Canadian P.M. Pierre Trudeau, 1974. Photograph by George Diack. Reprinted with permission of INFOLINE, Pacific Newspaper Group Library.

Reporter Kay Kritzwiser, voted one of 10 best-dressed Canadian women, 1954. Photograph courtesy of Kay Kritzwiser.

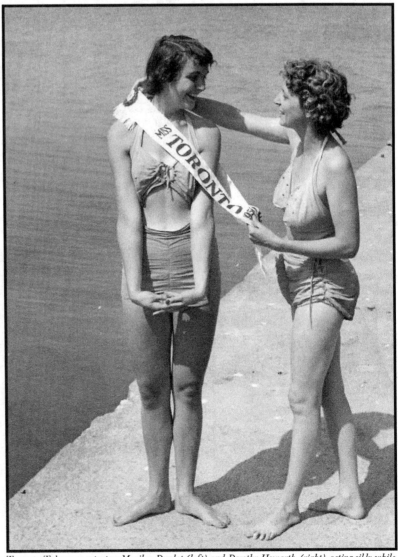

Toronto Telegram reporters Marilyn Dunlop (left) and Dorothy Howarth (right), acting silly while interviewing Miss Toronto, 1950. Photograph courtesy of Marilyn Dunlop.

Foreign Correspondent Marilyn Dunlop and photographer Boris Spremo covering Yugoslavian earthquake, April 21, 1979. Reprinted by permission of Torstar Syndication Services.

Reporter Dusty Vineberg interviewing Secretary of State Judy LaMarsh, 1964, at Dorval Airport. LaMarsh is returning from representing Canada at the Innsbruck Olympics. Photograph courtesy of Augusta Vineberg Solomon.

Joan Hollobon at rock face, Beaucage Mine under Newman Island, Lake Nipissing, May 7, 1955. North Bay Nugget.

June Callwood, Toronto Star *columnist, January 14, 1966. Photographer N. James. Reprinted with permission of Torstar Syndication Services.*

Reporter Joan Hollobon (foreground) throwing a pal at their judo club, North Bay, 1955. Photograph courtesy of Joan Hollobon.

Marilyn Dunlop tries water skiing at the Canadian National Exhibition. Her first assignment for the Toronto Telegram, *August 1951. Photograph courtesy of the* Toronto Telegram.

STASIA EVASUK

Glace Bay Gazette, 1942-1944. Toronto Star, 1944-1960 & 1964-1991.
Vancouver Sun, 1960-1962. Toronto Telegram, 1962-1964.

1924-2009

"I'm like a Jesuit. I go straight ahead."

A diminutive seventy-one-year-old in a designer peasant skirt and full maquillage, Stasia Evasuk was nestled on a sofa in her downtown Toronto apartment where she had resided for some thirty years. She was surrounded by paintings, oriental carpets and classy bric-a-brac, souvenirs of her travels as a fashion reporter and reminders of the famous people who had flitted through her life.

Stasia looked so perky in the daffodil yellow interior that it was easy to guess she was a Gemini. In fact, Anastasia Evasuk was born on June 12, 1924, in Glace Bay, Nova Scotia. Her father came from the Ukraine before the First World War and was a construction worker in a local coal mine. Stasia's mother's family had emigrated from Romania. Stasia never married and remained devoted to her mother, who ruled the family roost from her Cape Breton domain until her death at ninety-one.

"I was gently brought up. We obeyed and respected our parents," said Stasia in the tone Princess Anastasia Romanoff would have used had she survived the family execution in 1918. As she relived the past, the Anastasia voice faded away and was replaced by the tough-talking clipped tones of a Damon Runyon moll. Stasia told her story in short staccato sentences, just like the girl reporters in the old flicks. It was easy to picture her sitting on the city desk, devilishly swinging her legs in time to the clack-clack of the old Underwoods.

"I was fast on the manuals and at the *Star*, I used Ernest Hemingway's old typewriter," said Stasia before launching into one of her favourite stories.

"When I returned to the *Star* in 1964—my second time there—I had to see the managing editor Marty Goodman. He tried to haggle me down $5. Our eyes never stopped locking. The *Telegram* wanted me back. In the end, he offered me only $2 more a week to stay. But I took it."

A bit later, Goodman (1935-1981) offered Stasia a paltry $5 bonus. "I told him to keep it. The *Star* needs it more than I do."

Stasia was way ahead of her story. After graduating from St. Anne's High School in 1942, she found a general reporting job at the *Glace Bay Gazette* when she was 18. Stasia commented the war was good for women with newspaper aspirations. The men were away and labour was short. As a result, women had opportunities that were out of the question in pre-war days. Also, the notion of a degree in journalism as an entrée into a newsroom did not yet exist.

As a cub reporter, Stasia covered local happenings in Glace Bay and issues at the coal mines owned by the brutal Dominion Coal Company. Nathan Cohen was Stasia's editor at the *Gazette* and she always greeted him with a zesty, "How's it goin' Cohen!"

The Martin Goodman Trail, a twenty-kilometre hiking and cycling path along Toronto's waterfront, was opened in 1984 as a memorial to Goodman.

"He had a crush on me. Nathan was a great big guy in his early 20s and he would walk me home," Stasia recalled with fondness. Cohen moved to Toronto and went on to become one of the city's most influential drama critics. Their paths would cross again at the *Toronto Daily Star* where Cohen purveyed caustic theatre reviews from 1959 until his death in 1971.

Toronto

Stasia had a friend from Wolfville whose boyfriend was in the army and stationed in Ontario. In 1944, she talked Stasia into going to Toronto for a holiday. The two young ladies stayed at the YWCA residence on Elm St.—now the Bangkok Gardens restaurant and the Elm St. Spa. They decided to stay in Toronto and both found jobs at a Canadian Bank of Commerce on St. Clair Ave. W. Once employed, the girls moved to a boarding house on Margueretta St. where there was always dinner at six and bread pudding for dessert.

One day, Don Reid, a *Toronto Star* reporter, came into the bank. Reid had also been a reporter on the *Gazette* and he helped Stasia get her foot in the front door of the *Star*. "I wanted to write. I couldn't care less about the bank work. I was always buggering up the books," admitted Stasia who lasted only a few weeks at the bank.

From her fledging days as a *Star* reporter, Stasia remembered most vividly summers on Centre Island where she roomed with Ruth Andrew Hammond, who was Women's Editor. From May to October, the friends rented a room in Mrs. MacDonald's Respectable Establishment. Every day throughout the summer, the two girls took the ferry to Bay St.: "I dressed up, hopped on my bicycle and pedaled to the ferry, sometimes eating my breakfast as I went. It was fun. Those were the best years of my life," recalled Stasia.

Stasia fell into a reverie and emerged animated as she contemplated the long-gone golden days full of cycling, parties, youthful liaisons and picnics on the shore of Lake Ontario. "We would buy a mickey of rye that lasted all of us the weekend. We went to tennis dances and ate scrambled egg sandwiches in the small hours of the morning. Those were our salad days," said Stasia mistily. She added that if the police didn't come at least once to quiet down the summer revelers, it wasn't a party.

Advertising man Larry Hammond's family had a house on the island and Ruth Andrew "stalked" Larry one whole summer, and married him by Thanksgiving, according to Stasia.

At the *Star*, Stasia sat in the *Star Weekly* and syndicate department because, in the 1940s, female reporters were not allowed a desk in the *Star*'s newsroom. But like most of the women working at a newspaper in the World War II era, Stasia did not concern herself with employment equity—a term not yet coined. "I was having all kinds of dates. We were young. I couldn't care less. It was just the way it was."

Ruth Hammond had signed on with the *Star* in 1943 when there was a shortage of men due to the war. They needed an editor, so the *no girls* rule was waived that one time.

Ruth Hammond was the first woman to sit on the news *rim* at the paper. City Editor Tommy Lytle shouted, "make way for the lady" and sat her down between two veteran newshounds—one with a glass eye.

"I had made it. I was in training to be a news editor, or so I thought," recalled Hammond. "Then the publisher, Harry Hindmarsh, called me into his office and said I was to be editor of the *Women's Section*. I burst into tears and wept. I was so disappointed. But at least I was the first woman to be the editor of the women's pages."

While Hammond was Stasia's gal pal, it was Hindmarsh, known for his gruffness and remoteness, who took very good care of Stasia. "When I first joined the *Star*, I was twenty and he was an old man. I kept seeing this tall man. Finally, one day in the hall, I said 'aren't you too old to be working?' It turned out to be H.C. Hindmarsh," she said.

Star reporter and later editor, Ray Timson, once described Hindmarsh as a giant of a man "who smoked huge cigars and carried a foot-long fountain pen that reportedly took a bottle of ink to fill."[1]

Stasia remembered Hindmarsh, whom reporters called *The Great White Father*, as a grandfather figure and a benefactor. It was Stasia's good fortune that *old Hindmarsh*, who was

---

Before Ruth's appointment at the *Star*, the standing joke was the paper had a female sports editor, Alexandrine Gibb, and a variety of male women's editors, including Gordon Sinclair. Gordon Sinclair (1990-1984), was a *Star* reporter, off and on, from 1922-1964, and a news broadcaster at CFRB and *Front Page Challenge* panelist for CBC, 1957-1984.

In the days of yore, the *Toronto Star* was run by the Five Atkinson Principles. 1. Get the new first. 2. Sew it up so the opposition cannot get it. 3. Leave not a crumb or a morsel or a tidbit uncollected. 4. Play it big. 5. PLAY!

fifty-six at the time, took her under his wing. He treated her like a daughter and went so far as to supervise Stasia's money. In later years, when Stasia had a serious operation, Hindmarsh called every day to check on her condition. He also sent her an affectionate letter about his concern for her health.

Meanwhile, Ruth Hammond had introduced Stasia to Catherine Smyth who was writing fashion pieces for the *Toronto Star* on a freelance basis at the same time that Stasia was a cub reporter. The two gals became life-long friends. "One year, Cathy Smyth and I went to Europe for a holiday and Hindmarsh wouldn't let me have my vacation pay. He said, 'I'm keeping it in the bank for you.'"

Smyth recalled that trip to Europe with hilarity. On their first day in Paris, she and Stasia marched into the front room of a fancy establishment. There were potted plants and a piano in the corner, so Les Girls expected a bit of cocktail music. Perhaps some Cole Porter. After sitting comfortably for a while in a window seat, surrounded by plants and no waiter appeared, they suddenly realized they were in the living room of a private house. "We were thrilled sitting there. We kept saying to each other, 'this is exactly what a Parisian café should be,'" recalled Smyth. "Well, when the truth dawned on us, we beat it out of the house and giggled and giggled until we were sick."

Smyth also recollected one whole year when Stasia wore a yellow wig to work, and another period when she penciled double eyebrows on her face.

In her early days at the *Star*, Stasia always seemed to have a cigarette hanging from her lower lip as she worked on her stories. She was famous in the newsroom for flicking butts into her wastepaper basket and starting mini-fires. By the mid-1980s, Ontario had banned smoking in offices, putting an end to these mishaps.

Stasia stayed at the *Star* for almost fifteen years, most of it writing and re-writing articles for the *Star Weekly* under Gwen Cowley. During that stint, Stasia noticed that the dour Hindmarsh visited Cowley every lunch hour until he died. At one point, a couch was ordered for Cowley's office causing much speculation in the newsroom about what went on behind closed doors.

Creating the Right Path

In 1960, Stasia left the *Star* and went to Vancouver to marry Tom Mohr who turned out to be en famille with a nice young man and a dog. Stasia worked at the *Vancouver Sun* for two years while waiting for Mohr to confirm their wedding date. The whole thing came to a head when Hammond visited Vancouver and discovered that Stasia still had her wedding dress hanging in the closet waiting for the big day, almost two years after she was supposed to marry. Hammond confronted Mohr at a lunch about Stasia's expectations, and when Stasia arrived for dessert, Hammond forced him to admit to his fiancée that he would never marry her.

"My mother went to bed for three days. And I was worried about the gifts. Ruth had thrown a big bridal shower for me before I left Toronto. She said 'keep the presents,'" said Stasia, with a shudder, thirty-five years later.

After the two years at the Sun, prodded by Hammond, Stasia moved back to Toronto. "Anyway, I realized Toronto was the place to make a mark and I returned in 1962. I spent a summer as a sophisticated bum- sailing and going to parties galore. I had a string of boyfriends including Prince Michael Oblinski," she said with a coquettish toss of the head. "Then one day, Cathy Smyth phones up and says, 'listen Stasia, there's a job going at the *Toronto Telegram*. Apply for it.' And I did."

"I started at the *Tely,* and I see Helen Worthington. We were working for Beth Dingman (1918-2010) whose favourite phrase was '*can it.*' She knew nothing about being an editor. She couldn't make up a page. Oh my god, it was all so dull. Beth was a dull woman. They were still covering weddings and club meetings. At the *Vancouver Sun*, we were quite avant garde. We were writing features."

Today, this may seem incomprehensible, but the boys who ran the newspapers believed that women only wanted to read about their neighbours' weddings. It was weddings or nothing

Catherine Smyth (1925-1997) became a top publicist in Toronto. Her clients included the Canadian Opera Company and the Royal Ontario Museum. In the '80s, Smyth created the slogan: "ROM wasn't built in a day."

Newsgirls

in the *Star's* ladies' pages, according to Hammond. "It was brides, brides and more brides. One June, we were backed up with announcements. We ran so many small head shots of brides, they all looked like rabbits. Every day, a male editor checked the *Globe and Mail* to make sure the *Star* did not miss a wedding, engagement or a Women's Institute meeting.

"Then one day I went to Hindmarsh and said this is a big town and we are doing small town stuff. I told him I had made an agreement with the *Globe and Mail*; if they wouldn't run free wedding announcements, we wouldn't either," said Hammond.

From 1950, wedding announcements were paid for at the *Toronto Star*, but still took up far too much space, according to Hammond, who stayed at the *Star* until 1951 when she became pregnant and had to give up her job. In later years, Hammond reinvented herself as a public relations woman and ran her own firm for fifty years.

Meanwhile at the *Telegram*, reporter Helen Worthington (wife of fellow reporter Peter Worthington), whose *nom de plume* was Helen Parmalee, and Stasia alternated on a 6 a.m. to 2 p.m. shift at the old *Telegram* building at 80 King St. West and Melinda St. The type was set overnight in the composing room and in the early morning, the girls made sure the copy in the *Women's Section* was in the right place. After finishing in the composing room at 10 a.m., Stasia would run out to cover a society tea party or a fashion show, race back in to her desk and plunk out her copy on a manual typewriter for the late afternoon edition. In those days, both the *Toronto Star* and the *Telegram* printed six editions per day and copy had to be refreshed for each one.

"The pressmen were always waiting. If Helen or I were ten minutes late, they would hold up the paper as a union ploy against management. And ten minutes, in those days, were pretty precious because they were setting type by hand," explained Stasia, who had learned layout in Glace Bay.

Until the *Telegram* folded in 1971, the rivalry between Toronto's two dailies—the *Star* and the *Telegram*—was fierce. The object of the battle was to get a scoop or a bigger and better story than the competition and to get it on the street first. Thus, every minute in production counted. In order to hook the readers, anyone and everything was fair game— even if you had to simulate pictures and make up stories. Journalistic ethics rarely entered into the picture. Most newsies were not university-educated philosophers; in fact, the old-time editors were highly suspicious of education and anyone who was pretentious enough to call himself a journalist. Most of the members of the press corps were tough-guy tipplers who had been to war rather than to school. As a result, they were most at home in a warzone, a Montreal speakeasy or a poker game in the Yukon.

Hammond witnessed several sleazy scenarios. A classic occurred when a *Star* photographer paid a waif five dollars to weep by a tombstone of his supposedly dead brother so they could squeeze money from readers for the *Star's Fresh Air Fund*. On another occasion, a northern Ontario town was snowed in and the inhabitants were starving. Hindmarsh told reporter, Frank Tesky, and a photographer to charter a plane and take food. But all they could find at 10 p.m. were two loaves of bread and four quarts of milk. Their mission was to distribute food and get shots of *Father Star* as benefactor. When they arrived at the disaster site, Teskey gave out the bread and milk and then took it back again and re-distributed the same grub, over and over again, while the photographer snapped pictures.

In the meantime, a *Telegram* crew arrived and they photographed the *Star* team taking back the supplies. The *Telegram* plastered the photos all over the front page and the *Star* was unmasked. One up for the *Telegram*, which was just as unprincipled—given half a chance.

At the *Telegram*, there was the usual cast of quirky characters found in all newsrooms in pre-J-school days. Rosemary Boxer (1921-2008), a sophisticated *gal-about-town* known in Toronto society as Posy, had a peripatetic career during the 1950s and '60s that included fashion editor at *Chatelaine* magazine, exercise instructor on CBC TV and owner of a beauty clinic.

Stasia recalled the day Boxer announced to the girls in the women's department she was marrying Robert Chisholm, a millionaire grocer who was vice-president of Dominion Stores. Apparently, Lillian Foster, the *Telegram* fashion editor who dressed like a washer woman and was addicted to the horse races, asked Boxer, "Are you going to live above the shop?" Much laughter from the Telegram Peanut Gallery.

In 1956, Ruth Hammond launched her career in public relations. Clients included the YM/YWCA, Xerox, and Metropolitan Life. She organized PR courses at Ryerson, York and Toronto Universities. A *Ruth Hammond Scholarship* established in 2004 is awarded annually to outstanding students studying PR. Hammond passed away in October of 2015.

Boxer went to live in Rome, and as a well-connected FOOF (Fine Old Ontario Family), was given the post of Roman correspondent for the *Telegram*. There appears to be no extant records of her reportage, but Boxer did drop into the newsroom from time to time.

Stasia rejoined the *Toronto Star* in 1964 because she felt there was an opportunity there for her to become the Canadian Susie Knickerbocker. Knickerbocker was a famed gossip columnist for the *New York Tribune* and, in the 1940s and '50s before TV talk shows and the Oprahs of this world existed, the public hung onto every word about the rich and famous through insider gossips and Hollywood tattle-tales like Louella Parsons and Hedda Hopper.

Stasia also admitted her constant feuding with Dingman—who had been parachuted into the *Telegram* as women's editor after meeting owner, John Bassett (1915-1998), at a Montreal cocktail party—was another reason she defected from the *Telegram*. As for Dingman, she despised her staff as much as they despised her. "I used to look at them and think, these people are there to carry out my ideas and there they are with their pink plump bottoms stuck with mucilage to their seats," Dingman said in a 1997 interview. When Dingman suddenly appeared at the *Telegram* noses were out of joint and there was a sour atmosphere in the women's department.

When Stasia left the *Telegram*, she left a finished front page behind for Thursday, the day the *Star* and *Telegram* both published fashion spreads. "Then the same week, I wrote my first section front for the *Star*. They came out together and my by-line was in both papers. The whole news desk was in an uproar and editor Tommy Lytle, who drank a bottle of gin every day, was yelling at Mo Keller, the *Star*'s women's editor."

Shortly after Stasia left the *Telegram*, a juicy scandal broke out involving Peter Worthington, husband of Stasia's friend Helen Worthington. Worthington, the *Telegram*'s foreign correspondent, was sent to Moscow in 1965 to open up a Russian bureau. It seems that Worthington got involved with "Olga from the Volga" and eventually smuggled her out of Moscow. At the time, Helen and Peter Worthington had a young son. "Poor Helen found out that Peter was mixed up with a translator in Russia where he was on assignment," recalled Stasia.

The next thing Stasia heard was Yvonne Crittenden, also a reporter in the *Telegram*'s *Women's Section*, was involved with Worthington. "Time goes by and I am at a party at John Bassett's country estate, and I meet Yvonne Crittenden there and she says, 'Peter and I are getting married.' In the meantime, Helen is still in love with Peter. But it all worked out for Helen in the end. She left the *Tely* after me and eventually married a nice man who had been a childhood friend." After Olga faded away, Worthington married Crittenden in 1970.

This tale reappeared again in 2013. Peter Worthington, revered as a swashbuckling reporter á la Hemingway, died on May 12, 2013. On his deathbed, Worthington had his version of the Olga saga published by the *Toronto Sun*. By chance, Olga Pharmakovsky had died ten days before Worthington, leaving him to tell his uncontested version of his stint in Moscow in the mid-'60s smuggling Olga out of Russia. In Part I of his two-part epistle, Worthington's explains due to his close connection to Olga and the fact it was the height of the Cold War, the Russians suspected Olga of being a spy and intending to defect—which she did with Worthington's help. Worthington pointed out Olga had a husband, but her marriage broke down during the time he was in Moscow.[3]

In Part II, Worthington wrote the Russian assignment cost him his first marriage and he was in the middle of a divorce during the situation with Olga. "My wife Helen didn't want an absentee husband. We were divorced and she bettered herself by marrying a judge and living happily...I later married Yvonne Crittenden, whose husband had run off with another *Tely* staffer. (Caligula's court in those days and we all benefitted accordingly.)" Reeead all about it in the Sun![4]

Interestingly, even Worthington's boss at the *Toronto Telegram*, Doug MacFarlane, referred to Olga as "Olga from the Volga." Apparently, Worthington had not been "popular" with the Russians and Olga's defection from the Soviet Union "ruffled KGB and diplomatic feathers." The upshot: The *Telegram*'s Moscow bureau struggled on until it was shut down in 1970.[5]

Stasia's gossipy scuttlebutt illustrates how small the world of Canadian newspapers was in the '40s, '50s and '60s. The same dramatis personae appear in everyone's memoirs as reporters are reacquainted, as they move to and from the *Winnipeg Free Press* to the *Globe and Mail*, to the *Telegram* and to the *Star*. Thus Canadian newsrooms were rampant with salacious gossip, clandestine love affairs and meaty incestuous rumours.

Foster was a pal of financier and thoroughbred breeder, E.P. Taylor, and regularly went to the races with him.

Hedda Hopper was played by Helen Mirren in the movie, *Trumbo* (2015). Mirren portrayed Hopper as malicious and manipulative.

In the '80s and '90s Elizabeth (Beth) Dingman edited *Fusion*, a Toronto arts and crafts magazine.

In 1952, John Bassett bought the *Toronto Telegram* for $4.25 million. He published the first Sunday newspaper in Canada in 1957, but this initiative was challenged under Ontario's prudish Lord's Day Act. Thus the Sunday paper folded after four months. The daily *Telegram* died in 197 after a long, bitter strike by the Typographical Union.[2]

The new Mrs. Worthington became book editor at the *Toronto Sun* in 1978. Yvonne Crittenden continues to publish freelance pieces and on January 28, 2014, she posted on the *Huffpost* blog a lament about supermarkets banning the sale of marmite titled, *How Will I Survive Marmageddon*.

About two years after Stasia went back to the *Star*, Helen Worthington surfaced in the *Women's Section*, and by 1969, she was assistant women's editor working with Maureen "Mo" Keller, also editor of the *Fashion Section*. "Killer Keller we called her. Betty Stapleton (reporter) tagged around everywhere with her. They even went to the bathroom together. Lunch was Mo's social life and she always had to have someone to go with her for alcoholic lunches. When Helen Worthington came to the *Star* and started working for Mo, we figured she wouldn't put up with her. But Helen did and after Betty Stapleton, she became the designated liquid lunch companion," Stasia said caustically.

Nevertheless, from the late 1960s into the 1970s, Helen Worthington wrote a litany of stories about social change for women. Throughout February 1971, Worthington, under Keller's mandate, conducted *The Star Travelling Forum* designed for women to discuss *new* social issues such as teenaged drug problems, working mothers and families on welfare. In June 1971, Worthington's stories based on her forum experience were still appearing weekly in the *Star*. One shone light on child abuse, another on the plight of a family with a child suffering from cerebral palsy and yet another dealt with the trials of a disabled mother in a wheelchair.

When Stasia first went to work for Keller, she claimed her new boss looked her up and down and said, "I'm jealous of people like you. You know everybody."

"And there she was with a nice husband, a house and two sons," declared Stasia.

The relationship between Keller and Stasia was more of a catfight than anything else. Stasia described Keller's office as decorated like a bedroom and added Keller's clothes were awful. Keller's outlandish outfits, always with a hat to match, were the source of much merriment at the *Star*. They ran the gambit from Spanish senorita to frilly circus elephant. "We sent her to Shoppe D'or in Yorkville where they had very good second-hand stuff, but out of fashion. Mo and her first sidekick, Betty, came back loaded down with bags. Mo thought it was wonderful and often shopped there," said Stasia.

Stasia also claimed Keller was always pulling stunts on her. "I found out Nora McCabe, who wrote a social column, *What's Happening*, was getting a $500 clothing allowance. So I thought because I'm the fashion reporter, I should get one too. Marty Goodman okayed it. I bought a few outfits. Then Mo wouldn't pay. We didn't speak for a year. I just handed in copy. Then I forgave her," Stasia said magnanimously.

Keller, who could hold her own, had a thing or two to say about Stasia. "She wasn't that bright and not a great writer, but tough, tenacious and dependable. Stasia never let you down."

Keller was also tough and tenacious. She started her newspaper career in England at the *Middlesex Advertiser*. At age twenty, she shipped alone to Canada and, in 1955, found work at the *Etobicoke Press*. After marriage to sports reporter Arlie Keller, an assortment of jobs at newspapers across Canada and two children, in 1966, the Kellers were both hired by the *Toronto Star*. Mo Keller always said she had a photographic memory and that had helped with her career. In fact, all through her life she loved reciting by heart the great narrative poems of Keats, Tennyson and Browning—learned during her school days. During a 1997 interview at her home, Keller launched into *The Eve of St. Agnes* (Keats), followed by Yeats's *Cloth of Heaven*, complete with dramatic gestures.

Indeed, Keller had her eccentricities and questionable habits, but in many ways she and Stasia were alike. Both had her own pithy slogan. Stasia liked to say, "I'm like a Jesuit. I go straight ahead." And Keller was famous for exclaiming, "I sell my talent. They buy it."

Fashion, Frolic and Scoops

Despite Keller, the Trudeau years—the '60s and '70s—turned out to be Stasia's golden era as a fashion reporter. She described one Trudeau reception at Rideau Hall hosted by the Prime Minister himself. "I ended up in the receiving line and everyone thought I was Trudeau's date. He knew me a bit. But he didn't have a date and we were chatting. The press ended up photographing me with Trudeau because they thought I was his date." And sure enough, there is Stasia caught in the lens by a freelance photographer, looking flirtatious and very comfortable with Trudeau. She is wearing an exquisite pink frilly dress by Toronto designer, Maggy Reeves

(1923-2008), who over the years created some of her most glamorous frocks for Stasia. Reeves and Stasia indulged in wet gal-pal lunches most Saturdays until Reeves went to a nursing home about three years before her death.

Maggy Reeves's atelier in Yorkville catered to celebrities and Toronto's high society. Local clients included Susie Cohon, wife of the McDonald's hamburger man, George Cohon, artist Harold Town, ballerina Karen Kain, author Iris Nowell and skater Toller Cranston. One of the highlights of Stasia's career was travelling to Hollywood in 1977 to cover a fashion benefit that featured Maggy Reeves's designs. Under the headline, *Maggy Reeves in Hollywood is an Instant Sensation*, Stasia told *Star* fashion readers that 1,500 guests attended the sell-out show. "Magnificent Maggy's clothes captivated the audience of film stars and top Los Angeles buyers."

The Hollywood triumph had been organized by Loretta Young as a fundraiser for the movie star's favourite charity, *St. Anne's Maternity Home for Unwed Girls*. Stasia's extensive reportage in the *Star* put Reeves on the fashion map.

Twenty years later, all Stasia could say about the star-studded gala is she wasn't the least bit impressed with the fabulous receptions or the famous personalities like Candace Bergen and Cynthia Hayward, fiancée of Hollywood movie star Glen Ford, who modeled the clothes. After all, you can't take the Cape Breton out of the girl.

Reeves, who Stasia always referred to as *Maggy the Magnificent*, described Stasia as tough and hardworking. The friends travelled to Paris on a few occasions in the 1970s to attend the runway shows and view the latest designer collections. Stasia was oblivious to the impression she made in Paris. When she wanted something, she screamed in English in the time-worn ugly tourist style until people responded. Reeves recalled her French vocabulary consisted of "monsieur" and "chocolate mousse". But Stasia was aggressive and always got her fashion story. In those days, stories were filed by wire. Reeves recalled, in a 1996 interview, the time Stasia dragged her out into the Paris streets at midnight to accompany her on a hunt for an all-night post office. "There was a taxi strike and we walked and walked until 4 a.m., but she got the story through," Reeves said.

On another occasion in Paris, three hours before their flight back to Toronto, Stasia decided she wanted a blouse with wooden beads. She had seen one in the window of the Galleries Lafayette. "She can't speak a word of French, but insists on finding the window decorator. Stasia ran from floor to floor shouting *monsir*—looking for him to get the blouse out of the window. She was even looking into an Aboriginal teepee on display in the store. It took over an hour, but she got the blouse. An ugly thing. We just made the plane," said Reeves still exasperated twenty-five years later.

It seems Stasia's need to file stories at night became the bane of Reeves' existence. Another time Stasia, the inveterate newshen, convinced Reeves to leave a big lobster dinner hosted by actress Natalie Wood in a Los Angeles restaurant.

"Again we walked for hours. Stasia had no idea where the post office was. I missed the dinner and we got back to our hotel at about 3 a.m. this time," said Reeves, with a big sigh.

But Stasia's defense was she had to file daily, by wire or phone, the stories she had pounded out on the small typewriter she lugged everywhere. "It was work, work, work and rush, rush, rush. Get the job done. I went to the Paris and New York collections, but it wasn't glamorous. The fashion shows started at 8 a.m. and ended at 5 p.m. and then I had to write the copy. That was in the '60s and '70s. I was never invited to the parties that the *Vogue* people went to. Nobody in Europe had even heard of Canada or the *Toronto Daily Star*."

In June 1969, Stasia was on assignment again—this time covering the New York collections—when word came through the wire service that Judy Garland had died in London, England. The body was shipped to New York and thousands lined up to view Garland's casket. The *Star* told Stasia to write a story. "Maggy was there with me and, with my press credentials, we got into the funeral home to view the body. What I remember most is the white face and the red, red lipstick. Judy had a following of homosexuals and they were camped outside the Campbell Funeral Home singing her hits, accompanied by mouth organs." Stasia reported all for *Star* readers.

Not only local socialites beat a path to Reeves' Yorkville door, but so did Hollywood Glitter Gals such as Zsa Zsa and Eva Gabor, Vivien Leigh, Mrs. Sammy Davis Jr. and Tove Borgnine, the wife of actor Ernest Borgnine. As a result, Maggy's atelier walls were plastered with photos of her glamorous Hollywood clients wearing her creations. Currently, the ROM owns a collection of Maggy Reeves' garments and so does Ryerson University's fashion faculty.

Reeves remembered going with Stasia to a party in the 1960s at the home of Rosemary Boxer Chisholm, Stasia's former *Telegram* associate. Reeves had designed for Stasia a stunning peasant outfit with a full skirt and had it made in a wine-coloured fabric. Stasia complained she needed boots to match. Instead, at the last minute, Reeves dyed the pantyhose a deep burgundy colour to complete the outfit. As it turned out, the living room furniture was upholstered in a luxurious white material. Suddenly Reeves realized that everywhere Stasia sat there were perfect wine-hued imprints of her *little stick legs*. "I said, 'Stasia we have to get out of here.' I realized that I hadn't properly rinsed the dye out of the stockings. Finally, I dragged Stasia away from the party after pointing out the mess on Posy's furniture," said Reeves still laughing about the incident a few decades later.

Reeves also found a sensational coat for Stasia made of fluffy dark feathers. She wore it everywhere. Sometimes Stasia didn't even bother to take it off when she sat at her desk to write her daily assignments. There she was hunched over the typewriter, looking like a giant ostrich chick, tapping away. A few of the mean-spirited *Star* reporters referred to the garment as Stasia's "turkey coat."

Also in the '60s, the *Star* assigned Stasia to cover a lavish fundraiser in Venice where the glitterati had banded together under the patronage of Princess Grace and Prince Rainier (Grimaldi) of Monaco to raise money to bolster up the sinking city.

"Roloff Beny (jet-set photographer and socialite) was my date. Peggy Guggenheim invited us to stay with her, but I wanted to be freer. I loved the way Peggy dressed: black and white print dress and black stockings. That was very avant garde back then," declared Stasia.

Guggenheim also invited Beny and Stasia to a writers' lunch at her palazzo. Stasia was ever so impressed with the waiters who wore white gloves and served three wines during lunch and emptied the wine glasses by throwing the dregs over the patio railing into the garden. It was no wonder Stasia was impressed. In the 1960s, Canadians were still drinking sweet wine with overcooked beef and al fresco dining was considered an indulgence by only the most decadent foreigners—like the mysterious Hungarians who swarmed to Yorkville to sip café au lait at the Coffee Mill, Toronto's first outside café. Those Hungarians, who arrived after the uprising in 1956, persisted in crowding into the Coffee Mill until it closed in September of 2014.

Returning to Stasia's Venetian tale, Guggenheim's son, Sinbad, was also at the lunch. "He had four kids and just landed his first job at forty-four, and was very excited. And Peggy's daughter, Peggen, had just committed suicide," said Stasia like a relative. "Peggy had an art gallery in her palazzo, and after lunch the guests looked at the pictures and then most had a siesta. But Sinbad and I went to a park and drank wine all afternoon." Not too bad for a girl from an obscure Cape Breton mining town.

Before the Grand Ball on September 9, 1967, Beny and Stasia went to a cocktail party hosted by a Madame Volpe. All the beau monde was there, including the Monaco Grimaldis and Rose Kennedy, her first appearance since the assassination of her son John F. Kennedy. "After the party, it was pouring and all the guests rushed for the barges with Madame Volpe screaming in the background. Everyone forgot protocol and Princess Grace and Prince Rainier were left behind on the quay along with Roloff and me. We travelled in the same gondola together and here I saw the ugly part of Grace. Her face was all snarled up with anger."

It got worse. When the gondola arrived at the ball venue, there was no one to greet the regal couple because all eyes were focused on Richard Burton and Elizabeth Taylor. Liz stole the show. Because Taylor and Burton had married in Montreal in 1964, Stasia had the wit to introduce herself as a Canadian reporter and consequently got a pretty good quote from Richard Burton. "Then there was a fat little man who kept poking my elbow. Finally, he said, 'Do you know who I am?' I realized it was Aristotle Onassis. He said, 'see that yacht out there. That's mine. You're from Canada and I want to go there for business,'" recounted Stasia, adding that it was 11 o'clock at night and Onassis was wearing very black sunglasses.

Stasia was also on the ball in 1968 when the engagement of Jackie Kennedy and Onassis hit the news. "At 2 o'clock we heard that Jackie Kennedy was going to marry Onassis. At 4 o'clock Mo said, 'Marty says you are going to New York to get an interview.' He's crazy. I'll never

---

It is interesting to note that *Toronto Globe and Mail* art critic, Kay Kritzwiser, later met Guggenheim in Venice at the art Biennale in 1972. She said she was horrified to see the great art patroness wearing a frumpy printed house dress and ankle socks.

get near her, I said. I was a sophisticated woman and I knew Jackie Kennedy wasn't sitting around New York waiting for reporters. So I phoned a contact at *Women's Wear Daily* who stalked Jackie all the time. And sure enough they had an exclusive and agreed to sell it to the *Star* for ten cents a word. I told Marty Goodman to buy it. Marty said, 'We've never spent ten cents a word, not even on Pierre Berton,'" recalled Stasia.

In the end, Stasia managed to convince Goodman to buy the WWD story. It was on Page One and the *Star* scooped the country. "The next day I said to Marty, 'where is my bonus?' He gave me a hug and a kiss."

The lot of a fashion reporter wasn't always chic soirees and glamorous runway shows in regards to filing, as Stasia pointed out several times. No matter what the beat, when something big or unusual happened, every reporter at a newspaper like the *Star* becomes a news gatherer. On one occasion, Stasia was in Vancouver covering a Pierre Cardin show when there was a warning that a tidal wave from Japan would hit British Columbia. The word was that an atomic bomb went off and activated a giant wave. The *Star* told Stasia and photographer, Reg Innell, to get the story and pictures. Soon the pair found themselves holed up in a roofed bunker on the Pacific Coast, north of Vancouver. The one tiny room already had a high water mark on the wall from a previous Japanese tidal wave and Stasia had orders to measure the height of the new wave. Innell's job was to get a photo of the threatening wave through the rain and clouds. It rained all day and the pair spent the hours in misery waiting for a big wave that never came.

Innell was also on the job when the *Star* sent news reporter Frank Jones and Stasia to Ottawa to cover the opening of the *National Arts Centre* on June 2, 1969. "There was a ballet performance. Prime Minister Pierre Trudeau was there and Innell and I ended up with a front-page picture and story. Then when I got back to Toronto, Marty Goodman said, 'I send my best reporter, meaning Frank, and you get front page,'" Stasia commented with a sly grin on her face.

Apparently the press was to be allowed into the formal reception at intermission for fifteen minutes. But that minx Stasia contrived to over-stay. "I had my eye on Trudeau. I knew what my job was. A security officer tried to throw me out, but Trudeau said to let her stay. I was looking for a front-page picture—just doing my job. I asked Trudeau to do something odd. He was there with his girlfriend, Madeleine Gobeil. He grabbed her evening bag and threw it over his head."

Stasia started her front-page copy with a cameo of the irreverent Prime Minister. "The swinger hung his date's handbag around his neck, loosened his tie and started dancing like a teenager," she cooed. Stasia goes on to say that Trudeau and Gobeil, a Carleton University professor, "quick-stepped to *Winchester Cathedral*, but Trudeau rocked like a teenager to *Can-Na-Da*." Stasia ended her report in a manner that only added to the aging politician's image as a with-it-guy. "The Prime Minister kept at it till 2 a.m., leaving most of his cabinet colleagues huffing on the sidelines."

Stasia commented dryly, "I charmed Trudeau. I liked him, but neither of us had any illusions. He liked the publicity and I knew he was dealing not with me, but the *Toronto Star*."

During the period in Canada's political history—dubbed Trudeaumania—, Stasia scooped the fashion world with Margaret (Sinclair), Trudeau's trousseau. Simma Holt, a *Vancouver Sun* reporter and friend (later an MP in the Trudeau Government), called Stasia and said that she could get her an exclusive interview with the designer, Peter Plunkett-Norris, the man responsible for dressing Trudeau's glamorous young fiancée. And even better, she had procured the original sketches of the honeymoon duds.

Stasia managed to chat with Margaret's mother, Mrs. James Sinclair, about her daughter's secret meetings with the designer. She also snared a quote from the designer himself. "Mrs. Sinclair told me that if I should phone, only to speak to her or her daughter. She also said, 'I ask you not to show anybody these designs and not to tell anybody her daughter is getting married,'" Stasia reported on behalf of the designer who blabbed all to Stasia and thus the world.

It seems that Miss Margaret Sinclair started planning her wardrobe sketches months before she married Trudeau on March 4, 1971. According to Stasia's reportage in the *Star*'s *Family Section*, Plunkett-Norris was told that Margaret Sinclair was marrying a diplomat and

Pierre Berton (1922-2004), author of some fifty books on Canadian subjects, was a columnist for the *Toronto Star*, 1958-1962.

shortly after the wedding, the newly-weds would be touring Russia, so the bride wanted some of her clothes to be Russian-oriented. One of the highlights of the trousseau was a midi-coat made of royal blue and rust tapestry and "trimmed in ivory fur in the Zhivago manner." This scoop turned out to be one of Stasia's finest moments and she recalled with glee the flurry it caused in the *Star* newsroom. "The section page was already made up. I got the sketches just as Mo (Keller) and Helen Worthington were coming back from one of their liquid lunches. We had one hour and, by God, Mo and I changed that page by hand," said Stasia.

Giving "Killer" Keller credit where it was due, Stasia recalled that Keller refused to let the wire service—*Canadian Press*—have the pictures until they had appeared in two editions of the *Star*. "In the meantime, the *Telegram* copied our pictures from our page and they came out with the trousseau in their next edition. But it looked so amateurish and washed out that we had a good laugh on Beth Dingman. The competition was so keen. It was so personal. That was what was so great about newspapers in those days."

Throughout the '60s, the fashion scene was free-wheeling and volatile and Stasia was there. In her daily copy, she burbled about Carnaby Street and the mini-skirt in the *Star*'s fashion pages. One Thursday, she informed readers that zodiac rings were all the go. "The latest fad on the market is the zodiac ring bearing the sign of the month you were born in," she wrote. In another fashion feature, Stasia reported, "Flowered raincoats are the best fashion for *swinging* in the rain. With matching hat $3.98." All the duds pictured on the page were from Eaton's.

In March 1969, Stasia revealed that everything's coming up leather, from coats and dresses to bikinis. "Leather took a flight into fashion last summer and is still sailing high with no sign of landing even for the fall," she wrote airily. Flighty prose, perhaps. But hey, it was the '60s—the *Age of Aquarius*—and, like man, Stasia was making the fashion scene.

In March 1971, after viewing a fashion show in Eaton's Ensemble Shop, Stasia declared "elegance and femininity return to spring clothes." Interestingly, this trite pronouncement is right beside a piece in the *Family Section* with the headline: "Woman Fights Male Writers." The story is about a gal who was battling for admission into the professional *Hockey Writers Association*. She claimed that she was being discriminated against on the basis of her sex, an issue that never concerned Stasia.

It was during Keller's tenure, the name of the *Women's Section* changed to the *Family Section*. By 1978, after a stint as editor of the *Insight* section, Keller was moving on to oversee the *Star*'s lucrative *Special Sections* that specialized in advertising inserts for such things as Sick Children's Hospital fundraising campaigns, George Brown College promotions and Christmas shopping guides. These extra sections featured anything that could bring in more bucks for the *Toronto Star* coffers. In fact, in 1989 *Special Sections* grossed $7.5 million thanks to Keller and her staff of two.

Mo Keller was a girl who loved her beverages and whose cup often *ranneth* over. She bragged about her monthly bar bills. They were in the thousands and most of them were totted up in the dining room in the old King Edward Hotel. The *Toronto Star* paid all the tabs without question because Keller was bringing in millions in advertising revenue. The on-going stories of *Keller-in-her-Kups* kept the newsroom sniggering for years. Many of the incidences are unprintable, but one we all liked was the time Keller was observed, at a staff party eating blue corn chips. The chips were, in fact, potpourri.

When Keller retired, her farewell party was well attended by the *Star*'s composing room staff. Keller was greatly admired by the lads in the composing room—known as the back shop. Her skill at moving copy around and setting up photos on the stone were legendary. In pre-computer days, pages were handset and made up on a stone with a sharp knife, a keen eye and a lot of experience. One composer testified, "Mo was a whiz on the stone and she could make up a page faster than you can say roll the presses. Need a 10-inch trim. One stroke from Keller and it was done."

It would be remiss not to mention that in 1977, editor-in-chief, Martin Goodman, and Keller launched *Starship*, a special page for children. A revolutionary concept at the time, it appeared weekly in the *Toronto Star* until July 2008.

Richard MacFarlane commented in his book about his father Douglas MacFarlane's career at the *Toronto Telegram*: "The *Star* was adept at printing phoney front-page editions. When the opportunity arose to fool its opponent, it would do a small runoff a paper that looked like the preceding edition, having no changes in content. As it did each day, it would deliver a bundle to its competitor to make the *Tely* staff believe that the *Star* had nothing new on a developing story. Then shortly after, the real edition would be printed and delivered to readers."[6]

After Keller went to *Special Sections*, Bonnie Cornell was given the job of family editor. "Bonnie was very ambitious and always nagging. Bonnie didn't understand fashion. She always had her big fat legs up on her desk and her slip was always showing. Finally, she went to *Chatelaine*," said Stasia adding, "I felt bad when I later heard she had cancer and died." By 1982, Cornell was managing editor at *Chatelaine*. She died in 1994.

But issues like fat legs and chic attire did not concern a reporter new to the *Toronto Star*. In 1978, Michele Landsberg surfaced in the new *Family Section*. Landsberg was a crusading feminist columnist who garnered a huge following of female readers interested in everything she had to say. "Bonnie Cornell was one of the best editors the *Star* ever had. She had a bossy way and a lot of people made fun of her, but she had her ear to the ground. Bonnie knew what was important—what was hot and topical. The women's movement had a big impact in the pages of her section," Landsberg said.

The only memories Stasia, always the *fashionista*, recalled about Landsberg were two packs of cigarettes a day and clothes held together with giant safety pins.

When the *Toronto Star* approached Landsberg, she was writing social interest and motherhood stories for *Chatelaine* magazine. Cornell, who wanted a writer to deal with women's issues, asked Landsberg to submit some sample columns. Landsberg was hired and within a year, a *Star* survey revealed Landsberg was the best-read columnist.

Landsberg said, "I wrote pieces about quitting smoking and my problems of being overweight. They were staggeringly popular and reprinted in a booklet. The *Star* sent out 12,000 copies." Subsequently, it was Cornell who insisted Landsberg, the first feminist in Canada to have a newspaper column, submit work for a National Newspaper Award. "The *Star* said they are not going to give a feminist writer a NNA. Wrong. I submitted three columns including one on losing socks. I was sky high. I was so thrilled. The *Life Section* sent me a glamorous bouquet and I had a special gown made for the awards ceremony."[7]

Moving On

Throughout her career, Stasia was an *oo-la-la* party girl with gobs of black mascara on her big bright eyes. Surely, along with the *Globe and Mail's* Kay Kritzwiser, she was one of the most frivolous reporters ever. Stasia hunkered down at her desk, habitually, dressed in a bright frou-frou frock—ready to hit the cocktail circuit at 5 p.m. In contrast to this aspect of her persona, perhaps because she was a Gemini, she was always feuding with someone. Marty Goodman, Beth Dingman, Bonnie Cornell, Mo Keller, just to name a few.

It seems Stasia may have had legitimate reasons for these contretemps. In Walter Stewart's book, *Canadian Newspapers: The Inside story,* his profile of the *Toronto Star* newsroom is scathing. "The *Star* has not been a happy place to work in the memory of man... Many of the finest journalists ever to grace a newspaper have been through the *Star*'s mill. It uses up reporters and editors the way other newspapers use up pencils... When former *Star* reporters meet, they always exchange horror stories, like veterans of Dieppe, except that the wounds are psychic, not physical, and the machine guns were self-protecting memos from a galaxy of superior editors... Survivors like to believe they are better and stronger persons for having passed through the flames."[8]

In 1981, Stasia's world came crashing down. From fashion doyenne with six Judy Awards, the ultimate accolade given by the Canadian fashion industry, and three American fashion awards under her sequined belt, Stasia was stripped of the fashion beat and offered a sop—the delicately entitled *Age of Reason* column. Or as it was called in the newsroom, the *Age of Raisin*. The column had been the territory of Lotta Dempsey until she left the *Star* to marry Dr. Arthur Ham. Lotta had worked at the *Star* for twenty-two of the fifty-seven years she spent as a newsgirl. Dempsey died in 1988. Over the years, there were many hilarious stories about her including one told by *Star* medical reporter Marilyn Dunlop. "I remember one time I went to lunch with Lotta. We were waiting to be seated. She was so busy talking and laughing she didn't notice she had set her purse down, not on a table, but inside the lobster tank."

Back to Stasia's saga; "One day they called me in. Bonnie Cornell, Tom Curzon and John Honderich. I hated the idea. I was happy. I didn't want to be bothered with old people. It was a shock. They were all against me."

Stasia thought the situation over for two days and realized the decision had been made. So, ever the practical little trouper, Stasia figured—why not? Change is necessary. But after taking on her new gig, when in her cups, Stasia was often heard to lament like some bereft Shakespearean heroine, "I am wearing Lotta's mantle."

For ten years, Stasia produced a tri-weekly column about the interests of the silver-haired set. An up-beat photo of Stasia often appeared with her column. Photos show Stasia doing everything from mushing a team of sled dogs to delivering Meals on Wheels. Stasia received several awards for her *Age of Reason* reportage. Just as she was leaving the *Star*, she won her final award from the Ontario Association for Community Living. It was for *Who Will Care for Them?*, a piece about aged parents caring for adult children with learning disabilities.

By 1985, Ellie Tesher was in charge. She had climbed the ladder from reporter to family editor. During her tenure, the section name was changed to *Living*. Tesher left the newsroom in 2002 and began writing an advice column for the Star. Currently she and her daughter are producing *Ask Ellie*, a syndicated column.

In the *Toronto Star*'s Centennial year, Tesher wrote a piece about the voice of women at the paper. She reported, 100 years after the *Star* was launched, there were 161 women out of a staff of 426 in the newsroom (editorial department). This worked out to be 38 percent of editorial workers.[9]

When the *Star* terminated Stasia's staff position in 1991, she was heading for her 68th birthday and had spent fifty years as a newsgirl. However, she did continue with her *Age of Reason* column on a freelance basis for two more years.

In 1998, as a gathering of purple finches sang like a well-rehearsed choir on her downtown balcony, Stasia concluded her story. "I've lived a beautiful life. Nothing to complain about. I can look back with no regrets," she said softly as she added more vodka to her glass.

Stasia died May 2009 in Bradford, Ontario, tended by her sister. She was eighty-four.

AFTERWORD

In 1993, *Living* editor Linwood Barclay was given the job of firing Stasia and terminating *Age of Reason*. After Stasia died, Barclay—by then a celebrated novelist—wrote a piece about the firing for the *Star*. He explained how he dreaded having to push the old girl out. "I felt sick all week...Like everyone else I loved Stasia. She was this tiny dynamo of boundless energy...Those over-sized black eye lashes batting at you. I didn't want to give her the bad news."

It turned out Stasia felt so bad about Barclay's discomfort during the firing confrontation, she insisted on taking him to lunch at the King Edward Hotel. Over lunch and "some drinks," Stasia regaled Barclay with stories of all the famous people she had hung out with. "She's had some life, and telling me about it lifted my spirits. Stasia understood it's not every day you have to fire someone, and she was there for me...By the time lunch was over, and I'm not sure just when that was, I was my cheerful self again. I grabbed a train home and Stasia happily went off to plan the rest of her life."[10]

ANGELA BURKE

Timmons Daily Press, 1947. Globe and Mail, 1949-1950.
Kemsley Newspapgers, NYC, 1950-1951. Toronto Star, 1951-1959

1920-2014

> "I just had to wire the *Star* for money. I could go anywhere, I had a plane pass. I was told anything goes on the expense account."

Beside her byline, a tag identified reporter Angela Burke as "the blonde glamorous Angela Burke." And glamorous she was.

Her stint at the *Toronto Star* was a whirl of exotic travels, celebrity balls and reports on the movers and shakers of the 1950s. It was routine for Angela to receive an invitation from Her Majesty the Queen commanding her to attend highfalutin functions. One invitation, dated October 12, 1957, summoned Angela to Ottawa for a reception at Government House to meet Queen Elizabeth II. Another invitation, from the President of Yugoslavia, insisted she attend a gala reception at the White Palace in Belgrade for "Leurs Majestés Paul Roi des Hellènes et la Reine Frédérique." That was September, 1955.

Angela needed evening gowns to run with this crowd and evening gowns she had. A particular favourite was a beige silk taffeta model by Balenciaga, no less.

But Angela was not just a flighty party girl. After the Belgrade ball was over, Angela filed a sheaf of stories to the *Toronto Star* about conditions in Yugoslavia at a time when that country was terra incognita in the West.

"Burke of the *Star*," made even bigger news in 1955 when she attended the first press conference ever held in the Kremlin. She was the first member of the Western press in the Cold War era to shoot footage of the mysterious Soviet leaders. In the copy Angela wired to the *Star*, she said, "no one stopped me from bringing my cameras into the room which was remarkable."

Nikolai Bulganin was the first to enter the Kremlin hall allotted for the press conference; Angela described him as "looking as benign as someone's grandfather."

"Nikita Khrushchev followed and I thought he looked older and fatter than his pictures with his huge bald head and five feet three inches.

"As Bulganin began reading his statement, I decided to chance it and with my 16mm movie camera. The whir of the camera stunned the assembly for a second and I wasn't sure whether to continue or not, but Bulganin went on reading. Vyacheslav Molotov smiled, and Khrushchev looked with interest and whispered something to Marshal Georgi Zhukov. As I left the Kremlin, no one stopped me for taking photographs, moving or still."[1]

All her life, Angela treasured this black-and-white historical footage.

Newsgirls

Beginnings

Angela was born on October 3, 1920, in Buffalo, New York. It seems her parents, Frank and Ruth Burke, anticipated a difficult birth, as Timmins, Ontario, the Burkes' hometown, did not have a very sophisticated hospital. Because she was born in the U.S., Angela had dual citizenship.

Angela grew up in the 1930s. The world was in the throes of the Great Depression, but all the trials and tribulations of the Dirty Thirties passed her by. As the privileged daughter of an affluent druggist in Timmins, there was always money. The family wintered in Florida and Angela and her sister travelled overseas with a chaperone. Angela attended a series of private convent schools, including a French language institution in Haileybury, Toronto's Loretto Abbey, and Marymount, a Catholic school in Paris. During the war, Angela was a student at McGill University in Montreal. She graduated in 1943. As a result of her schooling, Angela spoke beautiful French.

After graduation, Angela worked as a file clerk in the Washington Press Office of the British Embassy. When the war ended, she returned to Timmins and landed a job at the *Timmins Daily Press*. She lasted hardly a year and, in late 1946, headed for New York and went to work at the *New York Telegram*, a Kemsley Newspaper of London publication. Angela was on re-write, which meant she took copy off the teletype machine and re-wrote it. Ian Fleming who later wrote the thrilling James Bond books, worked in the same office as Angela. While in New York, Angela also enrolled in a post-graduate journalism course at Columbia University.

Angela's father Frank died while she was in New York and so she returned to Ontario, a decision made easy by the *New York Telegram*, as they had no intention of providing her with the foreign correspondent's job that had become her dream.

> Ian Fleming (1905-1964) was the foreign bureau manager for Kemsley in the 1940s.

Angela Follows Her Dreams

Angela's privileged and peripatetic girlhood had given her a sophistication and sense of independence far beyond what one would expect from a girl raised in a rural mining town like Timmins. Once her father's death was settled, the ambitious Angela hit Toronto and set her cap for a job with a big city newspaper.

She managed to snare a job at the *Globe and Mail* in 1949. There, she covered local politics under the critical eye of city editor, Doug MacFarlane.

"I was sent to Parkdale to cover a candidate's speech and I asked what he was going to do for the people of Parkdale. MacFarlane told me I did the wrong thing in questioning the candidate," recalled Angela in a 1997 interview in Montreal. At the time, Angela was seventy-six and as perky and glamorous as ever.

MacFarlane claimed he "saved her neck" from the repercussions of asking a blatant question. At that point, Angela realized she didn't fit into the *Globe's* vision of the world and, after a year, she left. Meanwhile, she had decided that the *Toronto Star* would be the right fit for her.

"I had a hard time getting on the *Star*. They offered me a job in the women's section but I wouldn't take it. I wanted to be a reporter," she said. "I pestered Borden Spears, the city editor, but they didn't have women in the general news department, so I went to the library and read everything I could about Harry C. Hindmarsh."

> One reporter from this period described Hindmarsh as ruling the *Star* like an ancient emperor—a "Genghis Khan."

Based on her research, Angela wrote a personal letter to Hindmarsh, the *Star*'s dour publisher. In it, she alluded to his reputation as "an ogre." But nevertheless, she assured him with all the brass and sass of youth that she wanted to work in his newsroom. The next thing the thirty-year-old woman knew, she had a call from the *Star* offering her a test assignment.

"I was sent to Red Lake, Manitoba. I flew with a photographer to Winnipeg and then we rented a small plane. I was supposed to find out why all the nurses kept leaving. Well, it turned out there were all these miners in Red Lake and the nurses kept getting swept off their feet and marrying. I got the story in right away and that's how I was hired."

The year was 1951 and Angela was determined that she was not going to the women's section to write about an endless string of weddings. Besides, Ruth Hammond, the women's editor, was a known dragon. Angela recalled that Hammond "had a fantastic temper and all she did was throw things." For the record, when Hammond arrived at the Star, the women's editor was Gordon Sinclair, most remembered by all Ontarians over fifty as not only a curmudgeonly newscaster, but a regular on CBC's *Front Page Challenge* along with another blustery aging newspaperman Pierre Berton.

Hindmarsh liked to keep his reporters from getting "too big for their britches" after a snappy foreign assignment by giving them a stint in a menial job. This meant that sometimes even aggressive swaggering newsmen like Sinclair would find themselves writing up weddings and social notices for the women's section.

Newsroom Pet

Hindmarsh was always known in the newsroom as Mister Hindmarsh. He was austere, aloof and formal, but for Angela, he was a dream boss. She had carte blanche to do what she wanted and all the staff knew it. As a personal pet of Hindmarsh, Angela managed to avoid the pariah status assigned to the lady reporters in the women's section. The gals were separated from the men in the newsroom and hidden behind closed doors in the old *Star* building on King St. West. Hindmarsh believed that a female sighting would distract men from their work.

Angela explained: "If you sent a suggestion to HCH, it would be back on your desk by morning. Once I sent fourteen and all were approved, except for one. Hindmarsh used to send notes to the editors saying: Let Miss Burke do this piece."

And so, she did.

Angela kept a few Hindmarsh notes. One, dated November 28, 1955, said "Mr. Kingsbury (managing editor) Could you have Miss Burke get busy for some articles for the editorial page. She has some ideas that she picked up in England and I fancy she will do a good job on them. She could come off routine work." Another one said "Mr. Kingsbury: Please compliment Miss Burke on her first provocative article. It is splendid. She might continue writing only articles which satisfy her and not try to write one-a-day if she feels it is too many."

No wonder Angela loved her years at the *Star*.

Although Hindmarsh looked after Angela, he never spoke to her. "Borden Spears did everything. Hindmarsh would send notes and then answers would go back through Borden, to Kingsbury, to Hindmarsh's inner sanctum. And then notes would come back out again with the initials HCH at the end," recalled Angela. "I remember how Hindmarsh would examine the obituaries every day. Once, he decided he needed a story on why all of a sudden so many people were dying and I had to research this. That's the kind of man he was. Interested in everything."

While Angela remembered Hindmarsh with respect, her fondest memories of her days at the *Star* were reserved for Spears, who as city editor, was Angela's immediate superior in the newsroom pecking order. "I really loved him. He was a real gentleman. Borden was also a good scholar and very fair. I called him Mr. Spears. He was so respected."

Our Gal in the Soviet Union

1955 was certainly a stellar year for Angela. She spent six weeks in the Soviet Union where she hobnobbed with some of the world's most dubious politicians and observed the Soviet leaders at their work as well as photographed them. Angela also talked with the women in the streets of Russia and attended galas. She described a banquet held for Vietnam President, Ho Chi Minh, on July 15, in the opulent St. George Salon at the Kremlin. Angela was the only woman in the press corps and she put her feminine powers of observation to work. Angela, a veteran gourmet and gourmand, told *Star* readers that guests dined on "caviar trays, salads, steamed sturgeon, followed by a delicious rice and meat entree which nobody at the table could identify." Angela consciously noted: "There were no wives or women Communists at the head table. Khrushchev sat between the Vietnam visitor and [Georgy] Malenkov. Wives of members of the central committee may have been seated at a special table but it was unknown to us."

Angela Burke

Hammond died in October, 2015. She was ninety-five. In 1956, Hammond began a fifty-year career in public relations. She established her own agency and later organized Public Relations courses for Ryerson University, York University and University of Toronto. A Ruth Hammond Scholarship, established in 1985, is awarded to outstanding students studying PR.

Spears' son, John Spears, currently toils at the *Toronto Star's* City Desk, as an Editor.

Angela also confessed to the reading public that Soviet living had cultivated her "capitalist tastes" for caviar, which sells for a fortune back home and is available at all meals. "I'm learning to distinguish between fairly good and best caviar. It's taste, I might add, is as remote from the salty fare one gets on canapés in Toronto as tree-ripened fruit from the green."[2]

As an interested spectator in child political indoctrination, Angela was granted permission to visit a Moscow nursery, kindergarten and pioneer camp. After the visits, she started a story with the pronouncement: "Courses in Marx-Lenin-Stalin thinking begin in the Soviet almost with a baby's first breath. By seven the child is conditioned for life.

"At the institutions I visited, children appeared healthy, happy and as they passed infancy, conformed almost like the Alpha, Beta and Delta babies Aldous Huxley wrote about in his *Brave New World*. Nothing essential is lacking and physical force is never a factor in making these assembly line children 'think correctly.'"

Angela also described how the state "usurps the role of parents" and how women went to work—most often hard labour—immediately after birth and deposited their babies in state care where the conditioning process starts.

In other stories, Angela examined the issues of education and censorship.

She told readers that one of the greatest drives for education in the world is going on in Russia. "Everyone there is keen on reading for learning. Bookstores in Moscow are crowded and stalls scattered along thoroughfares are humming with business." She informed the Canadian public that authors such as Shakespeare, Hemingway, Steinbeck and Galsworthy enjoy state approval. Angela concludes, "pursuing knowledge, of course, is conducted strictly along ideological lines, but nevertheless the new Soviet intelligentsia shows single-mindedness in their devotion to this one-track learning which is soul-shaking."

Later at a press conference at *Pravda*, where its editors were instructed to answer questions from the Western press, Madame Olga Tchetchetkina, editor of Asian and African news, explained that Cold War tension would lessen if there were more communication between Russians and foreigners.

Question: Then why can't Soviet people invite us to their homes?

Answer: They can. We like to have you. The great barrier is language.

Angela threw in her two-cents worth: "Speaking from my own experience this is not so. One young Soviet woman who works for the Communist party invited me to her room where she lives with her parents. We made arrangements in the lobby of a Leningrad hotel. Six hours after she had written out her address for me, she appeared at my hotel room cancelling the date and asking for her slip of paper back. A hotel spy had reported her."

Shortly after the *Pravda* conference, Angela listened to a speech Premier Nikolai Bulganin made to the 1,354 deputies of the Supreme Soviet. Angela reported, "With it, the Soviet Premier gave the iron curtain another roll-up and set the stage for a new era of Soviet-Western relations. Emphasizing the importance of personal contacts in removing distrust and suspicion, Bulganin spoke of the 'fruitful' atmosphere generated at Geneva through the meetings of a top leader at official and unofficial sessions.

Later, during a scrum, Angela asked Khrushchev why she couldn't go to the infamous salt mines in Siberia. He replied "If you'd like to walk, you can go Miss Burke."

In yet another report filed in Russia, Angela drew a detailed word-picture of Nikita Khrushchev for the curious Canadian public after being asked endlessly about him. "Here's what I know: Khrushchev is tough and is known for saying what he thinks. After meeting and watching Mr. K., during my six weeks in the Soviet, there is no doubt he is the real boss of Russia. He was the man who gave statements on Russian policy to foreign correspondents without consultation. He was the man who kept other presidium members waiting. On one occasion I saw Premier Bulganin waiting outside the French embassy in Moscow while Khrushchev conversed with newsmen. He was also the man who Bulganin deferred to as soon as protocol was laid aside on official occasions."

"I found him a man to fear; a man completely sure of his direction and an implicit believer in its rightness. On all occasions, he was on the offensive. Undiplomatic, he said what he thought. When the visiting French delegation, Burke made a reference to Russian women doing back-bending work on Moscow roads, to which Khrushchev replied: 'At least in the Soviet Union women are given a chance to earn their bread. In France they pick it up on Paris streets.'" [3]

In her analysis of Khrushchev's character, Angela pointed out that he had never travelled outside the Soviet satellites, except for one trip to Switzerland. She concluded that "he was limited in his imagination of how the Western world lives. He believes firmly that capitalism exploits the working class and that communism is the working man's only salvation. He is convinced that one day the whole world will be communist."

After her Russian stint in September, 1955, Angela travelled to Belgrade and declared, in her first file from Yugoslavia, that "After spending six weeks in Russia, life in this Communist state of Yugoslavia is, by comparison, like re-emerging into Western democracy." She told readers that cafes and churches are full, women are not pick-and-shovel workers and even the guards appear human. Besides singing the praises of the less-astringent form of Communism, she found in "Titoland" (as she called it), Angela reported that Yugoslavia has the best-looking men per capita than any other place in the world.

Frivolity aside, the *Star* had assigned Angela to cover the historic meeting of Bulganin and Khrushchev with Josip Broz Tito, the Yugoslavian dictator. Angela explained there were ten Western reporters, in the pool, outside the meeting chambers and they would pick out one "chap" to go in and report what was happening inside back to the rest. Then, the reporters would write as if they were one-on-one with the subject. "The *London Times* sent their top "*colour man.*" "The *Times'* colour man wrote that Bulganin had an eye for ladies' ankles. And he wasn't even inside," said Angela.

Years later, Angela was scanning Bulganin's obituary in the *New York Times* and there it was—the bit about an eye for a good ankle. So much for the integrity of eye-witness reporting. Angela managed to scoop the world when she wrangled an exclusive interview in Belgrade with the elusive Mrs. Jovanka Broz Tito. Angela recalled that Jovanka Broz was a large "Junoesque" woman of peasant stock. "Nobody knew anything about her. In fact, she was Mrs. Tito for six months before anybody heard of the marriage. It came out when Anthony Eden was on a state visit and invitations went out to an official party in the name of Tito and Mrs. Josip Broz Tito," said Angela. [4]

In April, 2011, Jovanka was interviewed by *Balkan Life* about her demands for the return of all the goodies confiscated from the dictator's mansion. Apparently, they had been locked up for more than three decades. Earlier, she had been insisting that U.S. President Barack Obama recognize her "abysmal treatment" by the Russians—she being a First Lady and all.

On the last leg of Angela's 1955 European trip, she stopped at Camp Friedland, Germany, where she dug up a chilling story or two. It all started in Paris at the Hotel Continental where Angela received an urgent telegram from Spears, dated October 11:

"PLEASE TAKE EARLIEST PLANE POSSIBLE FOR CAMP FRIEDLAND GERMANY WHERE HANS BAUR FORMER HITLER PERSONAL PILOT HAS BEEN RELEASED BY RUSSIANS FROM LABOUR CAMP STOP BAUR AND TWO OTHER RELEASIES WITNESSED HITLERS SUICIDE WITH EVA BRAUN"

A few days later a second telegram reached Angela at Hotel Muenchen in Germany:

"INTERESTED IN WOMEN AND CHILDREN NOW REPORTED RELEASED BY RUSSIANS STOP APPARENTLY CHILDREN BORN IN CAPTIVITY STOP PLEASE TRY LOCATE STOP.... THANKS FINE STORY TODAY=SPEARS"

Angela did not get to interview Baur, but she did interview three young German mothers who had given birth while working as slave labourers in Siberia. The women were part of a group of 9,000 Germans freed by the Russians in October, 1955.

"Only one knew the father of her baby had been repatriated. Married in a ceremony arranged by the prisoners themselves, Mrs. Horst Gruwes, 28, wore an iron wedding ring hammered out by her husband in the coal mines of the notorious Vorkuta prison camp," wrote Angela.

Gruwes, a trained ballerina, had been taken prisoner in 1945 by the Russians when she crossed from West to East Germany to see her mother. She was charged with espionage and sent to Vorkuta where she built streets, often in forty-below weather. Another female prisoner had been taken away while on a visit to relatives in East Germany and her family didn't hear a word from her for almost three years.[5]

The Homefront

Meanwhile at home, shocking tales like this reported in the Western press helped fuel the Cold War and instill Canadians and Americans with distrust, suspicion and loathing of the Soviet system. This impression was not helped by the uncouth image of Khrushchev banging his shoe on the desk at the United Nations like the thug he was.

When Angela visited Russia, the United States was still in the throes of McCarthyism, a curious mindset that overflowed into Canada. In 1950, Senator Joseph McCarthy whipped up fear of communist Russia to fever pitch and, in their anti-communist hysteria, had Americans looking under their beds for "Reds" and purging their own population of anyone who uttered a thought that could be interpreted as pro-Soviet.

One of the more tragic victims was civil rights' activist, Paul Robeson (1898-1976), a black American, who was a graduate of Columbia Law School. He was also a National Football League player, singer and actor. His most memorable roles were *Othello* on Broadway and Robeson's rendition of Oscar Hammerstein's, *Ol' Man River*, in the 1936 movie version of *Show Boat* has never been equaled.

Early on in life, Robeson had joined the Labour Movement and the Communist Party. He was blacklisted by McCarthy and after spending time in the USSR, the American Government seized his passport and his careers were over. The Americans erased Robeson from their history, and in the "Home of The Free," he was forgotten. But not in Canada. In 1952, 40,000 people attended a Robeson "concert," organized by several Canadian and American labour unions. This protest was held under the international Peace Arch on the border between Washington state and British Columbia. Robeson performed songs of solidarity from the back of a flatbed truck—the front wheels and cab in the U.S. and the flatbed "stage" in Canada.

On a lighter note, Malachy McCourt, in his book *A Monk Swimming,* offers an uproarious description of the Khrushchev's shoe furor as described by the Irish delegation present at that absurd incident. It seems in 1958, Frederick "Freddie" Boland, the Irish ambassador to the United Nations, was elected president of the General Assembly and after a day's work at the U.N., the Irish delegation, including Boland and journalist Conor Cruise O'Brien, repaired to Malachy's Irish pub on 14th St. to carouse. They knew rude songs, epic poems and bawdy stories and they told them.

On the evening of the Khrushchev shoe incident, the tale was told with much embellishment. It all started when Freddie Boland ruled Khrushchev out of order for interrupting another delegate's speech. The Russian refused to button his lip, so Boland started banging, authoritatively, with his gavel. Not to be outdone, Khrushchev removed one of his shoes (the left one, of course) and rapped smartly on top of the escritoire in front of him in rhythmic response to Freddie's challenge.

"Freddie rat-tat-tatted, with his gavel and Nikita, at a slight disadvantage in trying to match the decibel level with the rubber heel on the shoe, acquitted himself quite well. Musical interludes of this nature are rare at the U.N. sessions—especially drumming that utilizes everyday furniture of the workplace. Freddie tapped and Nikita whacked, and pretty soon the two disparate modes of drumming merged into a hypnotic rhythm that had the whole General Assembly swaying back and forth and at the point of clapping and giving thanks to God, Allah, Buddha.

"But lo and behold, in a tremendous, overwhelming victory for Atheistic Communism, Freddie's gavel broke, thereby ceding control of the rhythm to Nicky the K. and the Soviet Union. Seeing that he had triumphed, Nicky gave his trusty escritoire a few more hearty whacks,

---

This infamous incident occurred October 12, 1960. The shoe banging was Khrushchev's angry protest against a speech accusing the Soviet Union of "swallowing up" Eastern Europe.

Paul Robeson (1898-1976), after exile in Russia, returned to the U.S. where he died.

waved the victorious *sabot* at the cheering masses, and put it back on his foot. Questions were asked why a Capitalist-made gavel gave out before a silly old, factory-made Commie shoe, but the results of that commission were never published. Another Capitalist Conspiracy cover-up."[6]

Swanning Around Europe

In the 1950s, Angela interviewed dozens of the celebrities that filled the American gossip magazines. *Star* readers followed the adventures of the pert, Angela, as she took advantage of every opportunity to travel—on the *Star's* tab—and meet the most famous people in the world. They read, agog, as Angela partied with Frank Sinatra in Madrid and lunched with Randolph Churchill and Lord Beaverbrook in Monaco. She interviewed Hollywood pinup girl Jane Russell, star of *Gentlemen Prefer Blondes,* along with Marilyn Monroe. She flew with Hollywood TV star, Robert Cummings, in his private plane. He was a vegetarian and health food nut, according to Angela. The *Star* published a picture of Cummings and Angela in the cockpit. She is wearing a furry Sunday-go-to-meetin' hat and, yes, white gloves.

In 1956, once again, Angela headed for Europe. This time, with a wedding invitation in hand. Angela was assigned to cover the marriage of Hollywood starlet Grace Kelly and Prince Ranier of Monaco. In April, Angela travelled to New York City where she boarded the *S.S. Constitution*, along with a band of photographers in pork pie hats. She, herself, was sporting a smart little chapeau made of a band of artificial cherries. (Cub reporter Cathy Smyth lent Angela the hat.) Of course, the chic little Miss Burke was also wearing her white gloves.

Angela's fellow passengers included twenty-two journalists, Grace Kelly, her wedding party of eighty, Kelly's poodle Oliver and a bevy of handlers. During the nine-day crossing, Angela's job was to snap up every tidbit of information about Kelly and her entourage and get it back to the news desk in Toronto so *Star* readers wouldn't miss a turn on the deck.

Angela reported that Kelly arrived aboard the ship wearing a beige tweed suit, a white pillbox hat and a sable fur draped over her arm. Angela described how Grace walked the decks during the day in tweed skirts and cashmere twin sets and at night, dined in evening dress and horn-rimmed glasses.

"She was about the prettiest twenty-six-year-old I had ever seen, and the thinnest," commented Angela.

One *Star* story, datelined: "Aboard *S.S. Constitution at Sea*", April 7, featured a chat with Peggy Davis, elder sister of Grace Kelly. Davis admitted to Angela she had never heard of her future brother-in-law until the previous December. In one of the numerous wedding stories Angela filed that day, she quoted Davis as saying, "Until Ranier arrived in the U.S, I didn't even know there was a prince named Ranier or a principality called Monaco."

To the end of her days, Angela treasured her wedding invitation with its royal seal and the words *Marriage S. A. S. Le Prince Souverain de Monaco*. "I could have earned a lot of extra money filing for NBC, *Paris Soir*, *Gourmet* and the *Daily Mail*, but I didn't. You see I had an official invitation and the other reporters didn't," Angela said.

Not only did Angela wire wedding dispatches to the *Star* six times a day, but she took 16mm film of the Kelly-Ranier wedding on April 19, 1956, that she always kept in her possession.

On the same trip, Angela attended a luncheon hosted by Anglo-Canadian tycoon Lord Beaverbrook at his Riviera estate. Beaverbrook, born in Maple Ontario, started his working life in New Brunswick as William Maxwell Aitken. There he made his fortune in the pulp and paper business. Beaverbrook liked to call himself the "barefoot boy from the Miramichi."

"I met him in Monaco at the Hotel de Paris. He found out I was with the *Toronto Star* and said he would have his man phone me about lunch. He did ask me for lunch that day, but I couldn't go. I was working very hard. We had *six* editions and I had to file something about Grace's wedding for each one. Believe me, I knew every telegraph station in Europe. Beaverbrook phoned me again from his house outside of Monaco and we set a date. I arrived exactly on time and no one else was there. Beaverbrook showed me his orange trees and garden. He pressed a button and water from the Mediterranean flowed into a fountain. He asked me about the *Star* and politics. I was very open with him."

"Lord Beaverbrook (1879-1964), also known as "The First Baron of FLeet," bought the London *Daily Telegraph* in 1918 and grew the paper into a powerful print empire. Beaverbrook was also an influential British politician.

After Beaverbrook pumped Angela for Canadian political gossip, Randolph Churchill, who was working for Beaverbrook at the *Evening Standard*, arrived from Paris with a woman friend. Beaverbrook's Edinburgh secretary was also a guest. "We started with orange blossoms (gin-based cocktails) and then had a champagne lunch. I was on Beaverbrook's right. He exaggerated, terrifically, everything I had said about politicians during our garden walk. I would protest: 'But Lord Beaverbrook that's not what I said.' It was a power game. Beaverbrook was a real power player," recalled Angela with complete clarity. "And then he started on Randolph about six ongoing lawsuits resulting from his column. Beaverbrook taunted him about how he was going to pay for them. Then Randolph told a complicated story about Pamela Digby (Randolph was her first husband), who got an annulment from him so she could marry playboy Gianni Agnelli, the Fiat heir."

Although Pamela, an English socialite and "professional courtesan," had a passionate affair with Agnelli, they did not marry. She had dozens of lovers including Prince Aly Salmone Khan, Baron Élie de Rothschild and shipping tycoon, Spiro Niarchos. Pamela's final husband was Averell Harriman, an American railroad tycoon. U.S. President Bill Clinton appointed Pamela Digby Harriman American ambassador to France in 1993.

Angela got the impression that Beaverbrook was very worried about conjugal arrangements. "He talked about Clare Booth Luce who turned Catholic to marry Henry "Harry" Luce who was ambassador to Italy. It was of great concern to him," she said.

Clare Booth was appointed editor of *Vanity Fair* magazine in 1933. She is famous for her line, "No good deed goes unpunished." Booth married Henry Luce (her second husband), in 1935 and later entered politics. In 1942, Booth Luce was elected to the American House of Representatives. In 1954, President Dwight Eisenhower made her the American ambassador to Italy.

On one occasion, Luce commented: "In politics women type the letters, lick the stamps, distribute the pamphlets and get out the vote. Men get elected."

Angela Rocks On

Another spin-off from the Kelly wedding was an invitation from Stanley Kramer, the Hollywood producer of *The Pride and The Passion*, to join his film crew on location in Spain. Angela received the invitation in mid-Mediterranean while on board the *S.S. Constitution* as it steamed its way to Monaco. The *Star* said "go for it." During the shooting on the plains in Spain, Angela became a pal of movie stars Frank Sinatra, Sophia Loren and Cary Grant.

"C.S. Forester, who wrote *The Pride and The Passion*, arrived the same time I did. He was a man in his sixties and he took me to all the closed parties. This was Sophia Loren's first American movie. We went to parties with her, her sister and Frank Sinatra. Most events were al fresco, but others were in smart apartments in Madrid," recalled Angela.

Angela admired Cary Grant for "his good looks", but it was Frank Sinatra who won her heart during those days in Spain. Angela described for *Star Weekly* readers a late-night party in Madrid. The thirty guests, including Loren, Grant, Kramer and Angela, were all assembled when Sinatra made a late entrance. "He came in with a pretty dark-haired singer from California on one arm, and a bottle of bourbon in the other. Completely at ease, he was magnetic. In the background Sinatra recordings were being played with some of the party dancing, while in the foreground a knot of people gathered around Sinatra and he chatted away spicing his conversation with anecdotes. There was no doubt about what bobbysoxers had discovered back in the '40s. Sinatra was electric."

Angela concluded that Cary Grant was as "thoughtful" and quiet as Sinatra was "flashy." She tells readers: "Uncommonly handsome and tall, Grant could command attention solely by virtue of his appearance. Sinatra could do it in spite of his. Undoubtedly, he is the Rubirosa of the film world."

Once, a movie reviewer sent a short telegram to Cary Grant's Hollywood agent asking "How old Cary Grant." Grant sent one back saying; "Old Cary Grant fine. How you?"

Meeting in a doorway, Luce once said to Dorothy Parker, New York author and wit; "Age before beauty." Parker sweeping past: "Pearls before swine."

Porfirio Rubirosa, like Pamela Digby, was a favourite of international gossip columnists. He was an extremely handsome diplomat from the Dominican Republic who always had a glamour girl on his arm. During the 1950s, there he was in the glossy magazines pictured with one Hollywood beauty after another—Marilyn Monroe, Rita Hayworth, Ava Gardner, Kim Novak.

At one intimate lunch for five, Kramer was on Angela's left, Grant on her right, and Sinatra across from her. "Frank had enormous presence and was a marvelous raconteur. In fact the most entertaining conversationalist I ever heard. He took hold of the conversation and it ran the gamut of boxing to politics. He told us tales of Nat King Cole. He was most entertaining. At another lunch, Cary Grant asked me if I wanted to be the best newspaper woman in the world.

And of course, I didn't," Angela said decades later.

One celebrity that got away however was Princess Soraya (1932-2001), a gorgeous Ava Gardner look-alike who had just been ousted as consort of the Shah of Iran. Angela kept the collect telegram, sent by the *Star*'s news desk, alerting her to Soraya's whereabouts. Dated April 11, 1958, it said:

"LINER CONSTITUTION WITH PRINCESS SORAYA ABOARD ARRIVES IN NEW YORK FROM THE MEDITERRANEAN EARLY AM APRIL TWENTY SECOND"

Without further instruction on the 22nd, Angela was on the dock, but an interview never materialized. "As I recall, Soraya was broken-hearted about the end of the marriage. The Shah got rid of her because she couldn't have a baby," sighed Angela.

Angela identified Helen Keller (1880-1968) as the most impressive individual she ever interviewed. Keller was about eighty when Angela met her at the airport in New York. Keller was returning to the U.S. after an Asian tour.

"Helen Keller had the most beautiful face. She was just back from Japan with her companion Anne Sullivan. She had no speech, couldn't hear and was blind. I asked, if you could have one faculty, what would it be. She said hearing, because lack of it cuts you off more than anything else. Then, when I got back to the *Star*, Harry Hindmarsh Jr. was on the city desk and he asked who Helen Keller was," laughed Angela.

Arguably, much of the copy Angela submitted over sixty-five years ago may seem trivial today, but she was the first Canadian journalist ever to file on-the-spot reports of conditions in the great bête noire known as Russia.

> Keller, born in 1880, became blind and deaf after a childhood fever. But with the help of a dedicated teacher she learned to communicate and became an advocate for the blind, an outspoken suffragette and committed socialist. For decades, Keller was a popular lecturer due more to public curiosity about how she overcame her disability than to her radical political views.

> Bête noire: a person or thing very much disliked or avoided.

Money No Object

In those days, for favoured reporters like Angela, there was plenty of money to swan around Europe. "I just had to wire the *Star* for money. I could go anywhere. I had a plane pass. I was told anything goes on the expense account," recalled Angela.

Today's reporters in budget conscious newsrooms, where down-sizing and belt-tightening is rampant, can only drool over the money pots of the past. But times were different when Angela arrived at the *Star*. Television had yet to permeate North American lives. Information came in written form in a newspaper or in a specialty magazine. It was the era of *Life* magazine and movie magazines featuring Hollywood gossip columnists like Hedda Hopper and Louella Parsons who were household names. Everyone read these magazines and discussed their content on the same scale that the world talked about the O.J. Simpson murder trial or the Obama presidential campaign as seen on television. Meanwhile in Toronto, the *Star* and its rival, the *Toronto Telegram*, were riding high and spared no expense to gather stories for the insatiable reading public. The word was the message.

"We stayed in the best hotels and ate in the top restaurants. I went first-class everywhere, no questions asked. You know, I should have asked for a bigger dress allowance," said Angela, wistfully, forty years after the fact over a sublime lunch at Claude Postel's restaurant in old Montreal. "I was so pleased with my life. It was marvelous and so much fun. There was no limit on over-time pay, so I made lots of money."

And indeed, Angela, a single gal, was making a base pay of $100 a week by 1956, about $500 more per anno than the average family income reported by Statistics Canada for that year. By the way, in 1957, Angela wrote a story about the first woman *Hansard* reporter in Ottawa. She pointed out that Mrs. Joan Blair landed the job only because there was a shortage of trained men. But the fortunate Mrs. Blair was paid the going male rate of $6,400 a year, a fabulous salary for anyone in the '50s, never mind a woman.

Ben Rose (1922-2008), a veteran *Toronto Star* newsie, and later editor of the *Jewish Daily News* in Toronto, confirmed there was a money tree at the *Star*. "We threw money around like water in those days. There was an excess of profit tax. We would book hotel rooms everywhere. The *Star* brass would pay for any amount of booze, travel and cover the cost of fines and trashed rooms without comment."

Hard News

During her career, Angela also covered hard news along with the many hard-boiled male reporters of the 1950s, like the *Toronto Telegram's* foreign correspondent Peter Worthington (co-founder of the *Toronto Sun* and a *Sun* columnist) and Jocko Thomas, who was the *Star's* police reporter for fifty years. Angela said that she kept her bags packed because she never knew where she was going next.

"I remember a plane came down outside of Ottawa and it was thought that it had a nuclear warhead on it. When I arrived, I talked to a bomb disposal expert there to get the facts. I filed my story, but a new *Star* science reporter said I was wrong about the technical stuff and changed my story. As I walked into the newsroom, Mr. Spears was apologizing. My facts were right," said Angela, always a proud professional.

But Angela was careful to keep a low profile in what was a man's world.
"Yes it's true. I could rent a plane or a train. Do anything. Money was no object. But as a woman, I knew I had to be super careful. If I got special stories, they would blame me. I felt I couldn't give the men cause to resent me. They were very nice to me and never swore in front of me. I do remember one editor saying, we don't like to photograph any girl over nineteen. In those days, no one thought anything of that," commented Angela.

Legal entanglements—an occupational hazard—happens to just about any reporter if she handles enough news stories. Angela was no exception. She was hauled into court early in her *Star* career after a diary belonging to a murder victim disappeared. The Kitchener police charged Angela with theft and "unlawfully and willfully attempting to obstruct justice." A headline in the *Globe and Mail*, January 31, 1953, blared "Girl's Diary Gone, Woman Reporter for Star Charged."

In January, 1953, Marie Huras, a seventeen-year-old Kitchener girl, was shot to death and Toronto reporters ascended on the small town like locusts on a corn field. In the course of getting the story first—and a darn better one than the *Telegram*—Angela went to Huras's rooming house and sweet talked the landlady (still all in a day's work for general assignment reporters) into allowing her to go to the victim's room. In one drawer, Angela found a diary and allegedly took it. The teary landlady, Mrs. Balge, later lamented in court that "it didn't look like much," so she gave Angela permission to take the diary on the promise she would return it in a few days.
In court, it also emerged that Angela had coffee with the murdered girl's sister and asked for a photograph of the victim. Angela mailed the diary back on January 29, but wasn't charged with theft until January 30. When she reappeared in court on February 4, she was out on $200 bail and her case was remanded for a week. The same day a headline in the *Star* read "Girl reporter (Angela was thirty-three) Given Remand in Diary Theft."

During her trial, Angela's lawyer John J. Robinette (1906-1996) maintained there was no case against his client because the diary was in the mail before the charge. Also, there was no evidence that she willfully set out to obstruct justice. In the end, the obstructing justice charge was dismissed, but the magistrate found Angela guilty of theft. This ruling was appealed and, two months later, the Ontario Court of Appeal found that "perhaps Miss Burke was a little over-enthusiastic in her duties," and acquitted her. Angela was a free woman. [7]

It was Angela's first murder story and she looked to the *Star* for instruction. "I was with a photographer and the landlady showed us the diary. I phoned the *Star* and they said to send it to the library. So I put it in the mail. It was all so stupid. There was nothing in the diary of any use anyway," said Angela.

Newsy Women

With that behind her, the next year, June, 1954, the *Canadian Women's Press Club*, a dynamic force in the age of print, conferred on Angela the prestigious Memorial Award for her story about "Mamie, wife of President Eisenhower." Angela wrote in *Mistress of the White House,* "Judging from her performance to date, there seems no pretense to the U.S.A's top chatelaine and it's unlikely she'll play the grand dame role as did some of her predecessors." This profile appeared in *Star Weekly*, the *Star's* Saturday magazine devoted to pictures and features. After the press club awards' ceremony, the *Star* reported that "Miss Burke's story was the outcome of a chatty interview, in Washington, with the president's wife about her new life as presidential wife." The *Star* burbled on about Angela being "Janie-on-the-spot" when other prominent women hit the headlines. It told readers that Angela had interviewed Madame St. Laurent (wife of Canadian Prime Minister Louis St. Laurent) and also an Indigenous woman in Saskatchewan who took up her gun and warned male predators to keep off her trapping preserves. Miss Burke chartered an aircraft and flew to the hinterland to interview the aging Annie Oakley."

Angela also covered several royal tours, the bane of lady reporters along with the wedding beat. "Covering them was stupid. The information was totally controlled. But I liked the Queen Mother and the Duchess of Kent. I did a long tour with her."

Angela also covered the Princess Margaret Rose and Group Captain Peter Townsend romance. Stupid or not, the world was enthralled with royalty and in the '50s readers lapped up every word concerning the progress of Princess Margaret's love affair with Townsend. Would she marry Townsend or not? Townsend was an older man, but the biggest stumbling block was his divorce.

Angela was sent to London to observe the nuances of the romance. For a week in October, 1955, Angela filed daily from England. She reported in one story that Townsend had met with Margaret for the sixth straight day. "This time he didn't use the back door, but drove in boldly through the front gate of Clarence House, Margaret's official residence. Five minutes later, Queen Mother Elizabeth left by car, through the exit nearest Buckingham Palace, leading to speculation that she was consulting with Queen Elizabeth, who returned today from Scotland."

"Townsend had been very close to her father, King George. And it was obvious Princess Margaret met him before he divorced his wife," Angela said. "They were very much in love. It was really sad."

The next day, Angela's copy let *Star* readers know that everyone was anxious for "officialdom" to make a specific statement regarding the Princess's future. "Yesterday it was tea for two at Clarence House. Protocol, surrounding the Princess's meetings with the Group Captain, has been much curtailed. No lady-in-waiting accompanied Margaret when she dined with Peter at the home of the newly married Bonham Carters (parents of actress Helena Bonham Carter) the other night."

The cheap British press was really something, according to Angela.

"Once, Margaret and Townsend were in a country house and the London dailies were on a vigil. One reporter said to me, there's Peter standing in front of the fireplace and he's saying such-and-such. And then Margaret says so-and-so. Do you know he made it up—the whole conversation and there it was the next day in his paper printed as truth," said Angela, still in shock decades later.

On October 31, 1955, after reams of purple prose purveyed by the press corps and much soul-searching by Princess Margaret, HRH announced that she had given up Townsend for God and country. Townsend went into exile and married a Belgian woman. The former lovers did not see each other again until Margaret invited Townsend to dine with her two years before his death in 1994. After a tragic and debauched life, Princess Margaret Rose died in 2002 at age seventy-one.

Newsgirls

There is nothing glamorous about this type of assignment as Angela knows from experience. This brand of celebrity reporting involves a gaggle of reporters huddled for hours outside prohibited gates, hoping for some tidbit that can be used to frame a story. Things have changed somewhat from Angela's time. Today, rather than newshounds skulking around behind the shrubbery, there are photographers with high-tech equipment. In a world where the visual is all, the paparazzi now stake out the celebrities.

So fierce was competition among the different news' publications. Reporters of Angela's vintage were driven to get the story—at any price. As a result, reporting was only for the fit. Angela paints a picture of physically demanding working conditions both at home and abroad.

"In the Toronto newsroom, we worked on the oldest and rottenest (manual) typewriters. We'd yell 'copy boy' and wave the pages and he would come running and grab them and take them to the city desk. But when I travelled, I carried a little *Olivetti*. I would write out the first five paragraphs and then run to a telegraph office. Then the copy would be teletyped to Guy Birch, the telegraph editor. The copy had to be on the desk by 6:30 a.m. to make the first edition. By seven, they were panicky because the type had to be set by hand. Sometimes on a breaking story, I'd telephone, re-write and dictate it. I'd shout 'open your line.'"

It was essential when there was a breaking story to get it to the news desk for the bulldog edition, even if it was inaccurate and partly made up. This didn't matter. What did matter was the *Star* beating the *Telegram* and the *Globe and Mail*. The bulldog hit the Toronto streets shortly after midnight. Because there were five or six editions of the newspapers, daily, errors could be fixed, facts added, and details clarified as the day went on. The *Toronto Telegram* and the *Star* vied every night to be the first with any important snippet.

Politics

Despite Angela's off-putting *Globe* experience with municipal politics, a decade later Angela found herself quite fascinated with local and national politics and, during her *Star* years, she had a chance to meet many prominent politicians.

"I found politics great fun. Once I was sent to Elliot Lake. They had found uranium there and Dennison mines were just opening. There was a press train going for the occasion. I met Lester Pearson there. He had left external affairs and was the Member of Parliament for the area. Prime Minister of Canada was still in his future. Pearson was distressed because you couldn't get a drop of anything to drink. He knew I knew a lot of miners because I was from Timmins, so I was asked to find some drink."

Angela used her connections and after a pal visited the local bootlegger on her behalf, she arrived at the hotel where all the VIPs were dining with enough hooch to liven up the whole affair well into the night. There was a large group at the dinner and it was all quite jolly and wonderful, according to Angela. She remembered Pearson as "a delightful person and full of fun." But with his high-pitched voice and lumpy appearance, Angela admitted none of his bonhomie came through when he appeared in public as Prime Minister.

Angela started one story she filed from Elliot Lake on October 3, 1957, with a question. "What's everybody doing in Toronto. This is the town where killings are being made." She went on to tell readers that the motto of the uranium-boom town is "get-rich-quick."

"Two years ago nothing was here but wilderness and a few drill holes. Today a town has exploded, overrun with thousands of miners and construction workers with bulging pockets. Doctors are pulling in money by the shovelfuls. So is the only dentist who works in a trailer, for space is at a premium. So are the two young lawyers, both young and well on the road to early retirement. In six months they've made as much as they would ordinarily make in six years in the city."

"I also did a stint in the press gallery in Ottawa," explained Angela, flashing a press card printed with the Canadian coat-of-arms and the date, 1957. "I would write a positive story about the Conservative party and because the *Star* was Liberal, it would be on Page 8 instead of Page 1. Finally, an editor pointed out to me if I wrote negative stories about the Tories or concentrated on Liberal stories, I would be on page 1. But I didn't care. He said 'as long as you know.'"

However, Angela did her fair share of Liberal stories and even covered the Liberal

> Person did become leader of the Liberal Party and, in 1963, he was elected Canada's Prime Minister.

Convention in January 1958 where her old drinking buddy, Lester Pearson, was running for party leader against Paul Martin, father of Paul Martin Jr., who became Prime Minister from 2003-2006. After Prime Minister Louis St. Laurent delivered his retirement speech on January 14 in front of 2,500 Liberals, the race was on. Besides the two top contenders, there were two other men vying to lead the Liberals.

Before and during the Liberal Convention, Angela interviewed the wives of the four candidates and painted a verbal picture of each woman that is a revealing portrait of the role of political wives in the 1950s.

Angela spoke with Maryon Pearson in her home weeks before Pearson was flying to Oslo to collect his Nobel Peace Prize for establishing an international police force to resolve the 1956 Suez Crisis. This was the United Nations' first peace keeping mission.

The interview took place just before Pearson announced his candidacy for party leadership. Readers were told that the good wife and model homemaker, Mrs. Pearson, knitted throughout the interview. Angela described Mrs. Pearson as the "second diplomat in the Pearson home who trod the tightrope with nary a lurch as she finessed questions about her husband's political prospects. Queried about a predicted victory for her husband as Liberal leader at the January convention, Mrs. P. didn't even admit that her husband would be a candidate. 'I live from day to day,' she said with a smile, 'and I face these things just as they occur.'"

While the Liberal convention was in full swing, Angela reported that the first words Paul Martin uttered to delegates after finishing his elect-me speech were "How was it, Mother?"

"Being called mother, isn't that awful?" remarked Martin's forty-four-year-old wife Nell, with a broad smile. "I said to him it's one of the best speeches, you've ever made," quoted Angela.

And what of the two wives of the "low men on the totem pole" in that Liberal race? Angela described Mrs. Don Mackay of Calgary and Mrs. Lloyd Henderson of Portage La Prairie, in print for all the world to read, as "two of the most understanding, loyal little women in the country." Angela continued, "Neither of these two women can be described as overly ambitious and have no desire to live at 24 Sussex Dr., but they have no intention of puncturing their husbands' balloons." Angela also reported that Mrs. Mackay was caught early in the day "buoying her husband up as he sat like a busted bronco rider in his hotel room." And poor Mrs. Henderson was observed, still up at midnight, keeping the home fires burning as she waited for her husband to finish a long day of "button-holing delegates."

Angela also allotted some ink to Mrs. Gwendolyn Blair (*Bubbles* to her friends), secretary to the *Federation of Liberal Women*. The cute headline above Angela's story, written by a *Star* desker, read "Bubbles Wants Women at Liberal Convention: 'Twitterers' Has-Beens."

Bubbles, a budding feminist, told Angela that the convention is going "to give birth to a new type of being: women political wheels." Angela explained to be sure, "Bubbles does not mean the ladies are planning to put up a female candidate, but Mrs. Blair thinks it's high time Canadian women took their politics seriously." According to Angela's copy, Bubbles believed "that women are finally growing up to their responsibilities and today there are fewer *twitterers*. Women are realizing that politics concern them and their families. Today we have a tremendous number of women who would be excellent Members of Parliament, but people still worry about women candidates. So, when a well-established man comes along, the woman, no matter how able, is shoved aside."[8]

Unfortunately, Mrs. Blair offered no solutions.

Angela also reported some pre-election shenanigans. She recounted a delightful story about two geese Pearson auctioned off at a fundraiser for the Ottawa Philharmonic Orchestra. Apparently, the first goose only fetched $7, so Pearson took his trademark bowtie off and put it on the second gander's neck and it brought in $21. During the Liberal convention, the farmer who bought the geese had "Lester B." parading around his barnyard sporting the bowtie to show who he was voting for.[9]

> It was worth nothing that Bubbles Blair was using the word "twitters," fifty years before "Twitter," "tweeting" and "twittering" came into the E-word vocabulary.

Ottawa Beat

While in Ottawa, Angela filed dozens of other stories ranging from the revolutionary to the nutty, such as a piece published on November 23, 1957, about an Ottawa engineer who operated a flying saucer observation centre for the government. He told Angela that he believed that Canadians could be descendants of men and women from outer space.

That same month, Angela also reported that the Post Master General predicted that within five years, post offices across Canada will be equipped with machines to sort letters, read addresses and "in fact, do everything except walk down the street and make door-to-door deliveries." She also wrote "If you're a postal employee there's no need for panic. Mr. Hamilton says growth of mail is so rapid employees can be easily absorbed while bringing in machines with brains."

Interestingly, Angela made a big deal about Hamilton's "afflictions that doubtlessly would have vanquished most of us." She described him in this news story as a "slight man, badly crippled from birth." She underlined Hamilton's physical disability by telling readers that his father won a gold medal in the 1908 Olympics.

In the 1950s, television interviews were not wide spread and circuses like CNN weren't even dreamed of and neither was *political correctness*. Canadians had virtually one television channel and instant photographs were a technology of the future. As a result, it was *de rigueur* for reporters to describe a person's looks. Often, they were not flattering. Throughout her career, Angela described hundreds of women as plump, but being nice, Angela always added "pretty." Another government pundit also made a prediction in 1957. Donald Snowden of the *Department of National Affairs* announced that the new-fangled invention freeze-drying, would send droves of young Canadians to the Arctic. Snowden showed Angela a pound of raw beef in a cellophane bag that looked "like a thick block of porous wood." Snowden said, "this piece of beef could change living in the Arctic. It keeps a year and can weather any temperature."

Angela commented, "he visualizes the Arctic as a vast mining camp. Within ten years he predicts it will be one of Canada's most potent tourist attractions." Snowden also refuted the "foolish fallacy" that the Canadian Arctic is useless to Canada and, with the enthusiasm of a dreamer, he made a delightful jump in logic. He told Angela the freeze-drying process was sure to attract a flood of people who would start mines in the Arctic over the next few decades. But the whole thing hinged on the little woman. "When the housewife knows she can prepare the same type of meal in a comfortable home, she's not going to object to living up there." [10]

Angela confessed, while she savoured national politics, she was never interested in those of the newsroom and she took very little interest in her fellow reporters. She didn't socialize, mainly because she was involved romantically with a lawyer at the time. Angela's lack of social camaraderie was unusual in the tight-knit little newspaper world of Toronto, where wordsmiths flitted from one newspaper to the other and back again. The local newsrooms were rift with love affairs and infidelities. Many bloomed at the old Press Club, adjacent to the Lord Simcoe Hotel (on York St.), where mottled newshounds chug-a-lugged gallons of rye whisky.

Everybody from the era remembered *Toronto Star* reporter Marjorie Earl's obsession with Alf Tate, a raffish newspaperman, who disappeared in 1955. He flew into the eye of a hurricane while on a *Star* assignment in the Caribbean. "Marjorie was in love with Alf Tate. He'd whistle and she would crumble and walk out to meet him," said Angela.

Cathy Smyth, in the women's department at the time, described Marjorie, who, along with Angela, was one of the three female reporters in news, as the "biggest bitch on wheels." "She was always mad about everything—always hard done by. She was a big, big woman with a space between her front teeth. She always wore a black suit. She was the big newspaper woman with PRESS tattooed between her eyes. She had this tough manner, but when A.O. Tate called out, she would melt."

Ben Rose, a colleague of both Angela and Earl, remembered Angela as a very good reporter, "But she wasn't considered hard-nosed like Marjorie Earl. She was more of a feature reporter and much more feminine than most women in the newsroom," he said.

For the record, although Earl was not charming she had other strengths. She was a founding member, along with six men, of the Newspaper Guild at the *Toronto Star*.[11]

After 185 people signed up to unionize the *Toronto Star* newsroom, in November, 1948, Local 87 of the Newspaper Guild was certified by the Ontario Labour Relations Board. The new guild was represented by Marjorie Earl and Ben Rose, along with financial editor Beland Honderich, city editor Borden Spears, Dennis Braithwaite, Charles Crissey and Joe Beauclerc.

Touring Canada

In 1959, Angela landed a honey of an assignment thanks to her cheerleader, Hindmarsh. She was instructed to pick a family in each province and to write about their lives. The "How Canada Lives" series ran in *Star Weekly* through the spring and summer of that year. In British Columbia, Angela interviewed a "fruit" family outside of Vancouver who were very upset about the importation of cheap American apples that ripened earlier in the season than theirs. In Alberta, she visited a family of Mormons who made millions when oil was discovered on their farm. In New Brunswick, she delved into the lives of a fishing family on Grand Manan, and in Prince Edward Island, she visited potato farmers.

"I could choose whoever I wanted to interview. I went with photographer Norm James and filed from every little hamlet in this country. In Pelican Narrows, in Saskatchewan, I even ran into Trent Frayne's mother. He was a stringer for the *Star*," recalled Angela.

In Three Mile Plain, Nova Scotia, Angela interviewed the Upshaws, one of Nova Scotia's 10,000 "coloured families." Angela describes sitting at the kitchen table with Gertie Upshaw when her husband Norm "came through the door and placed his full lunch pail on the counter" and announced, "we're on strike." In her article, Angela talked about tough times in Nova Scotia for everybody and described how families, like theirs, managed in that society "despite prejudice."[12]

Angela also visited Newfoundland where she interviewed the family of a dragger fisherman who had just moved to Fortune on the mainland from an island twelve miles off shore where there were only three families. "I loved Newfoundland, but I had to hire an interpreter to go with me to the outports and to talk to people like the Millers because I couldn't understand a word they said. Imagine, Fortune only had 1,500 people at the time, but that family was absolutely lost and overwhelmed."

Then one day, in 1959, Angela up and quit the *Star*.

"I liked what I did and I was happy at the *Star*. But I had no executive ambition. We worked and filed six times a day from everywhere. I never intended to stay at the *Star*. After twelve years, I got tired of writing. I left the *Star* just like that and went into television," she said.

> Frayne was a sportswriter and husband of June Callwood, another prominent *Newsgirl*.

A New Path

But before her move to the visual medium, Angela got her own back in print for all the royal tours she was forced to traipse through. Angela wrote a vitriolic column for *Maclean's* magazine that created a national furor. In it, she criticized both the Canadian people for their unquestioning veneration of the Royal family and the "gobbledy-gook" written and broadcasted by the press.

"As a newspaper writer who contributed to the royal myth for years, who covered and travelled with principal members of the royal family, I have never ceased to be amazed at the voraciousness of the national appetite for the Niagara of royal trivia that gushes forth particularly during royal visits," wrote Angela.

Angela accused the press of delivering "paeans of praise and flattery" and "naive hosannas" on the basis of no information. She also observed, after weeks of seeing Princess Margaret on a Canadian tour every waking minute, she had "not one indication of the Princess's interests, character or opinions."

Angela told Canadian readers it was time court advisors dispelled the shroud of mystery and false glamour that the royal family are kept in. Angela also attacked the outlay of hundreds of thousands of dollars to promote royal tours and editors who deleted from copy observations even the slightest controversial in nature. After tearing a strip off Prince Philip as "inaccessible and antagonistic" to the press, while being wined and dined out of the public purse, she advocated "junking" the belief that Canadians want to read about royals "to relieve their dull little lives."[13]

The year was 1959 when Angela's rant was printed by *Maclean's* editor Ralph Allen—a brave editorial decision in the days of the British Commonwealth, Orange Protestant parades and the Union Jack. "My comment was definitely anti-royal family. People were horrified. This was iconoclastic stuff," commented Angela.

Newsgirls

Angela's column opened the floodgates of anti-royal sentiment and two other ladies of the press hopped on the bandwagon. A few weeks after the May issue of *Maclean's* appeared, Joyce Davidson, hostess of CBC TV's *Tabloid*, tried the same thing on television and was fired. Davidson was a guest on the *Today Show* in New York the morning Queen Elizabeth and Prince Philip arrived on Canadian shores. Apparently, the hapless Davidson said that she was indifferent to the royal couple and she believed most Canadians were as well. There was a general hue and cry across the country, led by Toronto's Mayor, Nathan Phillips, and Davidson was asked to leave the show—her career in tatters. Davidson did pick up the pieces and continued to work as a talking head in both American and Canadian television into the 1980s. Toronto freelancer June Callwood (Chapter 4) wrote a piece, similar to Angela's for *Look* magazine, a popular American publication, and survived.

Angela was thirty-nine when she left the *Star* and lovely in a Doris Day kind-of-way. She went to North Bay for two months where she worked at the local television station before auditioning for a spot with CBC-TV Ottawa. After the test, Angela landed a job as hostess-interviewer of *Afternoon Edition*, a twice-weekly women's show. This stint lasted for two seasons (1960-61) and featured a cooking class with Madame Jehanne Benoît, Canada's first celebrity TV chef. In the meantime, Angela was trolling around for other opportunities and hooked up with MacLaren's Advertising Agency. She left black and white TV and headed for Montreal, where her accounts included the Tea Council of Canada, Five Roses Flour and Chateau-Gai wine. She was also director of publicity for Bruno's Schools of Design, the National Ballet and the Amsterdam Tourist Association.

But her best gig was with the *Jolly Jumper* company. The company circulated a publicity shot of Angela with blonde bouffant, sleeveless sheath and the perfect pearls, kneeling beside an Indigenous baby, tricked out in fringed buckskin papoose garb and hanging in a Jolly Jumper. The Jolly Jumper was brand new. The inventor, Judith Poole, a Vancouver grandmother, based it on a West coast Indigenous baby-care device. Poole's company, on the verge of bankruptcy in 1958, was bought by Pat Ryan who sent Angela on a tour of the United States and Canada to flog the contraption. Angela spoke to radio and television audiences about babies' need for exercise and mothers' need for relaxation. The Jolly Jumper promotional material claimed it was "a scientific baby exerciser" that solved both these problems. The most famous baby to be photographed in a Jumper was John John Kennedy, son of U.S. president John Kennedy.

Angela stayed with the advertising agency for five years. In 1966, her career path changed, again, and Angela became part of the team that propelled the *Royal Commission for the Status of Women*.

By 1966 Canadian feminists had mobilized, spurred on by Betty Friedan and Simone Beauvoir. Even the boys in Ottawa couldn't ignore this social phenomenon, especially after women threatened to march on Ottawa demanding equal rights and wages. At this point, Prime Minister Lester Pearson saw the writing on the wall and appointed a commission to find out what the girls were fussing about. The designated chairman was Florence Bird, a fifty-nine-year-old Toronto CBC broadcaster who worked under the name Anne Francis. Bird, an American by birth and education, later landed a (Liberal) seat in the Canadian senate.

In December, 1967, Bird declared "We'd better stop thinking in terms of men's jobs and women's jobs and start building a society where everybody is judged on merit."

Angela had come to Bird's attention after she organized a seminar for media women in December, 1966, in Toronto. This seminar was designed to alert female writers and broadcasters to the scale of public activities planned for 1967; Canada's Centennial Year.

"The commission got very bad press for a while. It was an anathema to the press. It was a laughing stock. At one point, among the men I knew in newspapers, only Marty Goodman (*Toronto Star* managing editor) was very supportive. We got fair coverage at the *Star* in hard news, not from the women's department."

The commission organized hearings and travelled across the country. Angela remembered the first hearing in Victoria as somewhat of a disaster. A female professor from the University of Victoria stood up and advocated vasectomies for men. "This was a brand-new word; we didn't

---

Florence Bird (1908-998) was a Liberal supporter as was Angela Burke. Bird received the Order of Canada in 1971 and later rewarded with a seat in the Canadian senate (1971-1983).

know what it meant, but when it came out, you can image the sensation it caused in the press. It was important to have the press on our side. My job was to see that positive stories got into the paper," Angela said.

In 1982, long after the commission was a memory, Bird told a reporter that the commission "attempted to make an in-depth sociological study of the situation of Canadian women and to foresee the way society would be in the future." And indeed, it did. The commission made 465 recommendations to the Federal Government and the provinces designed to give Canadian women equal opportunity. In the next fifteen years, two-thirds of the recommendations were implemented, thus guaranteeing equality.

After the commission filed its report, women were up and running in careers and the professions known as "male dominant" and Angela decided to bow out. Meanwhile, Angela found love and married Richard Kerrigan in 1972, a classmate from her McGill days, and relocated in Montreal. At the time of these interviews, Angela Burke Kerrigan was living comfortably in Knowlton, Quebec, as tuned into news-making events as she ever was. She died on September 30, 2014. She was ninety-three.

An obituary in the *Globe and Mail* was published October 31, 2014, although nobody in Toronto Star newsroom recognized Angela Burke's name. After a call to the news desk, M.E. Michael Cooke assigned a junior reporter to cobble together a much-delayed in memoriam that appeared on November 3, 2014.

MARILYN DUNLOP
Toronto Telegram, 1949-1953. Toronto Daily Star, 1965-1992.

1928-Present

> "They had to get someone to do the dumb things guys wouldn't do. We were always doing crazy things. Another time...I had to drive a huge bus in February of 1953. The male editors thought it was hilarious for women to drive big vehicles."

As a teenager in London, Ontario, Marilyn Dunlop worked one summer writing wedding announcements for the women's pages of the *London Free Press*. It was there, over photographs of smiling brides, she fell in love with the newspaper business and set her cap for a job on a daily paper. In 1949, this ambition became a reality when Marilyn landed a job at the old *Toronto Telegram*.

By the time Marilyn had officially retired after forty-three years in the newspaper business, she had garnered a *National Newspaper Award* for her 1987 story about the first laser brain surgery, performed at the Toronto Western Hospital, and four *Canadian Science Writers Association* awards, including one for a feature about cancer research in 1983. Besides filing daily newspaper stories, Marilyn also found time to author three books on medical subjects.[1]

Marilyn Bell Dunlop was born in Detroit in 1928. There were no jobs in Ontario, so her Canadian parents had moved to the U.S. where her father, James Bell, found work as a travelling salesman for a brick company. When Marilyn was three, the Bells moved to Toronto and later on another job opportunity took the Bells to London. "Until my purse was stolen, I kept my American birth certificate in it. It said on it, '*Dear Baby: Welcome to the City of Detroit.*' It was charming," Marilyn said in a 1998 Interview.

James Bell had served in the Canadian Army during World War I and was gassed at Passchendaele, Belgium, in 1917. His brother was killed at Vimy Ridge the same year. Marilyn's adored father died in 1942 from pneumonia, his lungs weakened by the German mustard gas attacks when he was a young soldier. He was forty-nine when he died and Marilyn, fourteen. This left Florence Duffy Bell, Marilyn's gentle mother, to fend for herself and her only child. After her husband's death, Florence sold his car for $500. Most of this money was eaten up by the funeral expenses.

Before her marriage, Florence, whose nickname was *Fluffy Duffy*, had completed teacher training at the Normal School in Hamilton, Ontario. When widowed, she decided not to teach, but thanks to a friend, found work in a London bank. Florence turned out to be anything but fluffy and quickly moved up the ranks to management. When the war ended in 1945 and the warriors returned, Florence was just as quickly replaced by a demobbed bank employee and that was the end of her stellar rise in the financial hierarchy. Marilyn's mother had no option but to accept a lesser job as a teller. Ultimately, Florence was in charge of safety security boxes, a job she performed until retirement.

Newsgirls

In the post-war days, the Canadian *Charter of Rights* wasn't even a dream and there was no such concept as equal pay for equal work and no form of social assistance existed. As a result, people did what they had to do to survive. Marilyn helped out. During her high-school years in the winter months, she had a part-time job at Reitman's, the ladies' wear store. At the end of the war, she would ride in a truck with a gang of young people to pick crops in the surrounding farms.

After high school, Marilyn Bell enrolled in the new journalism course at the University of Western Ontario in London where one of Marilyn's instructors was the remarkable Isabel Turnbull Dingman, herself a print pioneer. Dingman had started her career at the *Winnipeg Free Press* in the 1920s. By 1932, she was social editor of the *Regina Leader-Post*. When she married, Miss Turnbull had to leave the paper as married and pregnant women were not allowed to hold jobs. She went East with her husband and, in 1936, created a column for the *Globe and Mail* called *Mrs. Thompson Advises*. It ran until 1960. Meanwhile, Dingman was hired at the UWO in 1948 as an associate professor in the journalism program—a new faculty launched in 1945. Dingman taught at the university until she retired in 1959. Three weeks before her death, in 1969, Dingman threw a party for the London branch of the *Canadian Women's Press Club*. Post mortem, the London newsgirls established a UWO bursary in journalism in her memory.

Isabel and James Dingman's daughter, Jocelyn Dingman, was the first wife of National Post columnist Robert Fulford.

Landing in a Newsroom

After Marilyn graduated in 1949 with her degree, her first newspaper job at the *Toronto Telegram* didn't just land in her lap. She knew what she was gunning for. A *rara avis*, Marilyn was only one of three girls from her graduating class who tried to break into journalism. "Helen Allen was the women's editor at the *Toronto Telegram*. I came down to Toronto to see her and discovered she was at a Tory convention at the Royal York Hotel, interviewing George Drew's wife. But there was no way I could get in to see her because I didn't have a badge," recalled Marilyn.

No problem. This enterprising young woman spotted a reporter from the *London Free Press* who was dead drunk. Marilyn simply took his lapel badge and walked into the convention floor. She rooted out Allen and asked for a job. Allen told Marilyn she would let her know. When Marilyn didn't hear anything, she wrote a terrible doggerel poem. Allen read it and was so amused, she offered Marilyn a job. It was still the 1940s so naturally it was the *Women's Section* at the *Telegram* for Marilyn. There she was confronted, like most female cub reporters of her generation, with "pages, pages and more pages of columns of weddings, weddings and more weddings." But Marilyn had her foot in the door and, in retrospect, she appreciates the experience gleaned from Allen. Under her tutelage, Marilyn learned to make-up pages by hand in the back shop during the days when lead type was in use and five editions of a newspaper landed on the street every day.

Helen Allen (1907-2006) joined the *Toronto Telegram* in 1929 and worked there for forty years. Her biggest claim to fame is the *Today's Child* column, launched in 1964. It was based on the revolutionary premise that handicapped children were worthy of adoption. Each day, Allen would highlight a child with some *imperfection*. As a result of this column, Allen was credited with changing the public's attitude towards disabled children. In 1967, Prime Minister Lester Pearson cited Allen as *Canada's Mother of the Year* and in 1971 was inducted into the *Order of Canada*. After the *Telegram* folded in 1971, the *Toronto Star* continued Allen's column.

Right off the bat in 1949, Marilyn won the *Junior Canadian Women's Press Club* award and $100 (Marilyn cannot remember what the story was about) and after a year of tulle, gardenias and the Granite Club, she moved to *City* as a general assignment reporter. By then, Marilyn was making $30 a week, up $5 from her starting salary. She paid $8 weekly for a room in a sorority house on St. George St. Marilyn and shared this with another girl from London. Her friend worked as a secretary, a job that paid $35 a week or $1,820 annually.

It's Interesting to compare Marilyn's wage to 2015 when annual salaries for Canadian reporters ranged from $45,000 to $65,000.

When Marilyn arrived at *City*, there were a few women in the newsroom. Besides Allen, there was Dorothy Howarth, referred to as "The Sponge" by city editor Doug MacFarlane because she soaked up every detail of a news story; Pearl McCarthy (1895-1964), the art critic; and Phyllis Griffith (1905-1978), who was on the photo desk.

Marilyn Dunlop

"I was delighted. At last I was covering spot news. One time, because I was Marilyn Bell then, I had a request from the *Toronto Star* to sign my name for them so they could put it on a story about the swimmer Marilyn Bell and call it a first-person story," said Marilyn, the reporter. She added that in those days, competition was so fierce between the dailies that scruples didn't matter. The name-of-the-game was to get the story first and to captivate those readers.

In Marilyn's novice years in the 1950s, women did not wear trousers to work. Marilyn wore cotton dresses in the summer and skirts and suits in the winter and always stockings and pumps—not clumsy running shoes like today.

Once in "spot" news, it seems as if Marilyn, a tall, leggy girl with a big toothpaste smile, never got out of a swimsuit.

Cheesecake

She laughingly held up one cute bathing suit picture after another, all published in the *Tely* during her early days there. "The first time I walked into the newsroom, Doug MacFarlane said 'Can you swim? Good, then you're water skiing at the CNE this afternoon.'"

Marilyn had never been on water skis before. On the day of the assignment, the water in Lake Ontario was 11° Celsius and her period had just started. No matter. There she was on the top of a page of the old pink *Telegram* whizzing by the Canadian National Exhibition Grand Stand, partnered by a Greek-god clone from Florida's Cypress Gardens.

Another time, the *Telegram* published a series of three pictures showing Marilyn in a one-piece bathing suit, á la Esther Williams, attempting log rolling at the Toronto Sportsman Show. Readers see her falling off a log, clambering back on and, in the third shot, hitting the drink again. The headline on Marilyn's story reads: *Log Starts Spinning, Lady Goes Swimming*. Marilyn good-naturedly started her story: "Just how easy is 'easy as rolling off a log?' Believe me, I know. I've just rolled off one, umpteen times today."

That same summer, our cub reporter acquired a pair of short-shorts after a man appeared at the office in shorts. Marilyn was assigned to walk down Bay St., Toronto's staid financial stronghold, in the scanty garment trailed by a photographer. In 1951, a woman in shorts was nothing less than shocking and it was unthinkable in *Toronto the Good* for any girl with self-respect to "go downtown" without hat, gloves and pearls. The photographer's job was to capture the reaction of men passing Marilyn. As a result, *Telegram* readers enjoyed several cheesecaky pictures of Marilyn, including a rear shot of her trim bottom. In the photos or "art," as it's referred to in newsrooms, Marilyn may have on canary yellow shorts, but she is still carrying her Queen Mother-style handbag—a lovely touch—and for modesty's sake, she is wearing a turtle neck with long sleeves.

The "shorts are short, but looks are long," said a cutline written by some clever copy editor. "Men Whistle, Clerics Don't Look and Women Tsk," he continued, referring to a gaggle of young women in frocks and proper pumps who are shown looking askance at the *Tely's* eye-candy.

In her story, Marilyn put a light spin on this experience. She told readers "Shorts are not the thing to wear if you wish to remain cool, collected and unflustered. They attract attention on downtown streets—but no more attention than a hat with a whirling dervish on top. Oh, there were a few whistles. Thanks a lot, fellas! And one goggling truck driver nearly dumped his load of gravel on a TTC trolley. Two parcel-laden ladies looked at me, looked at each other and clucked their tongues and three soldiers suggested I join them."

In this fluffy piece (called a *brightener* in newspaperese), Marilyn also described the commotion when she hit the *Telegram* in her shorts. "Frankly, I didn't know so many men worked in the building. The newsroom sounded like a baseball game in which the umpire was taking an awful beating. Don't know what's the matter with those guys. The girls didn't make all that fuss when the man arrived in shorts," she wrote, concluding that she would now wear a skirt down to her ankles.

Marilyn, to this day, has a glossy photograph of fellow reporter Dorothy Howarth and herself, clad in two-piece bathing suits that they didn't quite fill out. The suits were borrowed

---

Interestingly, the same day Marilyn's log-rolling piece appeared, the *Telegram* headline said: "City Asks $10 Million More Ontario Grants." The obvious question arises: has anything changed in Toronto's squabble with the province in almost seventy years?

By the way, on the same page as Marilyn's reportage, Lawrence Motors advertised a red fully-equipped Ford convertible for $2,695. The paper also reported that King Farouk of Egypt won $30,000 at a casino in San Remo and King George VI, who had been convalescing at Sandringham, would return to London for his first official engagement since May. Also, a third case of polio was confirmed on a Royal Canadian Navy ship, according to the *Telegram*.

from *Miss Toronto* 1950. "The beauty contest was a big deal in those days and the judging always took place at the Police Games at the CNE. Dorothy, thirty-seven at the time, and I, twenty-two, were sent out to interview Ruby Mann, *Miss Toronto*, for a big feature for Monday's paper. She lived near St. Catherine's, by the lake. It was a sweltering Sunday and we borrowed suits to have a swim. But before we went into the water, we put her banner over us. We didn't take winning the contest as a serious achievement. We were poking fun at it. I don't think Ruby appreciated our laughing," Marilyn said.

Marilyn admits to learning a lot about reporting from Howarth, a veteran with a *National Newspaper Award* under belt. Marilyn recalled, Howarth was always asking stupid questions. So one day she asked Howarth why. "I thought you only asked what you didn't know. Dorothy explained that she asked the most obvious things to capture a subject's personality. She wanted to hear the subject's own words. She had no qualms about making herself sound dumb. As a result, she made people come alive in her stories."

The photogenic Marilyn was sent out, yet again, to the CNE. This time, she was assigned to write about a collection of famous jewels worth $15 million that were on display in celebration of the Exhibition's 75th anniversary. Marilyn faced the camera wearing a strapless evening gown, a diamond tiara, an assortment of other opulent jewels and a million-dollar smile. On the front page the next day, readers saw a photo that not only featured Marilyn in her finery, but a guard aiming his gun in the region of her head in 1953. Another assignment called for the pert Marilyn to interview Francis X Bushman, an aging star from the era of silent movies. The *Telegram* photographer snapped Marilyn in Bushman's clutches in the time-honored swing-kiss pose, favoured by Hollywood matinee idols.

"They had to get someone to do the dumb things guys wouldn't do. We were always doing crazy things. Another time, I had to drive a huge bus in February of 1953. The male editors thought it was hilarious for women to drive big vehicles," commented Marilyn. Predictably, the *Tely* printed a picture of Marilyn with pony-tail in the driver's seat of a truck as "a frenzied" male pedestrian flees for his life.

"The *Star* and the *Telegram* were always trying to out-do each other for reader attention. In many ways, it was an innocent time and everyone got a big kick out of nonsense stories. It was fun and crazy. We didn't think it was exploitive. It gave the reader a laugh. It was entertainment. I was young and I had a wonderful time at the *Telegram*," said Marilyn, who is as full of good humour and energy as she ever was.

Marilyn did admit if she had been puffy and pimply, she wouldn't have been plastered all over the paper in shorts and swimsuits.

Peter Dunlop was the lucky *Telegram* photographer often assigned to photograph the attractive Marilyn and within two years of her arrival at the paper in 1951, they married. While the Dunlops were on honeymoon in Fort Lauderdale, Marilyn filed another bathing suit story, accompanied by the usual cheeky glam photos.

In April 1953, the *Telegram* assigned Marilyn to test a bathing suit with built-in buoyancy. It was modelled after a life-saving device used by the British navy during World War II. Marilyn wittily wrote a hilarious copy in letter form. It started: "Dear Boss: Remember that story you sent me out on last Saturday. Guess you've been wondering what happened to me, eh? Well you can stop worrying. To make a long story short, I am in Florida. Couldn't seem to find a pool in Toronto. And the old bay is mighty cold this time of year. Had quite a time crossing the border. The immigration man asked what I was going to do in Florida and I told him I was going to write a story for a newspaper. You could see all sorts of things going through his mind—atomic explosions and defense secrets, but I told him it was about a bathing suit that you could swim in, even if you didn't know how to swim. Needless to say it took quite a while to cross the border."

After explaining her experiences, floating under the Florida sun in the suit, Marilyn closes with a plea, "It's a dandy help for teaching you to float alone. And speaking of floating a loan, do you suppose you could, or else I don't know quite how I am going to get back to Toronto. Buoyantly Yours, Marilyn."

The suit was a gimmick that didn't go anywhere. When it was inflated, it made the wearer look five months pregnant, according to Marilyn. Beside a photo of her floating in a Florida pool, the headline read: *She Floats And Gloats*.

Reality

Marilyn did manage to climb out of her bathing suit once in a while to produce some hard news stories, something she did as competently as her male colleagues. The explosion on the Canadian steam ship, *Noronic*, while it was docked at a Toronto pier, was a major story of 1949. Marilyn was still in the women's department and a cub reporter when she raced out into that September night to the scene of the burning *Noronic* at the foot of Bay St.

"At the sorority where I lived, we didn't have a phone in our room. It was down the hall. It rang in the middle of the night and I heard it. It was Art Holland who told me there was a big tragic fire and I was to get to the Royal York. Everybody was called out that night. A couple walked in like zombies. The women's eyes were extended with shock. They had been on the ship when it happened. I interviewed survivors and the paper set up a communications centre for relatives of the passengers," recalled Marilyn.

The *Noronic* fire broke out at about 1:40 a.m., September 17. The victims' corpses were sent to a make-shift morgue in the Horticultural Building on the Canadian National Exhibition grounds. There were 119 victims.

Up into the 1970s, Toronto was still a small town. Everyone read newspapers and the people that produced the news were an incestuous, cliquish lot. After the daily papers hit the street, newsies of all stripes met at the Press Club or *Radio Artists Club* on Bay St., just south of the *Telegram*'s offices at Bay and Melinda Streets.

The only items on the agenda at these establishments were hard drinking, camaraderie and industry gossip. If you wanted to know anything about romances, entanglements or scandals, the club bars were the places to be. Pals who regularly drank together, when it came to business, indulged in scurrilous personal rivalries for *The Big Scoop*. These hacks were egged on by demanding city editors who did not look kindly on a newsie who allowed the paper down the street to *skunk* them on a story. As a result in those hairy days, *lotsa* booze, puerile tricks and outrageous behaviour fueled the country's newsrooms and turned reporters into legends.

One of the classic stories, told by every old newshound in Toronto, revolved around the *Noronic* tragedy.

It seems the *Telegram*, with Marilyn's help, scooped the *Toronto Daily Star* on that one. There are several versions of the tale as to why the *Star* didn't immediately send out a team of reporters. It seems frisky *Star* reporters were always playing tricks on Fred Troyer, the night desker. In their cups, the playful *Star* boys would call Troyer and report a horrendous disaster and he would immediately deploy staff to cover the event, only to find it was a false alarm. The night the *Noronic* blew up, an inebriated Jim Hunt called in to report it and it turned out he had cried wolf once too often. Troyer chalked it up to another nocturnal prank. The worst of it was the *Noronic* was anchored closer to the *Star* newsroom than to the *Telegram*.

Meanwhile, although the *Star* had more resources and pictures of the *Noronic* disaster, the *Telegram* was first on the street with photographs and a report. Apparently, *Tely* photographer, Nels Quarrington, and reporter, Allen Kent, were returning downtown by car and saw a glow in the night sky. They investigated and filed the very first photos and eyewitness accounts.[2]

Jim Hunt didn't fare much better on another occasion after the *Noronic* debacle. Marilyn had been at the University of Western Ontario with Hunt, who was also a Londoner. "I was driving home with him for Christmas and near Ingersoll was an accident that killed a family of five. It was awful. Christmas presents everywhere. Anyway, we went to the nearest farmhouse to use a phone. We tossed to see who would get the phone first—ensuring a scoop. Jim won the toss and using the old *Star* trick, he held the line open so I couldn't use it. So I moseyed off to the hospital and by chance, the medical staff thought I was one of the family. They told me number five had died, a fact Jim didn't know. I called the *Tely* and it was the front page, black-line story.

On September 17, the *Toronto Star* ran seven pages of photographs with sensational captions such as "Fear Bay Hides Bodies Of Many Who Leap" and "They Died... Pitched Headlong on The Scorching Deck as They Fled For Life."

Interestingly, beside the 5th floor elevators at One Yonge St., the home of the *Toronto Star*, there was a framed front page featuring a *Noronic* explosion story with Edwin Feeney's byline. Feeney toiled at the *Star* for over forty years. When he was sixty-four, his editors decided he was incompetent and management leaned on him, just before his retirement age, until he had a nervous breakdown. This is just one of the many sordid stories told by the few old-timers who recall "the good old days" in the *Star* newsroom.

We did five editions in those days, and when the *Star* went to press early that morning, Jim's story missed the first edition," said Marilyn, still gleeful for winning one for her side in the never-ending war between the *Star* and *Telegram* for front page news breakers.

In retaliation and in a madcap gesture, the *Star's* Hunt sent MacFarlane, the *Telegram's* city editor, a bill for Marilyn's motel and gas expenses.

Marilyn told another story about a bus that plunged into a river near Cornwall, killing several people. MacFarlane hired an amphibian plane from the island airport to take photographic equipment, a photographer and a reporter to the scene.

"Bob Wong, who ran the airport, said that he only had room for the pilot, a photographer and his 400-pound wire photo machine. But when he saw me arrive—five foot, nine inches tall and seven months pregnant—he unloaded half the fuel. That meant we had to set down in Peterborough to refuel before getting to Cornwall," laughed Marilyn, adding she got a front-page story and they all arrived back in Toronto safely, "despite her extra passenger."

Time Out and Back into the Swim

Marilyn left the *Telegram* at the end of 1953, a month before her first baby was born. "After my four years at the *Tely*, they realized I was no longer a novelty you could toy with. They didn't make me quit. But in those days, there wasn't daycare and no one with children worked. So I stayed home for eleven years raising two children. But it broke my heart. I'd look at the paper and wish I could have covered this and that story," she said.

Then, out of the blue, Helen Palmer, the *Toronto Daily Star's* women's editor, asked if Marilyn could fill in for three months while one of her reporters went on maternity leave. Marilyn did, but felt she couldn't stay on because her son wasn't in school full-time yet. By 1964, when Marilyn was ready to go back to work, she realized her husband was a hopeless alcoholic and the marriage broke up. Luckily, *Star* city editor Jerry Towner, a friend of Marilyn's husband, took her on as a full-time general assignment reporter. Two years later, Marilyn was assigned a story that would change her life and career path and catapult her into the role of award-winning medical reporter.

Marilyn was sent to the *Hospital for Sick Children* to cover the separation of conjoined twins. "I was terrified," she recalled. "I was up against Joan Hollobon from the *Globe and Mail*, and Ken MacTaggart from the *Telegram*. Both were incredible medical writers and hardly any information was coming from the hospital."

Soon the enterprising Marilyn telephoned Dr. William Mustard, the heart surgeon on the team, and was able to get enough details to put an account together. Although she was assigned several scientific and medical stories over the next two years, she resisted offers to take over the medical beat. Finally, in 1968, Marilyn was pushed—kicking and screaming—into medical reporting. "When I finally said okay, I found myself at a meeting of cancer experts and I didn't even know what chemotherapy meant. I read medical books and journals like crazy. But for the first nine months, it was all a foreign language," she said.

Marilyn caught on to the lingo alright and she received her first award for medical reporting in 1974 from the *Canadian Science Writers' Association* for a series of articles describing how a team from Toronto's St. Michael's Hospital performed six operations in Hungary to demonstrate teamwork in open-heart surgery. In 1983, Marilyn wrote another award-winning series entitled *Medicare on its Sick-bed: Is There a Cure?* It was about the medical crises in Ontario. Four decades later, the same old stuff is still being debated by the public, and the press is still thrashing it out.

Marilyn's seven-part series started on a personal note. Marilyn, who was old enough to remember Canada before universal medical coverage, recalled that in the 1950's, her aunt had a serious heart condition that persisted over a long period and bills mounted up. When her aunt died, Marilyn's uncle was left with a huge medical debt. When he died some years later, the man went to his own grave with outstanding doctors' bills. Marilyn told *Star* readers that paying his wife's medical bills was a life-long burden on her uncle. Marilyn contrasted this scenario with one even closer to home. In 1967, Marilyn's son Doug underwent brain surgery. By then, Ontario had Medicare and the $12,000 tab for her son's treatment was picked up by the taxpayer. No longer were people destroyed by impossible medical bills, all thanks to the Canadian House of Commons passing *The National Medicare Insurance Act* in 1966.

Although Marilyn was deeply immersed in doctors' grievances, miraculous medical discoveries and viscera of various sorts, the medical beat also meant she was on the spot, more than once, when there was breaking news. On these occasions, Marilyn proved, again, she was just as capable of producing front page hard news stories as the boys.

Marilyn had been assigned to write a series of background science stories related to the Apollo 13 spacecraft. While she was in Washington, *Star* foreign editor, Mike Pieri, instructed her to head to Houston to spell off the *Star's* Washington correspondent, Bruce Garby, just as the Apollo crew got into trouble. The Apollo 13 moon flight blasted off on April 11, 1970, from Kennedy space centre in Florida and shortly after, an oxygen tank exploded and the crew were instructed to abort the mission. The world was on the edge of its seat: will the Apollo land or not?

Marilyn was dispatched to Texas, the home of the flight commander James Lovell. Outside of Houston, she joined a rag-tag press gang that gathered in front of Lovell's house. Marilyn followed the entire survival drama from that vantage point. "Mrs. Lovett was inside watching the situation on television. She would come out and tell us what was happening," said Marilyn. "It was a remarkable situation. The space ship landed two days later with no casualties. We couldn't believe they got back safely."

Again, in 1970, Marilyn was Janie-on-the-spot when one of the biggest stories of the year broke. Marilyn just happened to be in Quebec covering a threatened strike by Montreal medical specialists when *le Front de libération du Québec* (FLQ) kidnapped Quebec cabinet minister Pierre Laporte. Five days earlier the terrorists had whisked away British diplomat James Cross. "I was spelling off our Montreal reporters who were exhausted from monitoring the FLQ crisis and I was staking out Cross's house when a report came over another reporter's radio that Laporte had been kidnapped. I ended up in Montreal for all the FLQ events. It happened accidentally that my stories were Page One stuff," Marilyn said, adding she was on the old St. Helene's Bridge when the kidnappers later released Cross. This enabled her to produce an eye-witness report. Another scoop for Marilyn.

These kidnappings and the murder of Laporte would go down in Canadian history as the "October Crisis" and as the only time in the country's history when the *War Measures Act* was invoked. The political leaders of the day, Prime Minister Pierre Trudeau and Quebec Premier Robert Bourassa, called in the army to enforce a curfew and help police guard key buildings in Montreal.

Marilyn emphasized that throughout her whole career she was lucky and believes some people just have an affinity for being in the right place at the right time. "There have been so many accidental fortuitous events for me."

Ireland Speaks

In 1976, Marilyn had travelled to Ireland at Christmas time and, from Belfast, filed a warm fuzzy story for *Star* readers: "In a small home in a bleak street, a bright-eyed baby gurgles happily at a Christmas tree glowing with lights. It is a miracle that she is alive to see them. Baby Catherine Gilmore was shot by terrorists before she was born and came into the world with two bullet holes in her back."

The tale goes on to tell how the infant's mother was shot on the street in her ninth month of pregnancy by an unknown assailant. The child apparently had one bullet removed but would go through life with the second one lodged in her—an eternal reminder of the tragedy of Northern Ireland.

This was the first time Marilyn had set foot on Irish soil. "I knew immediately that my soul lives in Belfast," she confessed over lunch, appropriately, on St. Patrick's Day, March 17, 1998. Talking about Ireland brought back memories of her early years and Marilyn began to chat about herself and family. In an introspective mood, Marilyn candidly said, after her father's early death, she was left with an anger that had manifested itself in various forms throughout her life.

Pieri retired after thirty years at the *Star* and wrote an adventure story, *The Amazing Adventure of Cholly Blake*, published August 2013.

Long before her trip to Belfast where she discovered her spiritual home, Marilyn had always identified herself as ethnically Irish—a descendent of Protestants from Tipperary. Marilyn cherished family letters from the 1850s, written to her maternal grandmother in Canada from kin still back in Ireland. She admits she handily dismissed her dour Scottish and Welsh forbearers on her father's side—from whom she probably inherited her toughness and tenacity.

Marilyn liked to think her stories are Irish in tone—"a little bit of blarney here and there"—and enjoyed telling her war stories; but unlike the macho reporters yarning in taverns around the world, she feared her tales of daring-do, cunning and scoop-grabbing were immodest. Brash or not, they won Marilyn Dunlop many awards.

In 1977, Marilyn's luck held. She had always dreamt of being a foreign correspondent and threw her hat in the ring, for the *Star's* coveted London bureau. "There were a lot of applications. But the *Star* had just formed a committee to encourage the promotion of women, so I got the bureau chief's job. Again, she said, rather modestly, it was sheer good luck, forgetting that she had already proved herself as a stellar newsgirl with her Apollo and FLQ reportage. Marilyn commented that it was one of the biggest shocks of foreign editor, and her new boss, Mike Pieri's life when a woman was given a prestigious foreign correspondence job.

Trouble and Triumph

But before she departed for her new life in June, 1977, Marilyn reported a medical study with a grabber headline, *Relax– Sex is Good for You*. She described a study of 161 heart patients conducted by the University of Toronto. It concluded normal sexual relations were therapeutic for most patients. However, there was a caveat: "The patients were middle-class men with long established marriages. Such men are unlikely to have pulse rates higher than 120 beats per minute during intercourse with their wives."

You can just hear the sniggers and guffaws from the boys in the newsroom! Marilyn pointed out that forty years ago, this kind of news—anything to do with male sexuality—was considered racy and even daring.

Marilyn was the second woman to *man* the *Star's* London foreign bureau. Previously, in 1960, Jeanine Locke (1925-2013) had been dispatched to London as bureau chief. Locke, who began her media career in Saskatoon at the *StarPhoenix*, eventually found her way to the *Star* newsroom. During her tenure in London, Locke covered important stories such as the rise of the Berlin Wall and the Adolf Eichmann trial on Nazi war crimes. In 1969, she joined CBC where she was a producer and writer until retirement in 1990.

Seventeen years after Locke's foreign appointment, Marilyn, at the ripe age of 49, her children grown up, excitedly packed her bags and sailed away on the luxurious *Queen Mary* for a two-year stint overseas. But the dream didn't play out quite as smoothly as Marilyn visualized. She no sooner arrived in London when she received a phone call from her Toronto physician, informing her that a mammogram taken before she left indicted she had breast cancer. Immediately, managing editor, Martin Goodman, ordered Marilyn home for treatment. "I told him: I'd cope with it two years from now. I've wanted to be a foreign correspondent all my life and I'm not coming home. Besides, I'll feel like a fool. There were all those going-away parties. What will I tell the foreign editor? Marty said he'd tell him I was on a special assignment. Marty also offered to send my records overseas, but in the end, I flew home and a day later, I was operated on at the Toronto Western. The doctor said I'd had a partial lumpectomy and he believed he had got all the edges," recalled Marilyn.

The only other people Marilyn told about her diagnosis were her lover, Rae Corelli, a hardened *Star* newsie and political writer in the 1950s and '60s, and her long-time friend Dorothy Howarth, the *Telegram's* intrepid newsgirl. After the surgery, Marilyn's doctor insisted on radiotherapy, a treatment she refused to consider. Itching to get back to London and her bureau, Marilyn said she had enough and left the country. Ten days after arriving in London she was informed that, in fact, she did not have cancer, but some funny cells. But she admitted the whole episode scared the *bejeepers* out of her and all she could think of throughout the scare was she would never be the foreign correspondent of her dreams.

As an aside, on the same page as Marilyn's sex and the aging-heart story, there's a large photograph of Maureen Forrester (1930-2010), one of Canada's most celebrated classical singers. She is wearing a black graduate's cap and is receiving an honorary *Doctorate of Music* from the University of Toronto.

The cancer episode ended well for Marilyn, but Marty Goodman, her rock and support throughout the ordeal, did not fare as well. Just as Marilyn settled into London, Marty phoned and told her he had pancreatic cancer. And indeed, within two years, the kindly Goodman was dead in 1981. Tears welled up in Marilyn's eyes as she remembered this sad event from thirty years ago.

Toronto Sun editor, Peter Worthington (1927-2013), recalled attending an awards event with Corelli and *Toronto Star* hockey columnist, Frank Orr. Corelli had a long coughing fit and Orr, renowned for his irreverent wit and ability to pun and spin a hilarious comment at the drop of a puck, commented: "Hey Corelli, you're famous. You've just coughed *The Girl From Emphysema*."

In London, Marilyn rented a flat on Ladbrooke St. in a tall Victorian house owned by a Polish couple. She loved the house and became fast friends with her landlords. Jan Levit and his wife knew what was to come and they left Poland in the late 1930s, according to Marilyn. After the war started, Levit created an alarm system for the British ministry of war that was designed to warn the war office if any German U-boats managed to get into the Thames estuary. It was never used, but forty-five years later Levit was awarded a Medal of Honour by the British Government.

While Marilyn was posted in London, Corelli's son, Stephen Corelli, boarded in another part of the Ladbrooke house while he attended school in London. Today he is a prominent New York architect.

Foreign Correspondent

In November of 1977, Marilyn was dispatched to South Africa. At the time, black activist Steve Biko was on trial and there was much unrest in the country. Marilyn's job was to interview the owner of the first restaurant in South Africa to allow black customers to mingle with whites. "I interviewed the building manager. It turned out his wife, a white woman, was advisor to the Zulu king. Minutes after I left the building, a bomb went off there. When I got back to my hotel room, Editor Pieri was on the phone telling me a bomb had gone off in Johannesburg. I recognized the building and lied, of course I knew about it, I'd just come from there. I was able to phone the manager directly and get the story first before any other news agency. That was plain good luck." In her account datelined, *Johannesburg,* Marilyn told *Toronto Star* readers that just two hours before the explosion, she had walked around the shopping centre with the manager, Nigel Mandy. A correspondent couldn't be more au courrant than that. In her copy, Marilyn explains that the restaurant, on the 52nd floor of the complex, not only opened its doors to blacks and coloured's but "without fanfare, it also changed a number of its toilets from whites only, allowing all races to use them."

Cynically, Mandy opined that the blast was probably the work of liberals because they knew that the centre was *newsworthy* and would thereby draw attention to their cause.

A few days later on November 28, Marilyn travelled to Rhodesia (now Zimbabwe) and filed an article about the woes and fears of white Rhodesians under the headline: *Rhodesia's Whites Worried by Smith's Latest Moves*. "John Martin, an architect, has raised his family here, but the prime minister's announcement last week that he would accept one-man, one-vote democracy and talks with black leaders has deeply troubled the Martins. The Martins are fearful of what lies ahead for the family. 'Our home has everything one could want,' Mrs. Martin said. 'What are we to do, give it all away? It is definitely not a seller's market.'"

Even if they could get a good price for their house, they could take little of their money out of the country. Their nephew who plans to leave can take only $400 Rhodesian (about $600). According to Marilyn's story, another family worried not only about their chattels, but wonder what will happen to their black servant who has been part of the family for 20 years. And others have no illusions that because whites are far out-numbered, a black government will strip them of their good jobs and give them to blacks. Robert Mugabe, who was elected president in 1980, and still is, changed the name of the country to Zimbabwe and, as they feared, many whites suffered from job loss and a land grab. Today, 40% of the farms seized belong to Mugabe or to his supporters.

Fast forward to 2013: The Rhodesian story isn't over, it seems. *One Hundred and Four Horses: A Memoir of Farm and Family, Africa and Exile*, covers the travails of one white farm family who did not leave in the '80s and agreed to look after the horses of other persecuted farmers heading for new homes abroad. Mandy Retzlaff and her family managed to hold on until 2002 when they were given four hours to leave their land. They packed up and headed out, with the horses, and were pushed eastward until they ended up in Mozambique. Today, only a few of the horses survive. Retzlaff's book, launched in 2013, provides an insight into the tribulations and attitudes of the displaced white South Africans and their struggle to survive Mugabe's racist policies.

A few months after her Rhodesian reportage, Marilyn found herself for the second time in Belfast, the home of her heart. By this time, the Irish Republic Army (IRA) and terrorist activities had escalated and Marilyn's news stories revealed more eloquence and emotional colour than normally found in files from hard-boiled foreign correspondents. But make no mistake, it was dangerous in Ireland. Marilyn recalls taking a train from Dublin to Belfast and it turned out part of the track had been bombed. When she arrived at her Belfast hotel, she found it had been bombed too.

In February of 1978, Marilyn covered an IRA bombing of another Belfast hotel where twelve Protestants attending a club dinner died. Marilyn interviewed Gerry Brannigan, chairman of Belfast Sinn Féin, the political wing of the IRA. Brannigan told her in defense of the killings La Mon Hotel was an economic target and "in the local capitalist structure, it is a bourgeoisie establishment." Marilyn also quoted him as saying: "The most difficult thing was for the IRA to say we did it and accept the consequences. It would have been simpler to deny it."

She also told *Star* readers, "Police were in the streets handing out posters displaying a torso of one of the victims, burned beyond recognition, in a bid to shock people into coming forward with information about the killers."

Marilyn ended her description of the daily brutalities in the religiously divided city of Belfast with an emotionally-charged paragraph: "In the eyes of the people of Ulster, there is a mute question: What next? They know more violence is as certain as the relentless rain that falls today. They don't know from which direction it will come or when. Unnerved by the lull in the aftermath of the horror, they can only wait."

On March 4, in another Irish piece, Marilyn reported more death and mayhem. "As three young men—a policeman, a soldier and a terrorist—were shot dead this week, the cries of outrage and despair grow loud, demand for tighter security and vengeance are strident and people everywhere say the senseless slaughter must end, but nobody really believes it. Like a fish in a bowl, Northern Ireland politicians circle around the same old waters finding no way out of the feud that has kept the people of this land divided for more than three centuries."

Marilyn also arranged a tête-à-tête with Andy Terry, another Sinn Féin officer. Marilyn described feeling like she was in a B-movie. She was picked up by an unmarked car, then transferred to another one before arriving in a park somewhere outside of Belfast. She spent a couple of hours walking with the terrorist and it seems he bared his soul to our reporter. "I really like Andy. He wanted out, but was stuck and couldn't get out of the Sinn Féin. There's nowhere he could go. He couldn't emigrate because no country would take him," Marilyn said.

Also during Marilyn's second year in London in July of 1978, a flaming gas tanker incinerated 140 people in a Spanish campsite, and horribly burned another 150. Marilyn was sent to San Carlos de la Rapita, 200 miles north of Valencia, to cover the story. She started her reportage with a sensational lead—the kind of purple prose the *Toronto Star* still thrives on: "A child's plastic wading pool decorated with a smiling cartoon tiger lies in the ashes of a tent.... Maybe the child, who happily splashed in it, days ago, is the same child whose ember of a body was splashed, in colour, on the front page of Spanish newspapers. No one really knows." Marilyn went on to describe scenes similar to the ones reported by the first people in Hiroshima after the atomic bomb was dropped on the Japanese city at the end of World War II.

"The shells of dozens of incinerated cars, so many that I stopped counting at 30, a woman and her husband look down at the ashes of a tent; her parents had been here, she believes. What is left of their car license plate is set up on the hood to identify it. Did they die here? Her husband kneels down and slowly sifts a handful of ashes through his fingers."

Marilyn wrote in this piece that the shocked look in the eyes of the survivors of this holocaust was the same as she had seen in the "eyes of the passengers who escaped from the *Noronic* when the ship burned in the Toronto Harbour. Death, in the midst of laughing carefree life, had grabbed them by the shoulder, then let them go."

While Marilyn was in Spain, there was an uprising in Basque country severe enough to cause the cancellation, no less, of the region's sacrosanct bullfights. The *Star* instructed Marilyn to go to San Sebastian to have a look. "The Basques don't speak English and I didn't have a clue

Marilyn Dunlop

about the history or any background at all. I didn't know what I would do. I got into conversation with a young man sitting next to me on the plane. He was from the BBC and was on his way to cover the Basque situation. I told him I didn't know a thing about it. He reached down, grabbed his brief case and handed it to me. "Read this," he said. It was all the BBC's background material. We became fast friends and split up his BBC's contacts. I would call people and say, loudly, "This is the BBC and', in a tiny voice, 'the *Toronto Daily Star* calling.' Well, it turned out the Basques knew all about the *Star* and Canada because of their Newfoundland fishing connections," said Marilyn. She added that the *Star* deskers couldn't believe the quality of the information in the stories she had filed.

"There's some magic in what's required in being a reporter," observed Marilyn, returning to her theme of good luck.

Marilyn had landed in San Sebastian, shortly after 200 Spanish policemen rioted in the streets, smashing windows and looting shops. Marilyn soon gleaned that the locals considered the Spanish police an occupying force and referred to them as the policía armada and treated them with much personal hostility. Apparently, the police went berserk after ten days of ongoing killings, riots, assassinations, railroad explosions and protest marches.

Marilyn, true to form, after explaining the politics for Toronto readers, went for the personal anecdote that put the news' story into perspective. One Basque nationalist told her that the Spanish police are so hated they are forced to live in little ghettos. "A butcher would not sell to a policeman's wife. Usually the Spanish send bachelors. And they get double pay here. There is not one policeman who is a Basque," she wrote.

Marilyn stayed in San Sebastian and filed several stories, in many ways similar to her pieces from Northern Ireland. Decades later, the IRA and Orangemen were still at it and in the north of Spain, Basque separatists are still singing the same old *we-want-independence* song.

After reminiscing about her Basque coverage, Marilyn promptly launched into another story about living under *the lucky star* reserved for newshounds. For some reason, the London bureau included Africa and Marilyn travelled to a Commonwealth Conference in 1978 in Rhodesia, with Canadian Prime Minister Joe Clarke and his wife, Maureen McTeer. Also in 1978, *the Pope died twice*, necessitating two trips to Rome—on the *Star's* tab—for Marilyn and Tom Harpur, the *Star's* religion reporter. The second time the pope died, Marilyn knocked on Harpur's hotel door and said, "We have to stop meeting like this. It's too hard on popes," a story she tells with an elfin grin.

Tom Harpur was not only a reporter but a former Anglican priest and he understood how things worked in the Vatican. He and Marilyn worked in tandem on the Pope stories.

Marilyn's first reportage in August, where she joined over 100,000 mourners in St. Peter's Square in 35° C of heat, was low-key and offered *Star* readers the usual details about the body lying, in state, in the Vatican Basilica and the splendour of eighty cardinals in full regalia.

In 1979, the *Star* sent Marilyn to Yugoslavia to cover an earthquake. Hundreds of hamlets were demolished and 121 people died. In Dubrovnik, Marilyn connected with *Star* photographer, Boris Spremo, and the pair picked up an Italian journalist who wanted to share expenses for the trip into the mountains.

"We had a driver who spoke Serbian; Boris who spoke Croatian and English; an Italian, whose only other language was French, and me who spoke English and some French. Boris translated everything to English for me and I translated to pidgin French for the Italian. I often wonder what appeared in the Italian newspapers," Marilyn said.

One of the more touching moments experienced by this little press gang was the time their driver stopped at a farm where the house and barn were rubble on the ground. The family had nothing left but a bag of oranges which they insisted on sharing with the foreigners. *Star* readers read Marilyn's report of this Easter earthquake and the tragedy of the Radovich family, filed from Titograd on April 22, 1979: "Risto Radovich lost his world. Yet it did not destroy the man. With nothing left but the clothes on his back and the rubber boots he stood in, the old man pressed into my hands, an orange from a bagful friends had brought him. A guest in his "home" must be offered hospitality."

John Paul I died suddenly on September 29, 1978, a mere thirty-three days after replacing Pope Paul VI. Immediately, there was much Machiavellian speculation about his demise. John Paul's death has never been adequately explained, according to Marilyn. And years later, in Hollywood's *Godfather III*, Pope John Paul I was depicted as dying at the hands of the Mafia.

The conflict between Serbs and Croatians began in 1990 and led to the Bosnian War (1992), a horror that involved ethnic cleansing. In 1999, United Nations took control of the region, formerly known as Yugoslavia.

Little did Marilyn envisage the terror and devastation that would befall Yugoslavia a decade later and leave it forever a shattered land when she wrote in the same piece: "Radovich's brother, Marko, a retired priest has come to the village to conduct the service as he did each Easter Day. Sadly, he looked at the ruined church. Some other priest will take his place Easter Day in a resurrected church. For him it was the end."

Two days later, Marilyn was back in London reporting on race riots in Southhall, a London suburb, where the National Front, a right-wing racist movement and 5,000 Asian and left-wing protesters went head-to-head with gasoline bombs, rocks and bottles. One dead and 340 rioters arrested.

Due to riots and unionist's insurrections, 1979 was destined to be known as the Winter of Discontent—a wonderful opportunity for a journalist's grist mill. Marilyn observed that conditions under Britain's Labour government had deteriorated to a situation where "the sick went unattended, the dead unburied and food grew short on grocery shelves."

Finally, in the May 1979 election, after thirty-two years—since 1945— Labour was swept aside and the Iron Lady, Margaret Thatcher, marched into 10 Downing Street. Marilyn was there. "I remember when Margaret Thatcher came to power, we were all hovering outside 10 Downing Street and all the lights went out. We all viewed it as symbolic." Nevertheless, Marilyn reported on Maggie's victory day: "At repeated requests from an army of photographers she smiles and waves. 'Give us a two-hand wave,' shouted one and she did. 'There it is, the victory wave,' another shouted."

Marilyn also wrote that trade unionists were dismayed by the election results. "Maggie Thatcher has promised legislation that could leave them feeling like Samson after his haircut from Delilah. Mrs. Thatcher promised to amend laws on closed shops and secondary picketing and to require unions to put out a bigger share of pay for strikers instead of forcing their families to fall back on public money."

Such is the life of a foreign correspondent, Marilyn once again hastily packed her bags for Ireland in August of 1979. Lord Louis Mountbatten, Prince Philip's uncle (also a second cousin of Queen Elizabeth), was assassinated in Ireland. Yes, Marilyn was off to Ireland again, but not to the Protestant north but to Southern Ireland and County Sligo—a hot bed of IRA support. Mountbatten, an old soldier, was murdered by the IRA who planted a bomb on his yacht. Later, Marilyn attended Mountbatten's funeral in Westminster Abbey and to this day has the *Order of Service* in her big box of memorabilia.

Award-Winning Medical Reportage

After almost three years of adventures in Britain, Europe and Africa, Marilyn returned to the medical beat at the *Star*. This time around, the paper sent her to all the important medical meetings in Canada, just as the *Globe and Mail* was sending its medical reporter Joan Hollobon. The pair, good friends by this time, were not above manipulating their bosses. "Once we were in Vancouver and we decided it would be fun to take the train back home through the mountains. We discovered that there was something medical happening in Banff, so I called my editor and said the *Globe* is sending Joan Hollobon and she called her editor saying the *Star* was sending me. We were both told to go to Banff. After we got off the phone we shook hands and said, gleefully: 'Done—a weekend in Banff.'"

Kay Rex (1919-2006), a *Globe* reporter and biographer of the *Canadian Women's Press Club*, sort of explained how newsgirls may be rivals on the job, but pals socially. "Each of us is a prima donna. We argue at any moment, but have fun talking to each other. There's very little jealously and practically no job-snatching. We're sometimes quite violent critics of each other, but when we dislike someone in the club, we dislike her in a loyal sort of way." [3]

Back at the *Toronto Star* (1980), the city editor was Ken MacGray, a dim man none of the rank and file in the newsroom ever had a decent word for. "There were a lot of women in the newsroom then and he was responsible for giving us assignments. He never gave the women anything worthwhile. So, at the Christmas party, we got up a song-and-dance routine targeted at Ken. We called it, *Girls Just Want to do Fluff*. Unfortunately, he didn't get the message and never did," recalled Marilyn. When MacGray retired in 1995 from the *Star,* a collective sigh of relief reverberated throughout the newsroom at One Yonge St.

After running around the world and often finding herself on the spot, at historical moments, Marilyn officially retired in 1992, but continued to produce a freelance column for the *Star* until 1997. By then, she had three books to her credit. Marilyn had left the newspaper short of her 65th birthday because the *Star* was cutting staff as a cost-saving measure. Marilyn felt if she left—and she was ready to—she would make a space for a young person breaking into the big wide world of news.

In her senior years, Marilyn continued to earn awards for her work. In 1990, both Marilyn and her friend and rival, Joan Hollobon, won the Royal Canadian Institute's prestigious Sandford Fleming Medal for outstanding contributions to public understanding of science. At the presentation dinner, Marilyn told the audience she was doubly honoured to share this evening with Joan. "When I started, Joan was an established medical writer for the *Globe* and already had a vast store of knowledge and she was more than generous sharing it with me." In 1993, Marilyn won another science journalism award for a series on DNA.

After her final retirement, Marilyn took up painting and developed into an accomplished figurative painter, as evidenced by the works on her walls.

At eighty-three, Marilyn was still living in North Toronto, not far from Hollobon and they regularly visit one another. In summer 2012, Marilyn was diagnosed with lung cancer. After she endured a series of radiation treatments, she moved to Kitchener the following September to be near her son and daughter-in-law. She now resides in a pleasant apartment in a deluxe seniors' residence. Marilyn is as cheerful and alert as ever and happy with her memories. She has no plans to write a memoir.

JOAN HOLLOBON

Kirkland Lake Northern News, 1952-1953.
North Bay Nugget, 1954-1956. Globe and Mail, 1956-1986.

1920-Present

"A school teacher asked when I was fifteen what I wanted to do. I said 'be a journalist.' She gave me a pitying smile and I was so crushed, I never told anyone else."

From the time she was a small child in pre-war Wales, Joan Hollobon wanted to write. The path that led her to the *Globe and Mail*—arguably Canada's most prestigious newspaper—would be impossible for a young person starting out today. Joan, with a high school secretarial education, and no journalism degree, doggedly did whatever work she had to do to pay the rent while grabbing every opportunity that came her way.

Joan spent thirty-one years in newspapering and along the way garnered a portfolio full of memories and awards. She remembers vividly her fledgling days as a reporter covering a Dionne Quintuplet story. When Joan was working on her second newspaper, the *North Bay Nugget*, one of the children died at eighteen years of age. This was the first of the many tragedies that would befall the world's most famous sisters, born on May 28, 1934, in the hinterland near North Bay. Joan recalls the story; not because of its newsworthiness, but because she was irked by the big city press who swarmed into North Bay and took over. At the time of this interview, Joan was ninety-two and her mind had drifted back to long-ago decades before the term "paparazzi" came into the language.

"Everyone in town was swept into the funeral. All the reporters from Toronto were there and this blonde vision from the *Toronto Star* swept in, wearing this gorgeous dress. It was summertime and it turned into a circus. There was so little space at the head of the grave, but *Life* magazine built scaffolding behind it and their photographers jammed in behind the priest. It was squashed with press. It was disgusting. The locals were trying to keep some order and we were outside the fence. I was trying to be well-behaved and cooperative in this rural graveyard, but they opened the gate to let the blonde reporter in. I was furious. If she could get in, so could I. But the poor old *Nugget* stayed outside the fence and the *Star* got in," said Joan, still peeved forty-five years later.

The brazen vision turned out to be Angela Burke. *Toronto Star* editors habitually inserted beside her byline the description, "the blonde, glamorous Miss Burke."

On March 23, 1936, the Toronto *Globe* reported on page one that the girls' father, Oliva Dionne, told reporters in New York where the quintuplets were on display that he had written a (sad) letter to King Edward asking to have the Canadian government return custody of the girls to him and his wife. "I told the King what was in our hearts. We see the babies only a little of time and we feel our family has been divided."

The quintuplets had become wards of the Ontario Government shortly after they were born and the province made millions of dollars from putting the five girls on display.

Not only does Joan's account of the North Bay invasion of reporters illustrate the rivalry between newspapers in an era when print was *The Medium,* but it also serves to illustrate the fact that old stories never die, but come back in a different form or with a new wrinkle, illustrated by the 1998 furor over the Dionnes after the Ontario Government offered a stingy compensation settlement to the three surviving women; they claimed the government stole money from them years before when it administrated their trust fund. In 1999, the Dionnes accepted a $4 million settlement from the government.

Humble Beginnings

As for Joan May Hollobon, North Bay and the Dionnes belonged to a future that was beyond her ken when she was growing up in her native Britain. Joan was born on the Isle of Wight in 1920 and grew up in North Wales where she completed high school. Her father, Ernest Frederick "Tony" Hollobon, was a career soldier and a gunner who won two medals in World War I.

"He was a very tough guy. In 1909, he had a row with my mother before they were married, over her dog, and ran off and joined the army. Those were the days of grueling field punishment. They used to tie men to a gun carriage and lash them. Anyway, in 1919, after the war, they married. In 1920, when I was six weeks old, Alice, my mother, almost died of pneumonia, but I'm told she said, 'I must survive, I must not let go because of Baby.'"

In our first interview in March, 1995, Joan described herself as a funny reserved kid whose only ambition was to write. "A school teacher asked when I was fifteen what I wanted to do. I said 'be a journalist.' She gave me a pitying smile and I was so crushed, I never told anyone else."

When World War II broke out, Tony Hollobon was commissioned and seconded to the Royal Welsh Fusiliers. After 1945, he left the army as a Lieutenant Colonel and did a crash course in theology at Oxford. He was ordained as an Anglican minister. Joan still has his army issue Bible from World War I and says, proudly, her father was a disciplined man who exercised all his life and could still wear his army uniform when he died at eighty-nine.

After the war, Joan, who had earned a certificate in the German language, landed a government job and, in 1946, found herself in Berlin working for the *Allied Control Commission,* a British Army bureau. There she served as the British secretary for a committee under the post-war allied government. Joan admitted she was in the middle of the dividing of Berlin, but as a young, untried woman she "didn't realize what she was seeing."

During her time in Berlin, she lived army-style and like everyone else in Germany. In the late 1940s, she lived on rations and depended on the Black Market for certain goods. Real coffee, at 500 marks a pound, was one of the most coveted commodities. Joan's mother sent coffee from England and, with this treasure, Joan made the barter of her life—a couple of pounds of coffee for a Baume et Mercier wristwatch that she wears to this day.

"During the war, the grocer kept his ration of coffee in the back for my mother and me. Later, at the *Globe,* I drank at least a dozen cups a day," said Joan who admitted to being a coffee addict.

Central to Joan's story and future career was her mother's death from cancer in 1948. This sad passage began Joan's odyssey to the New World. When Joan went through her mother's belongings, she found a school medal her mother, Alice Ford, had won in 1902 for an essay about Canada. Joan suspects this was the impetus that initiated the idea of emigrating from England to Canada.

In early 1949, Joan travelled to Toronto on a visitor's visa with a girlfriend who immediately found employment. Joan couldn't get a job and suffered through a long cold winter trying to find work. "I filled my pockets up with nickels and would call all the classifieds in the *Star.* Finally, I said to myself, 'if I don't get a job today, I'm going to take up charring.'"

Joan was saved from house cleaning by Simpson's Fur on Spadina Ave., a firm run by a kindly Jewish family who paid her $25 a week.

"I had a hard time because the place stank. Loads of raw furs not properly cleaned were placed in petroleum barrels. Part of my job, as the girl, was to go get permits in the deep freeze

---

It turns out the quintuplet story still has legs. The Toronto Star *reported on the front page on October 16, 2016, the city North Bay wants to move or sell the house. The Dionne quintuplets, Cecile and Annette are protesting and so are historians dedicated to the preservation of Canadian historical sites.*

in the bowels of Queen's Park where the Lands and Forests Department had its offices. I was freezing cold as I had no warm Canadian clothes. But I loved it. That first winter I was very poor, but I still sent food parcels to England. "

While Joan toiled for the furrier, she also babysat for a Jewish family in exchange for reduced rent on Hillmount Ave. "It was a bungalow and the brat and I shared one room. The mother was so Orthodox; she never came near me. But the kid and I stayed in the room and the two of us ate bacon and eggs for dinner off a card table."

Eventually, Joan and her friend went to Montreal where Joan managed to land a menial job at *Reader's Digest* putting advertising flyers on cardboard backs. Joan was so bored she conducted time motion studies—using her adored Baume et Mercier watch.

"In Montreal, I was pretty shabby. I had one dull grey suit. We were living on coupons. We were awfully hard up. We finally got a little apartment and furnished it with a metal trundle bed. At Christmas, I got a $100 bonus and we bought a winter coat for my friend and spent the rest sending food parcels back home."

Joan never intended to stay in Canada and went back to England in 1951 where she took a job writing letters for *Readers' Digest*. A year later, Joan decided to try her luck again in Canada. She arrived in her new country, unmarried and financially on the edge.

The Writer Flourishes

During her grim immigrant existence, Joan's dream of becoming a journalist stayed alive. She knew she was a writer. Even though the route appeared closed, she always believed that if she could work at a provincial paper, she could work her way up.

And, indeed, the route was closed—until Lady Luck smiled on Joan. A friend from England married Ken Rose, a professional fundraiser for the Toronto General Hospital. He sent Joan to Ken MacTaggart, an editor at the *Globe and Mail*. "He was a great talker and said he was going to help me. Ken sent me to Bass Mason, a perfectly horrible man in the *Telegram's* advertising department. He didn't like me. So he told me to go to the Thomson offices to see St. John McCabe and say Bass Mason sent me. I toddled off to Thomson's. There was a window with a receptionist and I thought 'she'll never let me in.' I asked for McCabe and was ushered into his office. I took a deep breath and told him my story. Then one day, he called and said: 'This is Mr. McCabe. Where have you been. I have a job for you.' And he mumbled something like women's editor, $30 a week and Kirkland Lake and I said, 'when do I leave?'" recalled Joan.

Joan had some idea where Kirkland Lake was because of her gig with the Toronto furrier. Joan filled out some forms and was asked how many words a minute she could type. She forgot what answers she gave, but in April, 1953, she headed to Kirkland Lake on the old Northland train, spending the night in an upper berth wide awake with apprehension.

When Joan arrived, she discovered no one at the *Kirkland Lake Northern Daily News* had been told about her arrival. Nevertheless, she was informed she was, indeed, women's editor and told to take wire copy, make up pages, write stories—none of which she had ever done. The management sent Margaret Alderson, a Toronto reporter from the *Galt Evening Reporter,* to teach Joan. Joan recalled Alderson arrived in a beautiful suit, hat and gloves. A no-nonsense professional, she taught Joan everything. Alderson fell in love with the north and later went to work at the *Timmins Daily Press*, where she eventually became Canada's first female managing editor.

"I was a very shy person and terrified. As women's editor, I had to go out to wretched teas and weddings and write it all up. And they all wanted their picture in the paper. I didn't have a clue. I didn't have the faintest idea what peau de soie was. I was so nervous that sweat ran down my ribs. My cleaning bills were horrendous," Joan said with a shudder, four decades later. "But there was an endearing quality to the social life in Kirkland Lake. Everyone went to the Catholic teas, then the WASPs had one and then the Hadassah had events and everyone went there. There was also a lively art club. It was a frontier with lots of Slavic miners. Everyone mixed in together."

> In the 1950s, there were few apartment buildings in Toronto, so it was common for single people to board in a family home or rent a bed-sitting room with a hot plate.

In her Lady-of-the-Press garb—a grey suit and tidy gloves—Joan drove the office vehicle, which was a beat-up Chevrolet panel truck, to the teas. Fortunately, a year before the outbreak of World War II, Joan's father had taught her to drive the family car, a 1928 Morris Minor that had two little levers to change the gears.

Joan was women's editor for a year and then became a general reporter. As a reporter in a mining community, Joan covered several mining tragedies as rock bursts in mines were common. In July, 1953, the *Northern News* published a thirty-page supplement about the progress of the booming Rouyn-Noranda mining town. Many of the pieces were written by Joan, but as was common back then, there were no by-lines. The theme of this special section was the prosperity mines were bringing to Northern Ontario.

After a year or so, Joan moved to the *North Bay Nugget*. In North Bay, Joan attended her first homicide, an experience that comes to every cub reporter sooner or later. "When I got to the house, the cops were scraping up the woman's brains with a piece of a Tide soap box. Her husband was a beast. He hit her on the head with an old-fashioned flat iron and killed her," Joan said.

Joan remembered another incident she investigated that was typical of the daily fare served up by small town newspapers. Her sidekick was the staff photographer, Frederick Karl von Bruemmer (1929-2013), a self-taught naturalist who would become well known for gorgeous books about the Arctic. Bruemmer, whose parents were executed by Soviet soldiers, ended up in a Russian labour camp when he was fifteen. Freddie and Joan became life-long friends.

One day, the pair was sent out to investigate a report that some old fellow had fired his rifle at his neighbour's cows. Joan and Bruemmer jumped into one of the paper's old panel vans and headed for a farmer's field, the scene of the alleged crime. "When the road petered out, we walked through fields to find the old guy. Finally, we came to a shack. He was an Englishman, an old trapper. He was wearing heavy long johns, even though it was boiling hot. He was quite affable and offered us tea and some old pound cake. He sat there in the filth in his underwear and we drank tea. It was a lot of fun. Things like that were always happening, but after that, I decided it was time to move on."

After more than two years in Kirkland Lake, Joan applied for a job at the *North Bay Nugget* and stayed there one year and seven months. Looking back, Joan commented, Kirkland Lake was really a mad, mad place where people went through the town "like a hot knife through butter."

"John Hart, the financial editor, had served time in Kingston Penitentiary. One day he disappeared and then re-appeared and disappeared again. He finally ended up in the Don Jail after he was caught carrying a gun. We found this out from a Toronto paper and we took up a collection for him."

Despite a shifty, but colourful, financial editor, Joan describes that period of her life in the backwaters of Kirkland Lake as quite dull. On the positive side, Joan's salary rose to $42 and she was able to live in a proper apartment building, owned by a Mr. David, a Frenchman who wore a dapper white suit and shoes. She had "a bachelor" with a little folding bed and a card table that she still uses. Joan only bought the absolute essentials as she had no intention of staying in Kirkland Lake.

North Bay also turned out to be studded with characters, remembered fondly by Joan. Joan was responsible for covering just about everything that happened in town; lands and forests, society, city council, police, courts and the air force. She also had to go regularly to New Liskeard to follow agricultural stories—a duty she detested. She also travelled to Cobalt to the county court where she soon discovered, after months of listening to the legal goings-on, that North Bay was a sink of iniquity. The characters were right out of Stephen Leacock's *Sunshine Sketches of a Little Town*, a delightful satire of provincial Ontario.

"In those days, judges didn't have to be lawyers. There was a funny little magistrate, Siegfried Atkinson, an English merchant. He had a big banana nose and looked like a draper. He was not averse to a little publicity. The press table was right beside his bench. He would look over the edge and lean and beam my way to make sure I got every bon mot that fell from his lips," recalled Joan.

During Joan's two-and-a-half-year tenure in North Bay, the mayor was the notorious Merle Dickenson, known to be corrupt and on the take. He was involved in several scandals and he too loved publicity. "He was an affable scoundrel. He would say, as long as you spell my name right, I don't care what you print."

Interestingly, Dickenson was still mayor in 1983 when there was talk of moving the log cabin where the Dionnes had been born to Niagara Falls as a tourist attraction. In the late thirties, over three million visitors trooped to North Bay to see the quintuplets. At the time, the girls were a bigger tourist attraction than Niagara Falls. Thus, it seemed to Dickenson his scheme to move their childhood home to The Falls was a natural fit. The plan never did hold water.

In those by-gone times in North Bay, Joan's day started at 8 a.m. with meetings. She would go home for lunch and dinner and sleep for a half hour. Most days she worked until 2 a.m., pounding away on a manual typewriter. As she had in Kirkland Lake, Joan did just about everything at the *Nugget*. One of her duties was to process pictures for the paper that came in on a wire service. She became acquainted with the purple plastic transfer method that involved taking an engraving off a machine. Instead of expensive metal, the pictures came in on a purple plastic material. It was also the days of hand-set linotype. This required a lot of time in the back shop and the ability to read upside down, a skill Joan still possesses.

"I enjoyed the police beat in North Bay. There were two detectives, both called Bill. I got on well with them. On Saturday, I had to make my police checks before joining the gang at the lake. I had bought a little Austin and after the checks one Saturday, it disappeared. Where was it? I'd left the keys in and one of the Bills took the keys and hid the Austin. I had to be a good sport and I was. And I got a lot of good stories out of it."

Probably the most exciting assignment of Joan's northern career was the day she and staff photographer, Stan Mulcahy, went underground at the Beaucage Mine on Newman Island in Lake Nipissing. In the 1950s at the height of the Cold War, everyone was hunting for uranium. Because of the rich deposits in other Northern Ontario locations such as Elliott Lake, it was assumed Beaucage, near North Bay, would also yield lucrative amounts of uranium. In the end, the riches did not materialize. But the day Joan and Mulcahy descended the 400 feet to the mine floor, investors and miners were still hopeful.

In the paper on May 7, 1955, appeared nine black and white photos of different machines that to contemporary eyes appear tremendously antiqued and clumsy. One of Mulcahy's shots shows Joan crouching on high grade ore dressed in oversized water-proofed garments and a helmet above her ever-present big, round spectacles. Joan wrote reams of copy describing her mining experience and impressions. "After the men got their kit and the shift had gone below, boots and helmets were produced for us. Made of plastic material, with leather inside, the helmets were not very heavy, but mine was too big and occasionally slithered down over my nose without warning. The only light was from the one on our helmets.

"We stood watching a cluster of men in the dim light and then all of a sudden all hell seemed to break loose just around a corner. Stan and I leaped three feet in the air and I know my heart was pumping like a sledge hammer. Convinced our last moment had come, we decided to take it bravely. The heroics were not necessary; a fellow had just started the mucking machine that's all. After that we didn't move a muscle no matter what violent and unexpected roars went off in our ears. In that setting I tried to imagine the feelings of the Cobalt miner, a few weeks ago, who was trapped in a tiny space and got out through ice-cool courage."

Naturally, at the end of that day, Joan was relieved to be back in the sunshine and opined that miners earn every penny of their pay.

Joan made many firm friends at the *Nugget*, including John McNeill, a young photographer who later followed her to the Globe. The Nugget boys started a judo club and McNeill insisted Joan join. Judo became a highlight of Joan's life in North Bay and there she is, in a marvelous black and white photo, looking fit and alert in her white judo kit. In another picture, she is flinging some poor chap over her shoulder.

"Johnny" McNeill, his wife, Aline, and Joan became pals and when the McNeills' daughter was born, she was given "Joan" as a middle name in honour of their close friendship. Joan recalled a winter night when a motorist was high-jacked by a hitch hiker and ended up in

Newsgirls

hospital in Huntsville. "Johnny and I had to drive there to interview him. The victim was so enraged, as he told his story he jumped out of bed with his broken leg. On the way back, late into the night, I was driving and there were lots of icy patches. I was holding the wheel firmly, but we hit a wooden railroad tie and the car bunny-hopped down the road and John woke up. The controller at the *Nugget* was very tight and prissy so, for fun, we put the offending piece of wood in the trunk to show George. It was almost morning when we got back to North Bay, but the first thing we did was put the tie on George's desk. I wrote the story and then went home to bed. I woke up later in the day—a little flighty—and went back to work. George wasn't amused with the wood."

Eventually, Joan was promoted to a *Nugget* columnist. Throughout 1956 in her columns, oddly called *Nuggets from a Topical Vein*, Joan presented readers with her thoughts on everything from the Prince Rainier-Grace Kelly nuptials to a diatribe about CBC radio.

Most of Joan's copy was free-flowing baffle-gab written in pretentious Edwardian language. Obviously, not edited by anybody.

In the Grace Kelly rant on March 12, a month before the actual wedding, Joan described Prince Rainier (Grimaldi) as a "pudgy prince" with a "tax-free lifestyle" and Kelly as a Plebian daughter of a bricklayer. Her final sneer—Joan wrote the wedding will take place in the "back yard of a gambling house."

Joan didn't hold back about how she felt about CBC programming.

"CBC has become a dirty word. To speak up in defense of the CBC is to invite incredulous glances, curled lips and sneers. Sneer on friend, here we go. First, let's make it clear we are not talking about television, which we never see, no, we speak purely and simply as a keen listener when there is anything on the radio that appeals. Also, we might add as a minority listener because the Hit Parade leaves us shuddering and westerns (cowboys) find us under the mattress both hands clamped over the ears." And on it goes.

Joan opened another column of *Tropical Veins* with a rather startling lead. "Whether this column ever gets read by anyone except the reporter who writes it is dubious, but that is not the point. At least, it may be the point to those Olympian beings known collectively by the august title "the desk," but it ain't no how the point to reporters. To them it is like a sound proof room to a cornet player, or steam valves to a boiler." This 500-word column deteriorated from there.

Anyway, producing this column for the five-week days left Joan time to relax and wander around. "One weekend I went to a party in Kirkland Lake. The editor at the *Nugget* was Mort Fellman. The North Bay advertising people got drunk and I mentioned I was thinking of leaving. This got back to Mort. He had the worst temper and I feared the worst. But he told me he'd be seeing Eddie Phalen at the *Globe and Mail* about a job and I applied too. Two weeks later, I received a very brisk reply saying no openings. I had already been warned they do not take women. But, I recalled one of the attributes of a good reporter is persistence," Joan said.

Damned determined to work on the *Globe*, Joan decided to make an orderly presentation. She made up a book with tags containing her editorial work and columns and sent it to the *Toronto Telegram*. No luck. Joan travelled to Toronto to retrieve her portfolio and marched to the *Globe* with it, expecting to get turned down in person. Phalen told her to see Margaret Cragg, the Women's Editor. "She gave me a quick grin and said, if I didn't want to be in the women's department and were prepared to wait, she thought there may be something in the news department. Then out of the blue, the Managing Editor, Bob Turnbull, offered Joan a job as a general assignment reporter. Thus, in October, 1956, Joan reported to the *Globe*. Joan said she badgered McNeill to apply at the *Globe* and eventually he joined her on staff.

North Bay was a close-knit society and when Joan left town for Toronto. Judge Jasper Plouffe, Chairman of the Police Commission, gave her a pen and pencil set that to this day remains a prized possession. On page three of the *Nugget*, dated October 11, 1956, there are three photographs of Joan's farewell dinner held at the Golden Dragon. She is shown with Plouff, Mayor Dickerson and also with a Mrs. Leatherdale, who presented Joan with a gift on behalf of the Hunters and Anglers Club. There is also a shot of Joan accepting a gift-wrapped parcel from managing editor, Mort Fellman. Slim, trim Joan is dressed in a straight skirt and a form-fitting suit jacket.

As an aside on February 1, 1955, the Daily Nugget published a page about the newspaper biz. "Ever think about starting a newspaper? A daily newspaper? Here's how much it costs. Starting from scratch. It shouldn't cost much more than $700,000, without frills."

On the rest of the page, Nugget staffers describe all aspects of how the newspaper runs and, in the bottom right corner, there's a three-column invitation to attend an open house at the Nugget's plant, sponsored by O'Keefe's Brewing Company Limited—now part of Molson Coors Brewing Company.

The story that accompanied the photos was choc-full of praises for Joan's contribution to the community and the newspaper. "Miss Hollobon, who hails from England, had the ability to extract every detail from any story to which she was assigned. A fast, accurate writer, she could turn out a story quickly once she assembled her facts." A reporter's job in a nutshell.

Endless Pressure and Deadlines

By the time Joan was hired by the *Globe*, she had a bit of a track or, perhaps more accurately, a *trap* record with the paper. While in North Bay, she had written a freelance feature for the *Globe* about a trapper. "I knew Dunc Halliday, the picture editor for the *Globe* was mad for animals and ships. I spent a whole day with a trapper as he trapped a beaver. The *Globe* ran the story, but never paid me. I was so proud to see my name in the paper, I never asked for the money. Then, one day, Frank McEwan was sent around to see the stringers. When he came into the Nugget and I told him about not being paid, he said 'Oh no, not another one.' Frank was the first person I ever met from the *Globe*. He was wacky, funny and generous. The first day he hailed me and gave me two pieces of information: the women's washroom is down the hall and the deadline is 6 p.m. The first Sunday, he invited me to lunch—a stiff, painful lunch. His wife didn't have a clue nor cared about newspapers. They were oil and water and eventually separated."

When Joan applied to the *Globe,* she was thirty-six and reckoned she was "too long in the tooth" to be a cub reporter on general assignment (GA). Accordingly, Joan knocked three years off and the *Globe* was under the impression she was a mere thirty-three. "I had to put the truth to the editor. I prattled—such a funny mistake. Isn't that foolish of me. I never heard another thing about it."

Once Joan landed the longed-for GA job, she found out it wasn't always what it was cracked up to be. GA meant Joan had to be available, at the drop of a telephone receiver, to race all over the city checking out everything from the most trivial social event to street crime. Once, Joan and a photographer, Art Bryden, were sent out to an armed robbery. The robber was supposed to be holed up above a pharmacy opposite St. John of Norway church. "I careened to the east end in my Morris Minor 1000—a lovely car. I got bored and decided to use the phone box opposite the shop to call the office. A policeman informed me the suspect with the rifle had a clear sight to the booth. He also said, "you're a damn fool. If you want to die with your boots on, go ahead."

Suddenly, a little boy appeared and told Joan the robber and police had gone into the church through a hole in the fence. She dutifully negotiated the hole and entered the church where she was spooked by heavy-thumping boots. They turned out to belong to police. In the end, it was a wild goose chase, but a lot of fun according to Joan. "When I got back to the office, the city editor, Fred Egan, came up to me. He was very conservative, always with a collar, tie and jacket, and a mean man—never comfortable with women reporters. He said 'Good work, Joan.' I hadn't done a bloody thing."

But soon after joining the *Globe*, Joan made her first mark. In December, 1956, she attended the Ontario Federation of Labor's fifth annual Human Rights conference in Hamilton. She quoted, profusely, the remarks of Kalmen Kaplansky, director of the *Jewish Labour Committee of Canada*, the gist of which centered round the fact Canadian employment agencies make a point of informing prospective employers about the race and religion of job applicants. "It is shocking to realize that qualified applicants can still be rejected for such irrelevant factors as race and religion," said Mr. Kaplansky.

Other labour speakers added that discrimination and segregation are luxuries North America can no longer afford and several accused the Canadian government of dragging its feet in enforcing laws against discrimination and failing to do anything about educating the public against discrimination.

That was over fifty years ago—a decade before activists would finally convince Ottawa a *Charter of Rights* was necessary. Meanwhile, the *Toronto Joint Labour Committee on Human Rights* was so impressed with Joan's reportage, it reprinted her article and distributed the text across the country. Joan still has a yellowed copy of the reprint.

Kaplansky (1912-1997), a trade unionist, received the Order of Canada in 1980.

The day after listening to Kaplansky, Joan found herself at a reception centre on Jarvis St. at 11 p.m. when sixty-seven Hungarian refugees arrived after a long exhausting trip from Vienna. Four pictures of cute, but bleary-eyed children, accompanied Joan's copy. The story was as close to a *Toronto Star*-style tear-jerker as the *Globe* ever got. Joan talked about fear, strain, red-rimmed eyes, pale faces and bitter tears. "They were blinking into the light from darkness, in fear. In a sense suddenly going into freedom was too sudden to grasp."

The next summer, when the new Shakespearean theatre opened in Stratford, Ontario on June 30, 1957, the *Globe* sent its theatre critic, Herbert Whittaker, and Joan. Whittaker was to review the dress rehearsal and opening performances while Joan's job was to cover the gala and celebrities attending opening night festivities. She recalled seeing *Toronto Star* critic, Nathan Cohen, and author, Robertson Davies, on a steel catwalk behind the stage in great dramatic cloaks looking very pompous.

After the inaugural play, Shakespeare's *Richard III*, all went well and Whittaker filed his review to the *Globe*: "The most exciting night in the history of Canadian theatre has ended with the final curtain on Tyrone Guthrie's production of *Richard III*. Towering over the occasion like an ill-fated bird of prey was the twisted, misshapen, spastic king portrayed by Alec Guinness."

According to managing editor, Richard Doyle, Whittaker missed the deadline for his review of the next night's show, *All's Well That Ends Well*, because the performance went on into night. "In one of the finest tributes paid to Whittaker in his long career, the Stratford festival moved its openings up a half hour to accommodate his *Globe* reviews."[1] Such was the power of the press in 1957.

Meanwhile, Joan had her typewriter with her and wrote her stories in the back of her beloved Morris Minor. Her front-page story describing the dedication of the new theatre starts: "Outside, the great circular roof flares away with a fine Elizabethan bravado. Indeed, the strangest thing about the Shakespearian Festival Theatre is, it is as if it had always been here, as if it had drawn to itself all the centuries of history." From there Joan proceeded to quote several clergymen and Ontario Premier, Leslie Frost, who were involved in the dedication ceremony. Frost compared the building of the theatre to "the spirit which inspired the Fathers of Confederation ninety years ago." Trying for some colour in her report, Joan noted that Siobhan McKenna, who was to perform a one-woman Hamlet on opening night was "alone among the women. Hatless in unrelieved black, except for white gloves and white necklace, her striking face mobile and interesting, "Butterflies in your stomach?" asked a laughing voice. "No. Not yet. The only thing which gives me...," but Miss McKenna's secret was lost in conversation."[2]

All-in-all, the official opening of Canada's most famous theatre appears to have been a very dull event. More interesting, on the same page as Joan's reportage, is a report about *Hurricane Audrey*, a catastrophe that killed five people in Ontario while the toffs yawned in Stratford.

Joan, still on GA a year later, found herself at the *Baptist World Youth Conference*. She reported that it was attended by 8,000 young men and women, "white and Negro and one speaker, a young Negro college student from Texas, said "Toronto is the only place I have ever been where people simply don't seem to notice I am coloured. Previously, I've met people who are rude or even too effusive. But here, colour just doesn't seem to count, one way or the other.'"[3]

Apparently, the conference brought together American whites and blacks from the still segregated south who would never have met in their own country. Joan also quoted two white people from Arkansas and Alabama who commented they had had a complete change of opinion since coming to the convention.

In December 12, 1958, Joan was back in familiar territory—up north in Sudbury, a mining town. Joan regarded the series of stories that came out of a bitter mining strike there as perhaps the highlight of her GA career. The strike against the International Nickel Company was in its 12th week and the miners' wives, with an empty Christmas on the horizon, held their own meeting and voted overwhelmingly for their husbands to abandon the strike and return to work. Joan told *Globe* readers the women were accused of being scabs and "not willing to fight for their men." Joan talked to one man about the women and he told her; "they don't know anything about union affairs. They'll only make matters worse."

For the record, Stratford's Shakespearian theatre was the dream of local journalist, Thomas Paterson (1920-2005). With a grant of $125 dollars from the town council, he started the ball rolling and the first season opened in a tent in 1953. Today, Stratford, Ontario's Shakespeare extravaganza is the world's largest.

At issue were a shortened working week, from forty hours to thirty-two hours, and benefits.

Instead of sticking to the union-management squabble, two days later, Joan went to the home of a union leader, Leon Breen, after the wives who attended the meeting received threatening telephone calls. In her page one story, Joan reported: "Strikers summoned to a meeting at 10:30 a.m. were told in no uncertain terms to bring their wives into line. Leon Breen, a tough and intelligent level boss, heads the union blacklist, because his wife headed the group that put forth the resolutions (two days before)."

Joan's story also referred to the mounting threat of violence with DPs (displaced persons/immigrants) and communists were named as the main perpetrators. "Breen has a borrowed 12-gauge pump gun, leaning against his refrigerator, and he has threatened to use it in self-defense. A call last night told him if he went to the meeting today, his life wouldn't be worth a plugged nickel and don't poke your nose outside the door. Another caller said, 'I blast you. I blast your wife, right out your house.'"

Joan stayed with the INCO saga until Christmas, putting what the newsroom calls a human face on a story. She wrote about the need and hardships of the miners' families and also about "infinite examples of generosity and Christian concern cutting across all barriers." Joan talked about $15 food vouchers and lack of fuel, never mind money for Christmas gifts. She mentioned fear of scurvy, rickets and skin diseases due to lack of nutrition. Joan also dug out how the strike was affecting everyone in the community, even the most sacred of all Canadian institutions, the hockey team. Apparently, attendance at hockey games went down and a $9,000 to $10,000 operating deficit was expected at the community arena.

Meanwhile the *Globe* reported that two Toronto firms had rallied to aid strikers' families. The employees of Dawson and Hannaford Ltd. collected $25 for Christmas groceries for one family and The Bata Shoe Co. donated 600 pairs of children's shoes.

On December 16, Joan's story was headed with "Sudbury Hopes for Settlement." It seems talks between INCO and the union were resuming in far-off Toronto. On December 19, Joan was still in Sudbury and reported the end of the strike and INCO agreed to pay its usual $25 Christmas bonus. Joan ended her story with the observation the telephone company was deluged with requests to reconnect phones and the liquor store was jammed. Finally, on December 22, the front page of the Globe published a wrap-up about the strike. Joan was one of four reporters who analyzed the economic and moral fallout in the community. They wrote Sudbury had lost $12,000,000 in wages and one million man-days of work.

On a lighter note, the only time in her newspaper career that Joan was aware she was conned was when an "African prince" blew into town. She was assigned a story on a Friday night for the Saturday paper. Joan was told a Toronto church on Bathurst St. was feting an African prince and she was sent to interview him. The ever-diligent reporter found a black man with a superior air dressed in corduroy and tweed. He claimed to be from a region called Sahari Chibangi—not unlikely, because in the 1950s all the places in Africa were changing their names.

"I was suspicious. He had something to do with the French embassy in New York, but, being Friday night, I couldn't get in touch with anyone to verify his tale. I checked the Atlas, there was a Sahari Chibangi. He seemed genuine and made sense. He was having some kind of passport difficulties. So I wrote about his plight and a double column story appeared on Saturday. A week later, I see my story pinned on the wall, along with a CP story and a quote from the prince's sister, somewhere in Kentucky: Has Edward been at it again."

When all was revealed, the prince turned out to be an American called Edward Woods. But Joan didn't feel so bad about being duped after she discovered even the American President, Harry Truman, was taken in. It seems Truman was opening up a museum in Missouri and the African prince showed up just in time for the President to give him a personal and special tour of the facility. "There was no money involved, just self-importance. He had cultivated the right shade of nonchalance, arrogance and a believable accent," recalled Joan. "The *Globe* never told me off, but there were lots of grins and smirks. I was mortified. It was my worst boob."

Wannabe African princes and Stratford openings aside, Joan hated the sporadic aspect of general assignment. In North Bay, Joan was used to doing a dozen things at once. Sitting around, on GA, waiting for *Globe* editors to dig up something for her to do was driving Joan batty.

> In the *Globe and Mail*, December 15, 1958, on the front page below Hollobon's INCO story, there is an ad for luxurious men's shirts. "Silky English broadcloth, 2 ply Egyptian cotton, $7.50," placed by Stollery's, a haberdashery that was a Toronto institution since 1901. The store, on Yonge St., was clandestinely demolished by condo developer Sam Mizrahi, on Sunday, April 18, 2015.

> Meanwhile, Simpson's Christmas advertisement on the back page of the same issue as this story, showed a white wool toy poodle for 89 cents, shoe shine kits, $1.89, Elizabeth Arden, gift boxed soap, $1.

Finally, she was given the church beat to do part-time. From being underemployed on GA, Joan soon found herself swamped. Not only was she covering church affairs, but also the medical beat.

"In 1959, David Spurgeon, the medical reporter, sat opposite me. He got a fellowship to Columbia. I was interested in the beat but the answer was "Oh, no we don't want a woman on the religion beat. They tried Walter Gray on the beat, but he was a politics' man and wanted to go to Ottawa. I went to England on a holiday and when I came back in September, my mail box was full of stuff including a memo to take over the medical beat until David got back. They were patronizing me," Joan said, archly. "I was juggling the two beats. It never occurred to me to complain. The church beat was so boring. The paper used to run in tiny type—not even 10 point—church financial statements. I asked why and was told because we always have. Bob Turnbull was city editor. He said, let the statements go and see if anyone notices. Not one complaint. Not a bleat. That was the end of that. Then, one day, I was late with my church briefs and the telegraph editor complained. I threw them across the desk at him and, calmly, Bob said "Joan, wouldn't you like to give up the church beat?" I did and Eric Dowd, a pop-eyed man with a Lancashire accent got it."

Medical Beat

Joan took to the medical beat and this is where she would make her name as a respected journalist. Once Joan was the medical reporter, she loved the beat but admits she was scared to death and felt like she was hanging on to a cliff by her finger tips. Joan invested in a medical dictionary and did not read anything except medicine for three years. In the end, she pinched Spurgeon's beat from him. "In fairness, he did everything to help me. *The Globe* was not cut throat about those things in those days."

In Joan's life, fear was a repetitive theme and a motivator, but she believes she is, indeed, her father's daughter and has inherited his grit and English ability of *muddling through* no matter how dire the circumstances. Looking back, Joan also admitted she had lots of good luck in her career and always seemed to be in the right place at the right time. And a few years into her "medical career," she too applied for a fellowship at *Columbia School of Journalism* in advanced science writing. Not university educated, Joan felt insecure about her lack of formal education, but decided to take the plunge anyway. "I had no academic qualifications and no background in biology. The only science I took was botany in high school, and that was all about water spiders skittering on the surface. Anyway, it helped me that Oakley Dalgleish was on the *Globe* board, and was keen on the medical beat. But still I had to have three sponsors for Columbia and, fortunately, I managed to get three outstanding ones," said Joan in what is perhaps the understatement of that decade.

Joan's work in the *Globe* was so highly thought of that no less a personage than medical researcher, Charles Best (1899-1978) of insulin fame, plus Roy Ferguson, professor of medicine at the *University of Toronto*, and managing editor, Richard "Dic" Doyle (later a Canadian senator), rallied around. On their recommendations, Columbia accepted her and Joan Hollobon, plucky medical reporter, packed for New York City. "I spent an academic year in New York. The lectures petrified me, but at least I understood enough to ask questions and was intelligent enough to keep my mouth shut when I didn't understand. It took me three months to settle down. There were forty-three on the course. I belonged in the middle. I wasn't the stupidest. I learned a lot," said Joan, who returned to Toronto, not only with a head full of medical facts, but with a fitted flecked tweed suit, purchased at Saks Fifth Avenue, for $25. Joan, always slender, loved it and in the coming years, she was often photographed wearing her Manhattan suit.

The Saskatchewan medical crisis of 1962, although now forgotten, was a watershed in Canadian social history and it was one of Joan's toughest assignments as a reporter. Under the government of Tommy Douglas, the leader of the *Commonwealth Co-operative Federation* (CCF) in Saskatchewan, the province implemented Medicare on July 1, 1962. Saskatchewan doctors immediately went on strike against state medicine. And the very first day of the strike, a nine-month old child died of meningitis, a death that was laid at the door of the medical profession. Feelings also heated up when Saskatchewan officials organized an airlift of ninety physicians from Britain to replace striking doctors.

Oscar Dalgleish (1910-1963) was a *Globe* character. He wore a black patch over one eye and looked quite dashing. During a business trip to New York, Dalgleish and his wife, Delsea, were introduced to an advertising executive who "appropriated" Dalgleish's look for the Hathaway shirt man and also Delsea's name for a new toilet paper—marketed as Delsey. Kimberly stopped producing this brand in the 1970s. [4]

The Globe sent Joan out west in mid-June to cover the story. She described, for *Globe* readers, the rancor and the digging in of the opposing camps. Joan was everywhere at once, fearful of missing something important. "I was told to go straight out to Regina. I was so compulsive and so terrified not to have something to write about, I went to two press conferences a day and filed two think pieces daily. One side of the debate gave a press conference at noon and deadline was 6 p.m. EST. The other was at 4 p.m., when it was already six o'clock in Toronto. I did evening interviews. This went on for three weeks. The *Toronto Star* had six people, a car and a plane on the job, but I never saw anything they were writing. The *Globe* finally sent Dave Spurgeon to spell me off. He was now the science writer. Dave and I were invited out to a relative of his for dinner where everyone wanted to re-hash the doctors' fight. At 2 a.m. we were still arguing the pros and cons. The doctors saw barbed wire and jack boots on the Saskatchewan border. This was the atmosphere at that time," recalled Joan.

Joan interviewed, listened, wrote and wrote some more, taking little time to sleep. She has a vivid memory of going to a cocktail party in Saskatoon and, after a few refreshments, finding herself in an argument with the hostess about weather in Ontario and Saskatchewan. At this point, Joan felt very ashamed of herself and realized after months of over-work, she had finally lost it. A doctor friend suggested sleeping pills and because she had never taken them before, she felt groggy and terrible. Things got so bad, managing editor, Clark Davey, came to the rescue and told Joan to take ten days' holidays and the *Globe* would pay for it. But Joan, although "all wrung out," insisted on staying on the job until the end of July.

Meanwhile, on July 23, after much acrimonious negotiation, the Saskatoon Agreement was signed between the doctors and the CCF Saskatchewan government, paving the way for universal Medicare in Canada. Two days later the *Globe* published Joan's erudite analysis of the agreement reached on the 23rd. After explaining the background; the controversy had really started. In 1959, when Douglas promised if elected, his government would set up a Medicare system. Against this, the *College of Physicians and Surgeon* claimed that doctors would lose control and power over their lives and profession.

In her story, Joan asked the question, "who won?" and put forth credible arguments to the effect both sides did and added, she suspected the bitterness over the dispute would not take long to dissipate.

Joan wrote "The trend toward provision of medical coverage under some kind of public sponsorship seems inevitably to be sweeping across the Western world." She goes on to say that the success of the Saskatoon Agreement depends on the good will and trust between physicians and government agencies. After documenting the claims made by both sides, Joan concludes "This has been a depressing vicious squabble to watch, and yet it has been a fight for principles as well as self-interest and fear of change. There has been a lot of dissension about this business, but damaging as it may be, dissension is healthier in a democracy than apathy and indifference. The agreement which ended this unhappy affair has a ring of magnanimity and reasonableness about it. If its provisions are carried out with good will, this document may prove to be a valuable guide for evolving Medicare plans suited to the Canadian scene and suited to doctors, patients and the economy."

Joan went back to Saskatchewan in November to check out the post-crisis atmosphere. After travelling thousands of miles all over the province, conducting dozens of interviews with the people, she concluded that everything had fallen onto place. "Then I was in the Hotel Saskatchewan worried about where I'm going to find authorities to interview and, by chance, the College of Physicians was having its annual meeting. I met their president. When I got back to the newsroom, I knew exactly what I was going to do and say and I wrote a *ten-part series*. The city editor was having fits running it, day-by-day. I was euphoric and told him not to worry."

This series, an intellectual and journalistic tour de force, was so successful and insightful that the *Globe and Mail* reprinted Joan's articles in a booklet, *Bungle, Truce and Trouble*. The stories, originally published in December 1962, cover everything from the background of the Medicare dispute in Saskatchewan to an explanation of the complex payment schedule, agreed on by the province and physicians, to the political implications of universal medical coverage for

> Now, in 2017, the story is eerily similar to the fears resulting from Trump's vow to dismantle Obamacare and build a wall on Mexican border.

the rest of Canada. In 1966, the House of Commons passed *The National Medical Care Insurance Act* and, by 1971, every Canadian province had universal Medicare.

Joan recalled sitting down, every day, and producing a feature piece for the next day's paper on a manual typewriter. In the early sixties, copy boys were still very much part of the process. Near deadline, she would take the copy to the city desk, page-by-page, where the slot would dole it out to copy editors. The editing was done by hand with a pencil. Reporters kept "blacks" (carbon copies) of everything they wrote, in case there was a problem with the published story. In those antique days, Toronto papers published five or six editions daily. As a matter of drill, reporters always checked the first edition for accuracy. This meant, if a name was misspelled or a fact slightly off, it could be corrected for the next edition. Today copy still goes through the same hands but it is shipped electronically from the reporter's computer to the city desk, to the slot and ends up on a copy editor's computer. Another thing has changed; because the big dailies only publish one edition, daily, reporters and copy editors only get one kick at the can. If there's an error, it stands, resulting in a list of corrections the next day, or an explanation by the ombudsman or worse—legal action by an offended party.

Although the pressure to produce copy was endless and deadlines always loomed heavily, for Joan, the *Globe and Mail* was a "fun place to be," she commented," it was a newsroom, *not a goddamn bank.*" The newsies were always having parties, attended by an assortment of denizens with ink-stained fingers. Joan often opened up her apartment on Fairlawn Ave., where everyone drank heavily. Back then, the beverage of choice was rye and ginger ale. Wine was equated with rubby-dubbies, according to Joan.

Back in the early days, before a typographers' strike in 1964, there were no security guards at the old *Globe* building on Bay St. The editorial department was wide-open and people wandered in. "There was the hockey-stick man. He was a big guy with a booming voice and he always came in with a couple of hockey sticks under his arm. He took a desk, made calls and all kinds of noise, but nobody ever tried to get rid of him," laughed Joan. "There were always people talking and laughing together. Walter Gray, he was an incredible gossip. Once he went to the Arctic for three weeks. He came back, at 10 a.m., and by 2 p.m., he was sitting on the edge of my desk and filled me in on everything that had happened to everybody in the newsroom while he was away."

Through the 1960s, Joan produced endless in-depth pieces on medical subjects. Cornea transplants, all manner of heart research, mental illness and cancer were all grist for Joan's insightful mill. One of her stories about the current research in cancer, that clearly explained the advances in this field, won accolades from *Globe* management. In a summary on cancer, Joan said "Proof will be found that at least some human cancers are caused by viruses and vaccines will, one day, be developed against these types." The next day, December 30, 1960, Miss Joan Hollobon received a typewritten memo from managing editor Doyle. It said "The page was splendid. You should be particularly proud." Joan kept this memo and stapled to a tear sheet containing that *splendid* work.

Joan also wrote a piece about "porridge in the arteries". She told readers that fatty deposits that build up inside arteries, causing coronary disease, look like mushy porridge. Later, in January, 1968, in the wake of Dr. Christiaan Barnard's first heart transplant in South Africa, Joan wrote a moral essay about heart transplants, under the headline *"Is it really ethical to transplant heart."* Joan also contributed regularly to The *Globe Magazine*, a publication that was inserted in Saturday's paper.

In June, 1963, Joan was sent to Oak Ridge, the maximum-security division of the Ontario Hospital for the criminally insane, at Penetanguishene. The result was a chilling two-part story that took up most of the space on succeeding Saturdays. Joan started: "Look into the face of the man who has killed another while insane, but later regains his right mind. What are his thoughts, his memories, his fears, his hopes, his future?"

Well, Joan interviewed such a man and told *Globe* readers in stark terms what it was like to be behind bars for thirty years after killing an ex-girlfriend without premeditation. Joan also interviewed a "brilliant" student who was depressed and killed his mother without warning. His psychiatrist told Joan the teen was obsessed with the idea he was failing and murdered his mother because he wanted to spare her the humiliation of his failure.

Joan examined the history of several prisoners and presented them to readers as sympathetic human beings who were not monsters but souls that needed help. One, named Wilkie, burned down his house, killing his wife and child, and had been in Oak Ridge for thirty years. Joan described him as a skilled mechanic and engineer. He told Joan "I feel my life has been wasted for no good cause. The doctors well know I wasn't a dangerous man. They said I was mentally defective. Do you think I'm defective now?" Joan responded for readers: "Logical and articulate, Wilkie clearly is far from defective," and she went on to pose the question of how do you return a man "to a world he left 30 years before."

In Part Two, Joan dealt with *untwisting* the minds of murderers and describes the day-to-day life and the rehabilitation work done at Oak Ridge, everything from brain surgery to ping-pong therapy. What made all this interesting is the societal context. In Toronto, in the early 1960s, mental illness and births out-of-wedlock were subjects never openly discussed by decent people. There was no Medicare, the birth control pill had just hit the Canadian market, "homosexual" was a term only used by the literati and the idea of voluntarily booking an appointment with a psychiatrist wasn't even considered an option, no matter how troubled a person seemed. Woody Allen had yet to make angst and therapy a trendy part of upper-middle class life

For the record, the cover of the Globe magazine, containing Joan's two-part series, featured a full-head shot of poet Irving Layton and a quote "I believe the poet at the best is prophet and a descendent of prophets." Yes, it was the Sixties—the Age *of Aquarius and Flower Power*.

Joan revisited the criminally insane story, in March 1967, in a series called *Behind the Bars on G Ward*. This time she and photographer Fred Ross (who ended his newspaper career when he was fired from the *Star*, in the late '80s, for financial improprieties) lived on G Ward, at Oak Ridge, for several days to experience the community from within. Joan explained the facility was "developing a therapeutic community where everything is open and every activity is directed at one goal—to get well."

Joan had curtains inside her cell for privacy, the only concession to the press in the all-male ward. Joan and Ross shared the daily routine with 38 inmates, half of them killers, the rest rapists and physically dangerous. "For 24 hours, I felt conspicuous and awkward as the only woman, but infinitely more as an eavesdropper. It is astonishing how rapidly an outsider begins to feel part of the community and begins to identify with the other patients. Listening, watching, one becomes as tense as the patients and begins to talk to the doctors and attendants with reserves—they are, after all, staff."

The group all consented to have everything recorded and their faces photographed for publication. Not only are there photos of group therapy sessions where all the inmates assess another's history, but one picture shows a patient in intensive care with cuffed ankles. Joan doesn't hold back to spare the sensibilities of readers. She explained that the men are partnered with a psychiatrist and no emotions are held back in the sessions. "The intensity of these experiences, the human hunger for love and communication, may slide emotions across the border into homosexual sentiments, which in turn create deep anxieties in patients who may have feared such tendencies in themselves, as well as creating jealousies and tensions among others."

The word *homosexual* in a Toronto newspaper. Shocking! All-in-all, the story was pretty raw stuff for polite Canadian readers in the 1960s.

Oddly, in view of the current situation in Ontario, where there is a chronic hospital crisis—shortage of beds and services—Joan thrashed out the same hospital bed and personnel shortage, in the pages of the *Globe*, in 1967. Her copy from forty-five years ago could be plopped in the *Globe and Mail*, verbatim, today. The only thing needing change would be the references from Ontario Premier John Robarts (1917-1982), in the '60s, to Kathleen Wynne, who became Ontario Premier in 2013.

Joan quotes a doctor: "Beds don't necessarily solve the problem. The concept we have to face is providing rounded service—active treatment, ambulatory, out-patient, chronic and convalescent care." She also deals with the different cultural patterns in Metropolitan Toronto and how this affects the way people seek medical care. Her story is anchored by a neat little chart showing how many beds Toronto and each borough can expect by the end of 1970. On April 23,

2015, reporter Theresa Boyle wrote in the *Toronto Star's GTA* section, "Ontario has one of the lowest per capita hospital bed number across the developed world." As the French say: "plus ça change, plus c'est la même chose." The more things change the more they stay the same.

Also in the 1960s, the *Globe* sent Joan to New York to attend a conference of American psychiatrists, when toute le monde was going hippy, and most of the shrinks wore the hippy uniform, a tie-dyed shirt and were bearded in the non-conformist fashion of the day. Joan recalls the irony of their appearance and the fact they were most concerned about rebellious youth. Joan had the nerve to ask in a forum if they preferred everyone took nice safe jobs at Bell Telephone and added that she believed it was healthier for young people to be rebelling. "They all stared at this strange creature and carried on as if I didn't exist," she said.

Joan, obviously, liked this image of herself as associating with the unconventional. In spring, 1972, she wrote a three-part series on transgender and sex-change operations. This was brand new territory and a testimony to the *Globe* editors' open-mindedness for allowing her to proceed. "A guy I'd known in PR sent me a tape. He was an odd ball. It was a biographical piece about being trapped in the wrong body. What he was building up to is he was seeking a. I thought it was a good story. I got to know this guy really well, although, I was fairly horrified by it all."

This series was published on the front page above the fold with a headshot of Joan with the tag, *Miss* Hollobon.

Joan became her colleague's confidante as well as the documenter of her story. As time went on, her friend became more and more adamant about having a and Joan became very concerned. She begged her not to do it. But, after she was refused at *Clark Institute of Psychiatry Gender Clinic* in Toronto, she went to New York and had an operation. Joan followed her to New York (for the *Globe*) where she met a community of trans people.

Joan described one of her interviewees as a stunning six-footer who favoured ladies' tailored suits in bright red. Karen (formerly Geoff) explained that her mother had always dressed her as a girl and her sister treated Karen like a sister. Joan felt she was a classic example of a woman caught in a man's body. Not only was she young and good looking, but she was well-employed when she met her. "But when he got to be a woman, doors closed on a successful career. I kept in touch. Unfortunately, *she* couldn't afford to keep up hormone treatment and *he* became unwell. And age isn't kind. He was a hand's breath away from starvation," Joan said.

In 1972, Karen told Joan that the estimated direct and indirect expenses involved in the operation had added up to nearly $100,000. Joan followed her friend's progress on a personal level. But Karen's situation also spurred Joan on to closely examine the medical and social factors involved in a sex-change. Joan spent six months talking to the trans community in New York and doctors in Toronto, Winnipeg and New York. After all the field research, Joan started her *Globe* series with a bang and with Karen's own words: "there was an ecstatic sense of relief, of well-being even though I was still woozy from anesthetic." Karen had died at 9:30 a.m. the day before in the hospital of unknown causes. "I thought about what I had achieved as a man. What would it be like facing society as a woman and coping with problems as a woman. I was nervous, but I also said 'Thank you, God, for allowing me to live two lives in one lifetime.'"

Joan spelled out for readers that, in a New York hospital, Karen's male genitals had been removed and a vagina constructed. In her three articles, Joan talks about the implications—legal, social, psychological and medical—of a sex-change. She pointed out that nowhere does the law define what is a man or a woman. She also revealed, before surgery, transwomen must take female hormones to develop breasts, re-train the voice and remove her beard by costly electrolysis. From there, she reports the alienation and disillusionment of those who choose to change their sex. After surgery, Karen quickly found a "no-man's land of pain, poverty, humiliation, lost friends, job anxieties, fear of discovery and legal struggles to establish a new identity."

Karen told Joan, "We are society's grey ghosts. A transsexual life is a fantasy. You daren't relate naturally to men or to women the way you feel. A male TS feels drawn to normal men, but as a woman he despises homosexuals and does not regard himself as a homosexual. It is in sexual relationships, with women, that he feels homosexual." [5]

Expert

Meanwhile, by the early '70s, Joan was no light-weight reporter. By then, Joan felt she had both her craft and knowledge of her subject down pat. This gave Joan enough confidence to organize the *Canadian Science Writers Association.* In the summer of 1976, Joan attended the joint meeting of the Canadian, British and Irish medical associations in Dublin. After filing her observations about the conference, Joan travelled to Belfast where she was shocked with conditions. She wrote several stories about Northern Ireland accompanied by evocative photographs she took herself. The first one appeared on page one of the *Globe* (July 27) under the headline: *Belfast; sudden death and a shocking life.* Joan wrote; "For a second or two, Elizabeth Gibson thought it was a car backfiring, but then her Belfast reflexes took over—it was a gun. She ran back to her office to look out a window. A man in blue jeans lay face down in a pool of blood at the corner of Falls Road while young children on their way home from school crowded around. The blood was washed off the sidewalk and Falls Road was once again just an ordinary, rather drab road in the bright sunshine."

Joan also interviewed doctors who dealt with the mutilated Protestant and Catholic partisans as well as ordinary housewives. All Joan's stories reveal an acute eye for detail and, fortunately, her editors left alone all the *colour* in her pieces. Joan shocked *Globe* readers with her description of the trauma endured by the ordinary people living in Belfast through this troubled time. She wrote: "people had forgotten how to go shopping, without being searched; to go for a Sunday drive, without being stopped by armed soldiers; to see teen-aged children go out without anxiety in their hearts."

Joan also profiled a survivor of a pub bombing, doctors on the frontline and took stark photographs of poor Catholic children playing in rubble beside bombed buildings. These photos of the children accompanied a story that describes the experiences of Catholic children when they were taken by volunteers from their ghetto to the Donegal Mountains. Joan followed along and reported it took three days to get the frightened city children to leave the security of the schoolhouse (where they were staying) to explore the fields and trees. [6]

By the time Joan returned from Ireland, Warren Barton was city editor and he took a shine to Joan and doled out front-page stories. He assigned her to cover the Manitoba floods of 1979. Not only that, but she was to be accompanied by Tibor Kolley, one of the best photographers in the newspaper business. By then Joan was fifty-nine and there was newsroom back-biting about Barton's choice of sending a vintage reporter to cover an important story involving breaking news. Joan felt the general tenure of the remarks were: "Why send old Hollobon when you have a newsroom full of young hotshots?"

As often happened with events like sudden flood, Joan was told to get to Winnipeg ASAP. In the rush to get her dog boarded out, another assignment finished and out to the airport, Joan forgot to pack her rubber boots of all things. It was like going on a fishing trip without a rod, according to Joan. When Joan and Kolley arrived in Winnipeg, they went directly to reconnoiter with Joan in street shoes. "We had to get into a rowboat to go anywhere. We soon saw a house with an entire earthen dam around it—a little fort—so I interviewed the guy in my sopping wet shoes. Then we heard about a Mennonite village next to a Roman Catholic village. When we arrived at the Catholic village everyone was huddled in the basement of the church. Meanwhile, the Mennonites led by an insurance man, who was a natural leader, brought food and supplies to the R.C. village. They later helped them rebuild," recalled Joan. "I was so impressed with all the people we met and we got good copy and pictures. People were so brave in the filth and mud half way up their walls."

Kolley's lovely photographs of Canadian ballerina Karen Kain and dancer Frank Augustyn, taken at a preformance, in 1976, are still selling on-line.

The stories ran in the *Globe,* daily putting a human face on the awfulness of the flood. As self-deprecating as Joan is, by nature, decades later, she still felt cocky about showing the kids from *J- school* that an old dog could still get the goods. And, probably, with more compassion and insight than the brash neophytes, trying to make a name for themselves.

Joan produced so much copy over the years that many stories are complete blanks when people mention them to her. Most long-time reporters suffer from this type of amnesia because of the nature of daily reporting. Due to never ending deadlines, an efficient reporter has to leave yesterday's assignment behind and move deftly on to the events du jour. As old newshounds say: "yesterday's news is today's fish wrap."

On one occasion, the Globe assigned Joan to write an obituary of a famous Polish Air Vice-Marshall who did spectacular things during World War II and later died in Toronto. "I had no idea who he was, but was told the *Globe* had done a feature piece on him in the past. So I went to the *morgue* to look at the story and to see whose byline was on it. It seems I had written the story. Not only that, the man lived on Rosemount, my street, and ran a grocery store in my neighbourhood. According to the story, I actually went there. I still couldn't recall a thing," laughed Joan, adding that the story was pretty good.

> The repository of old news stories, not dead vice-marshals.

As Joan approached the end of her career, Barton asked her to go on the City Desk and for a while, in 1983, she was assignment editor. "Seeing unedited copy was a revelation. I couldn't believe the low-level of copy from senior reporters," she said.

Then one day in September of that year, Joan was scheduled to make an after-dinner speech in Ottawa at the *American Medical Writers Association's* banquet. She took the Friday off, drove to Ottawa, spoke, drove back, slept a few hours and arrived in the newsroom at Saturday noon. Joan was told Barton had been fired. There was no city editor, but Geoffrey Stevens was suddenly managing editor. Joan described him as a "nasty young man, who never changed as he aged." In the new hierarchy, Shirley Sharzer (1928-2014) became deputy managing editor—a woman Joan found to be so indecisive, "she couldn't make up her mind what she wanted for breakfast." Suddenly, Joan stopped with her vitriolic remarks and uttered one of her old pet military mottos: "No names. No pack drill."

> Currently Stevens is a freelance columnist and teaches at Guelph and Wilfred Laurier Universities.

Nearing the end of her tenure, management paid little attention to Joan and she confessed she could not get on with Stevens after disliking him for 25 years. The intrepid Joan Hollobon retired in 1985, after twenty-eight years at the *Globe*. At her retirement party, she was given a collection of Mozart and an original political cartoon by Ed Franklin.

As a cartoonist, Franklin's favourite target was Prime Minister Pierre Elliott Trudeau who like to sport a flower in his lapel. Franklin once drew PET as captain of the *Titanic*, drinking the last glass of champagne in a sinking life boat. This appeared above a *Globe* editorial: "By the fall of 1979, many of Mr. Trudeau's old admirers believed that what he wore in his button hole was the last rose of summer." The *Globe* editorialists were wrong. Trudeau's Liberal party was not defeated until 1984.

Joan also received a new-fangled tape recorder that a manager took to his office for safe keeping; she never saw it again. He may very well have taken it to the *Toronto Star*, where he was moved to the next year. (Her rival at the *Star*, medical writer Marilyn Dunlop also threw a surprise retirement party for Joan.)

The gift of classical music could not have been a more appropriate gift. On one occasion, when Michele Landsberg was a cub reporter at the *Globe*, she heard "a cascade" of whistling in the ladies' room. "It was Beethoven. I never heard anything like it. But the gender barrier made me think there must be a man in the stall. It was Joan," said Landsberg, adding that she was sorry she never got to know Joan Hollobon.[7]

Admirable Work

After leaving the newsroom, Joan wrote a book, *The Lion's Tail*, a history of the Toronto General Hospital, published in 1987. She also became a contributing editor to the *Journal of Addiction Research Foundation of Ontario*. In recognition of Joan's contribution to medicine, the Canadian Medical Association presented her with a Medal of Honour, the highest award the CMA gives to a non-professional and non-member of its association.

A few years ago, someone called Joan and told her they were launching an award in her name. Annually, the Hollobon Award is given by the *Health Care Public Relations Association* to members of the media whose work has contributed significantly to the public's understanding of health care.

In retirement, Joan shared a Victorian house near Bellwoods Park with her long-time companion Kay Rex (1919-2006), another *newshen* who was also a *Globe* staffer.

Joan Hollobon

Rex started her print career in 1943 at the *Woodstock Sentinel Review* after a stint in a Hamilton munitions factory. At the Sentinel, she toiled at the switchboard and counting advertising lines. It was there in 1941, Kay first saw teletype, a medium she described as a form of magic that connected Woodstock to world-wide news. One day, Rex spotted a notice from *Canadian Press* stating it was looking for women who wanted to be writers. Bravely, taking the bull by the horns, Kay boarded a train bound for Toronto. "CP was close to Union Station, so I went there and saw Gillis Purcell. I had sent a letter and he held it up to the light and discovered it was perfectly typed."

Letters exchanged and some months later, CP hired Rex for the Toronto office. She spent six month getting to know the *Getstetner* duplicator. Rex had no illusions about her writing talents. She understood she was hired because she was a good typist and many male reporters were fighting in Europe. A year later, Rex was sent to CP's Vancouver office where she was the only girl and, naturally, covered women's news, dressed in her grey flannel suit, drab little hat and white gloves. When the war ended, Rex, twenty-four, went with CP to Ottawa where she produced a plethora of social articles. She earned $16, a week and paid $25 monthly for room and board.

> David Gestetner's duplicating machine, patented in 1913, was the forerunner of today's super-duper photocopies.

Rex recalled a fancy garden party she covered in Ottawa in 1946. "It was the first garden party I ever went to. The women in the air force were in somber, grey uniforms, but for others, out came the old prewar garden party gowns. They had been carefully put away and had little bleached lines from the folds, but nevertheless it was quite a show."

In the Ottawa bureau, the boys often played tricks on Rex. One slow Saturday afternoon, the men buzzed off to the local beer parlour and Rex was alone with the teletype machine. The phone rang and a voice said, "this is Prime Minister MacKenzie King and I want to give a statement." At first I thought it was one of the boys, then intuition clicked in and I realized this was real. I had my typewriter handy and took down 300 words. It was pretty trivial, but I was shaking. This shows how small a town Ottawa was back then. There was an openness and the press always had direct contact even with the top brass."

In 1958, Rex took a job in the women's section of the *Globe and Mail*. Joan and Rex became fast friends. Rex stayed at the *Globe* until her retirement in 1992. Three years later, she produced a history of the *Canadian Women's Press Club* called *No Daughter of Mine*. The book, launched at the Heliconian Hall in Toronto, was dedicated to Joan Hollobon: "My friend and fellow press clubber, whose encouragement and help made this book possible."

All through her career, Rex was an avid supporter of the Press Club and an activist who battled for women's rights in the newsroom. Meanwhile, Joan resisted the CWPC and wouldn't join for years. After much pestering, in 1968, Joan finally joined the club and soon became the treasurer. Joan claimed her only qualification for the post was "an intense dislike for owing money and the knowledge that if you only have ten cents, you cannot buy a dollar lunch."

> The book title came from an incident in Rex's own life. As a young woman, when she applied for a job at a daily paper, the editor growled. "No daughter of mine will ever become a reporter. Women don't belong in newsrooms. They restrict our language."

In a profile about Joan in a 1973 copy of the CWPC newsletter, Joan was described as "an inquisitive, rapid-thinking journalist with a lively and sometimes devastating wit." This story is also meant to portray Joan as a woman who "feels deeply and speaks passionately about issues that matter to her. The Joan who longs for more public parks in cities, who more often than she'll admit, lends a helping hand."

Ater Rex died in 2006, Joan sold the Bellwoods house and she and her cat, Tootsie, moved to an apartment on Heath Street where Joan brewed strong coffee and her spit-fire speech was as salty as ever. She lamented the fact that at her age, her old friends were no more. "They're all dead. Damn It! Now my friends are half my age."

Looking back over her career and all the lucky breaks, Joan said, "I had a wonderful time, but I wouldn't have hired me." Joan forgot about the hard work, long hours and the three decades of unstinting dedication she put into her job at the *Globe*.

Joan Hollobon, at ninety-seven, resides in Kensington Gardens, a nursing facility on Brunswick Ave. She is frail and cannot hear well, but she is still bright-eyed and longing for dark chocolate, strong coffee and raspberries.

AUGUSTA "DUSTY" VINEBERG

The Montreal Star, 1956-1973.

1926-Present

"I fought with the editors many times when I felt they were stupid. They were scared of me."

10

Dusty Vineberg Solomon stated right off the top, she had one regret: "I didn't have children. My mother, who lived to be 101, could have been a CEO. She was a perfectionist, a marvel and always said, 'you can only do one thing properly at a time.' And contrary to the evidence around me, I didn't believe you could do a good job and have children."

That out of the way, Dusty, an attractive, vigorous seventy-one-year-old, sat in her tastefully appointed Westmount apartment and commenced with the story of how she became a household name during the Swinging Sixties in Montreal.

During our conversation in 1997, Dusty's mind drifted to the past and the events that led to her tenure at the *Montreal Star*. She began her story at the beginning.

Augusta Myers Vineberg was born on December 21, 1926, into a well-heeled Montreal family that gave her a strong sense of security and her place in the scheme of things. Dusty's mother, Eva Friedman, was also born in Montreal, but in a tenement on what is now the McGill University campus. Her father was brought up in New York City and raised by his aunts. As a young man, he left New York and went to Montreal to work as a furrier in the Vineberg family's successful fur business. It was there that he met Eva Friedman and they married.

Augusta's mother knew her daughter would get a nickname and feared it would be Gussie, which she associated with a relative who ended up in a mental hospital. So, Dusty it was.

When most Canadian families were struggling through the soul-destroying deprivations of the Great Depression, followed by World War II, Dusty was ensconced on Avenue Elm, in Westmount, Quebec. There she lived a life of plenty in a grand house that was still in the countryside when it was purchased by her parents in the 1920s.

"Well, in 1944, I did wear a re-made dress of mother's to a dance. But then the dance was in Westmount," Dusty said, defensively, and then—realizing she could not deny that she was privileged—she admitted her affluent upbringing would forever affect the way she dealt with people and her career.

Dusty was impressed with her father's service in the *Royal Flying Corp* during World War I and was thrilled when he joined up again in 1939 to fight in the *Hitler* War.

Meanwhile, Dusty had heard Adolph Hitler's 1939, "Reichstag Speech" on the radio. It was a harangue, about the *Jewish Question*, and this influenced her decision to be a writer. Although she was still a child, Dusty believed if she became a writer she could right Hitler's pernicious hate mongering. With this goal in mind, after graduating from McGill University in 1948, Dusty went to graduate school at the Columbia School of Journalism. "They had quotas and I applied along with another Jewish girl from Montreal. I never figured they would take both of us, but they did."

Dusty commented that the sole thing her New York classmates remembered about her when she attended a reunion was her participation in a class skit, in which she played a woman of *easy virtue* in black knit stockings. The only thing Dusty recollected was an assignment to produce a story about the Fulton Street Fish Market and not being able to find it on the waterfront.

A year later in 1949, when Dusty was twenty-one years old, she travelled to Europe with her sister Trina—this was one of the many extended trips they would take together. Back home, deciding she ought to get to work, Dusty tried to land a newspaper job, but found no such luck. "So I took a job as public relations director of The Combined Jewish Appeal. When I did well, Edgar Bronfman patted me on the fanny," recalled Dusty.

> Edgar Bronfman (1929-2013), heir to the Seagram Empire that started with the family selling whiskey during the Prohibition Era. As a philanthropist, Bronfman was much involved in Jewish causes

There were several secretaries in the Jewish appeal office, so Dusty took to wearing a hat to distinguish herself from this lowly group of workers. But, she still had one of those fancy caps set aside for a position at a newspaper. She would take press releases, in person, into the *Montreal Star* so she could "rub shoulders" with the newsies. Finally, after seven years at the Jewish Appeal and making herself noticeable, Dusty wheedled a job offer from the *Montreal Star*. "I was making $90 a week at the Jewish appeal and I demanded $100 from the *Star*. They wouldn't give it to me at first. The managing editor, Walter O'Hearne, gave me a test: thirty books to summarize. I stupidly read them all, instead of summarizing the flap blurbs," recalled Dusty.

Even though Dusty desperately wanted the job, she tenaciously held out for the $100—and got it—a lucrative salary for a woman in 1956. Dusty was twenty-eight years old and living at home, which she describes as "comfortable and confined," and left her with lots of spending money for clothes and trips.

> At the time, teachers were barely pulling in $3,000 per year.

An Insubordinate Newsgirl

One of Dusty's first assignments was to write ten minutes' worth of news clips that were to be broadcasted daily on CJAD from the *Star's* news desk. The rookie recognized it as an assignment, designed to keep her busy. "Art Leonard, the announcer, barely tolerated me. They also found other things for me to do like summarizing the *bumpf* on press releases into one paragraph. It was torture." She readily admitted she was never assigned to cover a royal tour—a job that fell to most newshens at some time in their careers—because she was not reliable, fluid or speedy enough with her copy.

> Bumpf: Useless text.

"I was aware there were such things as deadlines, but they didn't apply to me," said Dusty, airily.

Despite a lack of reporting skills in those early days, Dusty wrote feature story after feature story, only ever telling them from a single-sided perspective. She laughed as she told me, "someone once said, to me, you ought to look at the other side of a story. It never occurred to me. And my editors never asked for two sides of an issue... Another time, Ed Romaine, one of the men on the re-write desk, said: fine job, but how about the name of the organization."

Dusty loved every minute of being a reporter. She confessed, all the local and newsroom politics would pass right over her head, "One day I said to the editor, Don Newman, I love working on a newspaper. And he said: when are you going to start."

She also commented how she realized that the *Montreal Star* was not the last word in journalism; she understood that if she were going to make it big, she had to go to Toronto. Dusty was never brave enough to leave Montreal and as a single woman who needed a salary to survive, she didn't want to take any chances of being without a job.

While Dusty may have played the role of fluffy airhead and used all the clichéd feminine wiles to get her way, she was no fool. "The *Star* was like a marshmallow. You pushed. It gave. I really did not manipulate, but...well, I figured out if you applied enough pressure, you could get your way. I fought with the editors many times when I felt they were stupid. They were scared of me."

And when the topic of feminism arose, she simply replied, "Feminist? What's that? I never experienced discrimination. I felt being female was an asset."

Augusta Vineberg

Throughout the 1950s and 1960s, Dusty pretty much got her way at the *Star*, by terrorizing her male superiors. "I would kick up a terrible row when I wanted something," confided the girl, with no dependents and no financial worries. And, on a whim, the spoiled brat in Dusty would take extended leaves from the *Star* to travel in Europe for three or four months at a time. She would then write about her travels and the *Star* would publish these articles.

Some of her travel pieces make interesting historical reading today. An early article described a trip Dusty and her sister Trina took to Vienna in 1959 for Passover. After observing that Vienna was "only now recovering its pre-war gaiety" and that some bomb-damaged buildings have been restored, she recounted a Seder Service arranged for Hungarian Jewish refugees in the only synagogue left standing. The Nazis only overlooked it because it was discreetly wedged between Aryan apartment buildings.

Dusty wrote, "The Seder was held in the heart of what had been the Jewish ghetto of Vienna, in an old, dank, un-restored building. There was no new paint here. Moisture oozed from the dark walls. Small as the synagogue was, it was able to accommodate the few hundred worshippers who survive today, of Vienna's pre-Hitler Jewish population of 180,000. We have no pictures, but I think we will always remember the humble congregation, singing so hopefully."

The sisters also spent time in Frankfurt where they looked at the impressive statue of Goethe. During her reportage on the post-war destruction, Dusty asked the unanswerable question: "We wandered through the bomb-damaged city and wondered *how*, in the face of tradition and culture, it could have happened."[1]

In the summer of 1966, one of Dusty's best pieces appeared in the *Star*. Dusty travelled ostensibly to the still new(ish) Stratford Festival, in Ontario. But instead of theatre, she focused on its local Mennonite country. This subject has been covered thousands of times since, but fifty years ago, the isolationistic Mennonite community had just come to light and Canadians considered it a very exotic topic.

Dusty told readers that she explored 750 miles of road around Stratford in one week. She exuberantly describes everything, from a fly-speckled grocery store in Milbank, where she sat on a kitchen chair for a soft drink, to bonneted toddlers babbling in German in Elmira. "This is Mennonite country [...] An hour's drive north of Stratford, you'll start seeing this strange sect on the road, clipping along in their black horse-drawn buggies. A rule of thumb, I was told, is that Mennonite men are clean-shaven; the Amish group, wear patriarchal beards."

Dusty concluded her piece with advice: "In this region, you must not rush. Stop the car and wander down a tree-shaded main street. You may find yourself outside the blacksmith's shop at Hawkesville where the Mennonite smithy shoes about 1,500 horses a year."

Dusty was equally fascinated with Cape Breton, but for different reasons. Her first night started in typical tourist fashion and, at Cheticamp, she spent an hour watching a spectacular sunset streak the "robin's egg-blue sky with flame." She wrote about driving the next day, through fields of wild flowers and thistle in "overwhelmingly sweet air."

In 1969, Dusty called her readers attention to the Cabot Trail, which was finally paved. She writes that gone are the days, "when the Trail was a dirt roller coaster so narrow that one prayed not to meet a car coming in the opposite direction." Then suddenly, Dusty was confronted by the task of covering the devastation done by a massive forest fire that roared out of control for fifteen long days. West of Ingonish as she was about to enter the Cape Smokey region, Dusty saw a sign: "Entering Cape Smokey Burn, June 1968, 42,000 acres started by carelessness."

It seems, due to all her pugnacity and trouble making in the newsroom, Dusty ended up being the first girl reporter to ever to sit in the City Room with the *Montreal Star* boys.

In Dusty's day, Donna Logan, Canada's first female managing editor, was also in the *Star* newsroom. Though she was management and not a reporter, Logan still posed a threat to Dusty's elitist position as the only female. "One day another woman arrived in the City Room and I didn't want her. I wanted to be the only one," Dusty confessed, shamelessly.

She explained, "We called the women's section *The Cage*. *The Cage* was a space with glass walls that separated it from the main newsroom. Fashion writer, Zoe Bieler, presided over *The Cage* and, inside, were other reporters, such as pioneer restaurant critic, Helen Rochester."

Donna Logan was Deputy Managing Editor of the *Montreal Star*, 1976-1979. Director of University of British Columbia's Sing Tao School of Journalism, 1997-2007. (Now Professor Emerita.) President of Canadian Media Research Consortium, 2005-2014.

Despite Dusty's snide attitude towards the gals working in *The Cage*, Bieler won a *Canadian Women's Press Club* award for her women's pages in both 1963 and 1964.

As a result of her fierceness, Dusty was left alone to do just about anything that appealed to her. She travelled on expense accounts, interviewed both local and international movers-and-shakers and became a well-known member of the local press corps, (but it wasn't all to *Princess* Dusty's liking).

"In the late '50s, I covered the Fontaine Zoo in the Mont-Royal district (closed 1989). It was zoo, zoo, zoo, until it came out of my ears. Baby animals, new animals, birth of animals. It's exactly what you would expect them to send a woman out to do," snorted Dusty. "Every time I was sent out to cover something, I came back with three ideas of my own and eventually they let me do whatever I wanted and they allowed me to explore. This enabled me to do culture, science and medical stories. I had pretensions about being knowledgeable and cultured," admitted Dusty, who in her senior years was, perhaps, judging her young self a bit too harshly.

Dusty's interest in culture was first stimulated while watching and lusting after Québécois sculptor, Armand Vaillancourt. Dusty used to ogle him from her office window back in her days at the Jewish Appeal as he carved an elm tree on the Appeal office property. This artwork is now a centerpiece in the Quebec Museum in Quebec City. "You should have seen him stripped naked to the waist," said the infatuated newsgirl with a gleam in her eye.

Years later, in September of 2009, poet-minstrel Leonard Cohen turned seventy-five. An event, which Dusty attended, was held in Montreal to celebrate the poet's birthday. Interestingly, Cohen was a friend of Vaillancourt, who was a passionate supporter of Quebec sovereignty. His wife, Suzanne Verdal, a passionate Flower Child, was the inspiration for Cohen's *Suzanne*, an anthem of the 1960s that reverberates today.

Party Gal

For the most part, in the 1950s and 1960s, Dusty's life as a reporter was a wonderful whirl of lavish press parties and sophisticated openings. "It was glamorous—lunches, taxis, cocktail parties. Always, the most sought-after invitations were for the showings at Irene's Hats. Irene's cocktail parties were so *lah-de-dah* that only the crème de la crème was invited. Tout le monde wore her hats in those days, and Irene was able to keep five milliners working for her," said Dusty.

Irene, the milliner, was Irene Burstyn, who made hats for the likes of the Molsons, Bronfmans and the rest of Montreal's high society. Olive Diefenbaker, wife of Canadian Prime Minister John Diefenbaker, also wore Irene's hats, as did Prime Minister Lester Pearson's wife. Burstyn launched her business in 1948, and by the time she closed shop, in 1978, she had a customer list of 8,000 well-heeled and well-hatted ladies.[3]

In the 1950s and early '60s, Enid Nemy, who would one day become an institution at the *New York Times*, was working in Montreal as a publicist. Nemy was in charge of organizing *Irene of Montreal's* exclusive fashion shows. These were held in Irene's *chi-chi atelier*, on Sherbrook Street, Montreal's most elegant address.

Nemy invited only a few members of the press to Irene's annual hat previews. "They were always small affairs. Enid was a very good writer and she wrote the commentary and spoke as the hats were modeled. The hats were gorgeous and the event was perfection. But I was too young and stupid to understand how unique these showings were," Dusty admitted.

Nemy started her career at the *Winnipeg Free Press* and later went into PR and, after a stint with CBC TV in '63, Nemy surfaced at the *New York Times*. There she was a correspondent and later, a columnist, renowned for her pithy observations. In her nineties, Nemy was still writing the occasional piece for the *Times*.[4]

When asked if she wore a hat to work, Dusty retorted as if the question were plain stupid, "Naturally, I wore chic hats and gloves."

In a 1964 photograph of Dusty, she is interviewing Secretary of State Judy LaMarsh at Dorval airport. LaMarsh was returning home after representing Canada at the Innsbruck Olympics. Even though it is winter, Dusty, ever chic, wears big sunglasses, a '60s fashion icon, along with the bouffant hair-do, made famous by Jackie Kennedy. In 1967 Dusty and LaMarsh

---

While Cohen was performing in Israel, the celebrants in Montreal sent him birthday wishes via satellite. The proceeds from the homage went towards the establishing of the *Leonard Cohen Poet Residence* at Westmount High School, which Cohen had attended. *The Canadian Jewish News* reported, "Two of Cohen's relatives were present; Dusty Solomon Vineberg, eighty-two, and her younger sister Trina Berenson. Their grandfather and Cohen's grandmother were siblings"[2]

Montreal's McCord Museum has a collection of eighteen hats and a few matching dresses, designed by Irene Burstyn. Burnstyn would say, in interviews, she made unusual and hats that were never out of style. One of her quirkier chapeaux was designed for Madame Jehane Benoît who was the Grande Dame of Québécois cookery until she died in 1987. Benoît's hat featured plastic apples.

would meet again, in Montreal, when LaMarsh was in charge of Expo 67.

Although Dusty never purchased a très chère chapeau from Irene, when her sister Trina married, Irene's *atelier* made a veil to match the bride's wedding outfit—a cocktail suit made from silk and shot with gold flashes. Dusty, the only bridesmaid, was in a shimmering silver dress and Irene created a matching veil for her as well.

Berenson worked for the *Family Herald,* a farm journal, under the same ownership as the *Montreal Star*. After the war, the *Herald* had a huge circulation across Canada. Trina wrote recipes and tested food under the watchful eye of editor, Frank Walker. She often cooked and baked the food for the *Herald* in Dusty's apartment. The culinary results were photographed in the apartment, despite Dusty's horror every time a boorish photographer dragged camera equipment across her exquisite Persian carpets.

Dusty commented, if a *Herald* reader complained that a recipe didn't work, Trina would send a cake to her, even if it were as far away as Calgary. The *Herald*, founded in 1869, folded in 1968.

Although Dusty liked to insist she really didn't have any political or feminist leanings, she joined the CWPC in 1958, and served as president of the Montreal chapter, from 1961 to 1963.

Dusty was no stranger to the Far North. Shortly before joining the Press Club, the *Star* sent her to the military base at Great Whale Bay to write about the Royal Canadian Air Force's annual Christmas party. The following year, Dusty persuaded the RCAF to fly Amita Malik, a visiting journalist from India, to the party. Malik, sponsored by the CWPC, spent ten months in Canada as a guest of different reporters across the country.

"I was in charge of Amita's month-long program, in Montreal, and I went everywhere with her. Amita was a flamboyant woman, always the centre of attention. She refused to remove her Indian dress. Amita, traipsing over the tundra in a pure silk sari and all her jewelry, topped by an air force parka and wearing mukluks, was a picture for my memory book," said Dusty, adding that as exotic as she was, the woman turned out to be a trial and never stopped complaining to her hostesses.

At one cocktail party, in Montreal, Malik arrived in a gorgeous bright silk sari and all the other women were in the little black cocktail dress that were fashionable in the early '60s. Malik was the only tulip in an onion patch. At the next press club party, the clever Malik swanned in, in a black sari, only to find all the Canadian newsgirls decked out in colourful dresses.

In Moncton, Malik became an honorary citizen. In Calgary, she was given the traditional white cowboy hat, and in Ottawa, Malik was introduced to Prime Minister John Diefenbaker, who was deaf and talked non-stop for a half-hour. The CWPC also arranged a visit to 24 Sussex Drive to see Olive Diefenbaker. Apparently, this outing was not a success as Malik was bored, bored, bored.

When Malik returned to India, where she wrote for English language dailies in Calcutta and Delhi, her observations about Canada were less than flattering. The gals in the CWPC were quite stunned by Malik's deportment in Canada. There is no record of the press club initiating a second exchange with a foreign female journalist.

The zenith of Dusty's career was Expo 67, held in Montreal, in celebration of Canada's 100th birthday. Montreal and the whole country were in party mode for a full year, as Bobby Jimbie sang *Ca-Naaa-Da* non-stop.

"The city was so exciting. Everybody came. Montreal basked as the *Centre of the Universe*. All the stops were pulled out. Money was no object for the arts and entertainment and there was no limit to public expenditure. It was a circus that Montreal was still paying for fifty years later," Dusty said.

Dusty's tenure took place during the *Swinging Sixties*. It was psychedelic, Pop Art, love-ins and sleep-ins à la Yoko Ono and John Lennon, and Dusty was there, at all the happenings. Montreal reveled in an orgy of celebrities, novelties and parties, topped with the Exposition. It was the first time a Canadian city ever played host to a World's Fair.

As Montreal geared up for this exposition, it became a Mecca for swingers in bell-bottoms, Twiggy bodies and asymmetrical Sassoon haircuts. Every young person in the country spoke of Mountain Street with the same awe as London's Carnaby Street and The Beatles.

Augusta Vineberg

In 1967, as Secretary of State, judy LaMarsh (1924-1980) was in charge of Expo 67, Canada's Centennial celebration. LaMarsh was in the army in WWII and served as a Japanese translator. After the war, she became a lawyer and a Cabinet Minister under PM Lester Pearson.

Jean Drapeau, Montreal's mayor for thirty years, financially mismanaged both Expo 67 and the 1976 Summer Olympics, also held in Montreal. Both events were scandal-ridden and citizens were left with over a $1 billion in debts. Montreal wasn't in the black until the late 1990s thanks to Drapeau's bungling.

Newsgirls

In 1965, pre-Expo, a Montreal pharmacist opened a drug store that was part psychedelic disco, part shop and a shrine for anyone who knew "where it was at." *Le Hot Drug* swung all night, and the Montreal scene left visiting hayseeds from Toronto and points west with their mouths agape.

Dusty wrote a column about opening night at le Hot Drug Discothèques. "There was a happening in a Montreal drugstore last night that rallied the jet-set, the far-outers, the hips, the heps and hautes [...] The occasion was the opening of William Sofin's new drugstore-discothèques-art gallery on Mountain St. This establishment had attracted interest for months thanks to the "habitable sculpture" that cloaks the entrance. Last night it became clear that the drugstore, where even the squarest square would not hesitate to pick up his prescriptions, is just a front."

Dusty described scenes that are now '60s clichés, but as she watched guests doing the *frug* in "their little black discothèques dresses" against a "dead kitchen-tile white" backdrop in the discothèques, it was all fresh and new. In the gallery that night was an art piece made of broken mirror with a price tag of $500. Dusty commented at least one guest gazed at the shards and gasped, "Oh dear, what happened."[5]

Dusty also mentioned Liberal MP, John Turner, who became Canada's Prime Minister for four months in 1984. He did the opening honours—not by cutting a ribbon, but by cutting a chain *barring passage* to the nether regions. "As he stepped away from his official functions, Turner demanded, 'Now where are the drugs?'" Like man, that was the Sixties!

Dusty's description of the frenetic soirée for a privileged 1,000 caught the eye of the *Star's* political reporter, Bob Lewis. Lewis wrote Dusty a note on parliamentary press-gallery stationery saying that he had just finished reading her column with great delight. "It was, I assure you, a welcome break from all those drab reports on crime and politics [...] Not only is it nice to see people excited, it's pleasant to read copy that swings."

> Later Lewis was editor of *Maclean's* magazine: 1993-2000.

Leading up to Expo, Dusty interviewed all the respected personages who swanned through town, including artists Alexander Calder and Henry Moore. Moore was unveiling one of his signature abstract sculptures at *Place Ville Marie,* Montreal's spanking new city centre. Dusty remembered the great sculptor declaring, to a philistine *Montreal Star* photographer, "No! I will not stick my head in that hole."

Dusty was bowled over when she interviewed Buckminster Fuller, the American architect responsible for the design of the geodesic dome, la Montreal Biosphère, at the United States' Expo pavilion. "He explained what a geodome was in twenty minutes," said Dusty, quite breathless, thirty years later.

The great geodome became a matter of controversy after the fair opened. There were four main exhibits in Fuller's gigantic bubble—two of which focused on space research and exploration, one featured Hollywood memorabilia and another, called *The American Spirit*, displayed everything from Canadian Indigenous bead work to patchwork quilts. In *The Spirit Hall*, an exhibit featuring 250 men's hats became a serious bone of contention due to the Russian presence at Expo.

The Russian pavilion, a no-nonsense warehouse affair, was stuffed with hardware, machinery and weapons illustrating the prowess of *Mother Russia.* Outraged American *hawks* called their country's effort a "hollow bubble" and the displays inside superficial. The Cold War was still a reality and the Berlin Wall had yet to fall. In 1967, Russia and the U.S. were overtly jostling each other for supreme military power. The frivolous hats that Jack Masey of the United States Information Agency installed inside the pavilion enraged American pundits. As the bureaucrat responsible for the exhibits, he was called to Washington to answer for the flippant way he chose to portray the U.S.

Dusty came to the defense of the American pavilion and its delightful display of hats and American folk-art collections. After all, she had a special affinity to hats thanks to her education at Irene's hat shop. After describing the American pavilion itself as, "making an overwhelming statement about American Architecture and engineering genius," Dusty declared the contents of the structure "elegant, witty, beautiful and fun."

She further wrote in the *Star*: "This has displeased visitors who appear to feel that anything that is fun cannot be serious. The hats—from cowboy to hard hats—are intended to represent in a lighthearted way the diversity of American life. There are some among us, it seems prefer hard facts to hard hats [...] In short, the pavilion is fun and it really does feel like Buckminster Fuller described it, like going aboard an ocean liner."

"The U.S.S.R. jam-packed its pavilion with every last nut and bolt manufactured in the Soviet Union, thus illustrating the might of Russia. Can anyone really imagine that the Americans are unable to lay out as much hardware as the Russians. The designers of the U.S. exhibit, civilized and world-oriented as they are, simply take it for granted their country's ability to achieve, technologically, whatever is necessary."

Dusty concluded, "The pavilion stands as a reminder of American diversity which resists generalizations about the country [...] What the world expects these days is more in the military line—rockets, napalm, the blindfold blunder into a quagmire from which it is impossible to extract the nation and where hate, fear and fanaticism are bred, dark companions of the qualities of love, hope, optimism, grace and joy which have built the American pavilion."

The column, "Hats off to the Americans," which ran on May 13, was so eloquent that it was later read into the *Congressional Record* in Washington when Masey was called on the carpet for shaming the U.S.

After Expo wrapped up, Dusty penned a television column for two years. "TV was just coming in and all I had to do was write about what I saw on television—not criticism, just bright observations and comments. I didn't do it well, but, interestingly, it was popular. I was always afraid of boring people. Also I filled in on the radio and talked about TV when Pat Pierce, who was a household name in Montreal, went on vacation."

One of Dusty's TV columns dealt with a CBC program, called *Viewpoint*, that one night featured the Toronto *Globe and Mail's* best-known columnist, Richard J. Needham (1912-1996). Dusty wrote, "Mr. Needham, in print, is biting, satiric and often wildly funny. In person? Well, if bad man Peter Lorre had turned into *Alice in Wonderland*, I couldn't have been more astonished [...] I'd pictured a *Mack the Knife*, but there he was a self-confessed 50, comfortable, solid-looking person wearing grey hair and big black horn-rimmed glasses." Dusty also commented that this "professional debunker," in print, was all "sweetness and springtime message" on television. Apparently he babbled on, offering all kinds of platitudes concerning sunshine in our lives and quoting Thoreau and Zorba the Greek to make his point. Needham, known as a rake in Toronto's journalistic circles ended his TV appearance with wishes for "maple sugar houses and a prolonged bout of spring fever to all at CBC."

Dusty concluded her review on a somewhat sarcastic note about what a tonic Needham's "happy little essay" was, in a spot, normally reserved for political and economic analysts.[6]

As an aside, Needham did write for the *Globe and Mail*, an amusing account of his visit to Expo 67 and the annoying long lines to get into pavilions. "Far more people are coming than anyone planned and they have to wait their turn for everything. The lineup has its own language, which might be called Exporanto—'I spent the afternoon drinking beer in Hai. The last time I saw my wife was when she went to the washroom in Britain [...] I met this fascinating woman in Yugoslavia, but then I lost her in the Atlantic Provinces."[7]

Another column featured Danny Gallivan, a hockey commentator in the early days of television and radio, only second in fame to Toronto's Foster Hewitt. In the post-war era, both radio announcers were revered as national institutions. Their roles, as embodiments of the only passion Canadians had ever had—hockey—were celebrated across the nation. To this day, nothing has filled the void left in the Canadian soul after the six-league NHL expanded into the U.S. and became Big American Business. Just ask any Canadian-born male over the age of fifty.

Dusty observed Gallivan (1917-1993) at work in the Montreal Forum, from a catwalk "tucked up near the Forum roof, sixty-five feet above the ice." She began her hockey piece with self-mockery. "That, said my mentor (Gallivan), who knew that I wasn't positive who exactly the Stanley Cup contenders were, is the ice."

Although Dusty didn't really say which teams were playing in her piece, a savvy reader could glean that it was the Montreal Canadiens and the Chicago Blackhawks by the names of the players she listed.

In her reporting style that made much use of compound sentences, Dusty wrote, "Up

Dusty painted a dramatic word picture of Gallivan, known as The Voice of Hockey. He narration of the Canadiens' home games went out over the airwaves for thirty years (1952-1983).

Newsgirls

there you're aware of noise, colour, crowd, noise: organ music, skates hissing down the ice, sticks thwacking boards and bodies, and a roar that irresistibly recalls the madding crowd the poet wanted to be far from. And it's with that roar in their ears that the broadcasters translate sixty minutes of lightening play into the King's English."

"Danny sucks cough drops and squeezes his left ear between the thumb and forefinger of his left hand. As the game starts, he assumes a semi-permanent crouch, his long torso rising out of his seat with his voice, until he hangs over the ice."

Dusty asked Gallivan how he could keep talking through entire games. He told her he studied the rulebook and the players' histories. Dusty concluded, after her first-hand Forum experience, that next time they wouldn't have to point out the ice to her.[8]

Interestingly, beside Dusty's columns was a photo of her, with her teased, bubble-hairdo and next to this, were the TV listings for the 1960s. Fifty-five years ago, Montrealers were watching *The Adventures of Rin Tin Tin*, *Red River Jamboree*, Pierre Berton, *Gunsmoke*, *Ti-Jean Caribou* and Marshal Dillon.

It would seem, at thirty-five, Dusty had the world by the tail. She was enjoying a career with credentials, local fame and financial independence. Then one day, Dusty felt a great emptiness. "I thought, sitting on the subway, here I am going home to watch TV and other people are going home to their children and their lives. But before Dusty left her entertainment beat, she learned a valuable journalistic lesson. She made the mistake of attacking Canada's "Singing Sweetheart Juliette"—one of the biggest stars of black and white Canadian television. Juliette, a robust blonde, was always introduced as *Our Pet Juliette* and Dusty referred to her in a column as the "overweight" Pet Juliette.

"The reaction was awful. The whole country came to Juliette's defense. But I learned something. I knew it was not a fair comment. It was a lesson in how not to provoke people. My comment was gratuitous. It was an abuse of power. In those days we manipulated people. The press did not examine itself. We had unbridled power." Having said that, Dusty admitted she wasn't sure she approves of an ombudsman's position (in a newspaper), and a press where everything a reporter writes is scrutinized and held accountable.

As exciting as the Expo period had been, Dusty's fondest memory was of Keith Andrews, the Montreal public relations man for the McClelland & Stewart publishing house. "He was very glamorous and, when he came to Montreal to promote a new book, he would round us up and take us out to a lavish lunch at the Mt. Royal Hotel. He would also bring authors to the hotel for us to interview. I interviewed everybody. There was a tremendous vitality. It was the best of times."

But it Wasn't Always Champagne and Frivolity for Dusty

In 1963, seven years after Dusty joined the *Star*, the public relations people put out a blurb about her career—its theme revolved around the old clichés, the unpredictability of women, as shown by Dusty's quirky career, and the "feminine prerogative to change her mind." The writer said that Miss Vineberg dislikes being confined to any one beat and she has run the "gamut of reportorial tasks from riding a tractor during a farm assignment to editing a book review page."

The promo also indicated that Dusty had a particular interest in medicine and her groundbreaking story, about a heart operation involving a heart-lung machine, earned Dusty the *Canadian Women's Press Club's* Memorial Award for the best news story of 1958.

In 1966, Dusty earned her keep when she wrote another award-winning story *Heart and Hope*. It was about Dr. Arthur Vineberg, a cardiac surgeon at the Royal Victoria Hospital in Montreal and a professor of surgery at McGill University. Vineberg pioneered an artery operation that increases the flow of blood to the hearts of patients who suffer from coronary artery disease. In her lengthy feature, Dusty explained the technology, quoted a woman whose life changed because of the operation, and talked about a group of doctors from Massachusetts General Hospital, who arrived in Montreal to observe Dr. Vineberg's team at work in the operating room.

In order to keep readers from suspecting Dusty was promoting a relative, she used the name Eva Friedman (her mother's maiden name) as her byline.[9]

For the record, a *Montreal Star* sports' reporter, Harold Atkins, was the one who dubbed the Montreal Canadiens' top scorer, Maurice Richard, the "Rocket." Later, when Rocket Richard's spunky little brother, Henri, made the team, he was dubbed "The Pocket Rocket."

Augusta Vineberg

The Voice of Feminism

As time went on, Dusty learned her craft and wrote her fair share of serious features. And sporadically in her newspaper copy, Dusty revealed that she had a few feminist stripes. In the spring of 1969, the Ford Motor Company twigged to the fact that girls were actually buying cars, and Dusty, along with a few other lady reporters and business writers, were flown on the company DC3 to the Ford plant in St. Thomas, Ontario. They were to preview the Maverick, a compact car designed to compete with the Volkswagen. It was the first vehicle the company built with women in mind.

The idea was that the newshens would deliver an opinion on the car. Racing drivers were assigned to take the females under their wings and help them with the technical jargon. Dusty commented in her copy that it was a good thing too; because all she knew after the test drive was that the car "rides smooth." Dusty also wrote, "you should have heard the men. The steering was the best of any American car. It was not a wallowing pig like the Sting Ray with a 427 (You'd better tell Dusty what a 427 is!). The brakes worked very well. (Fool, that I was, I had taken that for granted.) It was a perfect car for a woman because it parked and didn't stop there." Ford must have rued the day it put her on that corporate flight. Dusty looked over the plant and told Montreal readers, "this emphasis on appealing to women struck me as comic later, when we toured the spanking new plant, one of the most modern on the continent—from which women are strikingly absent."

"There can be few more totally masculine environments than an automobile factory. The place pulses with vitality. The place is skull-cracking, a clamour of screeches, hisses, bangs and beeps interrupted by the heart-stopping shriek of the crash truck racing to a point somewhere in the plant's 1.5 million square feet."

Dusty questioned the dearth of females in the plant and her Ford guide told her American factories employ some women but there are none in Canada. "Maybe that's why we are the number one division," he added, "the women work happily, outside in the offices as clerks and receptionists." Dusty described the offices "as in another world and as depressingly quiet and gray as those in any government building."[10]

Dusty often made her point, in print, about the double standard for men and women, but she was not always above doing the "girly" thing herself. In the mid '60s, she indulged herself in a cutesy life-style column about shopping for a new outfit. "It was in a vulnerable mood perilously poised between doom and despair that I found myself the other day on the threshold of a chic little shop...The shop was the sort of place where the solitary shopper tends to be swept off her feet by the enthusiasms of the proprietor, a charming lady that could sell sunlamps in the Sahara [...] I knew that, yet I tried on and tried on [...] And then it happened, I almost heard the leash snap as the adventurer that lurks in every woman streaked to the surface screaming, "Buy! Buy!"" The piece goes on to tell how the newly clad Dusty pranced around the newsroom and picked up the telephone receiver, "with a theatrical gesture worthy of Doris Day," in the hope of drawing attention to her new jewelry and duds. But no one responded except the cafeteria cashier—the lowest employee in the *Montreal Star's* food chain—asking, where did she get her bracelet?

In 1970, Dusty won an award for a four-part series about learning disabilities. Fifty years ago, these disabilities were generally not diagnosed nor talked about. A child was retarded or backward and that was that. Dusty is very proud of this series as this particular subject had not yet been discussed before in a public forum. Her four, full-page features, won a nod in the United States from the *National Council for the Advancement of Education Writing* and the *Star* made her features into a booklet that was widely distributed to parents, social workers and educators.

Dusty commented: "I spent months on that and it appeared in four consecutive issues. The psychologist I was working with said the work I produced was the equivalent to an M.A thesis."

An assignment that Dusty identified as one of her most memorable was one that turned out to be a *Mission of Mercy* in the Arctic. McGill University had a contract with the Federal Department of Health and Welfare to care for the people dwelling in the Baffin Island region. Dr. Douglas Cameron, who was responsible for the program, arranged for Dusty to fly to Frobisher Bay (now Iqaluit) to record for the reading public the university's work with Eskimos at Frobisher General

Hospital. As luck would have it, Dusty arrived in the Arctic just as a mysterious virus surfaced in Igloolik and killed two children in the settlement of 600 people, 150 miles inside the Arctic Circle. It was decided that the best course of action would be to evacuate three other desperately ill infants to Montreal, and treat another thirteen young children at the Frobisher hospital.

Dusty flew out of Frobisher with a team of nurses and a doctor from Montreal Children's Hospital. She held one of the babies in her arms throughout the three-hour flight because the nurses were busy with the other two. The story Dusty filed on June 1, 1972, focused on a week-old baby named Daniel Angilirq. Dusty explained that the disease caused severe coughing and respiratory distress and little Daniel was given a 50/50 chance of surviving. The child was fed intravenously through a vein in his scalp to compensate for severe dehydration. Dusty reported that the doctors managed to contain the infection in Igloolik, and within a couple of weeks it burned itself out.

In the early 1970s, Dusty was forced to interview author Robertson Davies, although she did not like his books. She visited him in his role as founding Master of Massey College, at the University of Toronto. Davies was launching *World of Wonders*, the third book in his Deptford Trilogy. "I had to read *Fifth Business* and *The Manticore*. This changed my mind about his writing. He turned out to be one of the loveliest people you could ever imagine. He served tea—Lapsang Souchong, mixed with Earl Grey. It became a favourite in our house. We call it the 'Robertson Davies' brew'," Dusty said.

On February 3, 1973, Dusty's exhaustive coverage of Davies' literary achievements and Davies, the man, were given a well-deserved full page in the book section of the *Montreal Star*. Professor Davies talked about his Presbyterian up bringing that "still remains a brake on pride and self-promotion. You were never supposed to talk about your own things or push yourself forward too much. Don't stick your neck out—if you're proud, God will strike you."

This early religious training also coloured Davies' view about accepting *Canada Council* grants, something the Presbyterian mind views as odious as welfare handouts. He admitted he would rather die, than take a charitable grant.

More interestingly, at the time of the interview, feminism was still in its infancy and equal opportunity was not yet a major issue. There was no question about Davies' views on the fair sex in a man's world. He told our reporter that the basic element in male nature is *Logos*, or law and reason; while in women, it is *Eros*, or feeling. As a result, women do not shine at research, but often make special doctors. "They're brilliant healers though they're not very often initiators in discovering new techniques."

Davies pointed out that in ten years of teaching graduate students he found, "they (women) don't initiate new or venturesome ideas in this realm either." Warming to his subject, Davies declared that to educate women, like men, is to do them an injustice. He would rather see the poor dears study the things they are good at, like psychology. "And I think they should study it as women without having to have a sort of competition, with men, whose notions about psychology are very different and tend to be mechanistic," says the Great Man of Canadian Letters.

Dusty, no lightweight, suggested to Davies that women might like to live at Massey College, a community of sixty-five male post-graduate students. And if they did have equal educational opportunities and the same learning environment as males, they might become better researchers and innovators. The result of this impertinence: "He looks at you silently over his glasses for a moment. And then he says, "who's going to bear and raise the children if they're all having careers?" Another pause. And then, "what women will never believe is that, in a man's estimation, one mother, with three children, outweighs twenty presidents of companies."

It is worth noting that Davies, who died in 1995, was a husband blessed with a wife who devoted every minute of her life to him, and a father of three indulgent daughters. Obviously, his is the voice of experience speaking.

After the story was published, Davies wrote Dusty a note congratulating her on her reporting. Dusty recalled that Ina Mayer, the entertainment editor, who was not very impressed with her effort, commented in a saccharine voice, "Robertson Davies is, indeed, a very nice man." Dusty added she was so impressed with Davies that she wrote a long letter to him in her imagination and has always regretted not sending it.

For the record, a column beside Dusty's Arctic medical flight story featured a follow up of the Sir Harry Oakes murder in the Bahamas in 1943. Throughout the 1940s, this story was huge in Canadian papers. It was suspected Sir Harry ran afoul of mafia gambling interests. To this day, the murder has not been solved, but it has been the inspiration for many books. The *Star* news flash of June 1, 1972, reported an American author "charged yesterday that the Duke of Windsor, as governor-general of the Bahamas in 1943, helped cover up facts behind the murder of Canadian mining magnate Sir Harry Oakes." The author claimed the duke, Queen Elizabeth II's uncle, was involved with gambling concessions and Sir Harry was upsetting the apple cart by promoting gambling interests of his own.

Another newsgirl, June Callwood, had a different reaction to Davies' view of the status of women. In the 1950s, fifteen years before Dusty's experience, Callwood interviewed Davies. In a profile in *Maclean's* magazine, she wrote, "Mrs. Davies is horrified when admirers suggest she must be a great help to her husband. But she does permit him to work un-interrupted evening after evening. 'Permit!' snorts Davies. 'I'll have you know that I am master in this house and it is run to suit me.'"[11]

After Callwood's interview appeared in *Maclean's*, Davies was outraged, not by his own sexist remarks, but by the fact that Callwood mentioned he had a cancer scare.

When Dusty had interviewed Davies, he indicated he couldn't understand why she wasn't married because this state was "so fortuitous a thing" for him. That was a few months before Dr. Samuel Solomon came into Dusty's life—permanently.

Change is Growth

Dusty was in her mid-forties when she married Solomon in 1974, the same year he divorced his first wife. Solomon, the director of the Endocrine Laboratory at the *Royal Victoria Hospital* and medical professor at McGill University, was also an early specialist in steroid biochemistry. In 1987, Solomon was a scientific advisor on the *Dubin Commission* on the banned practices in sport. He was partially responsible for having Canadian sprinter, Ben Johnson, stripped of the Gold Medal he won at the 1988 Seoul Olympics. After a celebrated career in medicine, Solomon was appointed an Officer of the *Order of Canada* in 1997. He lived until 2008.

On the fluffier side of the news—for years, Dusty had the privilege of originating short pieces for the *Montreal Star's* op-ed page. These lightweight scribbles, about whatever struck her fancy, were published under the heading, *Vignette* or *Potpourri*. Dusty described them as "ego-gratifying."

One commentary, penned in 1965, is a defense of all things English and the importance of England in an outraged there'll-always-be-an-England tone. A whippersnapper, who claimed that The Beatles put England on the map, inspired Dusty's diatribe. Our reporter lists England's contributions to the civilized world—Crown Derby china, Liberty prints, English jam, machinery, pipes, leather and Hepplewhite and Sheraton furniture. The list also included Chaucer, Shakespeare, the King James Version of the Bible, the Magna Carta, Lawrence Olivier and the Industrial Revolution.

Denying she is a Colonel Blimp, Dusty concluded: "What, in the name of Winston Churchill, are they teaching in history and literature classes these days." Plus ça change, plus c'est la même chose.[12]

Another piece offered musings on the family next door as observed by Dusty from her second-floor apartment. "The family lives in a real house, with a basement, and they have loaded the family jalopy for a weekend ski trip." Dusty explained she didn't really spy on them, just sort-of "kept an eye on them."

After years of a self-absorbed life filled with travels, opportunities and adventures—not open to many women of her generation—Dusty admitted, at the end of her career, she began to feel guilty about not doing anything for her community. Hence, she joined the Montreal's preservation movement in an effort to save the Van Horne Mansion on Sherbrooke Street. Cornelius Van Horne, president of Canadian Pacific Railway, occupied the house, built in 1870. He was responsible for adding trading ships to the CP Empire, and also for the chain of deluxe hotels that includes the magnificent *Château Lake Louise* and *Château Frontenac* in Quebec City. In 1973, Van Horne's historical house was demolished in the middle of the night because Drapeau, Montreal's moronic mayor, ruled it was of no cultural value in Quebec because the house was associated with Anglophones and not French Canadians.

In 1976, Dusty, by then well married, resigned from the *Star*—three years before the paper folded—and shifted to magazines. She helped launch *City Woman*, in the early 1980s, and worked as a copy editor at *Decormag*. She later edited *Polish Canadians* (Her husband, Solomon, was a Polish immigrant) for Tundra Books (1981).

Newsgirls

Before the strike, the Montreal Star, *founded in 1869, had been the biggest newspaper in Canada, with a circulation of 900,000. After the* Star *collapsed, Thomson newspapers bought the FP Newspaper Group that included the* Montreal Star, *the* Family Herald, *and the Toronto* Globe and Mail.

"Donna Logan always said, 'because of the population of English speakers was dwindling, one of the English dailies had to go.' But don't worry, it won't be us," said Dusty, with a snort, fifty-two years after the fact. "Everyone always believed it would be the *Gazette* that would go. In 1979, there was a strike by the *Star's* pressmen that lasted eight months. The scuttlebutt around the newsroom was that the head of the FP Newspaper Group (based in Toronto) had a son who was a known a pedophile. Newsroom gossips also felt that, because the son's case was in all the papers, the FP owner was so preoccupied with that, that he didn't pay attention to the strike. When he turned his attention to the *Star's* labour issues, it was too late for the FP group to regain their advertising revenues."

Looking back over the decades, Dusty commented the *Montreal Star*, was not a great paper. "But it was more liberal and lively than the *Montreal Gazette*, which had no passion about anything. But there was very little competition, anyway, because the *Gazette* was a morning paper and the *Star*, an afternoon paper."

Dusty remained bitter about the demise of the *Montreal Star* and loathed the *Gazette*. "I was told when the *Star* was folding, *Gazette* management put a note on the bulletin board saying, *Congratulations to all staff. You did it*. I never got over that. But that was the extent of the rivalry between the two English language newspapers in Montreal."

But that was long ago. In her 70s, Dusty was still a shrewd observer of life in Montreal, the only place she has ever lived. "You know, last week Sam and I were in the coffee shop at the Queen Elizabeth Hotel, where there used to be a press room—and looking out and seeing a *Henry Moore* and *Mary Queen of the World* church, I thought it's all still here. Where else in the world would I want to be?"

Where else, indeed.

Fast forward to 2014: Dusty is eighty-six and mourning the changes in her beloved Montreal. She is stunned by all the wrecking and the new public buildings and condos popping up on familiar streets.

"When a new building went up, I would be there. In Montreal, it was news. There was a tradition when a building was finished there would be a tree—a fir or something—put on the roof and the press would all gather there to file a report and take pictures of the dignitaries," said Dusty in a telephone conversation.

Dusty's mind also wandered back to Eaton's Department store, once a Canada-wide institution. Founded in Toronto in 1869, Eaton's introduced catalogue shopping in 1884. The retailer lasted until 1999 when the company filed for bankruptcy. "You went to Eaton's glove department and they sold them, from $5 to $200. In that store you could get almost everything you ever needed," lamented Dusty.

But worse than the demise of the Timothy Eaton Company is the talk of Ogilvy, a historical Montreal department store, being sentenced to the wrecking ball, according to Dusty. "People come from all over the world to go to Ogilvy, where a Scottish piper traditionally ended the shopping day," Dusty said.

Contrary to Dusty's fears, Ogilvy continues to thrive and the store still hires a piper to play daily at noon. Should Ogilvy be closed down once and for all, surely the piper will march out playing a slow pibroch, a traditional lament for what is lost. Hopefully, Dusty will be there to see it.

Ogilvy Ltd. was founded in 1887. In 1927, the store introduced tartan packaging and a bagpiper who piped out the last customers of the day.

ENDNOTES

Introduction

1   David Hayes, *Power and Influence: The Globe and Mail and the News Revolution*, (Toronto: Key Porter Books, 1992), 96.
2   Ross Harkness, *J. E. Atkinson of the Star*, (Toronto: University of Toronto Press, 1963).

Chapter 1

1   Richard J. Doyle, *Hurly Burly: My Time at The Globe and Mail* (Toronto: MacMillan of Canada, 1989), 99.
2   Nellie McClung, *Sowing Seeds in Danny* (New York: Doubleday, Page & Company, 1908).
3   Kate Aitken, *Canadian Cook Book*, (Toronto: Whitecap Books Ltd., 2004).
4   Kay Kritzwiser, "Our Neglected Wheatlands," *Regina Leader-Post*, Oct. 5, 1948.
5   David Hayes, *Power and Influence: The Globe and Mail and the News Revolution*. (Toronto: Key Porter Books, 1992), 80, 184.
6   Douglas McArthur, "Lives Lived," *Globe and Mail* (Toronto, ON), Aug. 7, 1997.
7   Michael Ignatieff, "The Lobster Shift," *Globe and Mail* (Toronto, ON), Mar. 5, 2004.
8   Doyle, *HB*, 98-99.
9   Hayes, *PI*, 93.
10   Kay Kritzwiser, "The Language Barrier Stands Before the Degree," *The Globe* (Toronto, ON), Oct. 18, 1958.
11   Hayes, *PI*, 96.
12   Val Ross, "They Like him, they really like him" *Globe and Mail* (Toronto, ON), Oct. 24. 1998, C22.
13   Iris Nowell, *Harold Town* (Vancouver: Figure 1 Publishing Inc., 2014).
14   Kay Kritzwiser, "An Unyielding Love of Graphics," *Globe and Mail* (Toronto, ON), Oct. 28, 1978.
15   Bruce Blackadar, "Jack Pollock and the long voyage back to Toronto," *Toronto Star* (Toronto, ON), Sept. 3, 1988.
16   Doyle, *HB*, 65.
17   Hayes, *PI*, 97.
18   Doyle, *HB*, 70, 97.
19   Kay Kritzwiser, "An Eclectic Statement of Artistic Independence," *Globe and Mail* (Toronto, ON), Apr. 3, 1983.
20   Kay Kritzwiser, "Hong Kong Landmark," *Globe and Mail* (Toronto, ON), Aug. 2, 1980.

Chapter 2

1   Pierre Berton, "Forgotten Headlines," *Toronto Star* (Toronto, ON), Nov. 8, 1962.
2   Dale Brazao, "Human 'bloodhound' finds Edwin Boyd," *Toronto Star, Star Beat* (Toronto, ON), Nov. 1996.
3   Val Sears, *Hello Sweetheart...Get Me Rewrite*, (Toronto: Key Porter Books, 1988), 114.
4   Charles Templeton, "Inside the Toronto Star," Templetons, 1982, http://www.templetons.com/charles/memoir/chap5.html.
5   Sears, *HS*, 116.

6. Peter Worthington, "Not All Dinosaurs Were Chauvinists," *Toronto Sun* (Toronto, ON), Dec. 9, 1993.
7. Sears, *HS*, 28.
8. "Worthington: Eye Witness to History." *Toronto Sun*, November 21, 2011.

Chapter 3

1. Michele Landsberg, *Writing the Revolution* (University of Toronto Press, 2011).
2. Kay Rex, *No Daughter of Mine: The History of the Canadian Women's Press Club 1904-1971* (Toronto, Cedar Cave Publishing, 1995).
3. Iris Nowell, *Harold Town.* (Vancouver, Figure 1 Publishing Inc., 2014).
4. Olive Dickason, *The Myth of the Savage and the Beginnings of French Colonialism in the Americas* (University of Alberta Press, 1984).
5. Olive Dickason, *Canada's First Nations: A History of Founding Peoples from Earliest Times* (Oxford University Press, 1992).
6. Suzanne Fournier and Ernie Crey, *Stolen from Our Embrace: The Abduction of First Nations Children and the Restoration of Aboriginal Communities* (Vancouver, Douglas & McIntyre, 1997).
7. Dickason, "Failing the First Nations" *Globe and Mail*, Jan. 1998.
8. Olive Patricia Dickason and David T. McNab, *Canada's First Nations*, 4th ed (Oxford University Press, 2009).

Chapter 4

1. Leslie Scrivener, "Portrait of a Marriage," *Toronto Star*, Dec. 2, 1990.
2. "Journalist Salary Canada." *Living in Canada*, accessed Jan. 12, 2017, http://www.livingin-canada.com/salaries-for-journalists.html.
3. Richard J. Doyle, *Hurly-Burly: A Time at the Globe* (Toronto, Macmillan of Canada, 1990), 64.
4. Doyle, *Hurly-Burly: A Time at the Globe*, 64.
5. Richard MacFarlane, *Canada's Newspaper Legend: The Story of J. Douglas MacFarlane* (Toronto, ECW Press, 2000), 105.
6. David Hayes, *Power and Influence* (Toronto, Key Porter Books, 1992) 60.
7. Jack Brehl, "The titan of The Star's newsroom," *Toronto Star*, May 18, 1992.
8. Hayes, *Power and Influence*, 61.
9. Doyle, *Hurly-Burly: A Time at the Globe*, 65.
    Ross Harkness, *J.E. Atkinson of the Star* (Toronto, University of Toronto Press, 1963), 100.
10. *It's All About Kindness: Remembering June Callwood*, ed. Margaret McBurney (Markham, Cormorant Books, 2012), 146.
11. Robertson Davies, "Devil's Advocate," *Montreal Star*, Feb. 3, 1973.
12. Kurt Eby, "Hall of Famer," *Ryerson Review of Journalism*, Mar. 16, 2002.
13. Susan Crean, *Newsworthy: The Lives of Media Women* (Toronto, Stoddart, 1984), 37.
14. Doyle, *Hurly-Burly: A Time at the Globe*, 234.
15. Ibid., 232.
16. Ibid., 323.
17. Ibid., 233.
18. Interview by Mary O'Connell, *Sunday Morning*, CBC Radio Archives, April 19, 1987.
19. Hayes, *Power and Influence*, 225-226.
20. Barker, D. and Wright, C, "Women of Colour on the Nellie's Saga," *Toronto Star*, Sept. 3, 1992.
21. Michelle Landsberg, "Callwood Furror," *Toronto Star*, July 18, 1992.

22   June Callwood, "The Nellie's Furor," *Toronto Star*, July 23, 1992.
23   Nancy J. White, "Portrait of 'Saint June'," *Toronto Star*, Feb. 19, 1995.
24   O'Connell, *Sunday Morning*.
25   Doyle, *Hurly-Burly: A Time at the Globe*, 497-499.
26   Sandra Martin, "The Written Word was his Favourite Game," *Globe and Mail*, Feb. 13, 2012.
27   Jack Brehl, "The titan of The Star's newsroom," *Toronto Star*, May 18, 1992.
28   Trent Frayne, *The Tales of An Athletic Supporter* (Toronto, McClelland and Stewart, 1990).
29   Crean, *Newsworthy: The Lives of Media Women*, 38.
30   McBurney, *It's All About Kindness: Remembering June Callwood*, 164, 171.
31   Ibid., 56-57.
      Ibid., 58.
32   Catherine Dunphy, "June Callwood, 82: Writer, social activist" *Toronto Star*, Apr. 15, 2007.
33   McBurney, *It's All About Kindness: Remembering June Callwood*, 69.
34   Interview by George Stroumboulopoulos, CBC TV, Apr. 2, 2007.
35   Barbara Walters, *How to Talk to Practically Anybody About Practically Anything* (Doubleday, New York, 1970).

Chapter 5

1   Simma Holt. *Memoirs of a Loose Cannon* (Hamilton: Seraphim Editions, 2008), 30.
2   Ibid., 12.
3   Ibid., 41.
4   Tom Ardies, *Canadian Newspapers: The Inside Story*, ed. Walter Stewart (Edmonton: Hurtig Publishers, 1980), 176.
5   Ibid.
6   Allan Fotheringham, "A Bash to Remember," *MacLean's Magazine*, 2000.
7   Pierre Berton, *Starting Out* (McClelland & Stewart, 1987).
8   Holt, *MLC*, 62.
9   Greg Joyce, Webster Obituary, *Toronto Star (CP)*, March 3, 1999. A2.
10   Holt, *MLC*, 124.
11   Ardies, *CN*, 177.
12   Holt, *MLC*, 65.
13   Ardies, *CN*, 183.
14   Alicia Costa, *Simma Holt: Rosie the Riveter of Canadian News*. 2009.
15   Holt, *MLC*, 133.
16   "Killer Released by Appeal Court Hangs Himself", *Toronto Star*, n.d. A26.
17   Holt, *MLC*, 141.
18   Ibid.,155.
19   Ibid., 149-150.
20   Simma Holt, "The Ugly Truth About Chretien," *The Saturday Sun*, May 4, 1996.
21   Holt., *MLC*, 159.
22   Ibid., 194.
23   Ibid., 176.
24   "MP Tells Commons That She's No Lady", *Toronto Star (CP)*, Nov. 8, 1975.A3
25   "MP wants fines for Time Wasters, *Toronto Star (CP)*, March 24, 1976.
26   "CRTCs Faibish abuses MP", *Toronto Star*, Nov.1, 1978, A19.
27   George Bain, "You Can't Say that to an MP", *Toronto Star (CP)*, Nov. 3, 1978. A8.
28   Ibid.
29   Richard J. Doyle, *Hurly-Burly: My Time at the Globe and Mail* (Toronto: Macmillan of Canada, 1989).

30	"Killers for hire at $50 since end of hanging: MP", *Toronto Star (CP)*, July 13, 1976. A2.
31	"Execution will take place of hanging.", *Sunday Sun*, June 27, 1976.
32	"Back Home at Sussex Drive", *Toronto Star*, May 31, 1977. A3.
33	Holt, *MLC*, 198.
34	"Sun loses Appeal of Libel Decision", *Globe and Mail*, May 15, 1979, 10.
35	Frank Rasky, "Mind your Ps and Qs – They Tell All", *Toronto Star*, Mar. 21, 1980, C1.
36	Holt, *MLC*, 216.
37	Ibid., 220-221.
38	Holt, *"The Ugly Truth About Chretien"*, 13.
39	Holt, *Condominium Calamity*, 223-237.
40	Ibid., 236.
41	Cindy Chan, *Epoch Times*, Nov. 7, 2008.
42	Falun Dafa Minghi. http://tinyurl.com/j6mprzz. Vancouver, August 9, 2012.
43	Brian Morton, "Former Vancouver journalist, MP Simma Holt broke down newsroom barriers." Obituary, *Vancouver Sun*, January 24, 2015.

Chapter 6

1	Ray Timson (1928-1999), "Star Memories," *Toronto Star*, Nov. 3, 1992. S5.
2	Richard MacFarlane, *Canada's Newspaper Legend: The Story of J. Douglas MacFarlane* (ECW Press, Toronto, 2000), 125.
3	Peter Worthington, "Part I: The untold story of Olga's defection," *Toronto Sun*, Saturday, May 10, 2013.
4	Ibid; Part II, Sunday, May 11, 2013.
5	MacFarlane, *CNL*, 207.
6	MacFarlane, *CNL*, 203.
7	Michele Landsberg, *Writing the Revolution* (Second Story Press, Toronto, 2011).
8	"The Crazy Rat Syndrome," *Canadian Newspapers: The Inside Story*, ed. Walter Stewart, (Hurtig publishers, Edmonton, 1980), 112.
9	Ellie Tesher, "Voices of Women," *Toronto Star*. May 24, 1992. A1.
10	Linwood Barclay, "He had to fire this tiny dynamo," *Toronto Star*, June 2, 2009. E7.

Chapter 7

1	Moscow Staff Correspondent, Angela Burke, "Angela Takes Pictures of Kremlin Press Talk," *Toronto Star* (Toronto, ON), July 16, 1955.
2	Angela Burke, "Caviar," *Toronto Star* (Toronto, ON), Aug. 5, 1955.
3	Angela Burke, "Khrushchev is Real Boss To Whom Bulganin Bows Angela Burke Declares," *Toronto Star* (Toronto, ON), Feb. 1, 1955.
4	Angela Burke, "Untrained for Position Peasant Wife of Tito is Gracious, Dignified," *Toronto Star* (Toronto, ON), Sept. 29, 1955.
5	Angela Burke "Bitter German Women Return with Babies Born in Camps," *Toronto Star* (Toronto, ON), Oct. 13, 1955.
6	Malachy McCourt, *A Monk Swimming* (New York: Hypernion, 1998), 101-103.
7	"Star Reporter Acquitted of Charge in Kitchener," *Toronto Star* (Toronto, ON), Feb. 11, 1953.
8	Angela Burke, "Bubbles Wants Women at Liberal Convention: 'Twitterers' Has-Beens." *Toronto Star* (Toronto, ON), Nov. 26, 1957.
9	Angela Burke, "Gander Is Dandy, Wears Mike Tie," *Toronto Star* (Toronto, ON), Jan. 11, 1958.
10	Angela Burke, "New Food Treatment Step in Making Arctic Paradise for Tourists,"

Toronto Star (Toronto, ON), Nov. 14, 1957.

11 Ross Harkness, *J.E. Atkinson of The Star* (Toronto: University of Toronto Press, 1963), 373.

12 Angela Burke, "We Lived 13 Months on Strike Pay," *Star Weekly* (Toronto, ON), May, 1959.

13 Angela Burke, *For the Sake of Argument:* "Angela Burke Says We Need a New Set of Ground Rules for Royal Visits," *Maclean's* Magazine, May 23, 1959.

Chapter 8

1 Marilyn Dunlop, *Understanding Cancer* (Toronto: Irwin Publishers, 1985); Marilyn Dunlop, *Body Defenses: The Marvels and Mysteries of the Immune System* (Toronto: Irwin Publishers, 1988); Marilyn Dunlop, *Bill Mustard: Surgical Pioneer (Canadian Medical Lives)* (Toronto: Dundurn Press, 1989).

2 Richard MacFarlane, *Canada's Newspaper Legend: The Story of J. Douglas MacFarlane* (Toronto: ECW Press, 2000), 110-112.

3 Kay Rex, *No Daughter of Mine: History of the Canadian Women's Press Club, 1904-1971* (Toronto: Cedar Cave Books, 1995), 63.

Chapter 9

1 Richard J. Doyle, *Hurly Burly: My Time at the Globe and Mail* (Toronto: MacMillan of Canada, 1989), 193.

2 Joan Hollobon, *Globe and Mail*, July 1- 2, 1957.

3 Joan Hollobon, *Globe and Mail*, July 7, 1958.

4 Richard J. Doyle, *Hurly Burly: My Time at the Globe and Mail* (Toronto: MacMillan of Canada, 1989), 69.

5 Joan Hollobon, "Man Becomes Woman," *Globe and Mail*, Apr. 19, 1972.

6 Joan Hollobon, "Broken Belfast," *Globe and Mail*, July 29, 1976.

7 Kay Rex, *No Daughter of Mine: The Women and History of the Canadian Women`s Press Club, 1904-1971* (Toronto: Cedar Cave Books, 1995).

Chapter 10

1 Augusta Vineberg, "A Tale of Two Cities," *Weekend*, 1958.

2 Janice Arnold "Cohen gets birthday greetings from Outer Space." *Canadian Jewish News*, September 30, 2009.

3 Kay Rex, *No Daughter of Mine: The History of the Canadian Women's Press Club 1904-1971* (Toronto: Cedar Caves Publishing, 1995), 81.

4 Enid Nemy, "Happy Rockerfeller, 88, Dies; Marriage to Governor Scandalized Voters," *New York Times*, (New York, NY), May 20, 2015.

5 Augusta Vineberg, "Call Doctor Jazz – This Drug Store Really Swings," *Montreal Star*, (Montreal, QC), Mar. 25, 1965.

6 Augusta Vineberg, "Television and Radio," *Montreal Star*, (Montreal, QC), Apr. 12, 1966.

7 Richard J. Doyle, *Hurly-Burly: A Time at the Globe* (Toronto: MacMillan Canada, 1990), 243.

8 Augusta Vineberg, "Hockey Telecasting an Exacting Chore," *Montreal Star*, (Montreal, QC), Apr. 21, 1965.

9 August Myers, "Vineberg Team Gives Heart – And Hope." *Montreal Star*, (Montreal,

QC), Feb. 5, 1966.
10 Augusta Vineberg, "Mini compact runs smoothly and the colors are pretty." *Montreal Star*, (Montreal, QC) April 2, 1969.
11 June Callwood, "The Beard," *Maclean's*, March 1952.
12 Augusta Vineberg, "Pot-Pourri, England," *Montreal Star*, (Montreal, QC), Jun. 23, 1965.

Index

A

A Monk Swimming, 108
A.V. Roe company, 58
Aboriginal and Non-Aboriginal Histories: Parallel Paths and Convergences, 48
Aboriginal Life Achievement Award, 48
Afternoon Edition, 118
Agnelli, Gianni, 110
Aitken, Kate, 15
Aitken, William Maxwell, 109
    See also Lord Beaverbrook
Albers, Anni, 22
Albers, Josef, 21, 22
Alderson, Margaret, 137
Allen, Glen, 60
Allen, Helen, 39, 122
Allen, Ralph, 58, 59, 117
Almonte Millstone, 36
Alsop, Kay, 69, 78
Aly Salmone Khan, Prince, 110
Amazing Adventure of Cholly Blake, 127
American Medical Writers Association, 150
American Newspaper Guild, 53
Amies, Hardy, 35
Anderson, Doris, 10, 78
Anderson, Marian, 71
Andrews, Keith, 160
Angilirq, Daniel, 162
Apollo 13, 127, 128
Archer, The, 21
Ardies, Tom, 72, 75, 76
AGO (Art Gallery of Ontatio), 22, 26, 38
    See also Art Gallery of Toronto, 21
Arts and Letters Club, 21, 23, 26, 70
At the Crease, 20
Atkins, Harold, 160
Atkinson, Joseph, 11, 57
Atkinson, Siegfried, 138
Atlantic Ocean, 59

B

Bain, George, 81
Balenciaga, 57, 103
Balge, Mrs. (rooming house landlady), 112
Balkan Life, 107
Baptist World Youth Conference, 142
Barclay, Linwood, 102
Barnard College, 71
Barnhardt, Shirley Ann, 19
Barretts of Wimpole Street, The, 17
Bassett, John, 32, 36, 38, 95
Baume et Mercier, 136, 137
Baur, Hans, 107
BBC (British Broadcasting Corporation), 131
Beatles, The, 157, 163
Beauclerc, Joe, 116
Beauvoir, Simone, 116
Behind the Bars on G Ward, 147
Belfast; sudden death and a shocking life, 149
Belgrade, 103, 107
Bell, Marilyn (Canadian swimmer), 30-32, 51, 57, 123
Bell, Florence Duffy, 121
Bell, James, 121, 127
Belle River, 52, 67
Ben Casey, 54
Benoît, Jehane, 118, 156
Beny, Roloff, 10, 17, 21, 98
Berceller, Oscar, 25
Bergen, Candace, 97
Bernard, Christiaan, 146
Berton, Pierre, 8, 11, 29-30, 32, 39, 51, 55, 58, 61, 63, 73-74, 99, 105, 160
Bieler, Zoe, 155, 156
Biko, Steve, 129
Birch, Guy, 114
Bird, Florence, 118
    See also Anne Francis
Blackadar, Bruce, 22
Blair, Joan, 112
Blatchford, Christie, 19
Blunt, Sir Antony, 21
Boland, Frederick "Freddie", 108
Booth Luce, Clare, 110
Borgnine, Ernest, 97
Borgnine, Tove, 97
Bott, Ellen, 21
Bourassa, Robert, 127
Boxer, Rosemary, 94, 97-98
Boyd Gang, 28, 29, 32
Boyd, Doreen, 29-30
Boyd, Edwin Alonzo, 28-30
Boyer, Charles, 54
Braithwaite, Dennis, 53, 116
Brantford Expositor, 51, 52
Bratton, Jim, 67
Braun, Eva, 107
Brazao, Dale, 29-30
Breen, Leon, 143
British Columbia Penitentiary, 74
Bronfman, Edgar, 154
Brown, Helen Gurley, 78
Broz Tito, Josip, 107
Broz, Jovanka, 107
Bruemmer, Frederick Karl von, 138
Bruno's Schools of Design, 118
Bryant, George, 31, 32, 51
Bryden, Art, 141
Bulganin, Nikolai, 11, 103, 106-107
Bungle, Truce and Trouble, 146
Burke, Angela, Chapter 7, 11, 59, 135
Burstyn, Irene, 45, 156
Burton, Richard, 98
Bush, George H.W., 70, 82-83
Bush, George W., 82-83
Bushman, Francis X, 124
By-Liner, 30
Bonham Carters, 113
The Bata Shoe Co., 143

C

Calder, Alexander, 21, 158
Caldwell, Nancy, 17, 25, 26
Caldwell, Spencer, 25-26
Calgary Herald, 18
Callwood, Harold "Bing", 52
Callwood, June, Chapter 4, 8, 10, 11, 25, 49, 69, 117-118, 163
Cameron, Dorothy, 22
Cameron, Stevie, 62
Camp Borden, 53
Camp Friedland, 107
Camp, Dalton, 61
Campbell Funeral Home, 97
Canada Council, 162
Canada's Mother of the Year, 122
    See also Allen, Helen
Canada's First Nations: A History of Founding Peoples from Earliest Times, 48, 50
Canada's Sports Hall of Fame, 57
Canada's Woman of the Year, 77
Canadian Embassy, 59
Canadian Jewish News, 57, 156
Canadian Media Research Consortium, 155
Canadian Medical Association, 150
Canadian National Exhibition, 15, 30, 46, 123, 125
    See also Expo 67
Canadian Native Arts Foundation, 48
Canadian News Hall of Fame, 36, 39, 83
Canadian Newspapers: The Inside Story, 72, 101
Canadian Press, 38, 47, 71, 80, 100, 151
Canadian Press Gallery, 80
Canadian Science Writers Association, 121, 126, 149
Canadian Women Journalists Conference, 69
CWPC (*Canadian Women's Press Club*), 14, 15, 17, 30, 35, 47, 51, 70, 78, 113, 122, 132, 151, 156, 157, 160
    Memorial Award, 70, 113, 160
    No Daughter of Mine, 151
Capote, Truman, 20, 22, 23
Carey, James "Jimmy", 77
Carleton University, 11, 99
Carlson, Don, 53
Castro, Fidel, 78
CBC (Canadian Broadcasting Corporation), 30, 32, 42, 47, 53, 58, 59, 61-63, 65-67, 71, 74, 85, 92, 94, 105, 118, 128, 140, 156, 159
    French Language Network, 85
    Front Page Challenge, 74, 92, 105
    CBC Radio, 32, 42, 62, 66, 140
    Morningside, 32, 42
    CBC TV, 67, 71, 74, 94, 118, 156
CFRB (Canada's First Rogers Batteryless), 92
Chadwick, Florence, 30
Chamberlain, Marilyn, 30
Champlain Society Symposium, 48
Charles, Nick, 24
Charles, Nora, 24
Chatelaine, 10, 78, 79, 94, 101, 113
Cherry, Zena, 25
Chinatown Merchants' Association, 79
Chinese Benevolent Association, 79
Chisholm, Robert, 94
Chrétien, Jean (Prime Minister), 83, 84
Christensen, Erik, 18, 25
Churchill, Randolph, 109-110
Churchill, Sir Winston, 74, 163
City and Country Home, 25
City, 122
CJAD, 154
Clark Institute of Psychiatry Gender Clinic, 148
Clarke, Joe (Canadian Prime Minister), 131
CNN (Cable News Network), 116
Coffee Mill, 98
Cohen, Leonard, 61, 156
Cohen, Nathan, 91-92 142
Cohon, George, 97
Cohon, Susie, 97
Cole, Nat King, 111
Columbia Law School, 108
Columbia School of Journalism, 144, 153
Columbia University, 104
Combined Jewish Appeal, The, 154
Commonwealth Conference, 131
Company of Young Canadians, 60
Confessions of a Hotel Fancier, 58
Coo, Abby, 71
Cooper, Gary, 54
Corbin, Virginia Lee, 14
Corelli, Rae, 39, 128-129
Corelli, Stephen, 129
Coren, Michael, 64
Cornell, Bonnie, 101

171

Corruption and Greed in the Mulroney Years, 62
Cosmopolitan, 78
Cote, Phoebe Philomene, 41-43, 47
Country of the Poor, The, 64
Cowley, Gwen, 93
Cragg, Margaret, 44, 140
Cranston, Toller, 97
Crean, Susan, 66
Creed, Harry, 57
Creighton, Doug, 30
Crissey, Charles, 116
Crittenden, Yvonne, 95
Cross, James, 127
CTV (Canadian Television Network), 25
Crown Publishers Ltd., 78
CRTC (Canadian Radio-Television and Telecommunications Commission), 80, 81
Cummings, Robert, 109
Curzon, Tom, 10

D

Dafoe, John, 71-72
Daily Mail, 109
Daley, Ralph, 72
Dalgleish, Delsea, 24-25, 144
Dalgleish, Oakley, 24, 25, 144
Danby, Ken, 20
Davidson, Joyce, 59, 118
Davies, Robertson, 58, 142-143, 162
Davis, Peggy, 109
Davis, Sammy Jr., 97
Day, Stockwell, 84
Dempsey, Lotta, 101
DePoe, David, 60
Destry Rides Again, 54
Dewar, Elaine, 63
Dickason, Olive, Chapter 3, 7, 8, 10
Dickason, Tony, 41, 43
Dickenson, Angie, 80
Dickenson, Merle, 139
Diefenbaker, John, 45, 58, 156, 157
Diefenbaker, Olive, 45, 156, 157
Dietrich, Marlene, 54
Digby Harriman, Pamela, 110, 111
Digger House, 11, 60, 61-63
DiManno, Rosie, 19
Dingman, Elizabeth, 93, 95, 100, 101
Dingman, James Jeffery, 14, 122
Dingman, Jocelyn, 122
Dionne Quintuplet, 135, 136, 139
Dominion Coal Company, 91
    See also A.V. Roe Company
Don Mackay of Calgary, Mrs., 115
Doubleday, 58
Douglas, Shirley, 17
Douglas, Tommy, 15, 17, 144
Doukhobors, 77, 78
    See also Doukhobor sect.
Dowd, Eric, 144
Downton Abbey, 14
Doyle, Richard "Dic", 23-26, 13, 18, 19, 21, 25, 53, 55, 56, 60, 61, 142, 144, 146
Drapeau, Jean, 157
Drew, George, 122
Dubrovnik, 131
Dunlop, Doug, 126
Dunlop, Peter, 124
Dunlop, Marilyn Bell, Chapter 8, 39, 56, 78, 101, 150

E

Earl, Marjorie, 11, 53, 116
Earth Mothers, 62
Eaton, John David, 16
Eaton, Signy, 16, 17
Eaton, Timothy, 17, 57
Eden, Anthony, 107
Edinburgh, Arnold, 25
Eisenhower, Dwight (President), 59, 110, 113
Eisenhower, Mamie, 113
Élie de Rothschild, Baron, 110
Elizabeth Arden Award, 10, 46
Elizabeth II, Queen, 21, 59, 66, 78, 103, 113, 118, 132, 162
Elliot Lake, 114
Emperor Akihito, 12, 37
Emperor Hirohito, 37
Empress Consort Michiko, 12, 37
Empress of Lima, 23
Enright, Michael, 66
Etobicoke Press, 96
Evasuk, Stasia (Anastasia), Chapter 6, 7-10, 21, 69
Evening Standard, 110
Evening Telegram, 27
Expo 67, 21, 157, 156, 159
    See also Canadian National Exhibition
Eye Has to Travel, The, 17

F

Faibish, Roy, 80, 81
Falun Gong, The, 85
Family Herald, 157, 164
Famous Five, 15
Farquharson, Bob, 53, 55-56
Farrell, Glenda, 54
Federation of Liberal Women, 115
Feeney, Edwin, 125
Felicano, Jose, 60
Fellini, Federico, 21
Fellman, Mort, 140-141
Festival of Britain, 30
Fine Art Consultants of Canada Ltd., 21
Five Atkinson Principles, 92
Fogg, Phileas, 35
Fontaine Zoo, 156
FOOF (Fine Old Ontario Family), 94
Ford, Gerald, 82
Ford, Glen, 97
Ford Motor Company, 161
Forester, C.S., 110
Forrester, Maureen, 128
Foster, Lillian, 53, 94-95
Fotheringham, Allan, 73, 74
Francophone Community, 52
Fraser, John, 13, 25
Frayne, Brant "Barney", 60, 63, 64, 66
Frayne, Jesse, 64
Frayne, Jill, 64
Frayne, Trent, 11, 25, 56, 58, 63, 67, 117
Freedman, Adele, 63
French Indians at Louisbourg: A Study in Imperial Race Relations, 47
Friedan, Betty, 118
Fromme, Lynette "Squeaky", 82
FLQ (Front de Libération du Québec), 127-128
Frost, Leslie, 142
Frum, Barbara, 47
Fuller, Buckminster, 158-159
Fulton Street Fish Market, 154
Fur Trade Association, 45
Fusion (magazine), 95

G

Gabor, Eva, 97
Gabor, Zsa Zsa, 97
Galleries Lafayette, 97
Gallivan, Danny, 159-160
Galt Evening Reporter, 137
Garland, Judy, 97
Gardner, Ava, 111
Garnet, Mae, 75
Gehry, Frank, 24
George Brown College, 100
George Bush: Man of Integrity, 82
George VI, King, 113, 124
Georgi Zhukov, Marshal, 103
General Motors of Canada, 25
Gentlemen Prefer Blondes, 109
Gibb, Alexandrine, 11, 29, 32, 53, 92
Gibb, Camilla, 67
Gibson, Elizabeth, 149
Gilmore, Catherine, 127
Girl From Emphysema, The, 129
Glace Bay Gazette, 91, 92
Glass Menagerie, The, 17
Globe's bulldog edition, 54, 114
Gobeil, Madeleine, 99
Goethe, Johann Wolfgang von, 155
Goodman, Martin, 9, 91, 96, 98-101, 118, 128-129
Gordon, Joe, 77
Gourmet, 109
Gouzenko, Igor, 38
Governor General's Award, 19
Grace, Princess, 98
Grace Tinnings Dance Troupe, 17
Grand Manan, 117
Grand Old Woman of Letters, 48
    See also Olivia Dickason
Granite Club, 122
Grano, 26
Grant, Cary, 11, 110, 111
Grass Harp, The, 22
Gray, Beverly, 18
Gray, Walter, 144, 146
Greenberg, Nassa Rachel, 70
Griffith, Phyllis, 36, 37, 39, 122
Grimaldi, Prince Rainier, 98, 140
Group of Seven, 38
Guggenheim, Peggy, 10, 21, 98
Guggenheim, Sinbad, 10, 98
Guinness, Alec, 142
Gutenberg Galaxy, The, 19
Guthrie, Tyrone, 142
Gwendolyn Blair, Mrs., 115
Gzowski, Peter, 32, 42-43, 63

H

Haileybury, 104
Haines gallery, 38
Halliday, Dunc, 141
Ham, Arthur, 101
Hamilton, Bob, 42, 49
Hamilton, Mr. (postal employee), 116
Hammet, Dashiell, 24
Hammerstein, Oscar, 108
Hammond, Larry, 92
Hammond, Ruth Andrew, 57, 92-94, 104-105
Hansard, 80, 111
Happy Adventure, 34

Index

Harper, Stephen, 72, 85
Harpur, Tom, 131
Harriman, Averell, 110
Harris, Lawren, 38
Harris, Marjorie, 66
Hart, John, 138
Hart House, 28
Hayes, David, 9, 18-20, 24, 55
Hayward, Cynthia, 97
Hayworth, Rita, 111
Heathman, Charles, 77
Hebrides, The, 34
Hello Sweetheart, Get Me Rewrite, 31, 35-36
Hemingway, Ernest, 91, 106
Hewitt, Foster, 159
Hind, Cora, 15
Hindmarsh, Harry, 32-33, 56, 57, 92-94, 104-105, 117
Hindmarsh Jr., Harry, 111
Hitler, Adolf, 107, 153
HMCS Haida, 33
Hockey Writers Association, 100
Hoffa, James, 46
Holland, Art, 125
Hollobon, Ernest Frederick "Tony", 136, 138, 144
Hollobon, Joan, Chapter 9, 78, 126, 132-33,
Holt, Leon, 76-78, 82, 84
Holt, Simma (née Milner), Chapter 5, 8, 11, 37-39, 39
Honderich, Beland, 34, 53, 116
Honderich, John, 101
Hopper, Hedda, 95, 111
Horst Gruwes, Mrs., 107-108
Hospital for Sick Children, 126
House of Commons, 15, 29, 38, 77, 80-81, 84, 127, 146
Howarth, Dorothy, Chapter 2, 11, 12, , 51, 55, 74-75, 78, 122-124, 128
How Canada Lives series, 117
Howarth, Thomas, 27, 38
Hunt, Don, 30
Hunt, Jim, 125-126
Huras, Marie, 112
Hurly Burly: My Time at The Globe and Mail, 13, 24, 53, 56
Huxley, Aldous, 106

I

Ignatieff, Michael, 18
Independence Bill, 34
Innell, Reg, 99
INCO (International Nickel Company), 142-143
It's All About Kindness: Remembering June Callwood, 66

J

Jackson, Leonard, 29
Jackson, Marian, 53
James, Norm, 117
Jenkins, Anthony, 66
Jerome, James, 81
Jessie Dow Prize, 20
Jessie's Centre, 63
Jewish Daily News, 8, 33, 112
Jimbie, Bobby, 157
John, Jeremy, 32
Johnson, Ben, 163
Jolly Jumper company, 118
Jones, Frank, 99

Journal of Addiction Research Foundation of Ontario, 150
Judy Award, 46, 101
Junior Canadian Women's Press Club award, 122

K

Kain, Karen, 97, 149
Kaplansky, Kalmen, 141
Keller, Arlie, 96
Keller, Helen, 111
Keller, Maureen, 10, 96, 96, 100, 101
    See also Mo Keller
Kelly, Grace, 11, 56, 62, 98, 109, 140
Kemsley Newspaper of London, 104
Kennedy Space Centre, 127
Kennedy, Jackie, 61, 62, 98, 99, 156
Kennedy, John F., 39, 98, 118
Kennedy, John John, 118
Kennedy, Rose, 98
Kent, Allen, 125
Kent, Duchess of, 113
Kerouac, Jack, 60
Kerrigan, Richard, 119
Khrushchev, Nikita, 103, 105-108
Kilbourn, Elizabeth, 20, 21
Kilbourn, William, 20
King, Martin Luther, Jr., 39
King, William Lyon MacKenzie, 151
Kingsbury, Jim, 52, 105
Knickerbocker, Susie, 95
Knowlton (Quebec), 119
Kolley, Tibor, 149
Koshevoy, Himie, 72, 73
Kramer, Stanley, 110, 111
Kritzwiser, David, 16
Kritzwiser, Harold, 15, 16
Kritzwiser, Kay, Chapter 1, 7-8, 11, 36, 43, 88, 98, 101
    Betty Beehive, 15,
    Betty Beehive Show, 15
    Betty Lou of the Lighthouse, 14

L

La Mon Hotel, 130
Lalonde, Marc, 79
LaMarsh, Judy, 156, 157
Lamport, Allan, 37, 51
Lander, Jack, 71
Landsberg, Michele, 9-11, 18, 46, 47, 56, 63, 101, 150
Laporte, Pierre, 127
Laverock, Lily, 69
Lavoie, Gladys, 52
Lawrence Motors, 123
Lawson, Smirle, 28
Leacock, Stephen, 138
    Sunshine Sketches of a Small Town, 138
Leigh, Vivien, 21, 97
Leonard, Art, 154
Leonard Cohen Poet residence, 156
Leslie Bell Singers, The, 58
Letendre, Rita, 22
Levit, Jan, 129
Lewis, Bob, 158
Lewis, Stephen, 47
Liberty Magazine, 16, 57
Life and Times of Edwin Alonzo Boyd, The, 30
Life magazine, 111, 135

Lightfoot, Gordon, 60
Lloyd Henderson of Portage La Prairie, Mrs., 115
Locke, Jeanine, 59, 128,
Logan, Donna, 155, 164
Loman, Ron, 31
London Observer, 42
London Times, 42, 107
Look magazine, 59, 117
Lord Beaverbrook, 109, 110
Lord Louis Mountbatten, 132
Lord's Day Act, 95
Loren, Sophia, 11, 110
Loretto Abbey, 31, 104
Love, Hate, Fear, Anger and Other Lively Emotions, 58
Lovell, James, 127
    See also Apollo 13
Lovett, Mrs. (James Lovell's wife), 127
Lownsbrough, John, 67
Luce, Henry "Harry", 110
Luckenbooth pendant, 26
Lytle, Andy, 9
Lytle, Tommy, 9, 57, 92, 95

M

MacDonnell, J.M., 35, 36
MacFarlane, Doug, 28, 31, 32, 36, 37, 39, 95, 104, 122, 123,
MacFarlane, Richard, 100
MacGray, Ken, 132, 133
MacLaren's Advertising Agency, 118
Maclean-Hunter, 25
MacLean's magazine, 27, 51, 58, 63, 73, 117, 158
MacNeil, Penny, 77
MacTaggart, Ken, 39, 53, 126, 137
Mad Men, 24
Madame Olga Tchetchetkina, 106
Madame St. Laurent, 113
Maiwald, Josephine, 34
Malaya Independence Act 1957, 36
Malenkov, Georgi, 45
Malenkov, Georgy, 105
Malik, Amita, 157
Mandy, Nigel, 129
Manitoban, 71
Mann, Ruby, 124
Manson, Alec, 77
Marchand, Jean, 83
Margaret Laurence Memorial Lecture, 64
Margaret Rose, Princess, 45, 113, 117
Marshall, Jack, 80
Martin, Paul, Jr., 115
Martin, John, 129
Martin, Nell, 115
Martin, Paul, 114, 115
Mary, Queen of Scots, 26
Massey College, 13, 58, 162
Mayer, Ina, 162
McBurney, Margaret, 23, 66
McCarthy, Joseph, 108
McCarthy, Pearl, 20, 53, 122
McClelland & Stewart, 74, 78, 160
McClung, Nellie, 14, 15, 63
McCord Museum, 156
McCourt, Malachy, 108
McCullagh, George, 55, 56
McCullough, Colin, 19
McEwan, Frank, 141
McGill University, 104, 153, 160, 161, 163
McGuinty, Dalton, 67
McKenna, Joey, 77
McKenna, Kathleen, 10

173

McKenna, Siobhan, 142
McLaughlin Carriage Co., 25
McLaughlin, Colonel Sam, 25
McLaughlin, Isabel, 22, 25
McLuhan, Marshall, 19, 20
McNab, David, 50, 179
McNeill, John, 139, 140
McQuaig, Linda, 62
McTeer, Maureen, 131
Medal of Honour, 129, 150
Medicare on its Sick-bed: Is There a Cure?, 126
Megarry, Roy, 62
Meir, Golda, 80
Memoirs of a Loose Canon, 70
Mental Health Association, 60
Metropolitan Life, 94
Middlesex Advertiser, 96
Millay, Edna Vincent, 16
Miller, David, 67
Milligan, Doris, 75
Milner, Louis Simon, 70, 85
Milstead, Violet, 57
Mirren, Helen, 95
Mirvish, Anne, 22
Mirvish, David, 24
Mirvish, Ed, 22
Mitchell, Joni, 60
Mitchell, W.O., 27
Mizrahi, Sam, 143
Mohr, Tom, 93
Molotov, Vyacheslav, 103
Molson Coors Brewing Company, 140
　　O'Keefe's Brewing Company Limited, 140
Monroe, Marilyn, 74, 109, 110
Montreal Gazette, 164, 41, 44
Montreal Standard, 15
Montreal Star, 45, 58, 153, 154, 155, 157, 158, 160, 161, 162, 163, 164
Moore, Henry, 21, 23, 158, 164
Morriseau, Norval, 22
Mountain Prison, 78
Mrs. Thompson Advises, 122
Mugabe, Robert, 129
Mulcahy, Stan, 139
Mullan, Joseph, 13
Mullan, Kathleen, 14, 15, 26
Mullan, Lucy, 14
Mulroney, Brian, 26, 62, 83
Mulroney, Mila, 62
Munns, Tommy, 17
Murdoch, Bertha "Betty" (Howarth), 35
Murdoch, William, 35
Museum of Man, 47
Mussolini, Benito, 15
Mustard, William, 126
Myers, Arnie, 72

N

Nash, Knowlton, 83
National Action Committee, 62
National Ballet, 118
National Council for the Advancement of Education Writing, 161
National Council of Jewish Women, 81
National Democratic Party (NDP), 15, 62
National Energy Program, 81
National Gallery of Canada, 47
National Medicare Insurance Act, The, 127
National Newspaper Award, 35, 36, 101, 121, 124
National Newspaper Awards (NNA) Ceremony, 35
National Parole Board (Vancouver), 82
National Post, 19, 53, 122
NBC (National Broadcasting Company), 109
Needham, Richard J., 9, 17, 18, 25, 159
Nemy, Enid, 71, 156
New York Now, 22
New York Telegram, 104
New York Times, 71, 107, 156
Newfie Bullet, 33
Newman, Don, 154
Niarchos, Spiro, 110
Nichols, Jim, 39
Niven, David, 35
Niverville, Louis de, 26
Normal School, 27, 121
Noronic, Canadian steam ship, 125, 130
North Bay Nugget, 135, 138
Northern News, 135, 138
Northern Princess, The, 77
Notre Dame College, 42
Novak, Kim, 111
Now Magazine, 64
Nowell, Iris, 21, 47, 97

O

O'Brien, Conor Cruise, 108
O'Hearne, Walter, 154
O'Sullivan, Sean, 80
Oakes, Sir Harry, 162
Oakley, Annie, 113
Obama, Barack, 107
Oblinski, Prince Michael, 93
Ochs, Phil, 60
October Crisis, 127.
　　See also Pierre Laporte.
Ol' Man River, 108
Old Lady of Melinda Street, the, 55
Olympics, 116, 157, 163
Onassis, Aristotle, 10, 98, 99
One Hundred and Four Horses: A Memoir of Farm and Family, Africa and Exile, 129
One Yonge St., 32, 125, 132
Ontario Association for Community Living (Award), 102
Ontario Court of Appeal, 112
Ontario Jockey Club, 65
Ontario Labour Relations Board, 116
Ontario Medical Association, 53
Order of Canada, 43, 49, 62, 69, 118, 122, 141, 163
Order of Service, 132
Organized Working Women, 62
Orr, Frank, 65, 129
Osgoode Hall, 30
Oswald, Lee Harvey, 39
Other Mrs. Diefenbaker, The, 85
Ottawa Sun, 82, 83
Ottawa Philharmonic Orchestra, 115
Ottawa Valley, 19

P

"Père", Father Athol Murray, 42
Palmer, Helen, 126
Parker, Dorothy, 16, 66, 110
Parliamentary Committee, 82
Parsons, Louella, 95, 111
Paterson, Elizabeth (Beth), 71
Paul I, John (Pope), 131
Paul VI (Pope), 131
Paul, Edgar, 34
Pearson International Airport, 37
Pearson, Lester (Prime Minister), 45, 60, 81, 114, 118, 122, 156, 157
Pearson, Maryon, 45, 115
PEN International, 64
Penang Cricket Club, 36
Penny Farthing, 60
Peterson, Oscar, 23
Petlock, Bert, 37
Pharmakovsky, Olga, 95
Phillip, Prince, 36, 59, 66, 78, 117, 132
Philip, Marlene (Nourbese), 64
Phillips, Nathan (Toronto Mayor), 59, 118
Pierce, Pat, 159
Pieri, Mike, foreign editor, 127, 128
　　Editor Pieri, 129
Plant, Isobel, 52
Plaut, Gunther (Rabbi), 60, 61
Pleasures of Photography: The World of Roloff Beny, The, 21
Plunkett-Norris, Peter, 99
Polish Air, 150
Poole, Judith, 118
Porter, Cole, 93
Portrait of 'Saint June', 64
Post Master General, 115
Postel, Claude, 111
Potter, Gibb, 16
Pound, Ezra, 64
Power and Influence: The Globe and Mail and the News Revolution, 9, 19, 24, 55
Power, Tyrone, 54
Pravda, 106
Press Club, Radio Artists Club, 28, 125
Prince Edward Bar, 70
Princess of Wales theatre, 24
Proulx, E. Annie, 34
Purcell, Gillis, 72, 151
Purple Onion, 60

Q

Quarrington, Nels, 125
Quebec Museum, 156
Queen Mary, 35, 128

R

Ranier of Monaco, Prince, 109
Raymond, A.M., 14
Raymond, Ethel, 52
Rayner, Gordon, 22
Readers Digest, 137
Reagan, Nancy, 82-83
Reagan, Ronald, 82
Redinger, Walter, 21
Reeves, Maggy, 97-98
Regina Capitol Theatre, 17
Regina Leader-Post, 13, 15, 17, 27, 41, 43, 122
Reid, Don, 92
Reitman's, 122
Retzlaff, Mandy, 129
Rex, Kay, 47, 132, 151
Rhodesia's Whites Worried by Smith's Latest Moves, 129
Richard, Maurice, 160
Richardson, Harold, 39
Robert McLaughlin Gallery, 25

Index

Robert Simpson Co., 57, 92
Robeson, Paul, 108
Robinette, John J., 112
Rochester, Helen, 155
Rogers, David B. "D.B.", 14-16
Rogers, Ginger, 54
ROM (Royal Ontario Museum), 21, 45, 93
Romaine, Ed, 154
Romberg, Sigmund, 71
Ronald, William, 23
Roosevelt, Eleanor, 15
Roosevelt, Franklin, 15
Rose (Rosenberg), Fred, 38
Rose, Ben, 53, 55, 57, 112, 116
Rose, Ken, 137
Ross, Val, 20
Roy Thomson Hall, 64
Royal Alexandra Theatre, 24, 54
Royal Canadian Institute, 33, 133
Royal Canadian Navy ship, 123
Royal Commission for the Status of Women, 10, 48, 118
Royal Tours, 19, 23, 36, 58-59, 113, 117
Rubirosa, Porfirio, 111
Ruby, Clayton, 60
Russell, Jane, 109
Russia, Al, 44
Ruth Hammond Scholarship, 94, 105
Ryan, Pat, 118
Ryder, Gus, 31
Ryerson University, 94, 97, 105

S

S.S. Constitution, 109-110
Saary, Zoltan, 19-20
Sainte-Marie, Buffy, 60-61
Salterton Trilogy, 58
San Carlos de la Rapita, 130
Sandford Fleming Medal, 133
Saskatchewan Farmer, 27, 35, 145
Saskatoon StarPheonix, 27
Saturday Night Magazine, 63
Schlafly, Phyllis, 83
Scott College, 13
Scott, Barbara Ann, 57
Seagram Empire, 154
Senate of Canada, 15, 26, 118
Sex and the Teen-Age Revolution, 85
Shakespearean Festival, 23
Shipping News, The, 34
Short, Bill, 72
Show Boat, 54
Shuster, Frank, 61
Silcox, David, 25
Simcoe, John Graves, 30
Simon, Carley, 60
Simpson, O.J., 111
Sinatra, Frank, 11, 79, 109-111
Sinclair, Gordon, 92, 103, 105
Sinclair, James (Fisheries Minister), 78, 99
Sinclair, Margaret, 78, 99-100
Sinn Féin, 130
Sinner in Silk, 14
Slinger, Joey, 77
Smith, Earl T. "ETS", 75-76
Smith, Hannah, 82
Smith, Harold, 35
Smith, Nathan (Supreme Court Justice), 85
Smyth, Catherine "Cathy" 7, 9, 56, 93, 109, 116
Smyth, Conn, 65
Snowden, Donald, 116

Sofin, William, 158
Solomon, Samuel, 163
Soraya, Princess, 111
Sorokin (Head of Sons of Freedom), 77
Southern Ontario Newspaper Guild (SONG), 53
Sowing Seeds in Danny, 14
Spears, Borden, 53, 56, 104, 105, 107, 112, 116
Spears, John, 105
Spitfires, 57
Spock, Benjamin, 61
Spremo, Boris, 61, 131
Spurgeon, David, 144-145
Squires, John, 34
Squires, Joseph, 34
Squires, Walter, 34
St. George Salon, 105
St. Helene's Bridge, 127
St. Laurent, Louis, 113-114
Stanley Cup, 159
Stapleton, Betty, 96
Starting Out in the Afternoon, 64
Starting Out: 1920-1947, 73
Stella, Frank, 24
Stern, Isaac, 71
Stewart, Martha, 15
Stewart, Walter, 101
Stolen from Our Embrace, 48
Straight, Hal, 72-75
Stratford Festival, 23, 142, 155
Strean, Shirley, 80
Stroumboulopoulos, George, 67
Student Prince, The, 71
Stutt, Devon, 66
Suchan, Steve, 29
Suez Crisis, 115. *See also* United Nations, 60, 108, 115
Sullivan, Anne, 111
Sutherland, Keefer, 17
Swift Current, 16

T

T. Eaton Co., 17, 57, 100, 164
Tate, Alf, 116
Taylor, Bernie, 22, 23,
Taylor, E.P., 95
Taylor, Elizabeth, 98, 156
Tea Council of Canada, 118
Telegraph Hill, 34
Templeton, Charles, 33
Terminal City Club, 76
Terror in the Name of God, 74, 78
Terry, Andy, 130
Tesher, Ellie, 102
Tesky, Frank, 94
Thatcher, Margaret, 132
The American Spirit, 158
The Fraynes, 58
The Thin Man, 24
Thomas, Jocko, 30, 112
Thomson, Ken, 62
Tilley, Alex, 21
Timmins Daily Press, 104, 137
Timson, Ray, 92
Tinning, Campbell, 16
Today Show, 59, 117
Tong, Sergeant Edmund, 29
Toronto Centre, 62
Toronto Joint Labour Committee on Human Rights, 142
Toronto Life, 63
Toronto Pride Parade, 64

Toronto Royal Winter Fair, 45, 59
Toronto Sportsman Show, 123
Toronto Star
　　Age of Reason Column, 102
　　Ask Ellie Column, 102
Star Travelling Forum, 96
Toronto Sun
　　Saturday Sun, 83, 167
　　Sunday Sun, 81, 168
Town, Harold, 22, 61, 97
Towner, Jerry, 126
Trans-Canada Airlines, 23
Trent University, 43
Troyer, Fred, 125
Trudeau, Margaret Sinclair, 78, 81, 99, 101
Trudeau, Pierre Elliot, 38, 78, 79, 80, 81, 82, 83, 85, 96, 97, 99, 100, 127, 157
　　Trudeamania, 99
　　Trudeauboppers, 79
Truman, Harry, 143
Trumbo (2015), 95
TTC (Toronto Transit Commission), 18, 123
Tumpane, Frank, 53
Turnbull Dingman, Isabel, 14, 122
Turnbull, Bob, 140, 144
Turner, John, 80, 83, 158
Typographical Union, 95

U

Ugly Truth about Chrétien, The, 83
University of Alberta, 10, 41, 47, 48
University of British Columbia's Sing Tao School of Journalism, 155
University of Manitoba, 71, 85
University of Ottawa, 42, 47, 48
University of Toronto, 11, 17, 18, 26, 48, 58, 67, 105, 130, 164, 165, 166, 168, 180
University of Victoria, 118
University of Western Ontario, 125
Upshaw, Gertie, 117

V

Vaillancourt, Armand, 156
Van Horne, Cornelius, 163
Vanity Fair, 110
Vegreville Observer, 70
Viewpoint (CBC Program), 159
Vineberg, Arthur, 160
Vineberg, Augusta Myers, 153
Vogue, 17, 56, 97
Vreeland, Diana, 17

W

Waddell, Ian, 81
Walker, Frank, 157
Walter, Barbara, 67
War Measures Act, 127
Wead, Bill, 82, 83
Wead, Doug, 82, 83
Webster, Jack, 73, 74
West, Bruce, 53
White, Kayce, 81, 84
White, Nancy J., 64
Whittaker, Herb, 25, 26, 142
Who Has Seen the Wind, 27
Whyte, Bertha "Mom", 19

175

Williamson, Frank, 41
Williams, Esther, 123
Williams, Tennessee, 21
Willinsky, Bernard, 31
Winnipeg Free Press, 15, 43, 71, 95, 156
Wong, Bob, 126
Wong, Susie, 25
Wood, Natalie, 97
World War I, 52, 121, 136, 153
World War II, 9, 33, 37, 42, 57, 61, 67, 71, 74, 92, 124, 130, 136, 138, 150, 153
Worthington, Helen, 93, 94, 95, 96, 100
    Helen Parmalee, 94
Worthington, Peter, 30, 32, 36, 37, 38, 39, 77, 80, 83, 85, 94, 95, 112, 129

Y

York University, 50, 105
Young, Loretta, 97
Young, Neil, 60

ACKNOWLEDGEMENTS

I would like to thank everyone who contributed to the production of this book.

During the many years I spent collecting clippings, data, photographs and personal remembrances for *Newsgirls*, there were several people who made the journey with me. I owe much to a roster of dear friends, advisers and believers who propelled me to finish this project.

A big bouquet to painter and photographer Linda Kooluris Dobbs for the flattering photo-portrait of myself. A special shout-out to graphic designer Barbara Raider who created the first cover concept for Newsgirls, and to the ever-patient Deanna Dunn who helped with IT issues. Also, thanks to freelance editors Susan Walker and Sharon Crawford.

Other people to whom I am eternally grateful include forever friend Jane Tilley, sister Dorothy MacKinnon, cheerleaders Gillian McDermott, Dolores Pian, George Yemec, Susan Freeman, Rene St. Louis, Nancy Kennedy, Professor David McNab and Crystal Helms, who facilitated interviews in Kitchener.

Merci beaucoup to readers Marion Lord, Trudy Rising, Dr. Kathryn Horne, David Pearce, Doreen Armstrong, Kim Laudrum, Carl Shain, Heather MacDonald and Russell Smith. Much appreciation to all the extra help received from the staff at the photo archives at the Toronto Reference Library, Mike Kelly at Torstar Syndicate and Anne Dickason and Karon Shmon at the Gabriel Dumont Institution for access to photos of newsgirl and Professor Emerita Olive Dickason.

And above all, many accolades to publisher and York University Instructor Mike O'Connor and the diligent members of York's Book Publishing Practicum for making *Newsgirls* a reality.

Peace and Light to all,

DJM

ABOUT THE AUTHOR

Donna Jean MacKinnon was born in Cape Breton, emigrating to Upper Canada when she was an impressionable child.

After attending Victoria College, University of Toronto with a B.A. in English & Near Eastern History, MacKinnon paid the bills as a social worker, teacher, barmaid, department store buyer, antiques dealer and freelance writer before surfacing at the Toronto Star, where she toiled for 21 years as a reporter, columnist, and features' writer.

MacKinnon began work on her debut book, *Newsgirls*, in 1995.

Front-Cover Photo: Angela Burke in a scrum of newsies, heading for the wedding of starlet Grace Kelly and Prince Rainier, April, 1956.
Reprinted with permission by Special Collections and Archives,
Toronto Public Library.

Back Photo Credit: Linda Kooluris Dobbs

CPSIA information can be obtained
at www.ICGtesting.com
Printed in the USA
LVOW04s1702090517
533874LV00007B/442/P